The Republic
Shall Be Kept Clean

# The Republic Shall Be Kept Clean

How Settler Colonial Violence Shaped Antileft Repression

TARIQ D. KHAN

© 2023 by the Board of Trustees
of the University of Illinois
All rights reserved
1 2 3 4 5 C P 5 4 3 2 1
♾ This book is printed on acid-free paper.

Library of Congress Cataloging-in-Publication Data
Names: Khan, Tariq D., author.
Title: The republic shall be kept clean : how settler colonial
    violence shaped antileft repression / Tariq D. Khan.
Description: Urbana : University of Illinois Press, [2023] |
    Includes bibliographical references and index.
Identifiers: LCCN 2022060374 (print) | LCCN 2022060375
    (ebook) | ISBN 9780252045301 (cloth) | ISBN
    9780252087431 (paperback) | ISBN 9780252054822 (ebook)
Subjects: LCSH: Indians of North America—Government
    relations. | Indians of North America—Colonization.
    | Settler colonialism—United States—History. | Anti-
    communist movements—United States—History. |
    Imperialism—Social aspects—United States—History. |
    United States—Ethnic relations. | United States—Social
    conditions. | United States--Politics and government.
Classification: LCC E93 .K45 2023 (print) | LCC E93 (ebook) |
    DDC 973—dc23/eng/20230207
LC record available at https://lccn.loc.gov/2022060374
LC ebook record available at https://lccn.loc.gov/2022060375

# Contents

Acknowledgments   vii

Author's Note on Terminology   xi

Introduction   1

1  Class, Race, Gender, and Empire   11

2  "Civilization" versus "Savagery"   31

3  Cleansing the Republic   60

4  The Guns of 1877   88

5  Republicans and Anarchists   121

6  The Respectable Mob   151

7  Aliens and Mobs   171

Conclusion: "The Problem of the Proletariat and the Colonial Problem"   191

Notes   197

Libraries and Archives Consulted   243

Index   245

# Acknowledgments

I wrote most of this book while subject to a malicious far-right campaign of persecution, which lasted for more than two years. The right-wing mob targeted not only me, but also my partner and my young children. My family and I were bullied, threatened, harassed, stalked, misrepresented, and generally vilified by far-right activists, politicians, media personalities, conspiracy theorists, and outright violent neofascist gangs: all of whom derogatorily characterized me as "antifa," "socialist," "anarchist," "communist," and "leftist," along with vulgar, Islamophobic, and racist terms that I won't repeat here. That all of this was happening as I was researching and writing about US colonial violence, white supremacy, and antileft repression made this history all the more real and urgent.

The reason I was able to overcome these obstacles to this work is the many people from near and far who defended and supported me. I cannot possibly list everyone, as it was literally thousands of people, including academics, friends, family members, neighbors, university organizations, and student groups from the University of Illinois and other universities, community organizations, labor unions and other working-class organizing groups, anarchist groups, social-ist groups, antifascist groups, lawyers, mental health professionals, and faith communities. The solidarity of these thousands of people, which came in many forms, foiled the right's attempts to destroy me and made it possible for me to continue working on this project.

This work benefited tremendously from a truly brilliant community of his-torians and other scholars to whom I am grateful. They generously gave time, suggestions, and critiques that improved this work to a level far above what I would have been able to produce on my own. First and foremost, I must ac-knowledge Kristin Hoganson, who read and thoughtfully responded to more drafts than anyone else. My conversations with her led to some of the most fruitful avenues of my research. She was, and continues to be, supportive in several ways beyond what I would have expected. I also thank David Roediger, who was supportive of this project from the first time I contacted him. He remained committed even after moving to another institution, reading every draft I asked him to, and always offering useful feedback and suggestions.

Erik McDuffie encouraged this work, offered useful critiques, and reminded me to pay closer attention to the ways gender politics played a central role in the history I was researching and writing. Kenyon Zimmer's generous feedback on my drafts was invaluable. His knowledge of the anarchist movement in the United States in the era of this study's focus is unmatched. I am also fortunate that Steven Salaita, an intellectual I tremendously respect both personally and professionally, took time to engage with drafts of my manuscript. His sharp anticolonial analysis has significantly influenced and sharpened my own analysis. I am grateful to him for his generosity, encouragement, and suggestions as I completed the work.

Other academics, intellectuals, and working-class organizers who have provided helpful feedback on sections of this work, or earlier papers that evolved into sections of this work, include Nazneen Khan, Servius Tulius Gomez, Tariq Omar Ali, Muhammad Yousuf, Antoinette Burton, Candace Falk, Michael O'Malley, Laura Moore, and participants in the Labor and Working Class Reading Group at the Illinois Program for Research in the Humanities, which has since evolved into the Humanities Research Institute. This work has also benefited from feedback from and discussions with participants in the "Race and Gender in the Early Twentieth Century U.S." session of the History Graduate Student Association Conference at Loyola University of Chicago; the Chabraja Center for Historical Studies "Insurgencies" Graduate Conference at Northwestern University; the North American Anarchist Studies Network conference at the California Institute of Integral Studies; the Midwest Labor and Working Class History Conference, "Social Justice for a Global Working Class" at Purdue University; and the North American Labor History Conference, "Workers and Global Cities: Detroit and Beyond," at Wayne State. This work was made possible by funding from the Department of History at the University of Illinois at Urbana-Champaign and a fellowship from the Doris G. Quinn Foundation.

I must thank the team at the University of Illinois Press for helping get this work out into the world: especially Alison Syring for getting the project off the ground and being an early proponent of this book, Geof Garvey for his highly skilled editing, and Tad Ringo for managing the project. There are several other people at the Press who worked behind the scenes to make this book happen, and though I do not know who all of them are, I see and appreciate the fruits of their labor. I also thank Sheila Hill for her indexing expertise.

Support from Beth Grace and Kelly Raiser made it possible for me to undertake and complete this endeavor. Thanks also go to my parents Aman and Clara Khan. Above all, I express my deep gratitude for my partner Kristina Khan, who has been with me through this entire process and has been immeasurably supportive.

# Author's Note on Terminology

Because of the sloppy, contradictory, vague, and in many cases outright incorrect usage of terms such as *socialist, anarchist, communist,* and *leftist* in mainstream US culture and politics, discussions of radical left politics and antileft political repression are often rife with confusion. I use *anticommunism* as an umbrella term that includes anti-anarchism. Explaining answers to questions such as "What was anarchism?" and "How did anarchists differ from Marxists?" is not the project of this study, as there is no shortage of books and articles that deal with that type of question. I will simply say that in the period of this study's focus, socialism was a large umbrella under which several overlapping strains of socialism existed, ranging from mild reformist to revolutionary strains. Anarchism was the antistate strain of revolutionary socialism.

The best way to understand what anarchism meant to its adherents in the era of this study's focus is to read their own words. Much of their writing is easily accessible in the form of autobiographies and several easy-to-find anthologies of anarchist writings from the period of this study's focus.[1] In addition to the anarchists' own words, there are hundreds of excellent secondary works that contextualize anarchist primary sources.[2]

Suffice it to say, for both anarchists and Marxists, the state was an institution that primarily existed and functioned to uphold class society. Communism, as both anarchists and Marxists envisioned it, meant a classless *and stateless* society, even while they differed significantly on the question of how to get there. Ending class society meant ending the state. As Marx's accomplice Friedrich Engels wrote that, as class distinctions are abolished, "The state must irrevocably fall with them. The society that is to reorganize production on the basis of a free and equal association of the producers, will transfer the machinery of state where it will then belong: into the Museum of Antiquities by the side of the spinning wheel and the bronze ax."[3] A leading theorist of anarchism, the Russian scientist Peter Kropotkin, wrote, "Every society which has abolished private property will be forced, we maintain, to organize itself on the lines of anarchist communism. Anarchy leads to communism, and communism to anarchy, both alike being expressions of the predominant tendency in modern societies, the pursuit of equality."[4] While not all communists were anarchists, anarchism emerged in the mid-nineteenth century on the leading edge of the communist movement, with anarchists and Marxists as part of the same circles and organizations. Indeed, anarchists have as much claim to the legacies of the First International Workingmen's Association and the Paris Commune as Marxists.[5]

In the period of this study's focus, the overwhelming bulk of the anarchist movement in the United States and globally was communist in orientation—in that it was resolutely anticapitalist and envisioned a classless, stateless society. Many participants in the anticapitalist movement used the terms *anarchist*, *revolutionary socialist*, and *communist* interchangeably. More important for this book's focus, state agents and capitalists used the terms *anarchist*, *socialist*, and *communist* as interchangeable pejoratives against working-class insurgency, regardless how individual working-class participants self-identified politically. Anti-anarchism was a form of anticommunism. It did not matter what, if any, ism an individual worker subscribed to. If she was with the strikers, as far as men like Theodore Roosevelt, John Hay, and police captain Michael Schaack were concerned, she was an anarchist, a socialist, and a communist.

I also use the term *anarchist-adjacent* to describe people and organizations who were not explicitly anarchists but were nonetheless involved in anarchist networks. For example, Ghadr Party cofounder Pandurang Khankhoje did not self-identify as an anarchist, but he organized with anarchists and was involved in the anarchist movement. The Ghadr Party itself was not explicitly anarchist, but some of its leaders, including its most influential cofounder, Har Dayal, were anarchists, and it was part of the anarchist movement. Bhagat Singh, who remains one of the most celebrated martyrs of South Asian anticolonialism in both India and Pakistan, was influenced by anarchism. He studied the works of Kropotkin and Bakunin. He hung up a portrait of Bakunin in the Naujavan Bharat Sabha headquarters in Lahore and wrote articles about anarchism for a leftist Punjabi newspaper, but he did not call himself an anarchist. Another example of an anarchist-adjacent individual was the Jewish-American pacifist and journalist Martha Gruening, who served as an assistant secretary of the NAACP but also socialized in the anarchist circles of New York's Greenwich Village and contributed to Emma Goldman's anarchist journal *Mother Earth*. The term *anarchist-adjacent* is to acknowledge that there were people and groups who were part of, or overlapped with, the anarchist movement but did not necessarily self-identify as anarchists.

In addition to using *anticommunism* as an umbrella term, throughout the text, I use the terms *anti-anarchism*, *antisocialism*, and sometimes the clunky *anticommunism/anti-anarchism* because agents of the state and bourgeoisie used the terms *anarchist*, *socialist*, and *communist* interchangeably. There are authors who simplify it by using the term *antiradicalism*. They are not wrong to do so, but I have chosen against it because of the confusing way the term *radicalism* is used in present-day US politics and culture. While, in a traditional socialist sense, *radical* simply means to approach social injustice by attacking the roots of the injustice, wider US society often uses the term as a synonym for *extremism* or *militancy*. There is no particular political position to extremism. For example, violent extralegal right-wing vigilante groups are extremists, and media often identify them as radicals when they are simply zealous conservatives, extreme not in their politics but in their willingness to go to violent extralegal lengths to uphold the existing order. The term *radical Islam* is another example of the political incoherence of the term *radical* in mainstream US culture and politics. Switching back and forth between the terms *anticommunist*, *antisocialist*, and *anti-anarchist* is more cumbersome and less elegant, but more accurate. All these terms as I use them fall under the umbrella of anticommunism.

Concerning the terms "Indigenous," "Native American," and "American Indian," there is no one standard "right" term for all situations. Because several Indigenous organizations and governing bodies use the terms interchangeably, I use these terms interchangeably throughout this book. When referring to one specific Indigenous nation, I use the appropriate specific name.

The Republic
Shall Be Kept Clean

# Introduction

In the 2019 State of the Union Address, the president of the United States, Donald Trump, declared, "Here, in the United States, we are alarmed by new calls to adopt socialism in our country. America was founded on liberty and independence—not government coercion, domination, and control. We are born free, and we will stay free. Tonight, we renew our resolve that America will never be a socialist country!" The well-heeled audience, ranging from lawmakers on the far right of the Republican Party to the progressive wing of the Democratic Party, responded to the antisocialist line with a standing ovation and chants of "USA! USA!" This moment exemplifies not only US capitalist ruling-class solidarity but also the deeply anticommunist ideology that unites the highest-ranking policymakers across party lines. The violent historical development of that ideology, and its attendant policies, is the subject of this study.

There are several useful studies on the development of US anticommunism.[1] As worthwhile as these studies are, they contain little to no discussion on the centrality of US settler colonialism to the development of US anticommunism. The present study centers US colonialism-imperialism and anticommunist repression and illuminates the close relationship between the two. It applies the findings of anticolonial scholars, who are cited throughout, on the nature of empire, colonialism, and the United States to internal repression and social control. This book argues that there is a direct relationship between the outwardly-facing so-called "Indian Wars" of the United States on the "frontier" and class war within the metropole. The former structured the latter and both were part of the same project of capitalist domination.

More telling than the bipartisan ovation for anticommunist rhetoric at the 2019 State of the Union address was the applause for the preceding line, "America was founded on liberty and independence—not government coercion, domination, and control." Here, the president equated capitalism with liberty and independence and equated socialism with government coercion, domination, and control. The bipartisan applause for that equation is indicative of the ahistorical shared delusion, shared mythology, and shared distortion about what the United States is and how it developed. As in any bloodstained empire, rulers tell themselves lies to justify their existence. In the context of the United States, settler colonial militarization and war were accompanied by a mythological/ideological structure that imbued genocide, land theft, and enslavement with purpose, justifying and sanctifying the settlers' position within the system.[2]

Rather than being born solely from social enlightenment and persecuted people's aspirations for liberty and equality, the United States developed directly within the genocidal context of European empire, militarization, and warfare. The US landowning class's War for Independence was far less a defining event for the United States than the three preceding centuries of unceasing European colonial warfare to enslave and control African people and to eliminate or contain Indigenous American peoples. By 1776, Britain's American colonies were already thoroughly militarized societies of armed settlers with "well-regulated militias" that served the two-pronged purpose of preventing and quelling revolts of enslaved and bonded laborers and expelling Indigenes.[3]

The War for Independence was an extension of, rather than a break from, previously-existing settler colonizer aims. The Declaration of Independence, the founding document of the United States, vilified Indigenous peoples as "merciless Indian Savages." The declaration grieved that the king of Great Britain's 1763 Proclamation limited the settlers' "liberty" by imposing boundaries beyond which settlers were forbidden to establish slave labor camps and colonies. The crown further hindered the settlers' supposed liberty by restricting migration of aspiring European enslavers to seize those coveted Indigenous territories west of the Appalachians and Alleghenies. This is what Thomas Jefferson meant with his seemingly innocuous language in the declaration, that the king of Great Britain refused "to pass others to encourage their Migrations hither, and raising the Conditions of new Appropriations of Lands."[4] Settler colonial expansion was a primary aim of independence, revealed by the fact that the first law the Continental Congress passed, preceding the US Constitution, was "the blueprint for gobbling up the British-protected Indian Territory": the Northwest Ordinance.[5]

War and militarization, for the purposes of outward territorial expansion and inward labor control, shaped US institutions to a far greater degree than any supposed lofty ideals. Rather than being a break from Europe, and rather than being some new form of state based on supposed liberal, democratic ideals, the United States emerged as a European-style "fiscal-military state," a state that is designed primarily for war, not just militarily but also economically and politically.[6] Historian Roxanne Dunbar-Ortiz puts it quite simply

2    Introduction

that "The United States was founded as a capitalist state and an empire on conquered land." Underscoring the centrality of militarism and war to the US economic system, Dunbar-Ortiz continues, "The [US] capitalist firearms industry was among the first successful modern corporations."[7] Militarization was the cutting edge of US industrial development. Many technologies of industrial capitalism, such as interchangeable parts, the assembly line, and, most important, the hourly wage system, were first developed in US weapons manufacturing centers—such as the famous Springfield Armory, established by the Continental Congress in 1777—before becoming standard operating procedure in industries more commonly associated with industrial capitalism, such as the New England textile mills.[8] Further, the expansion of bourgeois rights and so-called enlightenment ideals in Britain's American colonies was itself geared for settler colonial warfare: a maneuver by the landowning class to construct a white identity politics to unite the ethnically, religiously, and culturally diverse European colonists to consolidate settler colonial control vis-à-vis Indigenous peoples and enslaved Africans.[9]

The lack of attention to the violent settler colonial structure of the United States in histories of US anticommunism has resulted—among other problems— in historians misperiodizing, and thereby misunderstanding, the roots of US anticommunism. What historians refer to as the first Red Scare was preceded by more than half a century of red scares. Those earlier red scares played out squarely within the larger context of US "frontier" militarization and war. Internal repression against proletarian insurgency was colonialism turned inward: meaning the tactics, weapons, mythology, and ideology the state wielded to control the foreign, migrant, multiracial, multilingual, multiethnic urban "rabble" were developed and refined in the Indian wars and other outward imperialist invasions and occupations.

In his fine work *The Broken Heart of America*, historian Walter Johnson writes that, in St. Louis, "the practices of removal and containment that developed out of the history of empire in the American West were generalized into mechanisms for the dispossession and management of Black people within the city limits" and that "whites in St. Louis used Indian removal as much as slavery as the model for dealing with their Black neighbors."[10] The present study shows that what Johnson discusses as colonialism turned inward on a local level in one city was part of a larger story of the ruling class on a national, and even international, level turning colonialist modes of thinking, methods of social control, and tactics of war toward internal proletarian control. It focuses on the time period when US politicians, policymakers, business leaders, rentiers, colonial officials, and military and law enforcement officials first began using terms such as *socialist*, *communist*, and *anarchist* to describe a specter haunting the United States. It illuminates the larger US colonial-imperial context—touch-

Introduction    3

ing at times on a broader transimperial discourse and policy orientation shared by the United States, Canada, and western European imperialist states such as Britain, France, and Germany—in which US anti-anarchist and anticommunist ruling-class rhetoric, policies, and tactics developed.

Historian Ranajit Guha, a founder of Subaltern Studies, recognized a problem in the historiography of South Asian anticolonial struggles: that insurgent currents that did not fit neatly into a bourgeois-nationalist or communist party narrative were ignored, resulting in some of the most important strains of insurgency and counterinsurgency going unstudied in the historiography.[11] Similarly, many scholars who have centered colonialism and anticolonialism in their studies of late-nineteenth- and early-twentieth-century histories have left out the significant presence of anarchists and anarchist-adjacent individuals and organizations in global anticolonial networks.[12] Part of the reason is the fact that many scholars whose work focuses on colonialism and anticolonialism in the era have written in a liberal nationalist tradition or a Marxist-Leninist tradition, both of which tend to downplay, misrepresent, or more often simply ignore or erase anarchists and anarchism.

In contrast, capitalists and statesmen in the late nineteenth and early twentieth centuries did not downplay or ignore anarchism and anarchists, and, as the present work discusses, were quite explicit in saying that anarchists were anticolonial insurgents whom the state needed to put down with counterinsurgency strategies. But many scholars who have written anarchist histories have touched very little on colonialism and anticolonialism, despite states' deployment of explicitly colonialist counterinsurgency rhetoric and tactics against movements they perceived to be anarchist and despite the presence of anarchism in anticolonial currents globally in the era.[13] The present book emphasizes anarchists and people and movements the state—often incorrectly—perceived and vilified as anarchist, because anti-anarchism was one of the main vehicles by which the state turned colonialism inward.

From the mid-nineteenth century into the early twentieth century, explicit anticommunism-antianarchism became a central part of US ruling-class ideology and remains so to this day. This book will show that the kind of anti-anarchist rhetoric the US political establishment employs in the twenty-first century is not an aberration in US-American values, but an expression of them as they developed out of the US history of imperialism and settler colonization. In fact, as will become apparent in the following chapters, the mainstream political establishment's more recent anti-anarchist rhetoric against popular antiracist, anticapitalist and anti-authoritarian social movements is quite similar to the nineteenth- and early-twentieth-century rhetoric of the likes of Theodore Roosevelt, and in both cases the context was white supremacy, capitalism, and settler colonialism.

4    Introduction

Anti-anarchist rhetoric historically accompanies state violence that takes the form of colonialist counterinsurgency. In other words, anti-anarchist rhetoric goes hand in hand with the state turning its external frontier violence—which the state developed for ethnic cleansing, to expel, control, contain, or eliminate racialized enemies and assert and control borders—on its internal population. This story does not begin with recent presidential administrations or even what historians call the first Red Scare. It begins much earlier, in US settler colonial warfare against Indigenous peoples.

In the United States, anticommunism emerged first in the context of the enslavement of Africans and the ethnic cleansing of the frontier. This contextualizes more recent examples of antianarchist-anticommunist rhetoric against social movements in which Black and Indigenous activists and organizers are at the forefront. Indeed, the 2020 Independence Day celebration, in which the US president stood in front of Mount Rushmore—a white supremacist desecration of the Lakota sacred site, Tȟuŋkášila Šákpe (Six Grandfathers)—railing against what he called a "left-wing cultural revolution" and "far-left fascism," while militarized police nearby threatened, intimidated, gassed, assaulted, and arrested Lakota land defenders who asserted their people's land rights according to the 1868 Fort Laramie Treaty, vividly epitomizes the relationship between US settler colonialism and anticommunism and signals the urgency of this history.[14]

The notion that settler colonialism structured not only US-Indigenous relations but US culture and politics on a deep level is nothing new to Indigenous Studies and Genocide Studies scholars. As Patrick Wolfe famously argued in the *Journal of Genocide Research*, the core principle of settler colonialism—elimination—is a structure, not an event.[15] The understanding that settler colonialism is central to US history has been gaining ground popularly, beyond fields of specialization, largely because of a growing body of work by public-facing anticolonial scholars.[16] More significant, awareness of the settler colonial structure of the United States is expanding because of the increasingly visible Black, brown, and Indigenous organizing exemplified by the movement against police violence and the carceral state; Indigenous resistance to pipelines and the resource extraction industry; migrant resistance to Immigration and Customs Enforcement and Customs and Border Protection; and the global trend of people from historically colonized populations and their allies defacing, toppling, and removing symbols of colonization such as statues that honor enslavers and practitioners of genocide.

Although settler colonialism cuts to the core of the very structure of the United States, US labor and working-class history, as a field, has been slower to incorporate the frameworks that have been developed by Indigenous studies, radical black studies, and anticolonial social movements in the streets. The present study of US anticommunism-antianarchism is in part an effort to do

Introduction    5

just that: to apply anticolonial frameworks and understandings to US labor and working-class history. It will become apparent in the following chapters that US repression of the working class in industrial centers was thoroughly intertwined with war, militarization, imperialist expansion, and frontier ethnic cleansing.

The chapters will proceed thus: Chapter 1 discusses the theoretical frameworks and approaches to history that shape this study's approach. It serves to clarify what the much-abused and often-misunderstood category "working class" means, and why the category of class cannot be treated as separate from other important categories of social analysis such as race, gender, and, crucially, relationship to empire. Chapter 2 begins with the earliest examples of explicitly anticommunist rhetoric in the US *Congressional Record*, showing that it was southern proponents of enslavement and northern US Indian agents who first raised the specter of communism among US policymakers. US anticommunist rhetoric emerged from the context of settler-colonial militarism and war—the US invasion of Mexico and the Indian Wars—as a ruling-class defense of enslavement and a justification for genocide. By the time anarchists and socialists started to become influential in the labor movement in US industrial centers in the 1870s and 1880s, anticommunism already existed as an ideology of Indian killing. The mythology or ideology that accompanied the Indian wars then became the template for how the state would understand and deal with anarchism and the "labor problem." US police departments, relatively new on the scene and still struggling to gain legitimacy in the eyes of the public, relied on this mythological-ideological structure to bolster their authority, casting themselves as the heroic frontier Indian killers, and casting the anarchist "reds" as savages. Criminology and what was known as race science in the era likewise developed through colonial militarization, war, and genocide, as US and European violence against Indigenous peoples became the context for how anthropologists, criminologists, and law enforcers made sense of and dealt with urban proletarian insurgency.

Chapter 3 is a discussion of the relationship between counterinsurgency and the language and policies of ethnic cleansing—the language of cleansing, purification, removal, expulsion, containment, dirt, disease, contamination, infestation, animalization, and racialization—as they developed out of European colonialism and US imperial expansion. Exemplifying this language and policy orientation was Theodore Roosevelt—the ideological descendant of the English ethnic cleanser Oliver Cromwell—for whom conquering Cuba and the Philippines, ethnically cleansing the US West, and eradicating anarchism were all part of the same white man's war of civilization against savagery. Chapter 4 argues that the proletarian uprisings of 1877 were a significant turning point for the US bourgeoisie as they consciously turned the ideology, mythology, policies, weapons, and tactics of external settler colonial warfare on what they

6    Introduction

perceived to be an internal communist threat to civilization. It was an early example of what present-day sociologists call "imperial feedback."[17] It discusses US statesman John Hay to exemplify how colonialism turned inward. Hay is a useful example not only because of the influential and high-level positions he held in the US political, media, and literary establishments but also because he was a mild-mannered, refined political moderate, safely inside the mainstream of US culture and politics.

Chapter 5 argues that 1877 was as much a turning point for the working class as it was for the bourgeoisie. The preceding chapters discussed the process of US colonial violence and social control turning inward and did so largely through the words and actions of members of the ruling class, law enforcement, and their allies. Chapter 5 gives a view of this same process "from below" or, in other words, from the experiences of the people who were targeted by the forces of state violence, rather than the points of view of those doing the targeting. It focuses on the lives of Albert Parsons and Lucy Parsons, who both existed in the very center of the US history of white supremacy, enslavement, settler colonization, Reconstruction, the violent death of Reconstruction, the labor movement, revolutionary socialism, anarchism, insurgency, and counterinsurgency. US empire, settler colonialism, class war, and Black and Indigenous resistance influenced how Albert and Lucy Parsons imagined freedom and how they articulated and understood their own struggles against capitalism and the state.

Chapter 6 looks at all these currents as they converged in the San Diego free-speech fights of 1912. San Diego 1912 is a useful example not because it was exceptional but because it was a harbinger of what was to follow. It was representative of the unmasked brutality of the US ruling class toward "undesirables." The bourgeoisie rained down the cruelty of the intertwined forces of colonialism, capitalism, anti-anarchism, militarism, empire, police violence and right-wing vigilantism, white supremacy, class war, and gender/sexual violence on racialized, multiethnic, multilingual, poor, propertyless migrant proletarians who were asserting their humanity against private property and against the United States. And, like most similar episodes in US history, in which capitalism and the state remained intact, social progress did not emerge from it. The state did not become more humane. It became more effective at internal social control and counterinsurgency. Chapter 7 returns to the *Congressional Record* and looks at the period historians call the first Red Scare. It puts the Justice Department's anarchist deportations typical in the so-called first Red Scare within the larger context of ethnic cleansing, lynching, border control, and labor control in the US West. It argues in part that extralegal mob violence rooted in settler mythology and practices was the cutting edge of formal US state policy for internal capitalist social control.

## An Incident in Washington, DC

This introduction began with a vignette from above, about the bipartisan US political elite in Washington, DC, giving a standing ovation to the US president's antisocialist rhetoric. Let it end with a vignette from below, if for no other reason than to acknowledge that ruling-class narratives are not hegemonic, and that US history is not a history of national consensus, but of conflict.

In Washington, DC, in July 1877, onlookers witnessing a train loaded with soldiers from the Third, Fifth, and Second Artillery Regiments, two companies of infantrymen, two Gatling guns, and two caissons could have assumed with equal certainty that the cargo was destined for the Indian Wars or the Railroad War, the latter referring to the massive 1877 working-class uprisings sparked by wildcat railroad strikes. In this case, it was the latter. Either way, the troops were on route to exterminate "red savages," language that the US bourgeoisie in the era applied equally to Indigenous insurgents resisting colonialism on the frontier and proletarian insurgents resisting capitalism in the nation's industrial centers. In the capitalist imagination, both were part of the same war of civilization versus savagery, with civilization representing all that is bound up with the white man's property and savagery representing all that threatened white property. The train stood still on the tracks that ran along Virginia Avenue, just southeast of the Baltimore and Potomac Depot.[18]

Soldiers sat patiently, as the train seemed to be taking longer than expected to depart. Their mission was to deploy to Pennsylvania to crush the railroad strike with overwhelming firepower. The police did not have the capacity to deal with such a widespread, militant labor action, and the state militiamen—working people themselves—were largely in sympathy with the strikers. Politically influential wealthy industrialists, men such as Pennsylvania Railroad president Thomas Scott and railroad magnate Amasa Stone, called on the federal government to send in its professional Indian killers with their Gatling gun detachments. News circulated back to the passenger cars that an engineer up in the locomotive declared solidarity with the strikers and was refusing to transport any troops out of DC.[19]

A large crowd of mostly working-class Black men assembled on Virginia Avenue next to the train, in solidarity with the engineer and the railroad strike. According to the *New York Tribune*, "The crowd was composed largely of laboring men, two-thirds of whom were colored." It was an enthusiastic but peaceable assembly. The workingmen called up to the soldiers in the train cars, attempting to persuade them to refuse orders to fire on strikers in Pennsylvania. The *Tribune* reported that the crowd's comments to the soldiers were not threatening or belligerent but were "most of a good natured character." Nonetheless, chief of police A. C. Richards was uneasy about the situation and came out with a detachment of officers charged with "preserving order." About 4:30 p.m., the locomotive bell sounded and the train moved along as the crowd of mostly Black workers waved goodbye to the troops and "called out to the soldiers not to shoot at the strikers." This brief labor incident in the heart of the US capital city occurred at a time when settler colonialism was turning inward. US Army regulars armed and trained for Indigenous extermination were off to fight an Indian War against an internal threat to white supremacist capitalist order, the foreign communist proletariat, while the most historically exploited, politically disfranchised, and racially demonized sector of the US working class—Black workers—sounded the alarm against it.[20]

# 1

# Class, Race, Gender, and Empire

In the United States in the period of this study's focus, the sociologist's holy trinity—the intersecting axes of race, class, and gender—is insufficient, as they were not separate categories that intersected but were wrapped up in each other, producing and reproducing each other, all within the context of empire. Colonization, militarism, and war shaped the ways society constructed those categories of analysis, while those interwoven, coconstitutive categories simultaneously shaped how and why the state waged war.[1] While the following chapters vary in terms of subject matter: race, class, and gender are ever present, with empire as a common thread weaving through them.

This study rejects both a class reductionist and a race reductionist approach to US history. It recognizes that race and class are not separate categories, but are thoroughly entwined, as global capitalism, racial notions, and empire developed together, as part of the same whole. In the words of Nigerian anarchist Sam Mbah: "Racism is a key factor in this world and any working class analysis that seeks to deny this is only being escapist. Racism is simply endemic in capitalism."[2] Similarly, the anarchist, former SNCC organizer, and former Black Panther Party organizer Lorenzo Kom'boa Ervin argued in *Anarchism and the Black Revolution* that white supremacy is not about individual prejudice or any specific region of the United States, but that "Capitalist exploitation is inherently racist."[3] The prison abolitionist and geographer Ruth Wilson Gilmore writes that capitalism was "never not racial," not even in rural England, "or anywhere in Europe for that matter." And as much as capitalism was always racial, it was always imperialist, "its imperative forged on the anvils of imperial war-making monarchs."[4]

In the seminal work *Black Marxism*, Cedric Robinson challenged orthodox Marxist explanations of how capitalism developed, showing that contrary to Marx and Engels' description of the rise of the bourgeoisie putting an end to all feudal relations, there was never a clean break from feudalism. Instead, capitalism retained many feudal characteristics. The bourgeoisie sprang from feudal societies and cultures that were already infused with racial thought, and as global capitalism's class structure developed, it did so with racial thinking as a formative component. That is why Robinson referred to this economic structure as "racial capitalism."[5] Robinson also recognized that gender ideology and gender notions conditioned how capitalism developed and functioned, as well as how oppressed people resisted: that "All resistance, in effect, manifests in gender, manifests as gender. Gender is indeed both a language of oppression [and] a language of resistance."[6]

Preceding Robinson was the preeminent psychopathologist of colonization and decolonization Frantz Fanon, who recognized that "a Marxist analysis should always be slightly stretched when it comes to addressing the colonial issue." Fanon did not subordinate race to class, or vice versa, but described race and class as coconstitutive, producing and reproducing each other, particularly in the context of colonialism. Describing the dynamics of racial division under capitalism and colonialism, Fanon explained that "In the colonies, the economic infrastructure is also a superstructure. The cause is effect."[7] In this vein, the present study approaches race and class as historically entwined and coconstitutive. It will show that in the era of focus, notions such as working class, ruling class, bourgeoisie, proletariat, communism, anarchism, civilization, and private property were infused with racial meaning.

## Anti-Blackness and Anticommunism

Racial thinking in the United States is not only social and cultural but also political and economic, functioning to uphold capitalist and state power. In the words of political scientist Charisse Burden-Stelly, anti-Blackness and anticommunism are the *"legitimating architecture* of modern U.S. racial capitalism"(emphasis in original). The present study agrees with this insight but includes anti-Indigeneity on the list of what makes up that "legitimating architecture." To emphasize the historical relationship between anti-Blackness and anticommunism, Burden-Stelly points to a 1919 US Department of Justice report that vilified those the state identified as "Negro leaders" by associating them with the Industrial Workers of the World (IWW) and Russian Bolshevism.[8] In vilifying Black political consciousness as red, the state painted the anarcho-syndicalist IWW and Bolshevism Black, so that US anti-Blackness often took the form of anticommunism and vice versa.

The connection the Department of Justice report made between Black publications and the IWW was not mere scaremongering but was based on the fact

12 CHAPTER 1

that some Black socialist leaders in the era encouraged Black workers to join the IWW as a vehicle for both economic and racial emancipation. The Department of Justice singled out *The Messenger*, a magazine founded by Black socialists A. Philip Randolph and Chandler Owen, as "the most able and the most dangerous of all the negro publications."[9] The masthead of *The Messenger* boldly declared itself the "only radical Negro magazine in America." In the time period of the Justice Department report's focus, the "labor question" loomed large in the pages of *The Messenger*.

The magazine warned Black workers away from the anti-Black, top-down American Federation of Labor and encouraged Black workers to join the multiracial, syndicalist-structured IWW:

> In the great strikes which the I.W.W. has conducted at Lawrence, Mass. In the woolen mills, in the iron mine of Minnesota and elsewhere, the I.W.W. has brought workers of many races, colors, and tongues together in victorious battles for a better life. Not only does the I.W.W. differ from all organizations in regard to admission of all races, but there is a fundamental difference in form of organization from all other labor unions.[10]

In addition to its multiracial character and directly democratic organizing structure, the IWW emphasized the anarchist orientation to direct action rather than political action as the way to "get the goods." *The Messenger* argued that because the US political system systemically disfranchised Black people, direct action was the most practical option they had for winning bread-and-butter gains. In an article titled "Why Negroes Should Join the I.W.W.," *The Messenger* wrote that a Black worker has no power through the official channels of the nominally democratic state:

> Three-fourths of the Negroes in the United States are disfranchised. Over two million Negro men pay taxes but cannot vote. Therefore, the only recourse the Negro has is industrial action, and since he must combine with those forces which draw no line against him, it is simply logical for him to throw his lot with the Industrial Workers of the World.[11]

Further, argued *The Messenger*, the IWW and Black people in America had the same enemies: "Most of the forces opposed to the I.W.W. are also opposed to Negroes. John Sharp Williams, Vardaman, Hoke Smith, Thomas Dixon, D. W. Griffith, who produced *Birth of a Nation*—and practically all the anti-Negro group, are opposed to the I.W.W." *The Messenger* characterized the people who instructed Black people to avoid the IWW as white supremacists who openly hated Black people, white liberals who wanted to pacify militant Black resistance, and the Black bourgeoisie who likewise functioned to discipline and

Class, Race, Gender, and Empire      13

pacify militant Black struggle. "Negroes cannot afford to allow those Southern bourbons and race prejudiced crackers, together with their hand picked Negro leaders, to choose for them the organizations in which they shall go," proclaimed *The Messenger*. "We know that the American Federation of Labor is a machine for the propagation of race prejudice. We, therefore, urge the Negroes to join their international brothers, the Industrial Workers of the World, the I.W.W."[12] It is significant that *The Messenger* referred to Wobblies (members of the IWW) not as "our white brothers" but as "our international brothers." While it would have made sense to refer to the AFL's membership as "white," it would not have made sense to refer to multiracial, multiethnic Wobblies that way. The Justice Department seized on that kind of writing in the pages of *The Messenger* to vilify Black struggle as red and militant labor struggle as racially suspect.

US leaders' conflation of Black struggle with communism began much earlier than the first Red Scare. Historian Heather Cox Richardson recognizes this fact in her insightful discussion of the Paris Commune and Reconstruction in South Carolina, where US leaders vilified Black struggle as "communist" decades before the so-called first Red Scare. The present study, however, takes the conflation even further back. Richardson is quite correct that the US bourgeoisie was alarmed by the Paris Commune and feared the rise of a communistic element with the words of French anarchist Pierre-Joseph Proudhon on their lips, "property is theft." In the US context, policywise, white property owners' anxieties about communism translated into anti-Blackness. Northern Republicans began to abandon Reconstruction as they increasingly viewed Black political enfranchisement in South Carolina as leading to the "communistic" lower classes taking over the state: "South Carolina, whose elected government had a majority of African American legislators from 1867 to 1876, became the stage on which Northerners examined an America controlled by workers." In the wake of news of the Paris Commune, northern capitalists, represented by the Republican Party and its organs, began to equate Black suffrage and Black men in political office with working-class control over the means of production and Reconstruction efforts to economically enfranchise Black freed people with the anarchy of wealth redistribution.[13]

Richardson points out the irrationality of these anxieties, noting that many Black legislators elected during Reconstruction were, rather than communists, part of an emerging Black bourgeoisie whose interests were not those of the Black working class. Nonetheless, as this book discusses, there were indeed active Radical Republican Reconstructionists in the South, both white and Black, such as the Texans Albert and Lucy Parsons, who conceived of Reconstruction as a means of empowering the Black proletariat, and the Republican Party before it abandoned Reconstruction, as the party of Black workers and a vehicle

14    CHAPTER 1

for sweeping redistribution of wealth, property, and power. Richardson shows that white supremacist southern Democrats were effective in convincing northern Republicans to abandon Reconstruction by raising the specter of the Paris Commune to characterize Black southerners struggling for freedom as foreign communards laying siege to civilization.[14]

This book emphasizes that what Richardson insightfully observes in debates about Reconstruction in South Carolina was rooted in a larger and older settler colonial notion in which *communism*, as the property-owning class used the term, was a racial concept from the time it first entered the US ruling-class lexicon in the 1840s and early 1850s. This book further discusses US anxieties about the Paris Commune, and the commune's US version—in bourgeois imagination—the 1877 Railroad Uprisings, and how state violence to quell the uprisings was an extension of US genocidal war on Indigenous peoples.[15]

## The Bourgeoisie and the Proletariat

Some of the terms this book uses in relation to class structure, such as *working class*, *ruling class*, *bourgeoisie*, and *proletariat*, may seem outdated to some, but as will become apparent, they were very much in use in the discourse of the era under study, and were and are useful for describing the lived realities of the people in this history. This study uses the term *bourgeoisie* to describe people and institutions that owned capital: the class of people who owned and controlled the means of production, exchange, communication, and transportation. The term includes merchants, industrialists, rentiers, bankers, some professionals (such as railroad lawyers), the upper echelons of the military and law enforcement officer corps, and the economic, cultural, social, and political institutions that they controlled. Members of the bourgeoisie filled the seats of the legislative, judicial, and executive branches of the federal and state and territorial governments, exercising control over the military and law enforcement institutions. As US founding father John Jay's maxim went, "those who own the country ought to govern it."[16] For this reason, this study also refers to them at times as the *ruling class* or *capitalist class*. In layman's terms, they were the class of people who owned the country and made the rules.

The bourgeoisie's own internal rivalries and competing interests notwithstanding, by the 1880s they were a highly class-conscious, ideologically united group with common cultural and social institutions and a shared antagonism toward the working class.[17] That antagonism grew from the ruling class's older foundational enmity to Indigenous groups who were not proletarianized, existing—at least in the eyes of the bourgeoisie—outside and against the control of capitalist social relations and stood therefore as impediments to what the

Class, Race, Gender, and Empire    15

bourgeoisie called civilization. Later chapters will show that antagonism to Indigeneity, and its attendant mythological and ideological structure of the war of "civilization against savagery" preceded, accompanied, and shaped how the bourgeoisie conceived of and waged class war in US industrial centers.

As a result of the widespread misunderstanding of race, class, and gender as distinctly separate and narrow categories, the term *working class* can be very unclear. Many people incorrectly use the term *working class* as a synonym for white men in blue-collar professions. Class, however, is not about the socially defined "collar" of a person's profession—so-called blue, white, pink, etc.—but is about a person's power and position in relation to others and to the mode of production within the larger system. In the United States and globally, the working class cannot be properly characterized as primarily white or primarily male.

In basic Marxist and anarchist understandings alike, the working class, or proletariat, in the era of this study's focus, was that propertyless migrant mass of people who were displaced and driven by forces over which they had little to no control. They did not own capital, any significant amount of property, or the means of production, exchange, communication, and transportation and therefore were in the disadvantageous position of having to subordinate themselves to the capitalist class to survive. They were those who, in the words of working-class songwriter Ed Pickford, "never owned one handful of earth."[18] The working class was, and remains, multiracial, multiethnic, multilingual, and diverse in gender.

## White Identity

Further, many of the working-class people in the era under study, who would by today's standards be lumped into the category white, were characterized by the whites of the era—by those "respectable" people Jewish anarchist Emma Goldman derided as America's "arrogant whites"—as racially suspect outsiders.[19] Eastern European working-class Jewish migrants such as Goldman occupied a somewhat off-white racial position, what historian Matthew Frye Jacobson calls "provisional" or "probationary whiteness," as white US society decided whether such people belonged.[20] Discussed in later chapters, Goldman and her Jewish anarchist comrades failed that probation, as United States officials rounded them up, stripped them of citizenship, and deported them.

White was not something migrant groups simply were on account of skin color, but something they became by aligning themselves with ruling-class ideology and by actively participating in the project of white supremacist capitalist imperialist domination.[21] Historian Noel Ignatiev, in his classic work *How the Irish Became White*, showed how Irish migrants went from being a vilified, racialized, oppressed group, to becoming aligned with the oppressive white power structure of the United States in this manner. There is a price to becoming white, however, as doing so requires peoples to betray themselves. Ignatiev put it succinctly with the words, "In becoming white the Irish ceased to be Green."[22] When the Northern Irish civil-rights leader Bernadette Devlin McAliskey visited the United States in 1970 to elicit support from Irish Americans for her people's cause, she quickly realized that the Irish in America had long ceased to be Green. Remembering that visit later, she said,

> "My people"—and the people who knew about oppression, discrimination, prejudice, poverty and the frustration and despair that they produce—were not Irish-Americans. They were Black, Puerto Rican, Chicano. And those who were supposed to be "my people," the Irish-Americans who knew about English misrule and the Famine and supported the civil rights movement at home, and knew that Partition and England were the cause of the problem, looked and sounded to me like Orangemen. They said exactly the same things about Blacks that the loyalists said about us at home. In New York I was given the key to the city by the mayor, an honor not to be sneezed at. I gave it to the Black Panthers.[23]

She found more social, political, and ideological commonality with Black and brown freedom fighters and revolutionary socialists in the United States than with Irish Americans who had traded in their Irishness for whiteness.[24]

Second-generation, upwardly mobile Italians in the United States went through a similar process of becoming white, and thereby American, by aligning themselves with US patriotism, anti-Blackness, imperialism, and in some cases fascism. The process was likewise saturated with settler colonial mythology. By asserting themselves as whites, writes historian Jennifer Guglielmo, "Italians acquired preferential access through the denigration and exclusion of racial others." Like the Irish, Italians became white by betraying themselves, "as they did so against their own transnational history of racial stigmatization and class oppression." They did so to differentiate themselves, and racially distance themselves from, the earlier generation of migrant working-class Italian anarchists, socialists, and militant labor unionists—who lived, worked, and struggled for freedom in the era of this study's focus—who were racialized by whites as other-than-white, or at least a lesser kind of white, and "un-American" for their opposition to capitalism, white supremacy, imperialism, and the state.[25] That some prominent Italian-American associations to this day zealously champion Christopher Columbus and Columbus Day public celebrations as a way to assert their belonging and Americanness brings into relief the settler colonial foundations of white identity politics. Some Italian Americans asserted whiteness, and thereby Americanness, by proudly identifying themselves with the roots of European colonization of the Americas, despite its genocidal character.

## Anarchist Challenges to the Racial, Economic, and Colonial Order

Migrant working-class Italian anarchists in the United States—in contrast with those who sought to become white and thereby become American through political and cultural assimilation—were harsh opponents of Columbus Day celebrations. In *Immigrants against the State*, Kenyon Zimmer points out that as celebrations of Christopher Columbus became increasingly popular patriotic events, Italian anarchists in the United States, who believed in the abolition of borders and waging a "war on patriotism," disrupted Columbus Day parades and railed against Columbus in the Italian-language anarchist press. One of the main Italian anarchist newspapers in the United States in the early 1890s, *Il grido degli oppressi* (Cry of the Oppressed), denounced Columbus as a "pirate," mass murderer, enslaver, and "a man without principles, without any noble purpose, but consumed with the desire to plunder and command." These Italian anarchists as early as 1892—when US leaders were hyping up Columbus mythology in preparation for the 1893 World's Columbian Exposition—argued that Columbus's subjugation of the Indigenous population was the basis for "racial prejudices and hatreds" in America and "the martyrdom of negroes in the South." These working-class migrant Italian anarchists saw European colonization of the Americas and the anti-Indigenous massacres that such colonization was built on as the foundation for US-American anti-Black racism and therefore viewed celebrations of that colonization as something to condemn and oppose.[26]

Migrant working-class Italian anarchists in the era were developing sharp analyses of the intertwined nature of capitalism, colonialism, and white supremacy. A 1909 issue of the Paterson, New Jersey, Italian-language anarchist paper *L'era nuova*, charged that the "white race has acted against all the other races like a predatory animal." *L'era nuova* found that predatory behavior rooted in Columbus's "discovery of America": a "discovery" that, rather than marking the beginning of a period of enlightenment, "marks the beginning of a period of destruction, which lasts even today for the shame of humanity." *L'era nuova* saw white supremacy not as mere ignorance, individual prejudice, or bigotry but as the white race's "systematic destruction of the races of color." In another article, the Paterson anarchists called race science into question, arguing that the concept of race had more to do with historical and sociological factors, and the interests of the state, than it did with any objective biological reality.[27]

Scholars of US anarchism, such as Kenyon Zimmer, Jennifer Guglielmo, and Kathy Ferguson notice that the United States, in immigration law and in cultural representation, racialized migrant anarchists as a form of social control, labor control, and border control.[28] This study will discuss in part the relationship between racialization and the anarchists' opposition to the notion of private property and their challenges to dominant gender ideals, capitalism, empire, and the state. The anarchists' vision of freedom was not socialism under a US flag enacted through the nominally democratic channels of government, but a post–United States, and for that matter poststate, socialism. For example, in a speech to the IWW in 1913 in San Francisco, South Asian anarchist Har Dayal pointed to a US flag hanging in the lecture hall and called it a "sign of slavery" that should be done away with.[29] The anarchist Alexander Berkman wrote that "an anarchist knows that he has no country. . . . I recognize neither flag nor country."[30] It was not only US empire that anarchists opposed, but empire itself. The Japanese anarchist feminist martyr Kanno Sugako exemplified the anarchist spirit of the era in the defiant writings she penned in 1911 in a Tokyo prison while awaiting execution: "Persecute us! Persecute us as much as you wish. The old way is fighting the new—imperialism versus anarchism. Go ahead: Take your piece of stick and try with all your might to stop the onrush of the Sumida River."[31] Anarchists aligned themselves with, and were, internationalists who stood against capitalism and empire.

Anarchists understood capitalism, colonialism, and empire to be part of the same system. They argued that it was the duty of the labor movement to stand in solidarity with colonized peoples across borders against militarism, colonialism, and empire. Alexander Berkman, whom the Justice Department deported for his antimilitarist activities, wrote,

> Class-consciousness and solidarity must assume national and international proportions before labor can attain its full strength. Wherever there is injustice, wherever persecution and suppression be—be it the subjugation of the Philippines, the invasion of Nicaragua, the enslavement of the toilers in the Congo by Belgian exploiters, the oppression of the masses in Egypt, China, Morocco, or India—it is the business of the workers everywhere to raise their voice against all such outrages and demonstrate their solidarity in the common cause of the despoiled and disinherited throughout the world.[32]

The anarchist vision was an anticolonial vision.

Guglielmo, for example, mentions that Italian anarchists in Harlem joined in common cause with Black communists to oppose fascism and colonialism, in protest against Mussolini's 1935 invasion of Ethiopia.[33] The young J. Edgar Hoover's newly created FBI hired translators to find out what working-class migrant Italian women in Paterson, New Jersey, were writing in the pages of Italian-language anarchist newspapers such as *La questione sociale* and *L'era nuova*. The Justice Department was alarmed to find out that these women were railing against US patriotism, militarism, US "race hatred," and "the crimes of the white race." Italian anarchists—seeing the respectable whites of the United States

Class, Race, Gender, and Empire     19

carry out anti-Black pogroms and lynchings—scoffed at the whites: "They call this a free country!"[34] To refer to such working-class migrants as "white working class" is anachronistic and misunderstands the nature of white identity politics.

It should nonetheless be noted that these racialized, vilified, oppressed, "off-white" migrant groups still held a privileged position in relation to Black, Indigenous, and some Mexican and Asian groups in the United States in that it was possible for the off-whites to become white over time by aligning themselves socially, politically, and economically with the dominant white society. Black, Indigenous, and some Mexican and Asian groups remained racialized and oppressed regardless of how much they aligned themselves with US interests. Internal colonialism theory, particularly Robert Blauner's classic work, remains useful for understanding why some racialized groups were able to eventually become white while others remained racially oppressed. Blauner's thesis was that racial minority groups created by colonization experience more intense prejudice, discrimination, and systemic racism than racial minority groups created by immigration. Blauner argued that the United States developed economically through the enslavement of Black people, the conquest of Indigenous peoples, and the seizure of territory from Mexico, and so groups that were racialized through those intertwined foundational processes are racialized on a much deeper and foundational level in the United States than immigrant groups. This is not to suggest that immigrant groups do not experience racial violence and oppression, but it is not equivalent to or as intense and enduring as what groups minoritized and racialized directly face by US colonization.[35]

To clarify: as this study's following chapters discuss the racialization of anarchists, they are not equating the racialization of eastern and southern European anarchists in the United States with Black, brown, and Indigenous experiences in the United States. This study is not suggesting that anarchists became the "new Indians" or anything of that nature. It is arguing that settler colonialism and imperialism were so formative for US institutions that they structured internal political repression and internal proletarian control: that the culture, ideology, and policies of anti-anarchism and anticommunism, grew from, were shaped by, and overlapped with the larger settler colonial and imperialist structure of the United States.

It is also important to recognize that there were Black, brown, and Indigenous people in the anarchist movement in the United States, and in the militant labor and anti-imperialist orbit of the anarchist movement. Black, Latinx, Asian, and Indigenous anarchists were not mere passive participants in the movement, but they shaped the global anarchist movement's development. As later chapters mention, the organs of the bourgeoisie seized on the presence of Black, Mexican, Indigenous, and South Asian people among the ranks of militant labor to racialize and thereby vilify anarchist-influenced labor organizing and agitating.

20    CHAPTER 1

To treat the experience of eastern and southern European migrant anarchists as equivalent with Black, brown, and Indigenous experiences in the era would be false, but to treat anarchism in the United States as a purely European phenomenon completely separate from Black, Asian, Latinx, and Indigenous struggle would erase the presence of many of the people who were at the center of the social movement space that anarchism inhabited. Taken together, in the work of historians such as Christina Heatherton, Maia Ramnath, Kirwin Shaffer, Peter Cole, David Struthers, Kenyon Zimmer, and Cristina Salinas, to name only a few out of many examples, one can see US and European-born anarchists, Mexican and Indigenous anarchists and Wobblies, Black workers and union organizers, Caribbean anticolonialists, South Asian anti-imperialists, and working-class people of several tongues, nationalities, ethnicities, and races inhabiting the same social movement spaces in the United States and overlapping with each other socially and organizationally, at times targeted by the same laws, state agencies, and programs, sharing jail cells and prison yards.[36]

Take, for example, the Bakunin Institute, founded near Oakland, California. Named after the Russian anarchist Mikhail Bakunin, it was founded in 1913 by South Asian anarchist and Indian independence movement leader Har Dayal, who intended it to serve as a "monastery" for his Order of the Red Flag. The purpose of the order, Dayal explained, was "promotion of industrial organization and strikes (in cooperation with the I.W.W. and the Syndicalist movements)" and, "in Asia and Africa, it will further the movements of progress and revolt in various countries." Run by South Asian anarchists, the Bakunin Institute functioned as an anarchist "modern school"—based on the ideas of the Spanish anarchist educator and martyr Francisco Ferrer—as well as a training center for anarchist propagandists. Bakunin Institute members published journals such as the Urdu-language *Ghadr* newspaper, which was the organ of the militant anticolonialist South Asian Ghadr Party, and the anarchist paper *Land and Liberty*, which took an explicitly anticolonial position, aligning itself with what it called "the impending struggle in Mexico, Ireland, Egypt, India, everywhere." "Anarchists," proclaimed *Land and Liberty*, "sympathize with and do their best to assist national movements of revolt throughout the world."[37]

At the Bakunin Institute on any given day, one could find Urdu- and Punjabi-speaking South Asians associated with Ghadr, migrant Italian Wobblies, working-class Jewish anarchists, Irish Republicans, and Indigenous and Mexican revolutionists associated with the anarchist paper *Regeneración* training and sharing knowledge and friendship with each other. The Bakunin Institute did not last more than two years, as the state targeted its participants with Roosevelt's Anarchist Exclusion Act and other counterinsurgency policies, imprisoning and deporting many, and driving others, such as Har Dayal, into hiding. Though short-lived, the Bakunin Institute exemplified the multiracial, multiethnic, multilingual, internationalist, and anticolonial nature of the anarchist movement in the era. When the state deported Emma Goldman and Alexander Berkman a few years later for their antimilitarist activity, the prosecution pointed to Goldman and Berkman's association with Har Dayal as evidence that they were enemies of the United States.[38]

Anarchism, like Marxism, originated in the "workingmen's" movements in Europe in the mid-nineteenth century, but it quickly spread, to an even greater degree than Marxism in the era, to become an important part of the globe-spanning anticapitalist, anti-imperialist, and anticolonialist networks, movements, and social currents. The Marxist historian Eric Hobsbawm wrote that prior to the rise of Bolshevism, the anarchist movement was "the characteristic form of the revolutionary left." The Marxist left, wrote Hobsbawm, "had in most countries been on the fringe of the revolutionary movement, the main body of Marxists had been identified with a de facto non-revolutionary social democracy, while the bulk of the revolutionary left was anarcho-syndicalist, or at least much closer to the ideas and the mood of anarcho-syndicalism than to that of classical Marxism."[39] Nonetheless, even after those admissions, Hobsbawm in that essay downplayed the significance of anarchism for the development of global radicalism and underrepresented the timeframe of syndicalism's relevance.

Later scholars have shown that anarchism had a significant presence or important influence in anticapitalist, labor, nationalist, and anticolonial movements in Central and South America, the Caribbean, the Middle East, North Africa, southern Africa, South Asia, East Asia, Southeast Asia, and the South Pacific.[40] In his study of Filipino anticolonialism, Benedict Anderson writes,

> Following the collapse of the First International, and Marx's death in 1883, anarchism, in its characteristically variegated forms, was the dominant element in the self-consciously internationalist radical Left. It was not merely that in Kropotkin (born twenty-two years after Marx) and Malatesta (born thirty-three years after Engels) anarchism produced a persuasive philosopher and a colorful, charismatic activist-leader from a younger generation, not matched by mainstream Marxism. Notwithstanding the towering edifice of Marx's thought, from which anarchism often borrowed, the movement did not disdain peasants and agricultural laborers in an age when serious industrial proletarians were mainly confined to Northern Europe. It was open to "bourgeois" writers and artists—in the name of individual freedom—in a way that, in those days, institutional Marxism was not. Just as hostile to imperialism, it had no theoretical prejudices against "small" and "ahistorical" nationalisms, including those in the colonial world. Anarchists were also quicker to capitalize on the vast transoceanic migrations of the era. Malatesta spent four years in Buenos Aires [as well as time in Egypt and Cuba]—something inconceivable for Marx or Engels, who never left Western Europe. Mayday

22    CHAPTER 1

[observed by workers on every inhabited continent] celebrates the memory of immigrant anarchists—not Marxists—executed in the United States in 1887.[41]

Concerning the development of anarchism in South Africa, Anderson writes, "the anarchist and syndicalist movement never appealed to more than a small section of the whites. Indeed, its main success was when it developed as a popular, radical, union tradition amongst the Africans, Coloured, and Indians."[42] To characterize anarchism as purely European, primarily white, or concerned only with some imagined "white working class" is simply incorrect. The multiracial, anticolonial, and anti-imperialist nature of the anarchist movement is part of the reason that the bourgeoisie employed colonialist counterinsurgency strategies against movements it perceived to be anarchist.

With the exception of the work of Peter Cole—who has written about the important organizing of Black Wobblies on the Philadelphia waterfront in the early twentieth century—and Lucien van der Walt—who has written about Black syndicalists and multiracial unions in early-twentieth-century South Africa—labor and working-class history has largely forgotten the importance of Black syndicalists for the development of twentieth-century class struggle and Black struggle.[43] Nevertheless, working-class Black radicals drawing in part from the anarchosyndicalist tradition remained on the cutting edge of militant class struggle—certainly to a greater degree than the AFL's timid white "middle class" leadership—well past the heyday of the IWW. For example, the League of Revolutionary Black Workers, which was forged in the fires of the 1967 Detroit Rebellion, conceived of their organizing in Detroit's automobile factories and Black communities as part of the anarchosyndicalist tradition. In a 2020 interview, two of the league's founding members, Darryl "Waistline" Mitchell and Donald Abdul Roberts, reminisced:

> But the working conditions post–World War II was horrendous. When we look at the industrial history of America, we talk about the development of industrial unionism based on the IWW. They were like the original anarcho-syndicalists, the Wobblies. The IWW were the first Wobblies in America. We used to like to say in the League of Revolutionary Workers, we were the last Wobblies. Our initial development was as anarcho-syndicalist revolutionaries who were won over to Marxism. And even then, we loved the heritage of us being anarcho-syndicalists first. We would fight at the drop of a hat, man. There was none of that book shit for us. We loved intellectual development, man, but we liked fighting more than that. That was our heritage.[44]

To characterize the working class, working-class struggle, anarchism, and labor militancy as white is an erasure of many of the people who were at the center of radical labor and working-class history.

Labor and working-class history has likewise largely forgotten the significance of Indigenous anarchists and syndicalists in the development of twentieth-century class struggle and anticolonial struggle. In the late nineteenth and early twentieth century, Indigenous people were on the cutting edge of militant labor struggle. For example, Squamish and Tsleil-Waututh workers contributed significantly to a culture of militancy on the Vancouver waterfront, where there were at least sixteen strikes between 1889 and 1923. It was Squamish and Tsleil-Waututh syndicalists who formed the first official union on the Vancouver waterfront in 1906, Local 526 of the Industrial Workers of the World. Local 526 nicknamed themselves "the Bows and Arrows," signaling that they conceived of their labor organizing as part of their larger Indigenous struggle against colonialism and capitalism. Some Indigenous leaders who organized for the welfare of their people, against settler colonialism—such as Andy Paull, Chief Dan George, Chief Simon Baker, and Chief Joe Capilano—were politicized and gained organizing skills as young workers on the waterfront during that period. In the words of sociologist Jeff Shantz, "Indigenous organizing is a part of the history of syndicalism. Syndicalism is part of the history of Indigenous organizing."[45] When the lens is broadened beyond North America, to include Central and South America, the importance of Indigenous anarchists for anticapitalist struggle in the Americas is undeniable.[46]

## Mode of Production and Race

In addition to ideological and political factors, the overarching economic system, or mode of production, conditioned society's racial notions. This concept was explained by the Afro-Guyanese radical historian Walter Rodney, who challenged both "orthodox" Marxist and nationalist notions of race and class. Rodney argued that groups' positions in relation to the means of production conditioned racial thought, so that race and class in capitalist society were intertwined. The capitalist system, said Rodney, constructed race as a category for determining how people have access to the means of production. Rodney pointed to the way various capitalist societies delineated race differently and how that delineation tracked with the peculiarities of how labor was delineated in various countries. As an example, he pointed to the Portuguese in Guyana. In the 1830s–1840s, British landowners in Guyana had Portuguese peasants brought from the Madeira Islands and the Azores to serve as indentured laborers to replace enslaved African laborers. Guyanese society then racially delineated the Portuguese as a separate, distinct, lower race than the European landowners who were delineated as white.[47] Race, argued Rodney, was economically defined, so that, to the Guyanese population in a capitalist system, it seemed reasonable to refer to the landowning Europeans as white, but to the Portuguese—who were poor and propertyless—as a separate race distinct from the Europeans. Of the Guyanese population, said Rodney,

> Their perception of race was inextricably bound up with their perception of how people made their living, how they had access to the means of production. And initially the Portuguese, like the Indians, like the Chinese, like the Africans, came into our society as subordinated labor, as bondsmen, and that automatically defined them as a different race. This to my mind is a very useful insight into the way in which racism was essentially a factor developing out of a particular mode of production, not out of any aberration in people's minds about color, because if that were so, then there would be no distinction between a Portuguese and another European.[48]

This notion of the inextricability of race and class as Rodney articulates is applicable to the US context. Guglielmo, in her study of Italian anarchist women in New York and New Jersey, writes, "Southern Italian immigrants also received daily lessons that they were perceived as menial workers who were racially distinct from, and inferior to, northern and western Europeans."[49] Some of the migrant working-class groups in which anarchism found a home were delineated by the dominant society as racially inferior in part because they entered the United States into low-wage, low-status positions in the labor system. David Roediger shows that even within the same industry, companies in the late nineteenth and early twentieth centuries paid workers differently according to racial difference: for example, the Arizona copper-mining industry's wage differentials corresponded to workers' racial delineations as Mexican, Italian, or white.[50] Racial thinking was part of the mode of production.

This is all to say that the terms *working class*, *anarchist*, *socialist*, and *communist* as they are used in this book are not referring only to white workers, and when this study does refer specifically to white workers, it does so explicitly. Even in many cases of economically subordinated people who in the dominant racial thinking of the present would be considered white, their lived reality and social position was more complex than a term like "white working class" can encapsulate. Class reductionist and race reductionist narratives are both inadequate.

## Gender, Capitalism, and Empire

The notion that historians must reckon with not just race, class, and gender, but race, class, gender, *and empire* is not a new insight but has long been articulated by Black left feminism—a term coined by literary scholar Mary Helen Washington—as well as by Indigenous feminist scholars.[51] While the Black left feminist tradition is not monolithic, some common characteristics running through it that distinguish it from liberal feminism are anti-imperialism and a radical working-class orientation. Exemplifying the tradition is Claudia Jones's classic 1949 essay, which the Communist Party USA made into a pamphlet, *An End to the Neglect of the Problems of the Negro Woman!*, in which Jones wrote,

> The bourgeoisie is fearful of the militancy of the Negro woman, and for good reason. The capitalists know, far better than many progressives seem to know, that once Negro women undertake action, the militancy of the whole Negro people, and thus of the anti-imperialist coalition, is greatly enhanced. . . .
>
> Wall Street's boast [that US-American women enjoy unprecedented equality] stops at the water's edge where Negro and working-class women are concerned. Not equality, but degradation and super-exploitation: this is the actual lot of Negro women!
>
> Consider the hypocrisy of the Truman Administration, which boasts about "exporting democracy throughout the world" while the state of Georgia keeps a widowed Negro mother of twelve children under lock and key. Her crime? She defended her life and dignity—aided by her two sons—from the attacks of a "white supremacist."[52]

Jones continued in this vein, comparing US foreign policy, and the rhetoric of US leaders, with the reality of working-class Black women who were subject to both official state violence and extralegal mob violence within the borders of the United States. Jones did not have a race-reductionist, gender-reductionist, or class-reductionist analysis but rather talked about racial, gender, and class oppression as the same system and did so within a larger critique of US imperialism, all while keeping concern for working-class Black women at the center of her analysis.[53]

Another classic document of Black left feminism, and a staple of undergraduate Gender and Women's Studies courses, the 1977 "Combahee River Collective Statement," is an anti-imperialist and anticapitalist document. "We realize," wrote the collective, that the liberation of all oppressed peoples necessitates the destruction of the political-economic systems of capitalism and imperialism as well as patriarchy."[54] More than twenty years later, former CRC member Barbara Smith, reflecting on the tradition of Black feminism and its potential, said that "It is a mistake to characterize Black feminism as only relevant to middle-class, educated women." For Smith, the tradition of Black feminism was not an academic parlor game for intellectual discussion but "always encompassed basic bread and butter issues." The struggles that carried that radical critique were not liberal campaigns for a more racially and gender diverse ruling class but were the struggles of working-class women on issues of labor, immigration, environmental racism, the carceral system, sovereignty, "and opposition to militarism and imperialism."[55]

Along with Black left feminism, Indigenous feminist analyses are particularly useful for making sense of the racialization of those the state vilifies as anarchists and communists and for understanding the relationship between state violence and gender violence, as well as how and why state violence often plays out in the form of gender and sexual violence. Aileen Moreton-Robinson's work, for example, explores the relationship between race and property: being property, owning property, and losing property. Moreton-Robinson talks about the nation-state itself as white property, the possession of white people, and the intertwined nature of property and whiteness within colonial logic.[56] The anarchists of the late nineteenth and early twentieth centuries were self-declared enemies of the very notion of property. They championed the slogan coined by French philosopher Pierre-Joseph Proudhon, "Property is theft!"[57] To exist outside the logic of property was to exist outside the logic of whiteness. Settler society's understanding of Indigenous peoples as propertyless was central to settler notions of them as uncivilized. Anarchist organizing, which anarchists intended to collectively empower propertyless people and disempower the property-owning class, toward a society without property and without classes, fit neatly into entrenched settler colonial notions of savagery and racial otherness.[58]

Anarchists' provocative attacks on dominant white supremacist and cis-hetero-patriarchal gender notions set them at odds with respectable settler colonial society years before state authorities in Illinois executed Albert Parsons for his labor organizing and anarchist political beliefs, white supremacist vigilantes in Texas nearly killed him for the crime of miscegenation. Lucy Parsons flaunted society's racial and gender conventions by taking a lead role in organizing Chicago's multiethnic, multiracial, multilingual, migrant proletarian population against the wealthy property-owning class.[59] Indeed, as will be discussed later, the presence of women as leading voices of the anarchist movement was seized on by the capitalist press to vilify the movement as deviant and savage.

Policing sexual relationships played a central role in establishing and maintaining white settler society and reinforcing the cis-hetero nuclear family as it was threatened by so-called dark hordes of migrant laborers filling the needs of industrial capitalism.[60] Anarchist organizing ran counter to such sexual policing. Anarchist organizers, many of whom were foreign-born migrant laborers themselves, attacked outright the cis-hetero-patriarchal norms of bourgeois white society. Migrant South Asian anarchist anticolonialists in California called for "the establishment of the complete economic, moral, intellectual and sexual freedom of woman."[61] Interracial relationships, which the state criminalized during that era, were accepted within the anarchist movement. Anarchist women such as Emma Goldman, Voltairine de Cleyre, and Lizzie Holmes mercilessly assailed the institution of marriage and Christian notions of "purity" and "chastity." The state sentenced anarchists to prison for distributing information about free love and contraception in violation of Comstock laws.[62] Several participants in the anarchist movement, including Emma Goldman, Ben Reitman, and Alexander Berkman unashamedly had homosexual as well as heterosexual relationships.[63] Such actions and positions put anarchists at odds with the dominant white settler society.

Gender is a necessary category of analysis for understanding settler colonial violence and anti-anarchist and anticommunist violence. There were several organized vigilante attacks and some lynchings—much of which included gender and sexual violence—against people whom vigilantes and state agents perceived as anarchists or socialists in the early twentieth century. Work by Indigenous feminist scholars such as Sarah Deer and Dian Million, which focuses on the state, colonialism, and sexual violence, is useful for making sense of the deliberate employment of sexual violence by vigilantes—violence that may otherwise seem senseless rather than systemic—against those they perceived as anarchists.

Rape played a significant role in colonialist attempts to destroy Indigenous nations, which in turn led to a cycle of sexual violence. In the words of Sarah Deer, "Alienation from one's homeland provides a strong foundation upon which sexual victimization can take place."[64] The anarchist movement was largely made up of propertyless people who were alienated from their homelands. Dian Million argues that sexual violence, rather than being incidental, is constitutive of the nation-state, colonialism, and modern capitalism.[65] Indeed, the work of several Indigenous feminist scholars points to the significant role of sexual violence and gender politics in the formation and perpetuation of the settler-colonial state.[66] Understanding the significance and role of gender and sexual violence in US colonial suppression of Indigenous nations illuminates the widespread employment of gender and sexual violence by police and vigilantes against anarchists and militant labor. It is one of the many ways that settler colonial repression strategies became antilabor repression strategies.

US empire historically is a patriarchal project even when state officials employed the language of liberal feminist values as a smokescreen.[67] The dominant narrative in wider US culture and politics tends to water down, or even erase, harsh anti-imperialist, anticapitalist critiques, in the process watering down the historical actors who made the critiques, so that empire becomes invisible and radicals become symbols of the very system that waged war on them. Consider the reflection garden at the FBI academy in Quantico, Virginia, where etched in stone is the most insipid of all Martin Luther King Jr. quotes: "The time is always right to do what is right." Consider how the liberal establishment turned Pakistani girls' education campaigner Malala Yousafzai into a symbol of Western liberalism, when in reality she was a socialist and an anti-imperialist who visited US President Barack Obama not to seek Western salvation for Pakistani girls but to tell him that his drone attacks against the Pakistani people were making matters worse and increasing terrorism.[68] This study emphasizes the capitalist, imperialist structure of the United States and, where relevant, includes some of the strong voices from below—such as Lucy Parsons, Emma Goldman, and Ricardo Flores Magón—who challenged that structure, without turning them into symbols of US progress.

## Conclusion: Class War

There are no "better angels" in the nature of empire. Empire is violent and authoritarian. Empire is the context in which US military and law enforcement forces modernized: and they did so less in the context of war with other European powers than they did through militarism for two main purposes: internal labor control, and external frontier control. Before entering World War I, US forces were already well experienced in both urban warfare and frontier warfare—and the weapons of this type of warfare, such as machine guns and artillery—through outward war against Indigenous nations and inward war against proletarian insurgency. US labor history is in part a history of state terror: the agents of the wealthy slaughtering the working class. When the military, police, and right-wing vigilantes employed "Indian War" weapons and strategies to slaughter working-class people by the dozens in US cities to crush the 1877 uprisings, it was only the beginning.

The state violence of 1877 was followed by more massacres and lynchings, such as Haymarket, Homestead, Pullman, Lattimer, Virden, the 1905 Teamsters Strike, the Paint Creek Mine War, the San Diego free speech fights of 1912, and the 1914 Ludlow Massacre, to name only a few of many possible examples. The growth in the militarization of US society because of World War I intensified US war against the working class, as exemplified by the 1917 lynching of Frank Little, the 1919 lynching of Wesley Everest, the violence against the steel strikes of 1919, the 1920 Battle of Matewan, the 1920 Anaconda Road Massacre, the 1920 Alabama Coal Strike, the 1921 Battle of Blair Mountain, the 1924 Hanapēpē Massacre, the 1927 Columbine Mine Massacre, the 1929 Marion Massacre, and the executions of the migrant Italian anarchists Sacco and Vanzetti, to only scratch the surface.

And these executions, lynchings, and massacres continued through the 1930s, dramatically exemplified by the decade-long Harlan County War, the 1932 Ford Massacre, the 1933 San Joaquin Cotton Strike, the 1934 Toledo Auto-Lite strike, the 1937 Memorial Day Massacre, the 1937 Women's Day Massacre, and on and on. All this state violence occurred alongside unceasing anti-Black lynchings and pogroms such as the 1917 East St. Louis Pogrom, the Red Summer of 1919, and the 1921 Tulsa Massacre, to name only three of literally thousands of possible examples, and continual ethnic cleansing of the US-Mexico borderlands.

While these many incidents and episodes were not identical and each had its own histories specific to its time and place, none was a unique isolated incident, but each was an expression of an underlying social structure or system. When looked at together through a wider lens, they give a glimpse of the United States as a country with an economic, political, and social hierarchy maintained by unceasing violence, cruelty, and brutality.

Black radical sociologist Oliver Cromwell Cox pointed out in his classic work that most lynching and racial mob violence of the late nineteenth and early twentieth centuries was led by the most enfranchised, property-owning, "respectable" white citizens and was about upholding the class structure of the United States, which was thoroughly entwined with the white supremacist racial structure.[69] The executions of the Haymarket anarchists, often portrayed by labor historians and left radicals as the height of US class war waged by the wealthy against the poor, was relatively minor in comparison with some of the episodes of the following five decades. When Illinois governor John Altgeld pardoned the remaining Haymarket anarchists, it was not an omen that the United States was developing a conscience. Rather, state violence in the form of counterinsurgency against the working class only intensified afterward. The present work serves to historically contextualize the development of US anticommunist counterinsurgency as a method of internal social control. It places this counterinsurgency in the larger context of US warfare against Indigenous peoples and violent US imperial expansion.

# 2

# "Civilization" versus "Savagery"

In popular understanding, anticommunism is largely rooted in the Cold War between the United States and the Soviet Union, with the two states competing for political, economic, cultural, and military dominance in the post–World War II period. Those who are more knowledgeable of US history look further back to the wave of antileftist repression from 1917 to 1921 that historians call the first Red Scare, which includes the Palmer Raids, when Attorney General A. Mitchell Palmer subjected hundreds of suspected foreign-born anarchists to detention and deportation. Labor historians take it even further back, to the events surrounding the 1886 Haymarket Tragedy, the Great Railroad Uprisings of 1877, or even to the Paris Commune of spring 1871, an event that alarmed some sectors of the US ruling class. Most historical narratives about US anticommunism, whether they be serious scholarly studies or popular narratives, describe anticommunism primarily as a capitalist reaction to suppress the labor movement and the spread of European-born socialism.[1]

In the United States however, anticommunism is older than these examples, and it developed directly out of the context of the enslavement of African people, elimination of Indigenous nations, and imperial expansion. US anticommunism first surfaced as an ideological defense of the white supremacist, settler colonial state: as a weapon against both the antislavery movement and Indigenous resistance to colonization. This fact is crucial to understanding the racialization of adherents to a political ideology—anarchism—which this chapter will later discuss.

As a revolutionary communist movement began to emerge in Europe, the United States was carrying out a military invasion and occupation of Mexico, taking more than five hundred thousand square miles of land from Mexican and Indigenous peoples. The conquest made Indigenous communities stateless insurgent populations with no citizenship rights. Three weeks after US and Mexican authorities signed the Treaty of Guadalupe Hidalgo, the Communist League published Karl Marx's influential pamphlet *Manifesto of the Communist Party* in London. Just as a nascent communist movement was beginning to transnationally disseminate a coherent communist ideology, the United States was debating whether the ceded territories would allow slavery and what to do about the continued existence of Native nations. It was in these debates over slavery and the "Indian question" that anticommunism made its first appearance in mainstream US political discourse.

The word *socialism* entered the lexicon in the late 1820s with the proliferation of utopian social experiments such as the short-lived Owenite communities and offshoots in the United States, Scotland, Ireland, and England. As early as the 1830s, US statesmen, journalists, intellectuals, and political organizers were aware of a revolutionary socialist movement in Europe. By the late 1840s they knew of German radicals who called their movement "communist." Some of these German communists, such as August Becker, author of the 1844 book *Was wollen die Kommunisten?* (What do the communists want?), migrated to the United States in 1848 to flee political repression after the 1848 uprisings. Some of these Forty-Eighters worked as left-leaning, Republican-aligned journalists and newspaper editors in the US Southwest and Midwest. Mainstream US newspapers reported on the nascent European socialist movement, as did the US workers' movement. The organs of the workers' movement—newspapers such as *Subterranean*, *Plebian*, and *Working Man's Advocate*—regularly reported on and were sympathetic to the activities of socialists in Europe.[2]

Nevertheless, while US state and business leaders had concerns about mobocracy, they did not see the US workers' movement as communist or as a threat to the system of private property. The mainstream of the movement in the United States was not revolutionary, anticapitalist, or anticolonialist. Notwithstanding the agitation of marginal radicals such as Thomas Skidmore, formations such as the Locofocos and the Workingmen's Party were reformist, working not to end the system of private property, but to make it fair through electoral and legislative action. Workers' associations were among the strongest supporters of Andrew Jackson, a leader who built his career on enslaving Black people and exterminating Indigenous peoples. The leading intellectual of the Workingmen's Party in the 1830s, George Henry Evans, preached moderation, arguing that electoral, rather than revolutionary, action was the right course for the US workers' movement. Despite Evans's romanticizing of Indigenous people, he was a strong proponent of US settler colonization, seeing newly conquered Western lands as a relief valve for industrial workers by providing opportunities for cheap land and financial independence. Historian Shelley Streeby shows that prominent labor activists and popular fiction writers who championed the working

32    CHAPTER 2

class and opposed nativism and racism in the 1840–50s still internalized and popularized US settler-colonial values. Popular fiction writer and labor activist George Lippard, for example, idealized US imperialism and settler colonialism as providing propertyless urban industrial workers a way out of oppression.[3] And so, the US establishment in the 1830–40s did not employ explicitly anticommunist rhetoric against the workers' movement. US leaders were far more anxious about the antislavery movement and Indigenous resistance to colonization.[4]

The earliest example in the *Congressional Record* of anticommunism being used as a rhetorical tool was a speech by South Carolina congressman Robert Barnwell Rhett in the House of Representatives on June 1, 1848. Rhett—who would soon after become the leading "fire-eater" in Congress and later a representative in the provisional government of the Confederate States of America—asserted on behalf of the legislatures of South Carolina, Virginia, Georgia, and Alabama that they would not tolerate the South being excluded from "colonizing any of the territory belonging to the United States."[5] By this he meant the rights of whites to enslave Black people must apply in the territories acquired from Mexico, and that the fact that Mexico had abolished slavery did not mean that the territories acquired from Mexico should continue prohibiting slavery. Rhett argued thus:

> The conqueror can enter and occupy the conquered country, and by military force may disregard any laws existing protecting persons or property. As he is omnipotent over the persons and property of the conquered, he can take with him into the conquered country any institutions [particularly slavery] recognized in his own.

To emphasize the point that conquerors are not subject to the laws of the conquered, Rhett asked, "Suppose a law establishing communism in property [were in force prior to US conquest], would that prevent us from holding property separately in the Territory?"[6] Proslavery lawmakers conceptualized imperial expansion, settler colonization, white racial domination, enslavement, and an economic system based on private ownership of property as part of the same nation-building project. Rhett rhetorically employed communism as one of that project's foils.[7]

As early as 1847, Karl Marx was giving talks introducing the notion that under the wage system, the interests of capital and labor are diametrically opposed. Southern US proponents of slavery seized on this idea to argue for the expansion of the institution of slavery into the Western territories. On July 11, 1848, as the US Senate considered a bill to establish the territorial government of Oregon, Virginia senator Robert Hunter—who would later become the Confederate States secretary of state—argued along those lines in his impassioned plea that the institution of slavery be allowed to spread westward unhindered.

Sounding almost like a Marxist, Senator Hunter asked his colleagues to look at the conditions in the manufacturing cities in Europe and the US North, where the economy was running by the wage system: overcrowding, child abuse, crime, destitution, suffering, brutality, and exploitation of the poor by the favored classes. "Is it surprising," asked Hunter, "with such spectacles as these before the public, that the doctrines of communism should find a footing amongst the laboring classes?"[8] By contrast, he continued, "this spectacle of a man willing to work, and dying for want of bread, is not to be found in the slaveholding states. . . . On the contrary, the subsistence of protection of the slave, from the cradle to the grave, is secured to him by positive legislation, by public enactment, and last, but not least, by private affection."[9] The wage system, argued Hunter, naturally led to an unstable society because of conflict between capital and labor and the unjust distribution of the profits created by labor. This instability was fertile ground for communist movements to grow and threaten private property itself. No such instability, Hunter argued, could be found in the South: "The southern slaveholder represents fairly both capital and labor, because he owns both, and interest makes him impartial and conservative in disputes between the two."[10] In Hunter's reasoning, slavery then ensured social harmony and was the best defense the system of private property had against communism, for there could be no conflict between capital and labor while enslavers owned both.

While southern US politicians raised the specter of communism to defend and expand the system of slavery into the US West, agents of the Office of Indian Affairs employed anticommunist discourse to justify eliminating Native nations from the US West. In fact, the first "communists" US authorities mobilized to contain and eliminate were not Marxists or anarchists but were Indigenous peoples. In reports to Congress dating as far back as 1850, US Indian agents referred to the Native peoples they were charged with overseeing as communists.

One such example is Alexander Ramsey, who served simultaneously as the territorial governor and superintendent of Indian affairs in Minnesota. Ramsey was appointed to this position by President Zachary Taylor. Prior to serving as president, Zachary "Old Rough and Ready" Taylor owned slave labor camps in Kentucky and Mississippi, where he enslaved more than two hundred Black people. Taylor's popularity stemmed from his success as an Indian killer—indeed, he was known for using bloodhounds to hunt recalcitrant Seminole people—and later his success in the US invasion of Mexico. Taylor handpicked Ramsey to make the lands west of the Mississippi safe for white settler colonization.[11]

In a report to Congress, Ramsey wrote that he was having a particularly difficult time dealing with the Dakota, who "live almost without law" and who "have no courts, no officers, no statutes, no debts to collect, no damages to pay."[12] The colonialist tactic of appointing a pliable chief through whom to control the group was not working on the "tribes of the Northwest" because of their democratic political structure: chiefs could not sign treaties or do any act binding on their people "contrary to popular approbation," and, Ramsey complained, a large number of braves accompanied the chiefs in every dealing with white officials to make sure of it.[13] Ramsey interpreted the "lawless" economic and political structure—in which the Dakota people collectively shared resources and power—as communism. In this "communism," wrote Ramsey, "lies the grand defect in the institutions, and the principal impediment to the civilization, of the red man."[14] Senator Henry Dawes would echo the same sentiment as justification for the genocidal Dawes Act thirty-five years later, arguing, after a visit to the "five civilized tribes," that "the defect of the system" was that "they own their land in common. . . . There is no selfishness, which is at the bottom of civilization."[15]

A month prior to Ramsey's report, one of Ramsey's subagents, Major Nathaniel McLean, argued similarly in his annual report to Congress. McLean reported that Dakota communities could best be subdued by breaking up their society's collective ownership of land through laws that strictly enforced individual private ownership: "Laws of this nature would also strike at the very root of one of the greatest evils which exist among them—their system of communism."[16] Speaking of the Dakota peoples, McLean wrote, "The great hindrance to their civilization is that communism in which they live."[17] He continued, "The time is drawing near when the Indian must disappear before the overwhelming tide of emigration of the Anglo-Saxon race" unless he abandon that communism and "adopt the agricultural system of the white man for subsistence."[18] Here it is clear that the system of private property was racialized as white, and *communist* was likewise as much a racial term as an economic one.[19] To equate civilization with private property was not a new concept. Indeed, it was the foundation of John Locke's justifications for British settler colonization of the Americas.[20] To refer to Indigenous political and economic structures with the phrase "their system of communism," however, was a new development.

Historically, US anticommunist rhetoric has never been far removed from state terror. Unsuccessful in their attempts to eliminate Dakota peoples through assimilation programs designed to whiten and proletarianize Indigenes through the system of private property, US officials turned to policies of expulsion and extermination. In a special session of the Minnesota legislature, Governor Alexander Ramsey told his colleagues, "Our course then is plain. The Sioux Indians of Minnesota must be exterminated or driven forever beyond the borders of Minnesota."[21] US Army troops slaughtered Dakota civilians and rounded up hundreds of others into concentration camps. Three months later President Abraham Lincoln ordered the largest mass execution in US history, with thirty-eight Dakota men—reduced from the more than three hundred captives Ramsey wanted executed—hanged. Minnesota officials placed a bounty on

"Civilization" versus "Savagery"    35

Dakota scalps, thereby encouraging white settlers to attack the remaining Dakota people. An ordinary white settler-farmer found and assassinated Dakota leader Little Crow, for which Minnesota paid him $500, and $75 to his son, for turning in Little Crow's scalp. In this way, the Dakota were dispossessed of their homelands, which were in turn carved up into private property for federally subsidized white settlers.[22]

The first "red menace" the United States ruling class organized violence to eliminate was Indigenous existence, not European anarchists or communists, and US violence against the former structured and gave meaning to its violence against the latter. By the late 1870s, when a large, anarchist- and communist-influenced militant labor movement began to mobilize, US anticommunism was already formed—as an anti-Black and anti-Indigenous discourse—through the ongoing violent process of imperial expansion and settler colonization. The language and policies of Indian elimination became the language and policies of anti-anarchist repression. In the late-nineteenth-century United States, white terms such as "savage reds" referred simultaneously to Native peoples and anarchists.

## Reds

Historians often conceive of Gilded Age and Progressive Era urban and labor unrest as disconnected from the framework of US settler colonialism, but in the eyes of the agents of repression, these processes—of imposing urban social control and colonizing the West—were part of the same project. The law-enforcement literature and ruling-class press of the era vilified and equated Indigenous groups and anarchists as threats to civilization. In addition to Indigenous groups and anarchists both being "reds," anarchist women were "squaws," anarchist men were "braves," anarchist meetings were "war dances," anarchist-sympathetic neighborhoods were "reservations," and Indigenous insurgents were "anarchists."

Part of the reason for the terminological state of affairs is that the state targeted both groups simultaneously. As the US Army and civilian armed settlers hunted Chiricahua Apache in the Southwest, Chicago police hounded radical labor organizers such as Lucy Parsons in Chicago.[23] As President Grover Cleveland signed the intentionally genocidal Dawes Act into law, the soon-to-be executed Haymarket anarchists sat in the Cook County jail preparing for their upcoming appeal hearing. The external genocidal process historians misleadingly term the "Indian Wars" overlapped with the beginning of intense internal state repression against a newly radicalized labor movement. As historian Franklin Rosemont wrote, "For most of 1886, Apaches and anarchists were almost equivalent bugaboos in American newspapers and pictorial weeklies," and the US press described both Native resistance and working-class resistance as outbreaks of "savagery."[24]

Take, for example, famous Chicago police captain Michael Schaack—author of the 1889 book *Anarchy and Anarchists: A History of the Red Terror and the Social Revolution in America and Europe; Communism, Socialism, and Nihilism in Doctrine and Deed; the Chicago Haymarket Conspiracy, and the Detection and Trial of the Conspirators*—who relied heavily on anti-Indian tropes to describe anarchists. His book recounted his efforts as a police officer in 1880s Chicago to protect civilization from savage anarchists and the labor movement that they organized. Schaack derogatorily referred to metalworkers on strike as "braves."[25] When residents of a prounion, working-class neighborhood near McCormick Harvester Company complained about the heavy police presence in their community during a McCormick lockout, the police captain dismissed their concerns with the characteristic contempt of a colonial official toward colonial subjects, writing, "The police were on what these misguided people considered their own reservation."[26]

While presented as a serious exposé of the radical left in Europe and the United States, Schaack's book employed the same kind of rhetoric that was common in popular wild West adventure novels, in which hardy white men civilized the American West by defeating Indians, outlaws, and wild beasts. By casting anarchists and organized labor as the bloodthirsty Indians of popular white imagination, Schaack glorified the police as heroic white men taming a wild frontier. For example, he described a meeting of the International Carpenters Union in Chicago as though the carpenters were an army of Native warriors preparing to attack a white settlement. All 180 men, wrote Schaack, "were present with their rifles, and they were loud for war. . . . They refused to be quieted, and, like Comanche Indians about to take to the war-path, they examined their revolvers and brandished their guns. . . . In anticipation of blood, they screwed up their courage by frequent libations."[27] In equating carpenters' union members with Comanche warriors, Schaack employed the "drunken Indian" trope, which was a racist trope he relied on repeatedly throughout his book.

Schaack described a group of anarchists that he claimed plotted to bomb a police station thus: "The cut-throats skulked around the station like so many Indians around the cabin of a helpless settler. . . . True to their instincts, however, these Chicago reds could not do without their beer while awake, and they made frequent trips to the neighboring beer saloons."[28] Here Schaack used the term *reds* in the dual sense of Indians and revolutionary socialists. These kinds of tales of the violent depravity of the anarchists, which fill the pages of Schaack's book, were almost always followed up with descriptions of the courageous actions of the police to save the city from the Chicago reds. The story always had a happy ending: "But the dashing and aggressive movements of the police, backed by courage and discipline, soon demonstrated to the howling rabble the hopelessness of the struggle . . . and several revolutionists bit the dust, maimed and wounded."[29] Schaack employed the mythological structure of the Old West adventure tale: "The masterly courage and brilliant dash of the men soon sent the anarchists flying in every direction." *Anarchy and Anarchists* is thoroughly a product of US settler colonizer culture.

Schaack was far from alone with this slippery usage of terms like *reds* and, drawing on settler colonizer culture—e.g., the tropes found in popular Western frontier adventure tales—to give narrative structure and meaning to confrontations with anarchists. Joseph Pulitzer's newspaper the *New York World*—the leading national organ of the Democratic Party in the era—reported on an anarchist "den" within which the anarchists' "Queen," Emma Goldman, ruled over "Savage Reds."[30] Pulitzer's reporter cast himself in the colonial trope of the white traveler entering a stronghold of scantily clad, dark Natives to be surrounded by large and bloodthirsty armed savages calling for violence in their foreign language, and who refrain from tearing him to shreds only because the chief calls them off. The reporter entered the anarchists' lair and, "one by one," he wrote, "the swarthy, half-clad and grimy anarchists" filed into the room between him and their "queen":

> A dozen stalwart black and redbearded Anarchists stood a few feet back of the reporter. . . . One man stood near the table with an ice-pick in his hand. . . . The group grew larger. . . . One burly Anarchist, broader chested than Sullivan, clinched [*sic*] his fists and, with face aflame with beer, heat and anger, exclaimed in German that all reporters should be killed.[31]

Luckily for the reporter, the savages' queen, Emma Goldman, had a whim to let him live, and with a nod she called "her slaves" off.[32] Such narratives were not only yellow journalism but colonialist literature—in that their authors relied on culturally ubiquitous colonialist notions to construct them. Note terms such as *swarthy* and *redbearded*, both of which conjured up images of racialized others.

Compare these narratives to the popular frontier adventure tales of the era. One example is the Warren Wildwood book *Thrilling Adventures among the Early Settlers*, first published in 1862 and republished in 1890. It included tales of Daniel Boone, Davy Crockett, Texas Rangers, and other hardy white men who paved the way for civilization's spread westward by killing wild beasts, Indians, Black insurgents, Mexicans, and outlaws.[33] Wildwood's white protagonists asserted their manliness by sneaking up on and murdering savage Indians. In one scene, a white army scout, the hero of the story, "with the rapidity and power of a panther" seized two Native women by their throats and drowned the "elder squaw" in the Hockhocking River, to "inflict a noiseless death upon the squaws, and in such a manner as to leave no trace behind."[34] Soldiers, sheriffs, and of-

38    CHAPTER 2

ficial law enforcers were not the only heroes; so were ordinary white settlers, vigilantes, and lynch mobs. In one section, a heroic white lynch mob numbering in the hundreds prevented what "began to look like an insurrection among the negroes" by hanging and burning the ringleader, a man of "savage disposition" named "Black Dick."[35] Wildwood explained that lynch mobs were part of the state apparatus, which arose to protect civilization from savagery in times and places where formal state authority was lacking:

> In the absence of legitimate authority and regular organizations, lynch law usurps its place, and ofttimes visits a swift and terrible retribution upon the offenders. Anarchists and desperadoes are either exterminated or driven farther west, and the beautiful spirit of order and progress emerges from the chaos of confusion and blood.[36]

The civilizing process was one of extermination, containment, and expulsion.

Such are the tales that urban police, judges, lawmakers, soldiers, university students, and businessmen in the 1880s and 1890s grew up reading or hearing, and they are the narratives that informed their notions of manliness, duty, and heroism. By casting anarchists as Native savages and frontier outlaws, urban police cast themselves as the heroes of such adventure tales. Cultural historians such as Shelley Streeby and Michael Denning have observed that popular frontier adventure novels in the era were often related to class conflict and that "a working class audience may have viewed Western outlaws as figures of class conflict."[37] While working-class readers may have been entertained by such tales and viewed "Western" characters through a lens of class conflict, urban law enforcement inserted themselves outright into these frontier myths as a way of legitimizing their authority.

*History of the Chicago Police*, a book that the Chicago Police Department funded and published in 1887—when it faced a public-relations crisis—explicitly cast the anarchists as Indians, and vice versa, and the police as Indian killers, and vice versa: "The little garrison which we find sheltered inside the block house or behind the palisades were Chicago's first police force, and the Indians they had to contend with were her first anarchists, and a few years later, near this very spot, occurred the first riot and massacre."[38] The reference is to Fort Dearborn, an army post the United States established in 1803 as a base of operations for genocide against the Indigenous peoples who lived in the region. The authors recognized the fort's genocidal purpose, writing that the soldiers, weapons, and equipment the fort contained "were intended to bring about the destruction of their [the Illinois and Potawatomi peoples'] power and their final extermination from the hunting grounds along the river and by the great lake" through "grasping, unyielding, relentless and deadly" military force.[39] By the 1880s, Fort Dearborn—or rather, the settler mythology surrounding it—held special significance in Chicago public memory and still does into the present. The first red star in the Chicago flag represents and celebrates Fort Dearborn. The other "riot and massacre" to which the police narrative referred was the Haymarket "riot and massacre." In making that association, the Chicago Police inserted themselves, and their anarchist antagonists, into one of Chicago's major founding myths: the myth of the Fort Dearborn Massacre.

As the myth went, in the summer of 1812, savage and bloodthirsty tomahawk-wielding Natives massacred the good and defenseless God-fearing pioneers of Fort Dearborn, who became Chicago's first martyrs in the cause of civilization. The reality, as historian Ann Durkin Keating writes, is that the Potawatomi attack against the US Army at Fort Dearborn "was not a 'massacre,' but part of a declared war that the United States waged against Great Britain and their Indian allies. As such, the Potawatomis and their allies won a military victory."[40] The military attack against Fort Dearborn was part of Tecumseh's pan-Indian alliance response to an actual massacre that US forces, led by William Henry Harrison, committed against Prophet's Town. US forces killed more than two hundred Indigenous people in Prophet's Town, laid waste to crops, burned the town, destroyed the granary, and looted buildings and bodies. The looting included digging up graves and mutilating corpses. This, writes Roxanne Dunbar-Ortiz, "was the famous 'battle' of Tippecanoe that made Harrison a frontier hero to the settlers and later helped elect him president."[41]

Indeed, massacring noncombatants and attacking nonmilitary targets was Harrison's strategy for eliminating the Indigenous presence in the region. His forces exemplified what military historian John Grenier calls the "first way of war": a military strategy that included "razing and destroying enemy villages and fields; killing enemy women and children; raiding settlements for captives; intimidating and brutalizing enemy noncombatants; and assassinating enemy leaders."[42] Harrison's purpose in ordering rangers and US Army regulars to employ this strategy against Prophet's Town was that the influential Shawnee spiritual leader Tenskwatawa, who preached pan-Native unity and the rejection of European ways, lived there. Destroying Prophet's Town to the extent of digging up graves and mutilating corpses was calculated to demoralize and terrorize not just combatants, but the entire people, and thereby eliminate the social, spiritual, and ideological underpinnings of Indigenous resistance to colonialism in the Northwest.[43]

In response to that massacre, and similar activity by US forces acting under William Henry Harrison's authority in the region—activity that was, by US officials' stated intentions, genocidal—a pan-Indian alliance attacked the settlements and military bases that were supplying and supporting US forces. As part of this campaign, they destroyed Fort Dearborn. Fort Dearborn was a legitimate military target. The forces who attacked it, rather than being bloodthirsty villains, were resisting genocide, fighting for nothing less than the survival of their peoples. As Keating writes, "The Potawatomis and their allies did not see the arrival of American settlers and institutions as progress, but as catastrophe."[44] They were fighting to drive out the settler forces that were intent on eliminating Native territories.[45]

Nevertheless, the founding myth of a "Fort Dearborn Massacre" became particularly powerful in the 1880s-90s, as Chicago's law enforcers and well-heeled white citizens faced a new savage enemy in the form of dangerous mobs of "howling anarchists."[46] In preparation for the events of 1893, bitter enemy of the labor movement and wealthy industrialist George Pullman—whose workers the following year would initiate the famous Pullman Strike under Eugene Debs's American Railway Union—funded a Fort Dearborn Massacre monument to be unveiled during the Chicago World's Columbian Exposition.[47]

The exposition was a celebration of colonization and empire.[48] It was authorized and funded by an act of the US Congress, "to provide for celebrating the four hundredth anniversary of the discovery of America by Christopher Columbus."[49] The bill's final approval came from the grandson of genocider William Henry Harrison, President Benjamin Harrison. The layout of the fair was explicitly white supremacist to represent "the progress of civilization."[50] Fairgoers entered through the Midway Plaisance, which was lined with exhibitions of dark and foreign peoples arranged according to the dominant racial hierarchy of the era, leading into the White City, which represented the pinnacle of civilization, manhood, and whiteness. Historian Daniel Bender points out that in the design of the fair, class hierarchy and racial hierarchy were intertwined in such a way that the designers of the fair equated the industrial working-class with the dark "savages" of the Midway. On the most primitive end of the Midway, next to the "Dahomey village" attraction, stood a model of a workingman's home.[51] Such white supremacist, capitalist, imperialist representations were accurate reflections of the ideology underlying US institutions. Indeed, after the US invaded and occupied the Philippines the following decade, the Department of War commissioned the chief architect of the White City, Daniel H. Burnham, to design the homes and offices of US colonial officials in Manila and Baguio.[52]

With the exposition shining the national spotlight on Chicago, the city's ruling class took the opportunity to further entrench the mythology on which their own claim to legitimacy rested. With George Pullman's money, they hired Danish sculptor Carl Rohl-Smith—who was in Chicago working on a sculpture of Benjamin Franklin for the White City—to create the bronze monument to the "martyrs" of Fort Dearborn. Rohl-Smith's sculpture was directly the product of US colonial violence. As live models for the Potawatomi figures in the sculpture, he used prisoners of war Kicking Bear and Short Bull, Lakota—not Potawatomi—warriors and spiritual leaders captured by the US Army at the 1890

"Civilization" versus "Savagery"    41

Wounded Knee Massacre. The army held them captive at Fort Sheridan, just north of Chicago. Fort Sheridan was named in honor of Indian-killer General Philip Sheridan, who was famous for coining the US-American aphorism "The only good Indian is a dead Indian."[53] Kicking Bear and Short Bull, survivors of a massacre committed against their people by a white settler military force, would now have their bodies used by white settler society to represent both the bellicose Native murderer and the noble savage of white imagination.[54]

This imagination was on full display at the monument's unveiling ceremony, which was attended by the most prominent members of Chicago's social, economic, and political elite.[55] The president of the Chicago Historical Society, Edward Mason, opened the ceremony with a speech in which he praised the heroes of Fort Dearborn who rescued the region from its Indigenous inhabitants, whom he referred to as "the invader and the barbarian."[56] Former president Benjamin Harrison—the grandson of the man who designed and ordered the series of anti-Indian massacres, raids, and assassinations to which the Pan-Indian attack on Fort Dearborn was a response—spoke next. He spoke of the bronze memorial to Fort Dearborn in a reverent tone as though Fort Dearborn represented something sacred. It was "more a thing of magic" than the White City itself.[57] He praised his Indian-killer ancestors, whom he identified with the settler-colonizer euphemism "the pioneer."[58]

> Free and unconventionally brave and self-reliant, as responsive to the cry of distress as a knight-errant, he pushed the skirmish line of civilization from the Alleghanies to the Rockies. All honor to him! He labored and forever entered into his rest. We possess the lands he won from the savagery of Nature and of the natives.[59]

White settler colonizer mythology was central to the US ruling class's conception of itself. That being the case, it makes sense that the professional police force, still a relatively new institution struggling to gain legitimacy in the eyes of the public, would insert itself, and its enemies, into this mythological structure.

*History of the Chicago Police* is a colonizer story about the centrality of the police and their Indian-killer predecessors to the development of Chicago from a small "outpost of civilization" to one of the nation's largest and most modern cities.[60] It takes the reader from heroic white US forces "freeing Northern Illinois of the presence of savages" in the early nineteenth century to the successors of those heroes, the police, maintaining law and order in a city "infested with anarchists" in the late nineteenth century.[61] Referring to the establishment of Fort Dearborn in 1803–4, the authors wrote,

> We have now located at Chicago, firstly, a police department, in the nature of a garrison of United States regulars; secondly, a lawless mob in the nature

of Illinois and Pottawattamie Indians; thirdly, the rabble in the nature of adventurers, hunters and shiftless half-breeds, and fourthly, the prominent citizen, represented in the person of Mr. John Kinzie and a few small French fur traders.[62]

The authors equated Fort Dearborn's struggle against Natives and desperados with the police department's struggle against anarchists and the great proletarian rabble, both in service to the one category of person that mattered: the "prominent citizen,"—the white, wealthy property owner or businessman.

By equating anarchists with Natives and police with Indian killers, urban police asserted their own legitimacy at a time professional police forces were relatively new, and at a time the police were under heavy scrutiny and international condemnation from the left for their role in the Haymarket Affair. In casting themselves as the hardy white men who tamed the wilderness by exterminating the savages who threatened civilization, the police bolstered their authority and the public image of policing itself.[63] The casting of anarchists as Natives, and police as Indian killers, also suggests a similarity or common assumptions between the psychology underlying Indian killing with the psychology underlying late-nineteenth-century anticommunism.

## The Red Sisterhood

The kind of narrative that equated anarchists with Native savages was shaped heavily by the dominant gender ideology of the era, and that ideology was likewise deeply intertwined with white supremacy and colonialism.[64] Take, for two examples, police captain Schaack's description of anarchist women as "squaws" at an anarchist meeting and his reference to a "war dance":

A lot of crazy women were usually present, and whenever a proposition arose to kill someone or to blow up the city with dynamite, these "squaws" proved the most bloodthirsty. In fact, if any man laid out a plan to perpetrate mischief, they would show themselves much more eager to carry it out than the men, and it always seemed a pleasure to the Anarchists to have them present. They were always invited to the "war dances." Judge Gary [who presided over the Haymarket trial], Mr. Grinnell [the prosecutor in the Haymarket trial], Mr. Bonfield [the lead detective in the Haymarket investigation] and myself were usually remembered at these gatherings, and they fairly went wild whenever bloodthirsty sentiments were uttered against us.[65]

The police captain's description of the women at one meeting is telling:

There were thirteen of these creatures in petticoats present, the most hideous-looking females that could possibly be found. If a reward of money had been

"Civilization" versus "Savagery"    43

offered for an uglier set, no one could have profited upon the collection. Some of them were pock-marked, others freckle-faced and red-haired, and others again held their snuff-boxes in their hands while the congress was in session. One female appeared at one of these meetings with her husband's boots on, and there was another one about six feet tall. She was a beauty! She was raw-boned, had a turn-up nose, and looked as though she might have carried the red flag in Paris during the reign of the Commune.[66]

Besides being an artifact of a deeply misogynistic police culture, this passage is saturated with colonialist gender ideology. Notice that the author not only racially othered the women—largely playing on the anti-Irish sentiments of the era: red hair, freckle-faced, turn-up nose—but he pathologized and animalized them: they were not women or ladies, but were *crazy women, creatures,* and *females.* He described them as the opposite of the dominant standard of civilized white womanhood.

The depiction also contains an element of the old outside agitator narrative, with anarchist women goading working-class men on to acts of disobedience to authority beyond what men would otherwise be inclined to do. The origin of the outside agitator narrative, or at least an earlier frequent use of it, resides in slavery: enslavers and their allies often blamed enslaved people's revolts throughout the Americas on abolitionist propaganda and agitators from outside their region. It became a common anti-anarchist and antilabor trope in the United States and Western Europe in the era. US statesman John Hay—who two years previously had resigned his position as assistant secretary of state and was currently working as a *New York Tribune* editor—was vacationing in Paris in March 1883 when a mass procession of the unemployed through the Esplanade des Invalides—coordinated by the carpenters union affiliated with the radical *Chambre Syndicale* trade-union movement—left him feeling very uneasy. Unemployed working-class people looted loaves of bread from three bakeries during the march. The anarchist Louise Michel—who was a hero to revolutionaries internationally for her leadership during the Paris Commune and her subsequent anticolonial activity in the South Pacific with Indigenous Kanak people against French control of New Caledonia—was not involved in any looting, but John Hay, along with the Parisian bourgeoisie, blamed her because she carried the black flag at the head of the procession.[67] In a letter to his wealthy industrialist father-in-law Amasa Stone, Hay blamed outside labor-movement agitators: "The laborers have had the mischief put into their heads by trades-unions." Of these outside agitators, he singled out, pathologized, and dehumanized Louise Michel, whom he referred to as "a crazy creature named 'Louise Michel.'" Had cavalry soldiers not dispersed the crowd, claimed Hay, Michel would have led the crowd to attack the very Élysée Palace.[68]

The state likewise singled Michel out and charged her with being the instigator of the looting. There was something particularly deviant about a woman carrying an anarchist flag at the head of a procession. Just two months prior to the "bread riot," a court in Lyon sentenced more than sixty suspected anarchists, including the famous Russian geographer and biologist Peter Kropotkin, to five years imprisonment for the false charge of belonging to the outlawed International Workingmen's Association—an organization that was well on the decline and no longer existed in France. During the Lyon trial, the anarchists read from a statement written by Kropotkin, in which they said, "Scoundrels that we are, we demand bread for everyone."[69] The judge in the Paris bread riot trial harped on Michel's black flag and anarchist affiliation. He asked Michel, "What was your purpose in crossing Paris with a black flag?" She responded, "I wanted to make people see that the workers didn't have any [bread] and that they were hungry. The black flag is the flag of strikes and the flag of famines." At this point, the judge had his bailiff hold up Michel's makeshift flag—a broom handle with a black piece of cloth attached to it—as though it were a dramatically damning piece of evidence. It was clear that she was not on trial over a few stolen loaves of bread, she was on trial for being an anarchist, and worse, an anarchist woman who beguiled working-class men. The judge sentenced her to six years imprisonment in solitary confinement followed by ten years of police surveillance, a significantly harsher punishment than what the judge in Lyon sentenced the anarchist men with two months prior.[70]

"Woman as outside agitator" was a very familiar narrative to respectable Christian people in the Gilded Age and Progressive Era: after all, it was Eve, the first woman, who was the original outside agitator. Adam was perfectly content in the Garden before Eve entered the scene, so easily beguiled by the serpent Lucifer into disobeying authority. The idea of eating the forbidden fruit never entered guileless Adam's mind, but it was Eve who gave him the fruit and told him to eat: a crime that he, like a good union scab or colonial informant, immediately snitched about to the Lord God when questioned. God asked Adam, "Hast thou eaten of the tree, whereof I commanded thee that thou shouldest not eat?" To which Adam replied, "The woman . . . , she gave me of the tree."[71] Naïve, innocent working-class men could not possibly be so discontented in free, democratic America. Some daughter of Eve had to seduce them into the evils of anarchism.

This narrative was common in the newspapers of the era. "Women Anarchists Have Become the Terror of the World's Police," read one Rochester headline:

Their Daring Crimes Are Said to Have Outstripped the Deeds of Brothers of the Red. Search for the Woman is Becoming a Safe Rule in Crimes Proceeding From Anarchistic Violence—The Guardians of the World Nearly Always Find a Woman Implicated When a Ruler is Stricken Down—Emotional Women Lose Sense of Fear.[72]

Of course, "emotional women" posed against "rational men" trope is a staple of US and European patriarchal thought and draws from colonial notions of a masculinized "rational" West versus a feminized "irrational" East. The *Los Angeles Times* ran the Rochester story under the headline "Female Terrors: Most Bloodthirsty of Agitators Are the She-Dogs of Anarchy." The story was on the business page of the *Los Angeles Times* Sunday morning edition. In the center of the page was a large image of five of the supposedly most dangerous people in the United States, with the caption, "Female Terrorists of America."[73]

The featured so-called terrorists were Emma Goldman—identified as "Queen of American Anarchists," the Jewish immigrant socialist Rose Pastor Stokes—"Millionaire Socialogist" [sic], the Russian former political prisoner Katerina Breshkovskaya—"the famous Russian woman Anarchist," the IWW union organizer Elizabeth Gurley Flynn—"addressing a Socialist meeting," and the anarchist essayist and poet Voltairine de Cleyre—"noted woman red." Of the five women, two were Jewish, three were born in the Russian empire and thereby "foreign" in the dominant US discourse, and only one—de Cleyre—was "Anglo-Saxon" and thereby "true American" in the dominant US discourse. The *Times* described the only US-born Anglo-Saxon of the group as the most cultured of them, and as "a woman of considerably more culture than Miss Goldman." Gurley Flynn was also US-born, but the paper made sure to emphasize her Irishness, writing, "Her parents spring from Irish Stock, and in them can be seen some traces of the radical ideas of their daughter." Elizabeth Gurley Flynn was seventeen years old at the time, but the papers apparently had no ethical objections to publicly vilifying and animalizing a minor as a "she-dog" and a "terrorist."[74]

"When it comes to deeds of violence," said the *Times*, "the woman anarchist sees redder than her destructive brother." The article blamed women for crimes that they had no connection to. For example, it suggested that Emma Goldman incited the Haymarket bombing in Chicago in 1886. At the time of the bombing, Emma Goldman was a newly arrived sixteen-year-old immigrant working as a seamstress in a sweatshop in Rochester, New York. She had no connection to any Chicago anarchists at the time. She did not get involved in the anarchist movement until three years after the bombing, when she moved to New York City in 1889 and joined Johann Most's circle. Notwithstanding the facts, the story falsely claimed Goldman "was active in Chicago before the bomb thrown into the wagon full of policemen in the Haymarket riots resulted in the murder of a dozen bluecoats."[75]

The article did not label the women terrorists for committing any actual violence, but for their "eloquence," which, the paper charged, led men to acts of

46    CHAPTER 2

violence: "A President of the United States is assassinated, a Russian General is blown to bits, a riot mob parades the streets of Philadelphia waving the red flag, and in every case the investigations of the police show that it was the reckless eloquence of a woman red that incited the violation of law." The Philadelphia example referred to an incident in which Voltairine de Cleyre spoke before a march of the unemployed, after which the mostly "foreign" working-class migrants marched carrying red flags before being met by brutal police violence. As is often the case in the present era when the mainstream press covers police violence, the story used the passive voice to describe the police attacking the marchers: "pistols were fired and skulls cracked with clubs before the brands stirred by the fire of the woman's eloquence had been stamped out." The violence was not the fault of police who actually committed it, or of the "foreign mob" of men carrying red flags, but was the result of a "woman's eloquence."[76]

The article did not introduce a new notion but drew on already existing notions of women's criminality that pervaded dominant US discourse and fascinated US readers. During the 1877 Railroad Uprisings, a *New York Tribune* report on the communists in Chicago marveled that "A feature of the fights was the frequent participation in them by women, who fired shots from the inside and outside of their houses, and hurled stones and mud indiscriminately" at strikebreakers.[77] "Women are very rarely criminal when compared with men," wrote leading criminologists Cesare Lombroso and William Ferrero, "but when criminal they are infinitely worse."[78]

Respectable women stood in stark contrast to such criminals. The late-eighteenth-century ideal of "republican motherhood" and "wifehood" influenced US gender politics well past the early years of the republic.[79] It was an ideal of separate spheres for men and women—with men in the economic and political spheres and women in the domestic sphere—but women could influence the economic and political spheres by exerting a moral influence over men.[80] The Enlightenment, deeply intertwined with European colonialism, gave rise to the notion of stages of history, or stages through which societies develop over time from the lower levels of savagery to the higher levels of civilization.[81] Historian Rosemary Zagarri explains the concept: "as a society developed, women advanced the civilizing process, especially in the later stages, by cultivating men's higher instincts and pleasures and helping them contain their more ungovernable passions," and so women's primary contribution to the evolution of society from savage to civilized "was to improve and refine the manners of men."[82] So powerful was this discourse well into the early twentieth century that even the suffragists found it strategically necessary to argue within its bounds, basing their claim to a right to the ballot on the purifying influence refined, delicate, white women voters would have on US political institutions.[83] Emma Goldman complained of such suffragists that "they insist always that it

*"Civilization" versus "Savagery"*    47

is woman suffrage which will make her a better Christian and home-keeper, a staunch citizen of the State."[84]

Rather than cultivating men's higher instincts and containing their ungovernable passions, these "creatures in petticoats" at anarchist "war dances" fanatically encouraged their men to lawlessness and violence. Rather than being dainty, delicate, and refined, these hideous "females" were coarse, large, and masculine. They used tobacco—a manly activity—and one of them even wore men's boots. Describing women as masculine, or performing men's roles, was an old settler colonial strategy—dating back to some of the earliest New England settlers, for describing groups marked for extermination as savage. For example, in a 1674 manuscript, the Virginia and New England colonizer Daniel Gookin described Indigenous women performing men's roles, such as planting and carrying heavy loads, as evidence for why New England Indians were "very brutish and barbarous."[85] Literary scholar Roy Harvey Pearce noted in his classic study of settler understandings of American Natives that, in settler colonizer literature, from the time of the first European settlements in North America and into the nineteenth century, writers described Indian women performing men's roles as a characteristic of savage society.[86] Captain Schaack's description of anarchist "squaws" fit well within this settler colonial narrative.

In writing in such a way, Schaack contributed to a culturally pervasive notion of anarchist women as less-than-human hideous creatures. For example, an 1893 issue of the London-based popular magazine *Punch* featured an anti-anarchist poem and illustration that called anarchism the modern medusa.[87] Gorgon Medusa, the "Black bringer-back of Chaos" who crawled "malign in Civilization's path" had to be slain by the Perseus of state violence.[88]

> Civilisation armed with trenchant Law
> Must play the Perseus with thy monster maw,
> And all mankind be banded in the quest
> Of the worst enemy mankind e'er saw.[89]

The accompanying illustration was produced by the famous wood engraver Joseph Swain. It pictured Perseus as a heroic, muscular white man wearing the helmet of "Civilisation," wielding the sword of "Law" and the shield of "Justice." Medusa, dark, dirty, and serpentine, armed with a torch and a bomb, wore a sash emblazoned with the word "Anarchy." Perseus stood tall over her with one foot pressing her down as he raised his sword arm for a final blow. Civilization defeated savagery as state violence defeated anarchy.[90] Civilization was a white man killing a dark animalized woman.

This racist and misogynistic discourse exemplified by these passages from Captain Schaack and *Punch* was not mere rhetoric but was always a prelude to, an accompaniment of, or post-factum justification for violent repression.

CHAPTER 2

"The Modern Medusa," *Punch, or the London Charivari* 105, December 1893.

Indigenous feminist scholars have produced a large body of work illuminating the significant role of gender and sexual violence, and white supremacist misogyny in the perpetuation of the settler colonial state.[91] As Dian Million argues, gender violence, rather than being incidental, is constitutive of the nation-state, colonialism, and modern capitalism.[92] This being the case, it makes sense that when colonialism turned inward against anarchist "reds," the repression often took a violently misogynistic form.

Consider labor organizer Oscar Neebe's account of police detectives raiding, ransacking, and shutting down the office, where he worked, of the German-language working-class newspaper the *Arbeiter-Zeitung* the day after the Haymarket police riot. Upon storming into the office where anarchist women Lizzie Holmes and Lucy Parsons were writing at a desk, the police roughly assaulted the women while shouting misogynistic insults at them. When Lizzie Holmes verbally protested, the officer grabbing her barked, "Shut up, you bitch, or I will knock you down!"[93] The police spoke similarly to Lucy Parsons, but with the added *misogynoir* of calling her a "black bitch."[94] On the morning of the execution day of Lucy Parsons's husband Albert, when Lucy attempted to bring her children for a final visit with their condemned father, the police instead took her, the two young children, and Lizzie Holmes into custody. A male officer had a subordinate strip all four of them and search their naked bodies for bombs while he amusedly watched, and then he put them all, including the children, in cold cells, still naked, until after the hanging.[95]

Consider Emma Goldman's experience—which will be discussed in greater detail in chapter 6—in 1912 San Diego with a lynch mob—made up of the city's economically and politically enfranchised, respectable citizens—meeting her at the train station *en masse* to "welcome" her to San Diego with sexual harassment and threats of sexual violence. A liberal *San Francisco Bulletin* reporter who witnessed it, wrote that the mob "shouted threats, catcalls, and insulting remarks to the woman orator," and "the police did nothing to check the disturbance."[96] The pro-vigilante *San Diego Sun* gloated that a woman at the station who cheered in support of Goldman "was roughly handled" by men in the mob.[97] In one of the earliest automobile chases in US history, the wealthy vigilante mob went after the Grant Hotel bus that rushed Goldman away. They shouted at the bus driver "Give up that anarchist."[98] According to Goldman's account, even well-dressed, upper-class women joined in on the threats of sexual violence: "We will strip her naked; we will tear out her guts," and, added Goldman, "Many other things were said by those 'cultured' women which could not be repeated in public."[99] A colonialist culture that vilified, racialized, and animalized anarchist women is what made it socially acceptable, even heroic, for respectable citizens to treat anarchist women that way. Unable to capture Goldman, members of the mob later, with police complicity, kidnapped her tour manager, Ben Reitman. They ritualistically tortured, humiliated, and sexually violated him to the brink of death in place of her.[100]

The idea of the anarchist woman as the "outside agitator" pulling the strings, or as the "anarchist queen"—a term newspapers applied not only to Emma Goldman, but any woman red who appeared to be a leader, including Lucy Parsons, Louise Michel, Ernestina Cravello, Voltairine de Cleyre, and Irma

Sanchini—contributed not only to official state violence and political repression against anarchist women but also to violence in general against anarchist women. For example, in January 1888 in Le Havre, France, a Catholic fanatic named Pierre Lucas shot Louise Michel in the head during one of her speeches. Amazingly, Michel survived. Lucas reportedly said that his reason for shooting Michel was that "if he killed the anarchist queen, the revolutionary party will disappear [sic]."[101] Michel took pity on the failed assassin, seeing that he was poor and deceived by the church and state. In contempt for the justice system, which Michel despised, she forgave Lucas, refused to press charges, and in court she pled on his behalf, arguing that he was not evil, but was misled by an evil system. He was acquitted.[102]

Voltairine de Cleyre followed in Louise Michel's footsteps. In 1902, as de Cleyre was delivering a talk at a lecture hall in Philadelphia, a young man named Herman Helcher shot her three times at close range. De Cleyre recognized him as one of her former students from when she worked as a private tutor providing lessons in English, French, music, and penmanship. Though she was seriously and permanently injured from the attack, she refused to identify her assailant to the police. Like Michel, de Cleyre despised the justice system and thought that police and prisons should be abolished. She saw that Helcher was poor, malnourished, suffered from mental illness, and, in the words of de Cleyre's comrade Ross Winn, "was an unfortunate victim of one of those false and vicious ideas that form the basis of Christian ethics."[103] De Cleyre argued that Helcher needed proper food, decent employment, and proper mental health care, not punishment in a carceral system. "It would be an outrage against civilization if he were sent to jail for an act which was the product of a diseased brain," wrote de Cleyre.[104]

In 1903, after recovering somewhat from the attack—she never fully recovered and suffered health issues for the rest of her life as a result of it—de Cleyre delivered a lecture titled "Crime and Punishment" for the Social Science Club of Philadelphia. She argued against carceral logic and against policing and prisons. "Believe me," argued de Cleyre—an atheist who sounded more Christlike than most who claimed to be followers of Jesus—"forgiveness is better than wrath—better for the wrong-doer, who will be touched and regenerated by it, and better for you." Instead of a system based on "this savage idea of punishment," argued de Cleyre, we need a system based on ensuring that the needs of all are met, a system that does away with "the oppressions which make criminals, and for the enlightened treatment of all the sick."[105] Many ideas and critical approaches in the present day, which are considered to be cutting-edge, fresh new "abolitionist" takes on the carceral system, were things that anarchists argued for as early as the mid-nineteenth century and increasingly emphasized from the 1880s onward.[106]

## Race Science

In stark contrast to the anticarceral, abolition-minded anarchists of the era were the criminologists. Skull science, phrenology, and physiognomy gave the blessing of science to the racialization, animalization, and misogynist terror of capitalism and the state. Ruling-class Europeans relied on a kind of "race science" to give scientific justification to racial hierarchy, the enslavement of Black people, empire, capitalism, and genocide. Its development in Europe was thoroughly part of the colonial project. From 1881 to 1914, a period of wholesale slaughter that European states euphemistically call the "scramble for Africa," colonial forces shipped the remains of tens of thousands of African children and adults they massacred to fill scientific research collections in Germany, France, Belgium, Spain, Italy, England, and Portugal. The American Museum of Natural History bought prominent German "skull collector" Felix von Luschan's collection—a collection that is a direct product of the German genocide of the Herero people—and it remains with the museum to this day. Similarly, the development of phrenology and physiognomy in the United States was fully dependent on the settler colonizer practices of robbing sacred Indigenous American gravesites and torturing enslaved Black people in the name of scientific progress.[107]

An 1895 issue of the *Phrenological Journal of Science and Health* pathologized anarchist women using Emma Goldman and the French anarchist Marie Louise David as case studies. The journal argued that facial characteristics revealed that the women were genetically prone to anti-authoritarian criminality. In Goldman's case, "The facial signs of destructiveness and alimentiveness [a term phrenologists used for an overpowering instinct in so-called primitive peoples and animals for immediate self-gratification, especially regarding food and drink] are very pronounced in the mouth, and it is chiefly in the mouth and eyes that we may detect the signs of quality and temperament which account for the woman's disposition to attack the present social fabric."[108] The journal also employed *cheirognomy*, the "science" of determining a person's psychological and moral character from the size and shape of their hands, to suggest that Goldman's thumb and index finger evidenced a lack of both willpower and logic.[109]

The mainstream press was just as enthralled with the physiognomy of anarchists as police and race scientists were. The *Fresno Morning Republican* described Goldman as having a "masculine" face, with "heavy brows, and large mouth and jaws."[110] The *New York World* wrote, "Her lips wreathed into lines that were uglier than when her face was in repose. The two front teeth were set wide apart, and on either side there were dental hollows, making the interior of the mouth look black, or rather that dull opaque hue characteristic of the mouths of some snakes."[111] Comparing the anarchist "queen" to a snake alluded to classical mythology, popular in the era, of evil serpentine female villains such as

"Lucy Parsons, Anarchist Queen," *Sunday Inter-Ocean*, August 12, 1900.

the woman turned child-eating monster Lamia, the cave-dwelling half-woman and half-snake mother of monsters Echidna, and of course the venomous-snake-haired Medusa. As Patrick Wolfe argued, "elimination is an organizing principle of settler-colonial society."[112] Racialization and animalization—and their concomitant metaphors of pollution, contamination, dirt, and disease, which will be discussed in chapter 3—are the language of elimination.

The mainstream press spoke similarly of Lucy Parsons, referring to her, as to Goldman, as "the anarchist queen." While her face is well shaped, said Chicago's *Inter-Ocean*, "her ears are rather badly turned and show marks of what Max Nordau [the Zionist and author of the 1892 book *Degeneration*] would catalogue as degeneracy." It continued, "Her eyes are long and brown, and her hair is not straight black but kinky. Her hands are characteristically long and large [read: unfeminine], with pointed fingers. When she talks her rather thick nostrils dilate and her whole face and figure quiver with excitement." The "Anarchist Queen," said the *Inter-Ocean*, "is an American Indian, a mixture of the Aztec and the North American aborigine." The illustration on the page depicted Lucy Parsons being roughly grabbed, manhandled, arrested, and abducted by baton-wielding police officers, with the caption "Lucy Parsons in the Role of Anarchist Queen."[113]

According to the leading criminologists of the era, anarchists were of the "criminal type," which was not simply a social condition, but a biological one.

"Civilization" versus "Savagery"

The influential Italian criminologist Cesare Lombroso argued that the criminal type was the result of *atavism*—a devolution back to an earlier, prewhite, stage of human evolution. "Born criminals" and the "morally insane"—categories that included anarchists—in modern European societies shared many characteristics with nonhuman apes and modern "savages" such as people in Black and Indigenous societies.[114] Kenyon Zimmer goes as far as to argue that "by ascribing to [anarchists] a phenotypically recognizable genetic defect that threatened to undermine white supremacy through racial degeneration," Lombroso—along with the policymakers, law enforcers, and journalists aligned with his ideas— racialized anarchists "*as anarchists*."[115] Lombroso certainly did attempt to make anarchists, along with anticolonial insurgents, out to be a specific, biologically defined rather than politically defined, group. Lombroso published volumes of illustrations of criminals' faces, grouped according to their specific type of criminality, for scientists, criminologists, and law enforcers to use as a reference. He included illustrations of heroes of the anarchist movement, such as the French Louise Michel and the Russians Mikhail Bakunin and Sophia Perovskaya, in the same section as the anticolonial "half-breed" Louis Riel, who led two Métis rebellions against the Canadian state.[116]

Lombroso used skull science to pathologize and racialize anarchists who would otherwise have been considered white. In his famous 1891 study of anarchist criminality, he posited that the criminal type "again frequently appears among the communards [of the Paris Commune] and the anarchists."[117] It bears mentioning that the bulk of Lombroso's evidence for his conclusions about anarchist physiognomy in this study were based not on actual scientific examination of anarchists, or even on photographs, but on illustrations and descriptions from police captain Schaack's book. Lombroso's work exemplifies the fact that race science was not about scientific rigor and objectivity but rather served the social, political, and economic needs of the dominant class. That need being in this case to delegitimize working-class claims of social injustice by characterizing anarchist organizing and labor revolt as the result of individual biological degeneration rather than systemic, structural inequality. The positivist school of criminology was a defense of capitalism, imperialism, and colonialism.[118]

Lombroso asserted that a high percentage of anarchists in the United States were of the criminal type, and that "congenital criminals" were the result of racial devolution or atavism: "a revival of the primitive savage."[119] Labor leader Samuel Fielden and fiery propagandist Johann Most, wrote Lombroso, had "facial asymmetry, enormous jaws, developed frontal sinus, protruding ears. . . . Fielden has a turned up nose and enormous jaws; Most has acrocephaly and facial asymmetry."[120] As for the internationally famous Chicago Haymarket anarchists, they all had facial anomalies that indicated atavism:

54    CHAPTER 2

The ears are without lobes; the ears are also developed a little more than normally in all (except Spies), they are protruding in Lingg, Spies, Fischer, and Engel. . . . We find a Mongolic cast of feature in Engel and Lingg, both of whom should have much of the degenerative characters, enormous jaw and zygoma, and Lingg oblique eyes. . . . The physiognomy of August Spies is morbid. He has a senile auricle, voluminous jaw bones and a strongly developed frontal sinus. . . . [His] physiognomy corresponds with his autobiography, written with fierce fanaticism. . . . Fielden has a wild physiognomy, not without sensuality. . . . [They all] possess the degenerative characters common to criminals and the insane, being anomalies and possessing these traits by heredity.[121]

Anarchists were not mere common criminals. They possessed "a true moral insensibility, an innate cruelty" in accordance with their "criminal physiognomies."[122] Degenerative, morbid, fierce, wild, sensual, Mongolic: these were characteristics that evolution should have eradicated from white men through Victorian ideals, capitalist morality, and industrial discipline.

In using the term *Mongolic*, Lombroso drew on the work of J. Langdon Down, the doctor who classified and named Down syndrome. Down's 1866 paper "Observations on an Ethnic Classification of Idiots" associated Down syndrome with supposed nonwhite racial characteristics. Down argued that "congenital idiots" exhibited the physiognomy of lower, savage races. He wrote, "A very large number of congenital idiots are typical Mongols."[123] Notions of "idiocy" and mental disability developed directly out of the context of white supremacy, colonialism, empire, and the attendant discourse of civilization versus savagery.[124] This is the context that gave meaning to Lombroso's use of racial terms to pathologize and criminalize anarchists.

Three months after publishing Lombroso's study of anarchist physiognomy, the scientific journal *Monist* published a response written by convicted Haymarket anarchist Michael Schwab. Schwab pointed out many of Lombroso's errors, some of which were that Lombroso relied on illustrations from Chicago police captain Michael Schaack's book rather than photographs or actual examination; Johann Most did in fact have an unsymmetrical face, but that resulted from a botched surgery, not heredity; Lombroso's heavy reliance on a police captain's narrative for information about the anarchists, resulted in factual errors in much of what Lombroso wrote about the family histories of the anarchists; and rather than being cruel and unfeeling as Lombroso characterized them, many anarchists, such as August Spies, behaved in ways that were highly altruistic.[125]

Stephen Jay Gould wrote in his classic book *The Mismeasure of Man*, "Whenever Lombroso encountered a contrary fact, he performed some mental gymnastics to incorporate it into his system. This posture is clearly expressed in his statements on the depravity of inferior peoples, for again and again he en-

"Civilization" versus "Savagery"     55

countered stories of courage and accomplishment among those he wished to denigrate."[126] This certainly was the case with Lombroso's treatment of anarchists, among whom, his critics pointed out, examples of empathetic and altruistic behavior abounded. Rather than attempt to deny the existence of anarchist altruism, Lombroso explained it away as further proof of madness. He associated anarchist altruism with hysteria and epilepsy, arguing that the "hysteria" anarchists experience, "which is the sister of epilepsy," includes "certain bursts of excessive altruism, which is an outgrowth of moral madness and is dependent upon it—and reveals to us the morbid phenomenon within the warmest charity." In anarchists, he continued, "the tendency to evil is cloaked in an altruistic form."[127] Even the anarchists' altruism was evidence of physical and psychological degeneration. Likewise, as some prominent anarchists stood out in society as people of genius—scientists, intellectuals, writers, poets, artists—Lombroso reminded his readers that anarchist genius was likewise evidence of pathology: "I have proved how often genius is nervous epilepsy, and how almost all the sons of men of genius are lunatics, idiots, or criminals."[128]

Note also how Lombroso feminized anarchist "madness," describing it with the term *hysteria*: a notoriously misogynistic term: misogynistic not in itself but in the way it functioned in the larger discourse. "Hysteria" is from the Latin *hystericus*, which means "of the womb." The term *hysteria* largely functioned, and continues to function, in patriarchal society to delegitimize women's concerns as irrational. Using the term to describe the anarchist passion for justice and equality functioned to likewise delegitimize anarchist critiques of political, economic, and social injustice. Anarchist "hysteria" was further feminized as the *sister* of epilepsy. In the patriarchal society of the era, to pathologize anarchists and then to feminize and racialize the pathology was a sure way to delegitimize anarchist politics.

Lombroso was convinced that there was a relationship between anarchism and epilepsy. Of the Haymarket defendant Louis Lingg, for example, Lombroso wrote, "we see a truly ungovernable epileptoid idea driving him to political action."[129] This pathologizing of anarchists as "congenital idiots" and epileptics is important for historians to pay attention to because it was not mere rhetoric. It made its way into US immigration law. The 1903 Alien Immigration Act—also called the Anarchist Exclusion Act—which congressmen and President Theodore Roosevelt crafted specifically to create a legal basis on which to deport and ban anarchists from the United States, not only denied entrance of anarchists, but also "All idiots, insane persons, epileptics, and persons who have been insane within five years previous."[130] Governments enacted laws based on Lombroso's theories, and police, prosecutors, judges, and juries based decisions about guilt, innocence, and sentencing on the positivist school of criminology.

The Alien Immigration Act was not mere rhetoric. The state enforced it almost immediately, using the speaking tour of a British anarchist named John Turner as its test case. Turner was an anarchist labor organizer and a founder of the powerful Shop Assistants' Union in England and the Retail Clerks Association in Brussels. He did a speaking tour in the United States in 1896 without incident. When he returned for a second speaking tour in October 1903, things did not go as smoothly. Immigration officials, who monitored the anarchist press, learned of Turner's tour schedule ahead of time and hatched a plan to allow him to enter the United States but then catch him in the act of spreading anarchism to then arrest and deport him. Immigration inspectors arrested Turner after his speech at Manhattan's Murray Hill Lyceum and detained him for three months at Ellis Island. "I had a fine time in the pen at Ellis Island," Turner later said sardonically. "I was stared at as if I was a wild animal in an iron-barred cage nine feet by six."[131] In addition to the normal immigration security guards on duty, the federal government sent twenty-four armed Secret Service agents to guard Turner's cage.[132]

Labor unionists and anarchists, including Emma Goldman, who had recently formed a Free Speech League, rushed to Turner's defense, bringing in Clarence Darrow—who would later found the American Civil Liberties Union—to defend Turner. Darrow took the case to the Supreme Court to challenge the constitutionality of the Alien Immigration Act. The Supreme Court upheld the Alien Immigration Act and the deportation of Turner, arguing that constitutional protections do not apply to noncitizens. The decision laid the groundwork for the expansion of immigration restrictions to apply to not only racial, ethnic, and national categories but also ideological categories. Legal historian Julia Rose Kraut writes, "This legal precedent paved the way for the mass deportations of radicals after the 1919 Palmer Raids, the exclusion of alleged communist writers, actors, and professors under the McCarran Act of 1950 and the McCarran-Walter Act of 1952, and eventually for a visa denial barring entry to an Islamic scholar under the Patriot Act of 2001."[133] European criminology, which stressed the importance of ideological policing, informed the thinking of US lawmakers as they crafted such laws in the early twentieth century.[134]

European criminologists were significantly influenced by US settler colonialism. Skull science itself was a field that depended on US forces massacring Native people and robbing sacred Native gravesites for specimens. In 1865, one of the world's leading biologists, Harvard's Louis Agassiz, wrote to Secretary of War Edwin Stanton to request "the bodies of some Indians" to stock the nation's research collections with skulls.[135] That Agassiz made this request to the War Department speaks volumes about the relationship between science and imperialist violence in the era. The War Department obliged, and the nation's

"Civilization" versus "Savagery"     57

scientific collections over the following years filled with the skulls and bones of children and adults killed by US forces in the Sand Creek Massacre, the Mulberry Creek Massacre, and other incidents of murderous white settler violence. Archaeologist David Hurst Thomas writes that "US Army hospitals became laboratories for processing Indian bones."[136] Similarly, in 1906, leading German anthropologist Felix von Luschan sent letters to colonial officials overseeing genocide in German Southwest Africa to request they ship the bones of their victims to him in Berlin. Colonial officials obliged by forcing Herero women to work in concentration camps scraping flesh from the bones of Herero corpses to prepare the bones for shipping. Von Luschan later sold these bones to the American Museum of Natural History. It was a symbiotic relationship: genocidal white supremacist violence supplied the specimens to the anthropologists and criminologists who in turn produced the race science that justified white supremacy and colonization.[137]

By the 1880s and 1890s, European criminologists were accustomed to looking to the Americas. The main source that Lombroso cited as evidence for his 1891 study, "The Physiognomy of the Anarchists"—a study that criminalized, pathologized, racialized, and animalized anarchists—was Chicago police captain Michael Schaack's book.[138] Lombroso compared seditious anarchists to what he called "the least advanced peoples, as in Saint-Domingue," where enslaved Black people successfully rebelled against slavery and forced out the enslavers, "and those of South America."[139] He did not specify who the seditionists in South America were, but white readers in the era would have read "those of South America" as meaning foreign, dark-skinned "savages." The leading French criminologist of the era, Gabriel Tarde, argued along the same lines as Lombroso, writing that had these criminals lived in an earlier era of human evolution, rather than criminals they "would have been the ornament and moral elite of a tribe of Redskins."[140] While much has been written on the significant influence of French and Italian criminology on the US criminal justice system in the era, it is important to recognize that influence did not flow only one way. These same criminologists were influenced by US settler colonial history, practices, ideology, and culture. The settler-colonial ideology inherent in the work of men such as Tarde and Lombroso is likely a major reason that their ideas resonated so powerfully within US law enforcement institutions.

## Conclusion

In the 1840s and 1850s, state agents described Indigenous groups as "communists" to justify anti-Indigenous state violence. Three decades later and beyond, state agents would increasingly describe supposed anarchists as "Indians" to justify anticommunist state violence. Agents of capitalism and the state vilifying anarchists with racist terms such as "savage reds" and "bloodthirsty squaws," and equating them with supposed "Comanche Indians about to take the warpath," and the "moral elite of a tribe of Redskins," and the like was not a new development in ruling-class politics and culture but was an adaptation of an already existing and pervasive anti-Indigenous discourse. "Race science," psychopathology, and criminology were fully part of this anti-Indigenous and anticommunist discourse. The ruling class's application of "Indian War" language to class war was part and parcel with the kind of policy they conceived for addressing working-class insurgency. US "Indian War" policy and its accompanying language and ways of thinking were nothing short of genocidal, saturated with notions of cleanliness, purity, dirt, disease, contamination, removal, and extermination. As US anticommunism developed from such policy, language, and ways of thinking, it would become an ideology of "cleansing" the United States.

# 3

## Cleansing the Republic

### Patriotism

On April 26, 1908, US Army Private First Class William Buwalda, in uniform, attended an Emma Goldman speech in San Francisco. Buwalda had served five tours of duty and was a veteran of the US invasion of the Philippines. At the time Emma Goldman visited San Francisco on her western states speaking tour, Buwalda was assigned to the Presidio, a US Army fort in San Francisco. He was by all accounts an excellent soldier with an exemplary record of service. He had distinguished himself as a cavalryman and served as a blacksmith-farrier for Troop I, First Cavalry, in the Philippines.[1] In its 1902 annual report to Congress, the War Department credited Buwalda by name as one of the two soldiers responsible for making "a very important capture" of Filipino insurgent leaders Major Domingo Maratija and Lieutenant Braga in the vicinity of Rosario, Batangas. The US Army listed this capture as one of the "principal events in the Philippine Islands" for the fiscal year.[2]

Staunch antimilitarist Emma Goldman's visit to San Francisco, during which she gave a series of talks, caused a major stir in the city. Before her arrival, a rumor spread that she was coming to San Francisco to blow up the US naval fleet. San Francisco Police Chief William Biggy boasted that he would personally protect the fleet from "Emma Goldman and her gang." When she arrived at the St. Francis Hotel, she was greeted by a throng of newspaper reporters and photographers asking whether the rumor was true. She answered in her typical provocative style, "Why waste a bomb? What I should like to do with the fleet, with the entire Navy, and the Army too, would be to dump them in the bay. But as I have not the power to do it, I have come to San Francisco to point out to the people the uselessness and waste of military institutions, whether they operate on land or on sea."[3]

Her lectures in Walton's Pavilion in San Francisco filled the pavilion beyond its five-thousand-person capacity, with long lines of people forming hours before her talks. She described her meetings as "veritable battle encampments," with police in cars, on horseback, and on foot lining the streets for blocks around the pavilion. Several police officers also were posted inside the hall. At the Sunday-afternoon meeting, at which she was scheduled to give a talk titled "Patriotism," the situation reached a climax:

> The crowds struggling to get in were so large that the doors of the hall had to be closed very early to prevent a panic. The atmosphere was charged with indignation against the police, who were flaunting themselves importantly before the assembled people. My own endurance had almost reached break-ing-point because of the annoyances caused by the authorities, and I went to the meeting determined to vent in no uncertain terms my protest. When I looked into the faces of the excited audience, I sensed at once that very little encouragement from me would be needed to arouse them to violent action. Even the dull mind of Biggey [*sic*] responded to the temper of the situation. He came over to beg that I try to pacify the people. I promised on condition that he would reduce the number of his men in the hall. He consented and gave orders to the officers to file out. Out they marched, like guilty schoolboys, accompanied by the jeering and hooting of the crowd.[4]

Several plainclothes police remained, however.

One plainclothes police officer noticed in the audience a US Army soldier in uniform. The officer decided to keep a close eye on the soldier. After calming the crowd, Goldman began her speech, railing against patriotism and milita-rism. "What is patriotism?" she asked the audience. She answered by quoting the Russian novelist Leo Tolstoy, whom she called "the greatest anti-patriot of our times," who said that patriotism "is the principle that justifies the training of wholesale murderers; a trade that requires better equipment for the exercise of man-killing than the making of such necessities as shoes, clothing, and houses; a trade that guarantees better returns and greater glory than that of the honest workingman." The police officer was aghast that the soldier applauded along with the crowd during intervals in the speech. When the speech ended, the soldier, William Buwalda, enthusiastically approached Goldman to shake her hand. The sight of Emma Goldman and a US soldier shaking hands after an antimilitarist speech caused the audience to cheer gleefully, throw hats in the air, and stomp their feet. He said, "Thank you, Miss Goldman" and left. In her autobiography, Goldman wrote, "It was a dramatic ending to a highly dramatic situation."[5]

Cleansing the Republic 61

The police officer followed Buwalda back to the Presidio and reported him to military authorities. The US Army arrested and court-martialed Buwalda for "offenses against the flag and Army," specifically violating the vague 62nd Article of War. In the era, few things represented manliness and civilization more than a clean-cut white man in a US military uniform. The sight of such a man publicly applauding and shaking hands with the most notorious anarchist in the country was an affront to US American values. Philippine-American War hero General Frederick Funston called Buwalda's handshake "a serious crime equal to treason" and "a great military offense, infinitely worse than desertion."[6] Buwalda's first sergeant defended him, however, telling the court that Buwalda had a good record, and was "sober, reliable, always obedient."[7] Nevertheless, the army convicted Buwalda and sentenced him to five years hard labor. Because of his clean record in the army, authorities reduced his sentence to three years. Theodore Roosevelt pardoned Buwalda after ten months when he saw that the harsh sentence, rather than having its intended deterrent effect on enlisted soldiers, was arousing them to sympathy for Buwalda.[8] The point was to ensure that the civilized do not become contaminated, as Buwalda had been, with anarchist ideas.

Anarchists raised a public outcry against the treatment of Buwalda, using his case as an example of the hypocrisy of US democracy. After serving his ten months in Alcatraz, Buwalda became involved in the anarchist movement and helped set up more speeches for Goldman. He returned to the army the medal he earned for fighting in the Philippines, accompanied by a letter to US Secretary of War Joseph Dickinson explaining his reasons. It read in part

> After thinking the matter over for some time I have decided to send back this trinket to your Department, having no further use for such baubles, and enable you to give it to someone who will appreciate it more than I do. . . .
>
> It speaks of raids and burnings, of many prisoners taken, and like vile beasts, thrown in the foulest of prisons. And for what? For fighting for their homes and loved ones. It speaks to me of G.O. 100, with all its attendant horrors and cruelties and sufferings; of a country laid waste with fire and sword; of animals useful to man wantonly killed; of men, women and children hunted like wild beasts, and all of this in the name of Liberty, Humanity, and Civilization. In short, it speaks to me of War—legalized murder, if you will—upon a weak and defenseless people. We have not even the excuse of self-defense.[9]

The press reported that the soldier-turned-anarchist William Buwalda, who "recently was pardoned from the military prison by President Roosevelt," was arrested with Emma Goldman and Ben Reitman at the Victory Theater in San Francisco for "conspiracy to incite a riot."[10] To a respectable white US public, Buwalda represented the contagiousness of the disease of anarchism. None

62    CHAPTER 3

was immune, not even a US Army cavalryman. The disease would have to be removed from the body politic.

## Boomerang Effect

The language of dirt and disease is a significant component of racialization in the United States and Western Europe. Several scholars have observed that in the United States, historically, "Jews, blacks, Indians, Asians, and immigrants in general were named and organized in the nativist social imagery around pervasive images of dirt."[11] From the late 1870s onward, this nativist social imagery likewise included communists and anarchists. Political scientist Kathy Ferguson writes, "Anarchists were implicitly racialized in hegemonic discourse by the use of metaphors of disease and dirt."[12] Though correct, it should be added that this racialization was at times quite explicit rather than implicit. It is necessary to examine this language of dirt and disease in the context of US imperialism and settler colonialism and their relationship to the policies and practices of anarchist removal and exclusion.

The mainstream press in the United States was nothing short of murderous in its attitude toward anarchists in the era. Mexico, Missouri, nicknamed "Little Dixie" because it was first settled by enslavers from the South, applied a famous Indian-killing axiom to anarchists, printing on the front page of its leading paper "The only good anarchist is a dead anarchist."[13] The *Washington Post* recommended execution for anarchists, whether or not they committed any crime: "Since an avowal of anarchy has been found to be equivalent to an intention to commit murder . . . an anarchist is, in fact, a murderer, even before he has done the deed, and he should be executed accordingly."[14] The *San Francisco Chronicle* called anarchists "worthless as rats and far more dangerous" and argued that anarchists, including ones who were US citizens, be deprived of their citizenship and that all anarchist literature should be barred from the mails and interstate commerce. The anarchists' "damnable doctrine" was "conclusive proof of incurable insanity" requiring permanent incarceration.[15] In another editorial, the *Washington Post* wrote,

> It is imperative that the nests of these obscure and evil birds should be broken up. The states should cooperate with the government in making the country too hot to hold them. There should not be a nook or corner in this republic where three anarchists could gather together habitually. . . . They are always aliens born. . . . There can be no toleration of these hideous creatures. If they cannot be kept out of the country, public sentiment will require that their lives shall be forfeited as soon as they are caught.[16]

Cleansing the Republic    63

Historian James Green observes that, after the Haymarket police riot,

> Many editorialists relied on animal metaphors to describe anarchists, whom they branded "ungrateful hyenas," "incendiary vermin," and "Slavic wolves." Some commentators conceded that the anarchists were human but were from the "lowest stratum," as the *Washington Post* put it. Following this kind of reasoning, the alien incendiaries were often compared to other hated groups like the menacing Apache Indians. The *St. Louis Globe-Democrat* applied an old frontier adage about "savage" tribes to the new menace. "There are no good anarchists except dead anarchists," it proclaimed.[17]

This was the language of pathologization, criminalization, animalization, and contamination.

The most-often-referred to example of the language of dirt and disease as an accompaniment to political repression and extermination is likely German Nazi vilification of Jews in the 1920s–1940s. The Nazis, of course, did not invent anti-Semitism or racial thought, but drew on already pervasive European notions that stretch back to the Middle Ages, grew through the Christian Crusades against Islam, the expulsion and extermination of Moors and Jews in the Iberian Peninsula, Spain and Portugal's *limpieza de sangre* tests, the Vatican's fifteenth-century papal bulls that gave to the Portuguese God's blessing to conquer and enslave non-Christian peoples, and which the Spanish, Dutch, and English further solidified and codified into law through the processes of enslavement of Africans and settler colonization of the Americas in the sixteenth and seventeenth centuries.[18] Any study of the modern practices and language of genocide must begin not in Nazi Germany, but in European colonization.

Pulitzer Prize–winning historian John Toland observes in his classic biography of Adolf Hitler that Hitler himself began with English and US colonization of the Americas as his historical precedent:

> Hitler's concept of concentration camps as well as the practicality of genocide owed much, so he claimed, to his studies of English and United States history. He admired the camps for Boer prisoners in South Africa and for the Indians in the wild West; and often praised to his inner circle the efficiency of America's extermination—by starvation and uneven combat—of the red savages who could not be tamed by captivity.[19]

Historian Carroll Kakel points out that, within his own circle of confidants, Hitler was quite explicit about seeing himself as a "frontier" Indian killer. He referred to Slavic peoples as "Redskins" in the "wild east," who needed to be exterminated and replaced by Germans, along the lines of "the struggle in North America against the Red Indians."[20] Legal scholar James Whitman has shown that the Nazis modeled their race laws on US policies.[21] In *American Holocaust*,

64    CHAPTER 3

historian David Stannard shows that "The destruction of the Indians of the Americas was, far and away, the most massive act of genocide in the history of the world."[22] Britain and the United States set the standard for genocide that fascists would follow.

The language of dirt, disease, and infestation, along with the cure for these problems in the form of cleansing, removing, and purification, is the language of settler colonialism and genocide. Because settler colonialism is so formative to United States culture and politics, this language became the language of political repression in general, even when that repression was aimed inward. In December 1919, when US authorities, including the twenty-four-year-old J. Edgar Hoover, rounded up, imprisoned, and then forced 249 Russian-born "reds"—many of whom were Jews, such as Emma Goldman, Alexander Berkman, and Ethel Bernstein—onto the USAT *Buford* for deportation, US Congressman William Vaile celebrated "the cancerous growth about to be cut out of the American body politic," proclaiming, "the Republic shall be kept clean and in its cleanliness shall endure."[23] Discussing Vaile's remarks, Kathy Ferguson writes, "Anticipating Hitler's vilification of Jews in *Mein Kampf*, Congressman William Vaile reported in the Congressional Record that anarchists were an illness to be excised from the body politic."[24]

That the most immediate reference Ferguson finds to give historical context to Vaile's remarks was *Mein Kampf*—a book that was published five years after Vaile's comments and was not published in full in Vaile's language until twenty years after the anarchist deportations—exemplifies the problem in US political science and US historical consciousness at which this work takes aim. Why use German Nazism to contextualize Vaile rather than the much more immediate and appropriate context of US colonialism? It is as though Vaile was engaging in what patriotic US liberals might refer to as "un-American" rhetoric. Ferguson is quite correct that Vaile's language anticipated the way Hitler would later vilify Jews, but Vaile's language was thoroughly US American, rooted not in European fascism but in US colonialism. US American colonizers were not like the Nazis. It was the other way around: the Nazis were like US American colonizers.

It makes sense that European fascists adopted the language of colonialism. As the Afro-Caribbean anticolonial poet Aimé Césaire observed in his classic 1950 essay "Discours sur le colonialisme," all of Europe's monstrous techniques under fascist regimes for controlling, policing, surveilling, containing, imprisoning, torturing, expelling, and eliminating the state's enemies within were developed through centuries of colonialist violence. After centuries of inflicting these policies and practices on the natives on the frontier, explained Césaire, "the bourgeoisie is awakened by a terrific boomerang effect: the gestapos are busy, the prisons fill up, the torturers standing around the racks invent, refine, discuss."[25] To Césaire, fascism was the violence of colonialism returning home,

Cleansing the Republic    65

or in other words, fascism was not an aberration from what Europe was but an extension, with its roots firm in European colonialism. In the words of Zak Cope, "on its own soil fascism is imperialist repression turned inward."[26] This is all to say that the language of dirt, disease, infestation, cleansing, removing, and purification must not be characterized as something un-American, but as the language of US and European colonialism. When liberal US Americans describe such language as used in the present day by the far right as un-American, they are engaging, however unintentionally, in a patriotic denial of the processes through which the United States developed.

In the example of William Vaile, the connection to US colonialism is quite clear. After graduating from Yale University, Vaile joined the First Regiment of the Connecticut Volunteer Field Artillery in the Spanish-American War. He then went on to study law and graduate from Harvard Law School and became a lawyer for the Denver and Rio Grande Railroad Company and a county prosecutor. From June to December 1916, he patrolled the US-Mexico border as a second lieutenant in the First Separate Battalion in the National Guard of Colorado during a period of intense US ethnic cleansing of the frontier. Vaile's service to the US project of white nationalism—in invading Cuba, in defending the interests of the railroad magnates, as a prosecutor, policing the border, all before being elected on the Republican ticket to the US Congress—is the context for Vaile's use of the language of ethnic cleansing in reference to the deportation of Jewish and other "foreign" anarchists.[27]

A *New York Times* front page referred to the deportees as "The 249 undesirable aliens deported from the United States," and "Reds," who, upon arrival in Finland on the "Soviet Ark"—the US press's nickname for the USAT *Buford*—would be "marched to the special train which will carry them to the Russian frontier."[28] The "reds" would be returned to their natural habitat, the frontier. More than half of the "reds" shipped to the Russian frontier were members of the Union of Russian Workers (UORW), an anarchist federation that working-class Russian-born migrants founded in New York in 1911. By the time the young J. Edgar Hoover was on the case in his capacity as head of the Bureau of Investigation's new Radical Division—which carried out the Palmer Raids—the UORW had some sixty chapters across the United States and Canada and, according to records seized by New York State agents during the anti-anarchist raids, a membership of fifteen thousand.[29]

## The *Buford*

The USAT *Buford*, which carried the 249 involuntary passengers, was itself both an instrument and a symbol of US colonialism and empire. Originally it was the SS *Mississippi*, a civilian cargo and transport vessel. The US Army purchased the ship in 1898 to support US military operations in the Caribbean during the Spanish-American War. The army named the ship USAT *Buford* after the famous US cavalry officer, Indian killer, and hero of Gettysburg, John Buford. Buford graduated from West Point in 1848 and was immediately sent on frontier duty in the Indigenous territories recently ceded to the United States by Mexico. As a cavalry officer, Buford participated in ethnic cleansing campaigns against Indigenous groups. One such campaign was the 1855 "battle" of Ash Hollow, more accurately termed a massacre, in which 600 US soldiers attacked a group of 250 Sicangu Lakota people. When the soldiers attacked, Sicangu women took the children to safety in the nearby caves. The soldiers went after the women and children and fired indiscriminately into the caves, killing 86 people, half of whom were women and children, and took 70 women and children prisoner.[30]

Indian killer John Buford's namesake, the USAT *Buford*, sailed on in this tradition, first playing a role in the US invasion of Cuba; shortly thereafter it was refitted for service in the US invasion and occupation of the Philippines.[31] Over the next two decades, it was used in several US imperialist military operations, including operations in Hawaii, Guam, and Mexico before the army transferred the ship to the US Navy, at which point it became the USS *Buford*. Its final mission as the USS *Buford* was to support military operations in the Panama Canal Zone, after which the navy returned it to the army to again become the USAT *Buford*. At that point, the *Buford*, under US Army command, carried out the mission for which it became most famous: the removal of the anarchist "reds" back to their "Russian frontier," where they belonged.[32]

In 1923, the army decommissioned the ship and sold it to a commercial transport company, after which the film producer Joseph Schenck—ironically a Russian-Jewish immigrant like many of the *Buford*'s deportees—chartered it for use in the 1924 Buster Keaton popular silent film *The Navigator*. Keaton renamed the ship *Navigator*, and it became the center of his most popular and commercially successful film. Keaton's film was not an end but a continuation of the *Buford*'s function as a vessel of white supremacy, empire, militarism, and colonialism. The film was a blatant expression of US colonizer culture, rife with anti-Black and anti-Indigenous tropes.[33]

*The Navigator* was a story in which, in the words of the film's intertitles, "the entire lives of a peaceful American boy and girl" were "changed by a funny little war between two small countries far across the sea." From the outset, the film framed US Americans as mere "peaceful," neutral observers, while foreign nations were irrational and violent, engaging in "funny little wars." Spies from the "two little nations," continued the intertitles, "were at a Pacific seaport, each trying to prevent the other getting ships and supplies." The innocent, peaceful US Americans were then unintentionally caught up in this silly drama between irrational foreign nations.[34]

Cleansing the Republic    67

The film's lead role was Rollo Treadway, a wealthy, privileged, and comedically bumbling young heir to the Treadway family fortune, played by Buster Keaton. In the film, Rollo is the epitome of the overcivilized, soft, privileged gentleman, lacking in what Theodore Roosevelt called the "barbarian virtues."[35] Rollo proposes marriage to the wealthy young heiress Betsy O'Brien, played by Kathryn McGuire. So overcivilized and lacking in virility is Rollo that he has to be driven by his chauffeur to Betsy's house, which is directly across the street from his. Not only does this trip across the street require a chauffeur but it also requires another servant whose sole role is to open and close the door of the car for Rollo. Betsy, a conventionally attractive young white woman, unimpressed by such an unmanly specimen, rejects his proposal. Dejected, Rollo decides to go alone on the honeymoon trip to Honolulu he had planned for the two of them. Betsy's father, the wealthy industrialist John O'Brien, played by Frederick Vroom, sells the *Navigator* unknowingly to spies from one of the nations at war. The spies from the enemy nation decide to sabotage the ship and set it adrift the night before the new crew is to board it. On the intertitle is the classic trope in imperialist culture: "Under the cover of darkness the foreign agents prepared to carry out their plans." Through a series of coincidences and blunders, Rollo and Betsy end up on the *Navigator*, unbeknownst to the spies, just before the spies set it adrift.[36]

The two are at sea for weeks, during which time Rollo, forced to learn to live without servants pampering him, begins to develop manly competence. Eventually the two spot their salvation, a tropical island. Upon closer inspection of the island with binoculars, they see that the island is crawling with dark-skinned, scantily clad, painted, ferocious cannibals. The cannibals were played mainly by Black actors and non-Black actors made to appear Black, with the cannibal chief played by Black actor Noble Johnson. Johnson was typecast in Hollywood to play the role of racialized "exotics," such as the cannibal chief in *Little Robinson Crusoe* and Chief Sitting Bull in *The Flaming Frontier*.[37] "We're safer on the boat" reads an intertitle, but the ship runs aground and springs a leak. "We are sinking! It's just a matter of time until we're captured." Rollo dons a deep-sea diving suit and descends underwater to attempt to repair the ship. While Rollo is busy patching the hole in the underside of the ship's hull, and engaging in underwater gags, such as setting up a "Danger, Men at Work" sign and sword-fighting with a swordfish, the cannibals take a canoe out to the ship and kidnap Betsy.[38]

The image of the savage dark-skinned male predator pursuing the civilized, pure white young woman was a common trope in post-Reconstruction US popular culture and entered popular film culture with the first major motion picture in history, D. W. Griffith's *Birth of a Nation*. US President Woodrow Wilson favorably viewed *The Birth of a Nation* at a special White House screening in

1915. *The Birth of a Nation* contributed directly to the resurgence of the Ku Klux Klan, and *The Navigator* premiered and played in theaters almost ten years later during the height of Klan power. *The Birth of a Nation* was the epitome of serious drama, while Buster Keaton's films were the epitome of all that is frivolous and light-hearted in popular US culture. It therefore may seem out of place to compare Keaton to Griffith, but the trope of the white man as the hero against the dark savage threatening pure white womanhood is just as prevalent in *The Navigator* as it is in *The Birth of a Nation*, albeit far less serious in tone. The trope played on and catered to white supremacist fears of Black masculinity and white male status anxiety: a highly effective psychological device to emotionally engage white audiences in the era.[39]

Back on the island, Betsy is on the ground surrounded by spear-wielding Black Indigenous men who, wearing loin cloths, terrifying war paint, and exotic jewelry, stare down at her with malicious intent. Her light hair, white skin, and modest white sailor uniform contrast with the dark skin, thick dark hair, and nudity of her captors. She repeatedly tells them "No!" as they prepare to force themselves on her. At that moment, the hero Rollo emerges from the water onto the beach, wearing his deep-sea diving gear. To the superstitious natives he appears to be some kind of sea monster, and they flee in terror: the backward primitives defeated by the civilized white man's modern technology. Betsy rewards Rollo with kisses for saving her. A chaste white woman, her answer is "no" to the racialized savage but she remains sexually available to the civilized white man.[40]

As Rollo and Betsy return to the ship, the cannibals realize they have been tricked, and they paddle their primitive canoes after the couple. Wave after wave of cannibals attempt to board the *Navigator* as Rollo comedically fights them off, the lone white man standing bravely against the dark hordes to defend civilization and white womanhood. The waves of savages eventually overtake the ship, as Rollo and Betsy go overboard to escape. With the *Navigator*—a symbol of civilization—overrun by dark cannibals, all seems lost. Rollo and Betsy sink underwater in each other's arms. Just as they are about to drown, a US Navy submarine emerges from underneath them and rescues the couple: US militarism saves the day. The savages swarm the submarine in vain as it submerges again into the sea to carry the couple back to civilization. Betsy rewards Rollo with another kiss before the film ends. The civilized white man, initially rejected by the young woman, wins her over by proving his manliness in battle against savagery.[41]

In 2018, the Library of Congress added *The Navigator* to its National Film Registry: a project with the mission of preserving and archiving films that "reflect who we are as a people and as a nation."[42] Librarian of Congress Carla Hayden explains that the Library of Congress National Film Preservation Board chooses films for the registry on the basis of how well they reflect US American culture: "These cinematic treasures must be protected because they document our history, culture, hopes and dreams."[43] Indeed, if the purpose of the National Film Registry is to archive films which accurately reflect US American culture and values, then *The Navigator* absolutely deserves to be there.

Dominant US culture developed within the context of US imperialism and colonialism, along with the racial and gender notions with which those structures are intertwined. The *Buford* powerfully symbolizes this historical relationship between culture and imperialism: named to honor a genocider, functioning as a vessel of US empire and colonialism, and ending its military career in the project of cleansing and removing the disease of foreign radicals from the body politic, all before serving as the setting for a popular film saturated with anti-Blackness, anti-Indigenous tropes, and white supremacist gender anxieties. It is not just the film that reflects who the United States is "as a people and as a nation," but the ship itself.

## Matter Out of Place

The policies and practices of extermination, expulsion, and removal, symbolized by the USAT *Buford*, were accompanied by the language of extermination. For example, the *Washington Post* described the deportation of anarchists on the *Buford* as necessary for US national defense and spoke in terms of the "virus of Bolshevism" and "germs of anarchy" that were "breeding and multiplying in the body politic."[44] Ferguson connects this rhetoric of dirt, disease, and infestation to anthropologist Mary Douglas's classic 1966 study of the social concepts of purity and pollution, *Purity and Danger*.[45] Scholars often cite Douglas as coining the phrase "matter out of place" as a definition for the social concept of dirt. In using the phrase, and building on the concept, Douglas drew from the work of the anti-imperialist and anarchist-sympathetic "father of American Psychology" William James (1842–1910).[46]

James, who was highly critical of large, overarching systems that authorities or powerful institutions impose on societies, discussed dirt as a matter of classification within a system. From the point of view of a given system, elements that do not belong within that system are classified as dirt. Dirt, then, wrote James, is "matter out of place," or rather, elements that do not belong within the system at hand and, therefore, from that system's point of view, must be removed or cleansed from that system.[47] Building on James's discussion, Douglas wrote that societies classifying certain elements as dirt implies (1) the existence of a set of ordered relations and (2) the existence of a contravention of that order. She further explained

70    CHAPTER 3

> Dirt then, is never a unique, isolated event. Where there is dirt there is system. Dirt is the by-product of a systematic ordering and classification of matter, in so far as ordering involves rejecting inappropriate elements. This idea of dirt takes us straight into the field of symbolism and promises a link-up with more obviously symbolic systems of purity.
>
> We can recognize in our own notions of dirt that we are using a kind of omnibus compendium which includes all the rejected elements of ordered systems. It is a relative idea.[48]

Dirt is relative in that an element is only dirt within certain contexts. A hair on one's head, for example, does not make one's head dirty, but take one of those same hairs and place it on a restaurant table, and now the table is disgusting. The hair is out of place. "In short," wrote Douglas, "our pollution behavior is the reaction which condemns any object or idea likely to confuse or contradict cherished classifications."[49]

In the context of colonialism and capitalism, peoples and movements who do not fit within the system or who challenge it then become dirt, disease, infestation: in the words of Congressman Vaile, "an illness to be excised from the body politic." Indigenous nations were not dirt when they were out on the "wild frontiers" beyond the borders of the United States, or when they were safely contained, socially quarantined, on reservations under the control of the state, but, the minute they stepped off those reservations, they were, in the words of the *New York Tribune*, "infesting the country in all directions."[50] Eastern European Jewish anarchists were no cause for anxiety to US statesmen as long as they remained in their natural habitat, the "Russian frontier" but, in "civilized" US urban environments, they were a "virus."

## "Nits Make Lice"

This notion of "infestation" was deeply ingrained in English and US colonialism, exemplified by the heinous English and US colonizer axiom "nits make lice." In his study of seventeenth-century English colonialism, historian Gerald Horne writes that Oliver Cromwell's anti-Irish pogroms "created the template for republicans staring down the indigenous and slave revolts in the Americas."[51] The earliest known instance of the "nits make lice" metaphor is a 1675 English poem praising Cromwell's anti-Irish massacres in the 1640s, particularly the work of one of Cromwell's most brutal agents, Sir Charles Coote, who "Did kill the Nitts, that they might not growe Lice."[52] Coote was a military commander involved in Cromwell's Massacre of Drogheda. In the words of Irish studies scholar Kathleen Kane, he "was a military commander responsible for eradicating an indigenous population whose presence was inimical to the 'planting' of government-authorized settlers in a colonial space understood to be somehow empty, at least of a population of any value."[53] It is an assessment very much in line with Horne's argument that Cromwellian extermination and containment of the Irish served as an early template for English settler colonization of the Americas.[54] During the US invasions of Cuba and the Philippines, the US imperialist Theodore Roosevelt was inspired by Cromwell to the degree that he wrote a biography of Cromwell, praising him as "the greatest soldier-statesman of the seventeenth century."[55] In the words of Gerald Horne, "Roosevelt was completing what Cromwell had begun."[56]

Roosevelt likely would have taken such an assessment as an honor. Being a student of history, Roosevelt understood that English extermination and assimilation of Celtic peoples in particular was the template for English settler colonization of the Americas. In his race-history of the United States, *The Winning of the West*, he wrote, "The English had exterminated or assimilated the Celts of Britain, and they substantially repeated the process with the Indians of America." In the American case, however, extermination was much more prevalent than assimilation: "although of course in America there was very little, instead of very much, assimilation." Because of this emphasis on extermination over assimilation, explained Roosevelt, English colonizer society in the Americas, in contrast with Spanish colonizer society, retained "its general race characteristics. . . . The English-speaking peoples now hold more and better land than any other American nationality or set of nationalities," a direct result of the fact, in Roosevelt's racist logic, that the English settlers "have in their veins less aboriginal American blood than any of their neighbors."[57]

"Nits make lice" became a common justification that US frontier ethnic cleansers used to justify extermination, especially when children were among the victims of the massacres. In late August or early September 1864, the genocider Colonel John Chivington, who commanded Colorado's Third Cavalry Regiment, gave a speech to his men in which he reportedly summed up his policy as "Kill and scalp all, little and big; that nits made lice."[58] The phrase became an unofficial slogan of the men of the Third Cavalry, who put it into practice that November, most sadistically against captive Cheyenne and Arapaho people at the military camp at Sand Creek, Colorado.[59] In an unprovoked attack against a mostly disarmed population that was, under the leadership of the peace-seeker Black Kettle, honoring a truce with US forces, 675 US soldiers massacred and mutilated some 200 Cheyenne and Arapaho people, two-thirds of whom were women, children, and babies. The soldiers took scalps, ears, fingers, penises, vulvas, and fetuses as trophies, decorating their hats and weapons with them.[60]

Helen Hunt Jackson, a writer who worked to expose US government crimes against Indigenous nations, seethed with indignation that the respectable white public applauded such cruelty:

72    CHAPTER 3

When this Colorado regiment of demons returned to Denver they were greeted with an ovation. *The Denver News* said: "All acquitted themselves well. Colorado soldiers have again covered themselves with glory;" and at a theatrical performance given in the city, these scalps taken from Indians were held up and exhibited to the audience, which applauded rapturously.[61]

Congress appointed a committee to investigate the claims of people like Jackson that what the US Army did at Sand Creek was a massacre and a war crime. The testimony during the hearings was damning. Helen Hunt Jackson was present and compiled some of it in her report on Sand Creek. Witness after witness testified under oath of soldiers cutting off the private parts of women and children and murdering even babies in cold blood. One US Army major testified, "Women and children were killed and scalped, children shot at their mothers' breasts, and all the bodies mutilated in the most horrible manner. The dead bodies of females profaned in such a manner that the recital is sickening, Colonel J. M. Chivington all the time inciting his troops to their diabolical outrages."[62]

Another witness testified, "I saw a number of children killed; they had bullet-holes in them; one child had been cut with some sharp instrument across its side. I saw another that both ears had been cut off. I saw several of the Third Regiment cut off fingers to get the rings off them." Another testified, "I saw one squaw lying on the bank, whose leg had been broken. A soldier came up to her with a drawn sabre. She raised her arm to protect herself; he struck, breaking her arm. She rolled over, and raised her other arm; he struck, breaking that, and then left her without killing her. I saw one squaw cut open, with an unborn child lying by her side."[63] A certain Major Anthony testified,

> There was one little child, probably three years old, just big enough to walk through the sand. The Indians had gone ahead, and this little child was behind, following after them. The little fellow was perfectly naked, travelling in the sand. I saw one man get off his horse at a distance of about seventy-five yards and draw up his rifle and fire. He missed the child. Another man came up and said, "Let me try the son of a b—. I can hit him." He got down off his horse, kneeled down, and fired at the little child, but he missed him. A third man came up, and made a similar remark, and fired, and the little fellow dropped.[64]

Another witness testified of "men, women, and children's privates cut out" and "I heard one man say that he had cut out a woman's private parts and had them for exhibition on a stick."[65] This is "nits make lice" translated into action. After days of hearing such gruesome testimony, Congress's Joint Committee on the Conduct of War concluded that Colonel Chivington "deliberately planned and executed a foul and dastardly massacre, which would have disgraced the veriest savage among those who were the victims of his cruelty."[66] Nevertheless, the state did not charge Chivington or any of his men with even a single crime.[67]

Cleansing the Republic     73

Historian Paul Reeve points out that Sand Creek was not the first time the English colonizer axiom "nits make lice" was uttered as justification for a massacre in the United States. In October 1838, the Missouri State Militia attacked Mormons at Hawn's Mill, Caldwell County, Missouri, in what Mormons to this day remember as the Hawn's Mill Massacre. Anti-Mormonism is discussed further in chapter 4, but at the time, respectable white US society vilified and racialized Mormons as enemies of the United States who were in league with Indigenous nations. Among the many murders and other cruelties soldiers committed against Mormons at Hawn's Mill, one soldier found three boys, ages ten, nine, and six, hiding in a blacksmith shop. The soldier shot the ten-year-old in the head from close range, blowing the upper part of the child's head off, killed the nine-year-old boy, and wounded the six-year-old. Justifying this cold-blooded attack on terrified children, a militia member reportedly said, "Nits will make lice."[68]

The phrase also appeared in US popular culture in the 1850s, as "Tom Quick, the Indian Slayer" tales proliferated in US American folklore. Tom Quick tales were white US American revenge fantasies, in which Tom Quick, a US American "frontier" folk hero, traveled around killing Indians as vengeance for their supposedly having killed members of his family. In one tale, he saw an Indian family in a canoe in the Delaware River. He shot the father dead before sinking his hatchet "into the brain of the squaw" and did the same to the two oldest children: "The two oldest children, as Tom afterwards declared, 'squawked like young crows' as he killed them."[69] As he raised his tomahawk to kill the infant, he paused:

> Tom's heart was completely softened. He thought he would convey it to some white family, and have it taken care of properly, and fancied that it would be very pleasant to have such a pretty, innocent creature to fondle after he had been hunting, and when he returned to the settlements. But the fact suddenly thrust itself into his mind, that the child would in a few years become an Indian, and this so enraged him that he instantly dashed out its brains.[70]

He then fastened heavy stones to all five bodies to sink them to the bottom of the river, and destroyed the canoe, so as to leave no trace. "When asked why he killed the children, his invariable reply was, 'Nits make lice!'"[71] That is an example of a popular folk tale produced by US settler colonizer culture. The man who murdered a family of five in cold blood, who tomahawked an infant's skull, was the protagonist of the tales.[72]

Kathleen Kane writes that "nits make lice," a "cursory attempt to justify the slaughter of Native American women, elders, and children, was to achieve an axiomatic status in Native American popular memory—a status comparable only to that given to General Philip Sheridan's chilling remark: 'The only good

Indian is a dead Indian.'"[73] In response to the evil axiom and the practices it justified, anticolonial Sicangu Lakota woman Mary Brave Bird wrote,

> In the opinion of some people, the fewer Indians there are, the better. As Colonel Chivington said to his soldiers: "Kill 'em all, big and small, nits make lice!" I don't know whether I am a louse under the white man's skin. I hope I am.[74]

She likely was a louse under the white man's skin, at least in the minds of the leaders commanding the National Guard, federal marshals, FBI agents, local police, and other US forces armed with machine guns, helicopters, armored vehicles, explosives, and sniper rifles while she, along with other Indigenous Americans, stood boldly against them at Wounded Knee in 1973.[75]

## "Filthy Anarchists"

The language of extermination, of which "nits make lice" is but one example, is the language of colonialist violence. As chapter 4 more fully discusses, the state used colonial counterinsurgency, particularly the tactics and ideological framework developed through the Indian Wars, as its template for repression of proletarian social movements. Agents of the state and the bourgeoisie classified anarchists and communists, like other racialized enemies, as "matter out of place." The settler colonizer language of extermination, dirt, disease, infestation, cleansing, and purification became the language of anticommunism and antianarchism. The *Washington Post* said of anarchists, "These hideous creatures are not native to American soil. They do not spring from American parents. They are the degenerate offscouring of centuries of repression, ignorance, and vice in other lands."[76] In another piece, it called anarchists the "scum of foreign countries."[77]

Such editorials in the ruling-class press were well aligned with the way police captain Michael Schaack characterized anarchists two decades earlier. "The anarchists of Chicago are exotics," wrote Schaack, as in exotic plants, as in invasive species. He elaborated: "Discontent here is a German plant transferred from Berlin and Leipsic and thriving to flourish in the west. In our garden it is a weed to be plucked out by the roots and destroyed, for our conditions neither warrant its growth nor excuse its existence."[78] Schaack was an immigrant from Luxembourg, the same part of the world that many of the anarchists he vilified as "foreign" were from. It was not the anarchists' Germanness that made them exotics, but their communist politics. To Schaack, himself born in Europe, socialism in the United States was an "alien revolt," and anarchists "a contemptible rabble of discontents, un-American in birth, training, education, and idea."[79] By othering anarchists in this way, the immigrant Schaack asserted his own whiteness and Americanness, differentiating himself from the "bad" Germans.

Cleansing the Republic    75

In his autobiography, the Pulitzer Prize–winning author Carl Sandburg wrote of his memories of being an eight- and nine-year-old boy in Galesburg, Illinois, at the time of the Haymarket trial and executions. He recalled his childhood impressions:

> Then came the murder trial of the eight men and we saw in the Chicago papers black-and-white drawings of their faces and they looked exactly like what we expected, hard, mean, slimy faces. We saw pictures of the twelve men on the jury and they looked like what we expected, nice, honest, decent faces. We learned the word for the men on trial, anarchists, and they hated the rich and called policemen "bloodhounds." They were not regular people and they didn't belong to the human race, for they seemed more like slimy animals who prowl, sneak, and kill in the dark. This I believed along with millions of other people reading and talking about the trial. I didn't meet or hear anyone in our town who didn't so believe.[80]

Similarly the Pulitzer-winning novelist Upton Sinclair, who was the same age as Sandburg, reminisced about his childhood in the late 1880s. He remembered visiting a wax museum that included in its "chamber of horrors" an exhibit representing wild anarchists sitting around a table making bombs: "I swallowed these bombs whole and shuddered at the thought of depraved persons who inhabited the back rooms of saloons, jeered at God, practiced free love, and conspired to blow up the government."[81]

In contrast, John Most Jr. (1894–1987), the eldest son of anarchists Helene Minkin and the infamous Johann Most, in an interview with historian Paul Avrich, remembered being a child on the receiving end of such characterizations:

> We were very poor and lived in a series of basement apartments on the Lower East Side. The neighbors threw insults—and sometimes rocks—at us: "There go the filthy anarchists!" "There's that anarchist rat family!" We were abused continually.[82]

The phrase "dirty anarchist" followed him, he said, even into old age. It was not only neighbors but also the police that subjected the family to constant surveillance and harassment and frequently arrested or detained Johann Most. "Once when father was imprisoned on Blackwell's Island," remembered John Most Jr., "the police came and ripped up our whole apartment." One reason there was so much abuse against his family particularly at the turn of the century was that Theodore Roosevelt "was always denouncing the anarchists, and especially my father." The junior Most told Avrich, "Once in St. Louis Roosevelt was publicly criticizing father, who happened to be in the audience. Father hollered out, "*Halt Maul, Heisser Luft!*" (Shut your mouth, Hot Air!). He was arrested on the spot and kept in jail for five days until Teddy had left town."[83]

Indeed, Roosevelt despised Johann Most and at times publicly singled him out. For instance, in an 1894 essay titled "True Americanism," Roosevelt argued that "It is urgently necessary to check and regulate our immigration, by much more drastic laws than now exist" in order to "keep out races which do not assimilate readily with our own." He specifically named the anarchist Johann Most and the Irish Fenian Jeremiah O'Donovan Rossa—both of whom Roosevelt called "anarchists"—as examples of such "unworthy individuals."[84]

## Attentat!

Roosevelt frequently and zealously railed against anarchists, making the eradication of anarchism a top priority of his administration. His zeal is understandable considering that it was the assassination of his predecessor by an anarchist that put Roosevelt in the White House in the first place. In fact, Roosevelt assumed the office of the presidency following a string of anarchist assassinations of heads of state. In 1894, Sante Geronimo Caserio—named Geronimo by his Italian peasant father who admired the Chiricahua Apache military leader of that name—stabbed to death French President Marie François Sadi Carnot as retaliation for the French state's executions of Auguste Vaillant and Émile Henry. Caserio went to the guillotine shouting *"Coraggio cugini— evviva l'anarchia!"*—"Courage, cousins—long live anarchy!" In 1897, the anarchist Michele Angiolillo—aided by the Puerto Rican nationalist leader Ramón Emeterio Betances—shot dead the Spanish prime minister, Antonio Cánovas del Castillo, as revenge for Castillo ordering the imprisonment, torture, and execution of anarchists, socialists, and republicans at the dreaded Montjuïc Fortress. Angiolillo's final statement before being garroted was simply the word "germinal."[85] It was a word that carried deep meaning for revolutionaries. In the French republican calendar, it signified revolution and the beginning of a new world, and it was the title of an Émile Zola novel—a favorite among anarchists—heavy with the theme of proletarian resistance and martyrdom.[86]

In 1898 Luigi Lucheni stabbed to death Austrian Empress Elisabeth. Lucheni was of particular interest to criminologists. After his death by apparent suicide in prison 12 years later, scientists at the University of Geneva preserved Lucheni's head in formalin solution in a jar, thinking it might teach them something about criminality. In 1900, Gaetano Bresci shot dead Italy's King Umberto I, as revenge for the brutal 1898 Bava-Beccaris Massacre. Umberto I praised the general responsible for the massacre, awarding him the high honor of the *Grande Ufficiale dell'Ordine Militare di Savoia* (Great Cross of the Order of Savoy), for "the great service which you rendered to our institutions and to civilization."[87] The following year Leon Czolgosz shot US President William McKinley twice at point-blank range at the Pan-American Exposition in Buffalo, New York. Unlike most preceding anarchist assassins, Czołgosz did not give a specific reason for why he killed the head of state beyond, "I killed the president because he was the enemy of the good people—the working people." Two months prior to the assassination however, Czołgosz expressed to Abraham Isaac—a Russian refugee Mennonite-turned-anarchist who at the time was editor of the Chicago-based anarchist newspaper *Free Society*—that he was upset with the McKinley administration over "the outrages committed by the American government in the Philippine islands," and that he wanted to do something "more active" about it.[88]

Because of this, and perhaps because of the setting of the Pan-American Exposition, many anarchists understood Czołgosz's attentat in the context of US capitalist imperialism in the Caribbean and Pacific Islands. Under McKinley the United States greatly increased its imperial control over the Caribbean and Pacific trade networks with Asia, pushing Spain out of Cuba, annexing Hawaii, and establishing US colonial control over Puerto Rico, Wake, Guam, and the Philippines.[89] At the Pan-American Exposition, a celebration of US empire, McKinley announced that the United States would be expanding its foreign political and economic reach. One of the leading theorists and organizers of international anarchist-communism, the Italian Errico Malatesta—who had previously organized in places as far afield as Italy, France, Belgium, Switzerland, Egypt, Argentina, the United States, Cuba, and at the time London—saw Czołgosz's act, and individual acts of "propaganda by the deed" in general, as strategically foolish, nevertheless he refused to publicly condemn it, and discussed it in the context of US imperialism.[90] When the press asked him whether he condemned Leon Czołgosz, McKinley's assassin, he replied, "Why should anarchists condemn Czolgosz when the American government is the real teacher of violence? Anarchy wishes to abolish violence, but the Americans slaughter weaker people in the Philippines and Cuba."[91]

Reflecting on the attentat, the anarchist and anti-imperialist Voltairine de Cleyre likewise would neither condone nor condemn but instead placed the attentat in the context of McKinley's imperialism:

> Many offences had come through the acts of William McKinley. Upon his hand was the "damned spot" of official murder, the blood of the Filipinos, whom he, in pursuance of the capitalist policy of imperialism, had sentenced to death. Upon his head falls the curse of all the workers against whom, time and time again, he threw the strength of his official power.... Perhaps he was able to reconcile his Christian belief, "Do good to them that hate you," with the slaughters he ordered; perhaps he murdered the Filipinos "to do them good"; the capitalist mind is capable of such contortions. But whatever his private life, he was the representative of wealth and greed and power; in accepting the position he accepted the rewards and the dangers, just as a miner,

who goes down in the mine for $2.50 a day or less, accepts the danger of the firedamp. McKinley's rewards were greater and his risks less; moreover, he didn't need the job to keep bread in his mouth; but he, too, met an explosive force—the force of a desperate man's will. And he died; *not as a martyr, but as a gambler who had won a high stake and was struck down by the man who had lost the game*: for that is what capitalism has made of human well-being—a gambler's stake, no more.[92]

The comparison of McKinley to miners was not a random example but was powerfully meaningful because—in addition to the frequent deaths of miners by explosions and other accidents in mines—in the four years before the McKinley assassination, state forces massacred and otherwise killed and suppressed miners on strike in 1897 in Hazleton, Pennsylvania; in 1898 in Virden, Illinois; and in 1899 against the militant Western Federation of Miners in Coeur d'Alene, Idaho. Emma Goldman likewise drew a connection between Czołgosz's attentat, McKinley's massacres of Filipino people overseas, and capitalist massacres of miners within the United States. "More than any other president," wrote Goldman, McKinley "had betrayed the trust of the people, and became the tool of the moneyed kings." He had shamefully soaked the United States "in the blood of the massacred Filipinos" at the very moment the working class was raw with "the recollection of Hazleton, Virden, Idaho, and other places, where capital has waged war on labor."[93] For anarchists such as Malatesta, de Cleyre, and Goldman, it was not the anarchists who created the violence that led to McKinley's death but the social conditions of capitalism and imperialism.

It should also be noted that anti-Blackness contributed to the success of Czołgosz's attack. The president had a full security detail on duty keeping an eye out for suspicious behavior from the people in line to shake his hand. Czołgosz, standing nervously in line and holding a revolver concealed by a handkerchief, certainly should have aroused suspicion, but behind him in line was a large Black man named James Benjamin "Big Jim" Parker. The guards' eyes were on Parker, which allowed Czołgosz to simply walk up to the president and shoot. In the words of historian Moon-Ho Jung, "racial profiling facilitated this presidential assassination."[94] Ironically, Parker, whom the guards suspected of criminality, was the first to respond, apprehending the assailant and preventing Czołgosz from firing a third shot. The Secret Service and law enforcement seemed to resent the fact that many hailed Parker as the hero of the day. State officials refused to even acknowledge that Parker played any role. Despite being the closest witness and the first person to respond to protect McKinley, neither the prosecution nor the defense asked Parker to testify in the trial, and none of the Secret Service agents, law enforcement agents, or other witnesses who testified identified Parker as the person who took down the assassin.[95]

Cleansing the Republic    79

## Roosevelt's "War with Relentless Efficiency"

Roosevelt disdained the anarchists' explanations that the assassination was rooted in social injustice but found that the explanations carried enough social currency that he was obliged to address them. "On no conceivable theory," he told Congress, "could the murder of the President be accepted as due to protest against 'inequalities in the social order.' . . . Anarchy is no more an expression of 'social discontent' than picking pockets or wife beating." Perhaps drawing on the work of the psychopathologist Cesare Lombroso, who classified anarchists as a "criminal type," Roosevelt asserted that

> The anarchist, and especially the anarchist in the United States, is merely one type of criminal, more dangerous than any other because he represents the same depravity in a greater degree. . . . He is not the victim of social or political injustice. There are no wrongs to remedy in his case. The cause of his criminality is to be found in his own evil passions and in the evil conduct of those who urge him on, not in any failure by others or by the State to do justice to him or his. He is a malefactor and nothing else. He is in no sense, in no shape or way, a "product of social conditions," save as a highwayman is "produced" by the fact that an unarmed man happens to have a purse.[96]

Under a Roosevelt administration, there would be no introspection about questions of economic conditions or imperialism. Upon taking office, Roosevelt immediately set to work laying the legal framework for the removal of anarchists from US society. In his first official address to Congress, he called for anarchist speech to be curtailed: "Anarchistic speeches, writings, and meetings are essentially seditious and treasonable." Anarchism was "far blacker infamy" than both piracy and the slave trade. Further, he called on lawmakers to create laws to deport and ban anarchists from the United States:

> [Anarchists] should be kept out of this country; and if found here they should be promptly deported to the country whence they came; and far-reaching provision should be made for the punishment of those who stay. No matter calls more urgently for the wisest thought of Congress. . . . Anarchy is a crime against the whole human race; and all mankind should band against the anarchist. His crime should be made an offense against nations.[97]

It did not seem to occur or matter to Roosevelt or respectable white US society that the country whence Czolgosz came was the United States of America. Czolgosz's foreign-sounding name was evidence enough that he was "un-American."[98]

Before he fired his revolver, Czolgosz appeared to be an ordinary white man. As word quickly spread that an anarchist shot the president, Czolgosz ceased, in white public imagination, to be white or American. He was Polish, or maybe

80      CHAPTER 3

Hungarian, maybe Polish-Hungarian, or a German Pole, "as if double provenance would make him foreign twice and doubly guilty."[99] Though he was born in Detroit, his supposed foreignness was evidence enough that he was a villain. Georgia's *Statesboro News* captured the mood of mainstream white US society with the words "A man with such a name ought to be killed on general principle anyway."[100] Within minutes of the news spreading that a foreign anarchist shot the president, crowds of people reportedly gathered in the streets of Buffalo shouting the slogan "Lynch the anarchist!"[101]

Lynching was a ritualized form of extrajudicial torture and execution that contributed to a sense of white solidarity during the Nadir.[102] The state legally executed Czołgosz, but, historian Amy Wood argues, the execution shared commonalities with the spectacle of lynching in the public nature of the trial and execution. The respectable public cried for Czołgosz's blood. In Long Island, "a mob hanged Czolgosz in effigy before a crowd of over 1,000 people."[103] Thomas Edison produced a realistic reenactment of the execution on film, to profit from the public lust to see Czołgosz die and to promote the electric chair. Edison did not invent the electric chair, but he financed its use in New York state prisons.[104]

The execution of Czołgosz contributed to a sense of white national unity between North and South. Wood writes, "American imperialism in the Philippines and the large influx of immigrants from Southern and Eastern Europe at the turn of the century led many white northerners to express a new understanding for white southerners, as suddenly they themselves were grappling with a racially different and seemingly undisciplined labor force."[105] The white southern press recognized elements of the southern lynch mob in the northern mobs crying for the lynching of anarchists and gloated that the North could no longer claim moral superiority over the South: "The North has the anarchists, she is welcome to them, and with the anarchists and Filipinos on hand, they can let the South alone."[106] Here again was the conflation of anarchists, a politically defined group, with a racially, ethnically defined group that at the time was being subjugated by US empire. Theodore Roosevelt conflated all three groups—anarchists, Filipino independence fighters, and American Indians. In the same address in which he charged Congress with the task of anarchist exclusion, he equated Filipino "insurrectors" with "hostile Indians," announcing that the former would be treated as the latter.[107]

Theodore Roosevelt was the personification of the anti-anarchist public mood. He was not simply putting on an act to appeal to white public sentiment but sincerely despised anarchists, evidenced by the fact that he wrote the same way about anarchists in his private correspondence with close associates as he spoke in his public speeches. While William McKinley lay in critical condition in his hospital bed, Roosevelt wrote a letter to his friend Henry Cabot Lodge, saying,

Cleansing the Republic    81

Of course I feel as I always have felt, that we should war with relentless efficiency not only against anarchists, but against all active and passive sympathizers with anarchists[:] . . . Hearst [a newspaper editor who criticized Roosevelt
and McKinley] and Altgeld [the former Illinois governor who pardoned the
remaining Haymarket anarchists], and to an only less degree, Tolstoi [the
Russian novelist and Christian pacifist], and the feeble apostles of Tolstoi, like
Ernest Howard Crosby [president of the Anti-Imperialist League and author of
the poem "The Real 'White Man's Burden,'" which parodied Kipling's famous
imperialist poem], and William Dean Howells [author, editor, defender of
the Haymarket anarchists, and member of the Anti-Imperialist League, outspoken against the US invasion of the Philippines], who unite in petitions for
the pardon of anarchists, have a heavy share in the burden of responsibility
for crimes of this kind.[108]

That Roosevelt held a former mainstream progressive governor like John Altgeld and antiwar pacifists like Tolstoy, Crosby, and Howells partly responsible
for the assassination of McKinley shows how deep, emotional, and irrational
Roosevelt's hatred of anarchists was.

Congress rose to Roosevelt's challenge to legally exclude anarchists from the
United States. In the weeks following Roosevelt's speech, there was a flood of
proposals for anti-anarchist bills brought to the floor by the representatives of
the capitalist class. The debate within Congress was not about whether to expel
and ban anarchists, but how to most effectively do so. Even the progressives in
Congress were on board with the project of excluding anarchists. Senator George
Frisbie Hoar of Massachusetts, for example, was one of the most progressive
voices in Congress. In earlier years, he campaigned for Black political enfranchisement and, as early as the 1880s argued on the Senate floor for women's
suffrage. He opposed the Chinese Exclusion Act on the grounds that it was
racist. He was an outspoken opponent of McKinley's and Roosevelt's imperialist
policies, accusing the United States of committing war crimes in the Philippines
and establishing concentration camps, originally called "reconcentration camps."
He called for Filipino independence, tried to block US annexation of Hawaii,
and opposed US involvement in Panama.[109]

If anyone were to oppose laws excluding people on the basis of political ideology, it would have been Hoar. On the contrary, he caused a public debate with his
proposal to establish a penal colony for anarchists on a newly acquired Pacific
or Caribbean island. Anarchism could then be safely contained, quarantined,
under tight surveillance and control of the state. Roosevelt's staunch friend and
ally, the journalist Jacob Riis—famous for *How the Other Half Lives*—agreed with
Hoar's proposal, but others criticized it as being too merciful or untenable. The
Baptist preacher and president of William Jewell College, John Priest Greene,
argued that "every anarchist agitator" should be incarcerated in a work prison.

He asserted that "We should remember that anarchists and rabid socialists are as a rule (and without exception so far as I know) irresponsible worthless people, 'no good' to themselves nor to the country. It would spoil an island to put them on it." Though Senator Hoar's idea of an anarchist penal colony was hotly debated in the press, it did not get anywhere in Congress.[110]

Nevertheless, legislatures passed anarchist exclusion laws, first at the state level and then at the federal level. New York passed the Criminal Anarchy Act of 1902, which outlawed—with a punishment of a $5,000 fine and ten years' imprisonment—the printing, editing, publishing, or displaying of anarchist literature. New Jersey, Wisconsin, and Washington state passed similar laws. In 1903, the US Congress passed the Anarchist Exclusion Act or Alien Immigration Act, which banned from the United States any "alien" the state categorized as an anarchist and ordered immigration officials to deport such "aliens" within three years of date of entry.[111] It is important to note that these early anarchist exclusion laws were generally unsuccessful on a large scale. The vast majority of anarchists in the United States, although potentially subject to incarceration or deportation under such laws, remained at large. The more famous anarchists who were most subject to surveillance and state persecution had a lot of allies, and they were quite practiced at raising money and mobilizing a legal defense and public awareness campaigns to defend themselves. Nonetheless, these early anarchist exclusion attempts became the legal groundwork for Roosevelt's "war with relentless efficiency" against anarchism, and the state built on them to later create laws, policies, agencies, and strategies that would—in concert with extralegal vigilantism and extreme state violence, which will be discussed in later chapters—in less than two decades, become quite effective at taking the wind out of the sails of the radical left.

The language of "war with relentless efficiency" was the language of the Indian Wars. Before Roosevelt became the leading voice of anti-anarchism in the United States, and possibly the world, he was a leading Indian hater. The exterminationist rhetoric he used against anarchists and the militant proletariat in general was the rhetoric of Indian killing. In that same first address to Congress, in which he called for anarchist exclusion and the suppression of the Filipino independence movement, he called for the continuation of genocidal policies against Indigenous nations. Knowing that Indigenous nationhood was intertwined with the collective relationship of a people to their land base, Roosevelt's preferred method to erase the existence of Indigenous nations was to carve Indian lands up into private, individually owned lots. He addressed Congress thus: "In my judgment the time has arrived when we should definitely make up our minds to recognize the Indian as an individual and not as a member of a tribe. The General Allotment Act is a mighty pulverizing engine to break up the tribal mass."[112] Such language was nothing short of genocidal, in accordance with a policy that was nothing short of genocidal, inasmuch as genocide is a process intended to erase the existence of a people *as a people*.

Roosevelt's Indian hating preceded and informed his anti-anarchism. In Roosevelt's imagination, nothing better represented US American manliness than the Indian killer: the frontier cowboy or the US Army cavalryman. His colonialist gender politics directly shaped US imperialist policies and vice versa.[113] There were few atrocities US forces committed against "savages" that Roosevelt did not find praiseworthy. He engaged in outright denial of most US crimes against Indigenous groups, and when the evidence for the crimes was incontrovertible, he turned to the language of victim blaming. For instance, "The Sioux and Cheyennes," he wrote, "have more often been sinning than sinned against." The "so-called" Sand Creek massacre, said Roosevelt, "was on the whole as righteous and beneficial a deed as ever took place on the frontier." He belittled white men who mourned the US Army slaughter, torture, and mutilation of Indigenous children, women, and elderly people at Sand Creek as "emasculated professional humanitarians" who were "untrustworthy and unsafe leaders" on questions of "Indian management."[114]

Roosevelt praised what he called "armed settlers" who, decades earlier, "formed the vanguard of the white advance." He wrote that the strategy (championed by Thomas Hart Benton (1782–1858), a US senator whom Roosevelt admired as an architect of US settler colonization) of relying on armed settlers who would claim and hold the land permanently, rather than official military units who would be only a temporary invasion and occupation force, was the most effective way of establishing white dominion. Drawing on the ideas of Benton, Roosevelt asserted that this strategy was effective in establishing white control in Tennessee and Kentucky, and that white settlers did the same in Florida against "dangerous" Seminoles who were "prowling out at night like wild beasts from their fastnesses in the dark and fetid swamps." Benton, as quoted by Roosevelt, referred to Seminole people the same way Roosevelt would later refer to anarchists, as "assassins," "robbers," and "incendiaries" who "lurk about."[115] In January 1886, Roosevelt told an audience in New York that Indigenous peoples are "Reckless, revengeful, fiendishly cruel, they rob and murder, not the cowboys, who can take care of themselves, but the defenseless, lone settlers on the plains."[116] Only one caliber of man was designed to defeat such an enemy, the armed settler: "It is the settler alone, the armed settler, whose presence announces the dominion, the permanent dominion, of the white man."[117]

In the same January 1886 speech in New York, Roosevelt built on General Sheridan's exterminationist axiom, saying, "I don't go so far as to think that the only good Indians are the dead Indians, but I believe nine out of every ten are, and I shouldn't like to inquire too closely into the case of the tenth. The most vicious cowboy has more moral principle than the average Indian."[118] Even when

84    CHAPTER 3

Roosevelt was attempting to differentiate "good Indians" from "bad Indians," he ended up lumping them all together as suspect enemies. In his 1888 book about ranch life in Dakota, he compared the characteristics, in his hyperracial imagination, of Cherokee, Nez Percé, Apache, Cheyenne, Pueblo, and Arapaho peoples, arguing that some were better than others. When it came down to it, though, he concluded, "even the best Indians are very apt to have a good deal of the wild beast in them; when they scent blood they wish their share of it, no matter from whose veins it flows."[119] Roosevelt described his life in the Dakota badlands within the familiar US settler colonial framework of the struggle between "cowboys and Indians."

The myth of the so-called frontier cowboy played a powerful role in white US imagination. It served ruling-class interests in part by popularizing "rugged individualist" settler values antithetical to working-class consciousness and working-class solidarity. In the words of historian Greg Grandin, "In the mythology of the West, cowboys don't join unions."[120] In reality, cowboys were, in the words of labor historian Mark Lause, "grossly underpaid and overworked seasonal agricultural laborers" who developed a sense of class consciousness, organized to collectively bargain, and carried out a series of militant strikes in the 1880s.[121] Notwithstanding this reality, the cowboy fantasy persisted. And as historian Kelly Lytle Hernández observes, settler fantasies played a powerful role in trending the direction of US settler society, often in contradiction to reality.[122]

When the Haymarket affair alerted Roosevelt to the alarming fact that the "shiftless and squalid foreign mob" in US industrial centers was increasingly rallying under the banner of anarchism-communism, he inserted the anarchists into his "cowboys and Indians" narrative.[123] In a letter to his older sister and close confidant, Anna "Bamie" Roosevelt Cowles, he fantasized about himself along with his Dakota cowboy gang getting "a chance with rifles" at the anarchists. He bragged that he and his troop of frontier fighters could "take on ten times our number of rioters; my men shoot well and fear very little."[124] In his reminiscences of life on his Dakota ranch, in the midst of a tale about organizing a cavalry troop to fight Indians in his district, he recalled that the men in his troop were "very patriotic." To emphasize their patriotism, he wrote, "The day that the Anarchists were hung in Chicago, my men joined with the rest of the neighborhood in burning them in effigy."[125] These 1880s "frontier" vigilantes, as portrayed by Roosevelt, asserted their manhood and US American patriotism by fighting Indigenous peoples and lynching anarchists in effigy.

## Conclusion

Discussing Roosevelt's conflation of the Haymarket anarchists with Indians on the Dakota "frontier," historian Richard Drinnon observes, "Class was not race and anarchists were not Indians. Still, the concerted effort to apply Indian-hating directly to urban strife helps explain the intensity of virulence of the Haymarket Red Scare and those that followed, and helps account for the violence of American labor wars—all the Homesteads and Pullmans, Everetts and Centralias."[126] Drinnon ends his short discussion by musing on the appropriateness, given the ruling-class conflation of Indians and anarchists, of the escape from the law of Rudolph Schnaubelt, as told by historian Paul Avrich. Schnaubelt was the only man indicted for the Haymarket bombing to evade capture. Police questioned him on May 7, and after that, he mysteriously disappeared. A few false reports of sightings of Schnaubelt followed, including a news report that his dead body was found in Lake Erie.[127] What actually became of Schnaubelt was that, after the police questioned him, he fled the United States and, after a circuitous journey, ended up living in Buenos Aires, Argentina. He made it through the most sensitive and perilous part of the journey with the aid of Indigenous people who gave him food and shelter when he became lost in the woods trying to sneak across the US-Canadian border on foot.[128]

In equating the proletarian anarchist "foreign mob" with the Indian "tribal mass," Roosevelt was well within the mainstream of post-Haymarket white US American discourse. Both threats to the United States were "matter out of place," or peoples out of place. "Such foreign savages," said New York's *Sun* newspaper, "with their dynamite bombs and anarchic purposes, are as much apart from the rest of the people of this country as the Apaches of the plains are." Good "citizens of the republic," it continued, "would have the law forbid them to land on our shores, as they would keep out an invasion of venomous reptiles."[129] Just as such rhetoric justified massacres of Indigenous groups, in this case it justified the murderous state violence against strikers for the eight-hour-day in Chicago and Milwaukee. In Milwaukee, 250 National Guards, ordered by Governor Jeremiah Rusk to "shoot to kill," opened fire on a crowd of some fourteen thousand workers, many of whom were Polish immigrant laborers, gathered outside the Milwaukee Iron Company. The soldiers injured several and killed seven, including a child.[130] Such violence, according to the white press, was the strikers' own fault. The violence "was almost wholly the work of unnaturalized foreigners, many of whom could not even speak our language, and none of whom had become imbued with the spirit of American freemen."[131] According to the New York's Labor Bureau Commissioner, "Labor disturbances are almost entirely led by foreigners, and the cheaper and more ignorant class of foreigners are the most destructive and hardest to govern from mob violence."[132]

In *Gunfighter Nation*, historian Richard Slotkin points out that this formulation, which equated the proletarian "mob" with the Indigenous "tribe," was much more than mere rhetoric. It was directly connected to the militarized policy the state applied to the suppression of labor insurgency:

To defend itself against savage anarchy, society must organize itself as if it were an embattled army regiment of Indian-fighting cavalry. This way of symbolizing the social struggles of industrialization was realized in the events of the Pullman Strike of 1894, which saw cavalry regiments—among them Custer's 7th Cavalry, late of the Little Big Horn and Wounded Knee—drawn from the garrisons of Apacheria and the Sioux country to put down the strikers.[133]

From 1877 into the 1920s, time and time again, the state would call in its professional frontier Indian killers to suppress urban labor unrest. And, as events such as the 1914 Ludlow Massacre exemplify, they would do so with the same exterminationist weapons and tactics. Roosevelt's fantasy of manly cowboys getting "a chance with rifles" at the "urban mob" was a reality, only it was not only rifles, but also Gatling guns and artillery pieces.

# 4

# The Guns of 1877

How and why does the United States go from US Indian agents describing Indigenous North American peoples as lawless communists in the 1850s to US police casting largely urban, European-born anarchist-communists as American Indians in the 1880s? The transition was effortless, even natural, as the state turned the policies and logic of elimination inward. To people who had internalized the psychology of settler colonization, racializing anarchists and communists, and by extension the labor movement in general, made perfect sense. The social construction of race, as it functioned in US society, was historically intertwined with notions of private property and people's positions in relation to the system of private property.

The United States inherited this construction from English liberalism, as wealthy enslavers such as Thomas Jefferson, James Madison, and other "Founding Fathers" drew from the ideas of Enlightenment philosophers such as the "father of liberalism," John Locke. Locke had economic and political interests in the English colonization of America. Among other roles, Locke was a commissioner on the Board of Trade, which oversaw slave labor camps in the American colonies, and he was a shareholder in the Royal Africa Company, which controlled the slave trade to the American colonies. Locke's most influential work, his 1689 *Second Treatise of Government*, was largely a justification of the concept of private property and was specifically a justification for English colonizers to expropriate Indigenous lands and enslave African people. As historian Anthony Pagden writes,

> That so many of the examples Locke uses in his *Second Treatise* are American ones shows that his intention was to provide the settlers, for whom he had worked in so many other ways, with a powerful argument based in natural law rather than legislative decree to justify their depredations.[1]

Locke equated civilization with property, defining "the civilized part of mankind" as those "who have made and multiplied positive laws to determine property." The "civilized" stood in contrast to what Locke called "the wild Indian, who knows no enclosure, and is still a tenant in common."[2] Here one can see the underpinnings of nineteenth-century anticommunism, along with its racial connotations, embedded in much earlier Enlightenment liberalism, which emerged as part of the anti-Indigenous notions connected to the settler colonial project.[3]

As previously discussed, by the 1840s, the system of private property was "the white man's system of agriculture"—and later the white man's system of industry—in contrast with the Indians' "system of communism." Further, groups' positions in relationship to the mode of production within that system of private property simultaneously shaped and were shaped by notions of race. In the social chaos and dislocation of rapid industrialization, mass migration, and urbanization of the post–Civil War United States, neat categories blurred as latent social contradictions burst to the surface. The US ruling class relied on settler colonial thinking to make sense of this new world and settler colonial counterinsurgency strategies to impose order on it.

The white construction of the "wild Indian" became a convenient and culturally recognizable template for the racialization of the anarchistic proletarian "urban mob." American Indigenes, in ruling-class white imagination, proved incapable of submitting to white management, incapable of being saved—despite repeated attempts by supposed benevolent whites—and were therefore uncivilizable. If a group is uncivilizable, then it is incumbent on civilization to eliminate it. The proslavery social theorist George Fitzhugh wrote that "the Indian" in the mid-nineteenth century remained "as wild as those who met Columbus on the beach" and was therefore "doomed to extermination."[4] The enslaver William S. Price wrote in a letter to the editor of *Merchants' Magazine* that, despite having had "ample opportunity" to become civilized, the Indians "are Indians yet, and are likely to continue as such."[5] The Southern race scientist Samuel Cartwright—who argued that runaway enslaved people had a mental disorder he termed *drapetomania*, which could be prevented by whipping Black people who showed early symptoms—wrote that the Indigenous American "submits to government in nothing whatever."[6] What these Southern enslavers wrote about Indigenes was no different from what Northern US Indian agents, such as the previously mentioned superintendent of Indian affairs Alexander Ramsey, reported about Indians who lived without law and without government: "no courts, no officers, no statutes, no debts to collect, no damages to pay."[7]

What better racial template for organized labor than a race that whites characterized as incapable of submitting to management? What better template for anarchists than a race that, in white imagination, was incapable of government? In white imagination, Indigenous peoples and anarchists both rejected the state.

The Guns of 1877    89

The nation's leading Indian haters became the nation's first outspoken anti-anarchists, and the language of Indian hating became the language of anticommunism. This is not to say that anticommunism replaced anti-Indigeneity or that anarchists became the "new Indians." Indian hating and US anti-Indigenous policies and practices never disappeared, continuing unabated even into the present. This is to say that anti-Indigeneity and settler colonial ideology and culture were so pervasive and so formative to US institutions, politics, and culture that they informed and shaped internal political repression even when that repression targeted non-Indigenous groups and social movements.

## John Hay, the "Indian Wars," and the "Railroad War"

US statesman John Hay exemplifies the seamlessness of this shift from settler colonialism being an outward-facing project of eliminating other societies on the "frontier" to also being an inward-facing project of cleansing the United States within. Hay was a proponent of exterminating Indigenous peoples and an author of anti-Indian propaganda. He was also a leading opponent of organized labor, a member of what is perhaps the first explicitly antisocialist paramilitary organization in US history, and an antilabor propagandist.[8] His novel *The Bread-winners* pioneered what became a new literary tradition of capitalist fiction that later produced authors such as Ayn Rand, whose novels continue to influence the values and ideology of the United States ruling class.[9]

John Hay (1838–1905) was one of the most influential statesmen of his time. His political career spanned the years from the presidency of Abraham Lincoln, whom he served as a private secretary, to the presidencies of William McKinley and Theodore Roosevelt, whom he served as secretary of state. He was a key builder of US empire, through actions such as negotiating the Open Door Policy with regard to China and the series of treaties—Hay-Pauncefote, Hay-Herrán, and Hay-Bunau-Varilla—that led to the construction of, and US control over, the Panama Canal.[10]

Hay's political allegiance was first and foremost to capitalism. He was a Republican because, explained his friend and biographer William Roscoe Thayer, "the Republican Party was avowedly the capitalists' party."[11] It was the party for both the rich and "many others whom the dread of social upheaval turned into conservatives."[12] Hay both was rich and dreaded social upheaval. "He believed that the hope of the country, perhaps even of Western civilization, so far as this is based on property, depended upon maintaining the Republican Party as a breakwater against the rising tide of social revolution."[13]

Hay was also a prolific author, the unofficial "poet laureate of the Republican Party," who enjoyed fame and association at the highest levels of the US literary scene for his many works of poetry and prose.[14] One of his more famous poems was "Miles Keogh's Horse," a piece that played a role in the popularizing and mythologizing of a US Army horse named Comanche.[15] The horse was—according to myth, not reality—the only member of the US Seventh Cavalry Regiment left standing in the aftermath of the Battle of Little Bighorn, in which Lakota, Cheyenne, and Arapaho forces decisively defeated the Seventh Cavalry. The reality is that more than one hundred of Custer's regiment's horses survived the battle.[16] Nevertheless, Comanche became a celebrity and a mascot for the Seventh Cavalry. The regiment retired the horse and reverently ordered that he should never be mounted again. After the horse's death fifteen years later, University of Kansas professor Lewis Lindsay Dyche taxidermied Comanche for the regiment and displayed him at the 1893 Chicago World's Columbian Exposition. Mythmaking about the horse and the battle continued over the next century, exemplified by David Appel's 1951 popular fictional novel *Comanche: The Story of America's Most Heroic Horse*, the 1958 Disney film *Tonka*, which was based on Appel's novel, and the popular 1961 country song "Comanche (the Brave Horse)," by Johnny Horton. Presently the taxidermied Comanche remains one of the most popular exhibits on the fourth floor of the University of Kansas Natural History Museum, demonstrating the endurance of settler colonial mythology in US culture.[17]

Hay held US cavalrymen on the Western frontier in high regard, and he was bitter about the Indigenous victory. He wrote "Miles Keogh's Horse" in part to shame Congress for allowing Custer's troops to be outnumbered and not allocating more troops and resources to the project of exterminating the Native Americans. Indignantly, Hay wrote in one verse,

> Three Hundred to three Thousand!
> They had bravely fought and bled;
> For such is the will of Congress
> When the White man meets the Red.[18]

Hay sent the poem to his close friend Whitelaw Reid, owner and editor of the leading Republican organ, the *New York Tribune*—for which Hay worked as an assistant editor—to publish the poem anonymously. "It is a well-intentioned poem," wrote Hay, "calculated to make people kill Indians."[19] He added, "I think H. H. [Helen Hunt Jackson] ought to be a Ute prisoner for a week."[20] Helen Hunt Jackson—pen name H. H.—was a reformer, poet, and journalist and a harsh critic of US anti-Indian policies and practices. Reid himself had published some of her work in his paper. She accused the United States of violating international law and exercising cruelty in dealing with Indigenous nations. Men like Hay saw Jackson as an "Indian lover" and a race traitor who needed to be put back in her place. Ute men were vilified in US mainstream media at the time as being inclined to rape white women, so Hay's remark that she "ought to be a Ute prisoner for a week" implied that she needed to be taught a lesson by being raped by Utes. While only a short quip by Hay, it goes a long way in exemplifying the interconnectedness of US settler colonialism with the psychology of white supremacist patriarchy and violent misogyny.[21]

For Hay, as for so many white men of his class, the hatred of Indians to the point of wanting them exterminated was not simply about individual prejudice. Indian-hating was not about mere ignorance or personal distaste for cultural differences. It had everything to do with the system of land ownership and private property. For men like Hay, civilization at its core was about private property and the protection of private property. That is why so much of the "civilizing mission," exemplified in the era by the Dawes Act and abusive boarding schools filled with kidnapped Indigenous children, was geared toward destroying Indigenous identity by privatizing the land and replacing Indigenous values and diverse ways of life with capitalist values and cultural homogeneity. While the reality is that white settlers were the invaders in Indigenous territories, men like Hay saw Indians as the invaders attacking "civilization." Lakota and Cheyenne communities asserting their sovereignty and treaty rights along the Little Bighorn River stood as impediments to the designs of white prospectors who wanted to mine gold in the Black Hills for private profit, and that necessitated the Seventh Cavalry's merciless scorched-earth campaigns against civilian villages.

The concept of civilization sanctified this plunder. As Hay's friend Thayer wrote, in summarizing Hay's philosophy,

> The property you own—be it a tiny cottage or palace—means so much more than the tangible object! With it are bound up whatever in historic times has stood for civilization. So an attack on Property becomes an attack on Civilization.[22]

Simply by existing as peoples, and asserting their nationhood and sovereignty, Native nations were themselves, in the mind of Hay's class, an attack on property: stumbling blocks to Manifest Destiny. To Hay, as "an attack on Property" was "an attack on Civilization"; the anarchists, who championed the slogan "property is theft," were likewise "savages."[23] For men such as John Hay, just as it was for John Locke and Thomas Jefferson, a major piece of what made certain groups "savage" and others "civilized" was their position in relation to the white man's property interests.

For many North American Indigenous nations, the concept of nationhood was and is wrapped up in the community's collective relationship to the land. US settler colonialism, as historian Ned Blackhawk observes, was and is about destroying that relationship and replacing it with ownership and possession: ownership over both the land and the labor power of the people who work the land. Indigenous feminist Aileen Morton-Robinson writes about the nation-state itself as white property, as the possession of white people, and about the intertwined nature of property and whiteness within colonial logic. In the context of the United States, the power to own, to possess, is a power historically inextricable from violence and whiteness. Such was certainly the case with the notion of private property as held by men like John Hay—who, in defense of gold prospectors, in violation of an 1868 treaty, and in defense one of the most notoriously brutal units in the entire US Army—wrote a popular poem calculated to make people kill Indians.[24]

The Battle of Little Bighorn—what the Lakota remember as the Battle of the Greasy Grass—was one episode in a longer war of extermination that the United States waged against the Plains peoples, in large part in defense of the railroads that were essential to US empire and industry. As historian Sven Beckert points out, after the Civil War, the railroad industry was what made the New York Stock Exchange powerful, where more than half of the more than three hundred companies listed on the exchange were railroad companies. The rail industry made the US bourgeoisie "enormously wealthy and powerful," profiting from the federal government's giveaway of more than one hundred million acres of land to the railroad industry between 1862 and 1871.[25] Much of this land was inhabited and claimed by Indigenous nations who had no say in the process and did not recognize US government or private railroad company claims to the land. Historian Richard White observes that

> The government did not actually own much of this land; it belonged to Indians. But Indian ownership had never proved much of an obstacle to congressional schemes. Indeed, the very fact that it belonged to Indians initially seemed an asset in financing western railroads. Instead of land grants from the public domain complicated by competing claims from settlers, land might pass directly from Indians to the railroads.[26]

The persistence of Indigenous resistance to such blatant land theft by capitalism and the state complicated ruling-class schemes. The mechanism that made the land giveaways possible was a genocidal professional army.

General William Tecumseh Sherman of Civil War fame became the commanding general of the US Army in 1869, with his main responsibility carrying out genocide against Native nations that hindered the railroad companies and resisted US westward expansion. In the settler tradition of "playing Indian," Sherman's father, who was of the generation of settlers that displaced the Shawnee Nation from the Ohio Valley, "gave his son the trophy name Tecumseh," writes Dunbar-Ortiz, "after the Shawnee leader who was killed by the US Army."[27] Before taking over for Ulysses S. Grant as the head of the army, Sherman let Grant know that he prioritized the railroads, writing, "We are not going to let a few thieving, ragged Indians stop the progress of [the railroads]."[28] Lest there be any confusion about whether this US American war hero's intent was anything less than genocidal, in another letter Sherman wrote, "We must act with vindictive earnestness against the Sioux, even to their extermination, men, women, and children" and "during an assault, the soldiers can not pause to distinguish between male and female, or even discriminate as to age."[29] It was Sherman who charged Custer and his Seventh Cavalry Regiment with the task of eliminating the Plains peoples. Custer and his men waged total war on Indigenous nations, wiping out civilian villages and taking body parts from corpses as trophies, for nearly a decade prior to Custer's demise at the Greasy Grass. The mythology of Custer's Last Stand and Miles Keogh's horse served to make the victims and resisters of genocide into villains and the perpetrators of genocide into heroes, and not innocently but, as John Hay exemplifies, with the intent of intensifying the genocidal project.[30]

A year after Custer's death, the US bourgeoisie faced a new threat to the railroads, though this time it was from within US society. The Panic of 1873 and its concomitant Long Depression had hit the US working class hard. There were mass layoffs, evictions, wage cuts, and a significant deterioration in the standard of living, with many working-class people reduced to extremely unhealthy and dangerous living conditions. By 1877, some three million people were unemployed, roughly 27 percent of the working population. Many who were employed were only precariously so, often only able to find work six months of the year. Wages declined by 45 percent. As suffering people's faith in US institutions and politicians evaporated, previously marginal radical voices and ideas within the working people's movement began to resonate in the mainstream of the US working class. Socialists, many of them migrants and refugees with an internationalist consciousness, rose to leadership roles in labor organizations.[31]

At a July 4 celebration in 1876, the centenary of the signing of the US Declaration of Independence, the Workingmen's Party of Illinois made a new declaration: "That we are absolved from all allegiance to the existing political parties of this country, and that as free and independent producers we shall endeavor to acquire the full power to make our own laws, manage our own production, and govern ourselves."[32] At a packed workingmen's meeting in the Great Hall of New York City's Cooper Union in July 1877, the Amalgamated Trade and Labor Unions—with delegates representing the Custom Tailors, the Ladies' Shoemakers, the Cabinetmakers, the Carvers, the Cigar-Makers, the Fresco Painters, and the Typographical Unions—resolved "That the time has arrived for the working people of America to resist by all legitimate means the oppression of capital and the robbery which it perpetrates on labor."[33] No longer did these workers see labor organizing as a way to press for reforms geared toward harmony between capital and labor. After suffering four years of economic hardship with no end in sight, they resolved that the purpose of organizing a national federation of all trades was "so that combined capital can be successfully resisted and overcome."[34] Economic crisis and institutional failure to do anything substantial about it resulted in the left fringe of the labor movement becoming the center. Labor organizations that did not move left in step with the changing conditions and sensibilities of the rank and file became irrelevant to the rank and file.

Thus 1877 became a year of proletarian insurgency. It precipitated in July, after the B&O Railroad cut wages for the third time in a year. Railroad workers in Martinsburg, West Virginia, initiated a wildcat strike. They shut down the rail lines and declared that no trains would move until the company revoked the wage cut. Their action resonated powerfully, and soon railroad workers from all the major railroad companies across West Virginia, Maryland, Pennsylvania, New Jersey, New York, Missouri, Ohio, Indiana, and Illinois followed suit. Workers in other industries mobilized strike solidarity, and working-class support for the strikers was widespread. At a large working people's meeting in Cooper Union, the labor union delegates resolved "That we express our sincere sympathy with the railroad men and others who are now on strike, and pledge ourselves to use every effort to render financial aid not only to the men on strike, but to those workpeople who have suffered by it."[35] As the railroad company owners and managers remained obstinate, workers escalated their tactics to ensure the trains stood still, in some cases erecting blockades, destroying train cars, and burning down railroad company buildings, "giving some areas the appearance of a war zone."[36] As the railroad industry was, after agriculture, the main employer in the United States, and all major industry depended on the railroads, the wildcat strikes paralyzed the entire US economy.[37]

It must be noted, however, that there were also reactionary elements within the working class. While many workers, particularly in the East and Midwest, grew increasingly class conscious, aiming their anger and frustration up the social hierarchy, some white workers on the West Coast clung to their whiteness and turned instead to scapegoating and white supremacist terror. During the height of the railroad uprisings in Midwestern and Eastern cities, white workingmen and boys in San Francisco carried out an intensely destructive and murderous anti-Chinese pogrom, blaming the hardships of the Long Depression on "coolie" labor rather than on the bourgeoisie. Far-right demagogues rode this violence to position themselves as working-class leaders. For example, Denis Kearney, an Irish immigrant whom the Workingmen's Party denied membership for his reactionary politics, used the momentum of the San Francisco pogrom to form a competing union, the Workingmen's Trade and Labor Union of San Francisco. His organization dispensed with the international working people's movement slogan "workers of the world, unite," and instead rallied under the slogan "The Chinamen Must Go!"[38]

The Guns of 1877    95

The organizing and agitating of these white supremacists was a significant factor that led to the United States passing the Chinese Exclusion Act of 1882.[39] The railroad strikes, in which a multiracial, multiethnic, multilingual labor force mobilized along class lines, and the concurrent anti-Chinese pogrom, in which white workers mobilized along racial lines, represent the starkly different directions working-class people can turn in moments of economic crisis as a result of their level of political and class consciousness. White identity politics, which are rooted in settler colonialism, are historically the greatest barrier to working-class consciousness and working-class unity in the United States.[40]

During the railroad uprisings, most experienced professional US Army units were engaged with the project of Indigenous extermination on the frontier, expelling Nez Percé and Palouse communities from Idaho, Montana, and the Pacific Northwest, and so city and state governments that represented the bourgeoisie had to mobilize amateur local militias to take on the railroad strikers. Doing so proved difficult, as many of the men who would make up these units were working-class themselves and sympathetic to the strikers. In some cases, the militias refused to fire on workers, and some militia members joined the strikers, for which the labor unions praised them: "[We] offer our fraternal greeting to the volunteer soldiers who fraternized with their fellow workmen."[41] The Workingmen's Party newspaper, *The Labor Standard*, reported that a New York militia officer—whose men fraternized with strikers—said, "Many of us have reason to know what long hours and low pay mean and any movement that aims at one or the other will have our sympathy and support. We may be militiamen, but we are workmen first."[42] There were even local law enforcement officers who refused orders to quell the strike. The strike spread to other industries and began to look like a full-scale working-class uprising against capital. In St. Louis, where socialist labor organizers were particularly influential, the railroad strike developed into a citywide general strike to such a degree that one historian wrote that "no American city has come so close to being ruled by a workers' soviet, as we would now call it, as St. Louis, Missouri, in the year 1877."[43] The *Chicago Tribune* bitterly charged that of all the communists in the United States, "the St. Louis Communist seems to be the worst of the whole worthless class."[44]

As the strikes spread across states and industries, the demands of the strikers expanded. As these were wildcat strikes, largely spontaneous and without any single individual, committee, or organization in command, there was no unified list of demands, but rather a cacophony of wide-ranging demands: modest calls for better working conditions and an end to wage cuts and more ambitious calls for the eight-hour day and the abolition of child labor, and even full-on revolutionary demands for workers' self-management and collective control of industry.

The bourgeoisie was thoroughly panicked and outraged, fearing that the devilish spirit of the Paris Commune had finally reached America. While private property represented the white man's civilization, the Paris Commune, in bourgeois imagination, represented the opposite, and bourgeois US media characterized it with the same language with which it characterized Indigenous resistance—as "savage." The Commune, wrote the *New York Times* a few years earlier, was war "against art, property, and religion—against civilization itself."[45] "The Commune is the same savage beast the world over," wrote the *Missouri Republican* in reference to the railroad strike.[46] "It was feared," said the *New York Tribune*, that the strikers were "seeking to emulate the terrible deeds of the Commune."[47] "The very devil seems to have entered into the lower classes of working men," wrote John Hay.[48] "Those riots of 1877," commented Thayer, "burned deep into Colonel Hay's heart."[49]

Hay, like many men of his class, viewed labor unrest as a foreign phenomenon, out of place in the United States. While the Paris Commune alarmed the wealthy in the United States as much as it did the wealthy in Europe, men such as Hay believed that US democratic institutions provided some level of immunity against proletarian uprising.[50] It made sense to Hay that war between capital and labor would play out in autocratic, repressive Europe, but, Thayer explains, Hay "had reassured himself by the comfortable assumption that under American conditions—equal opportunity for all, high wages, equal laws, and the ballot-box—no angry laboring class could grow up."[51] The summer of '77 uprisings "blew such vaporing away: for they proved that the angry class already existed," and that the ballot box offered no defense against it.[52]

In a series of letters from July to September of that year, Hay, then living in Cleveland, expressed his strong feelings about the insurrection to his father-in-law, the wealthy railroad, oil, and steel magnate Amasa Stone, who was conveniently abroad on a European vacation as his workers rebelled against the harsh conditions he imposed on them. In Hay's thinking, foreign, outside agitators, rather than US working conditions, were the root of the problem: "the government is utterly helpless and powerless in the face of an unarmed rebellion of foreign workingmen, mostly Irish."[53] These "aliens," explained Thayer, came from countries where they had no experience in democracy, and they brought with them their "tribal, their racial, their religious, and their international feuds."[54] They "transplanted to America the creeds of discontent and revolution which had long kept Europe alarmed," introducing the pernicious word *proletariat* to otherwise content American workingmen.[55] These tribal foreigners "thrust the debate of the social revolution prematurely on the United States" and, being inexperienced in constitutional methods, "they saw no alternative to the Despotism from which they had fled except the Socialism or the Anarchism to which they would blindly leap."[56]

The Guns of 1877     97

In characterizing labor unrest as alien to the United States, Hay and Thayer were representative of the US bourgeoisie. Wealthy iron, coal, and steel baron James Ford Rhodes, speaking for the same class of businessmen, wrote that the 1877 strikes "came like a thunderbolt out of a clear sky, startling us rudely. For we had hugged the delusion that such social uprisings belonged to Europe."[57] Rhodes saw anything that threatened the white racial purity of the United States as a threat to civilization. He opposed Reconstruction, celebrated its death as the "restoration of home rule" to the South, and called the Reconstruction Acts, especially Black suffrage, "an attack on civilization," again demonstrating that "civilization," as many men of Rhodes's class used the term, was a white supremacist perspective.[58]

The bourgeoisie counterposed communism as civilization's foil. Trade unions were composed of "Communistic and law-defying men" who waged war "against all law and order and civilized society."[59] "The Communistic character of the riots is shown by every instance," said the *New York Tribune*, which zealously associated the strikers with communism.[60] "That the disorderly strikers are communists—enemies of all rights of property, and of all law or government that defend these rights—does not need demonstration."[61] Socialists in Milwaukee, scoffed the *Tribune*, were arguing that "all corporations should be dissolved, and that the Government should buy and run the railroads" and the fact that the strike was causing the proliferation of such ideas was precisely why it was so urgent to "put down the insurrection."[62] The bourgeois press vilified not only strikers but anyone who sympathized with the strikers as "communists," "professional agitators," "miscellaneous ragamuffins," "lunatics," "idlers," and so on.[63] They were not mere strikers, according to the capitalist press, they were savages who waged "warfare" on capital and whose acts were characterized by "wild rapine" and "murder of those who defend public order."[64] "This is the communist," said the *Tribune*: "His work in Paris is known. It is the blackest page in the history of the nineteenth century. His work in the United States we are beginning to know."[65] For a press that proudly declared itself a mouthpiece of capital—"Not to be in sympathy with capital would be a betrayal of the public interest"—it was not slavery or genocide but working-class insubordination that stained the century with blood.[66]

John Hay was particularly alarmed by law enforcement's seeming powerlessness in the face of a mobilized insurgent working class. He reported to Stone that Cleveland was "full of thieves and tramps waiting and hoping for a riot" and that, if the police were to provoke them in the least, "the town would be in ashes in six hours."[67] The following day, he reported that "There is a mob in every city ready to join with the strikers, and get their pay in robbery, and there is no means of enforcing the law in case of a sudden attack on private property."[68] He characterized the situation as having the potential to racially and ethnically darken and foreignize the United States, again demonstrating that the system of private property was racialized as white, and to threaten the system of private property was to cease to be white: "We are not Mexicans yet—but that is about the only advantage we have over Mexico."[69] In writing this way, Hay was representative of the mainstream sentiments of his class. The bourgeois press emphasized and exaggerated the racial otherness of the strikers. For example, in St. Louis, where Black rank-and-file workers—to the discomfort of some of the socially conservative white labor leaders—took the initiative in turning a railroad strike into a citywide general strike, the *Missouri Republican* referred to the multiracial strike processions as "squads of squalid negroes," and "whooping . . . dangerous looking" crowds of "brutal negroes."[70]

Racializing strikers was indispensable to vilifying them as "savages." For a society that had been continuously engaged in the project of Indian extermination, that had just come out of the so-called Sioux War, was fascinated with mythmaking around Custer's Last Stand, and was—in violation of the Treaty of Walla Walla—currently waging a war of extermination and expulsion against Nez Perce and Palouse people in the US Northwest, anti-labor discourse often took the form of "Indian War" mythology and metaphor. Custer's Last Stand was now playing out in major US cities, as respectable citizens, nay, Civilization itself was besieged by "barbarous" and "anarchical" foreign proletarians.[71] "The two events," writes historian Richard Slotkin in reference to Custer's Last Stand and the railroad uprising, "drew on the same language and became part of the same myth."[72]

The "Journal of US Civilization," *Harper's Weekly*, used Indian War language to describe the strikes. It was not a railroad strike, but a "Railroad War," and the editors placed the discussion of this war alongside news of the other US war with the Nez Percé.[73] The *New York Tribune* did likewise; for example, the front page of its July 20 issue had the headline "The Indian War"—a report by US Army General Oliver Howard about his pursuit of Nez Percé military commander Chief Joseph—directly next to the headline "The Railroad Rebellion"—a piece about US Army General William French's attempt to break the railroad strikers' blockade at Martinsburg, West Virginia.[74] As Slotkin discusses in *The Fatal Environment*, in the dominant ruling-class discourse, the wars against "Indian savages" on the frontier and proletarian "savages" at home were one and the same.[75] "Every striker," said the *New York Tribune*, "made war on upon all civilized society when he countenanced the stopping of trains."[76]

## Other Frontiers

The bourgeois comparisons between "communistic" and "anarchistic" working-class rebellion and Indigenous savages extended beyond Indigenous

American groups to "tribal savages" on other frontiers. Sharing headlines with the railroad strikes and the Indian Wars in 1877 was the Russo-Turkish War. British and US war correspondents informed the US public of the "savagery" of Britain's "Persian frontier."[77] From these war correspondent reports, US and British readers learned of a stateless Indigenous people called Kurds—which some correspondents spelled *Koords*—who were "a faithless horde of blood-thirsty savages," waging war on Christian civilization from horseback.[78]

At the height of the railroad strikes in the United States, US media received war correspondent reports of the "Koordish cavalry" seizing the northeastern Anatolian town of Bayazid from Russian forces.[79] The *New York Tribune* referred to the Kurdish fighters in the same language it used for the railroad strikers, as "an undisciplined horde of rioters."[80] According to the *Tribune*, the Kurds were "inordinately fond of fantastic costumes, and over-zealous in chasing American missionaries and decapitating spies."[81] Not to miss a chance to paint railroad strikers as un-American savages obstructing civilization's path, the *Tribune* commented that the Kurdish fighters "will make very picturesque strikers when the English engineers build their railroad from Constantinople to Calcutta."[82] In the column directly next to this news was an editorial vilifying labor unionists as Baltimore street thugs, Maryland "wild boat-men," Philadelphia "roughs," Pennsylvania "half crazed" miners, and "the crazy Communists of Chicago."[83]

Bourgeois discourse in other European colonizer states such as Britain and France similarly racialized anarchists in the era by equating them with the Indigenous "savages" of their own frontiers. For example, an 1881 issue of the popular London-based magazine *Punch* included a Joseph Swain cartoon titled "Time's Waxworks." It depicted Father Time giving Mr. Punch—a cartoon British gentleman that personified the magazine and appeared in several of its cartoons—a tour of Madame Tussaud's, the famous London wax museum. Father Time was showing Mr. Punch an exhibit featuring wax figures of the racialized enemies the empire had contended with over the preceding few years: for 1878, a wax representation of an Afghan; 1879, an Indian; 1880, a Zulu warrior; and 1881, an anarchist. The anarchist had a dark face, wearing a dark mask over the eyes, and cartoonish oversized lips drawn the same way popular white supremacist artists drew blackface minstrel characters. He had wild long hair, a tattered hat with the word *anarchy* on it, and a US Western outlaw-style duster coat poorly concealing a blunderbuss, a pistol, a knife, and dynamite. In bourgeois British imagination, proletarian resistance to capitalism and anticolonial resistance to empire were one and the same, and all belonged in the same chamber of horrors.[84]

French bourgeois discourse followed suit, associating anarchists with the Indigenous savages of France's North African frontier. *Documents d'études sociales sur l'anarchie* included Lombroso's article "L'Anarchie et ses héros," which

100    CHAPTER 4

discussed Paris's infamous criminal anarchist Auguste Vaillant. In Paris, in December 1893, Vaillant threw a homemade bomb into the Chamber of Deputies in retaliation for the state's execution of the working-class folk hero Ravachol. Ravachol had carried out a series of bombings targeting high-ranking members of the judiciary as revenge for their condemning anarchists and communards. French working-class culture romanticized and celebrated him as an avenger of the desperate and downtrodden.[85] One of the popular French urban working-class songs of the 1890s was "La Ravachole," with lyrics by Sébastien Faure and sung to the tune of the French Revolution song "La Carmagnole." Working-class Parisians sang *Dansons la Ravachole!*—Let's dance the Ravachole!—and called for *mort à la bourgeoisie*—death to the bourgeoisie—including magistrates, financiers, police, senators, deputies, generals, executioners, and all *bouchers en uniformes*. Ravachole's avenger Vaillant went to the guillotine shouting those same lyrics, "*Mort à la bourgeoisie*" and "*Vive l'anarchie!*"[86]

In "L'Anarchie et ses héros," Lombroso explained that Vaillant was a criminal by heredity, born to "degenerate parents."[87] He was "born of a former liberated Zouave who had seduced a young domestic."[88] Referring to Vaillant as the son of a "former liberated Zouave" racially othered him. Zouaves—elite soldiers in the French army of North Africa—had a reputation that bordered on savage. The original Zouaves were Indigenous North Africans—savages in the eyes of French imperialists—who were colonized by French forces. Zouave units later changed from North African soldiers to all French soldiers but retained the Indigenous North African–style uniforms and the reputation for wildness. Lombroso was tapping into this popular image of the "wild Zouave" when he characterized Vaillant as being born to "degenerate parents." Further, by specifying that Vaillant's father was not just a Zouave, but a "former liberated Zouave," implied that he was of the former type of Zouave, North African rather than French, and that is what made Vaillant not just socially but biologically a criminal and "degenerate." These examples of anti-anarchist representations in Britain and France suggest that US discourse equating anarchists with Indians was part of a larger global capitalist colonialist narrative that equated proletarian rebellion with Indigenous frontier savagery.

Agents of capitalism and the state in Central America and the Southern Cone countries—where US and British businessmen owned and managed operations in major industries such as mining, ranching, meatpacking, and wool—employed almost identical language equating labor militancy and anarchism to Indigenous savagery, foreign migrants, and frontier outlawry. And just as such rhetoric accompanied massacres and repression in North America and Europe, it accompanied massacres and repression in Central and South America from the late nineteenth century into the mid-twentieth century.[89] One of many possible examples is the Patagonia Rebelde, 1920–22, an uprising of rural workers in Patagonia, which the official and extralegal forces of capitalism and the state suppressed with extreme violence.[90]

Accompanying the mass executions and tortures committed by Argentina's Tenth Cavalry Regiment and extralegal right-wing paramilitary thugs such as the Liga Patriótica Argentina, were comparisons and equations in the conservative ruling-class press of strikers to Indians and frontier outlaws. The Argentine Army's official magazine *El soldado argentino* repeatedly referred to workers on strike with terms such as "savage bandits of the canyons and forests," who "like the Indian before them" laid siege to civilization in a "bloodthirsty" frenzy. And just as in the United States, the state relied heavily on the "outside agitator" narrative to delegitimize workers' discontent with the system. The workers rebelled not because they had valid grievances but because they were incited by "none other than the anarchists and communists who have been imported into our land."[91] Such examples from Europe and Latin America suggest that US rhetoric equating working-class insurgency with Indigenous savagery to justify capitalist and state repression was part of a larger, global capitalist discourse rooted in anti-Indigeneity. While this study focuses on the United States, it is important to recognize that anticommunism drew on anti-Indigeneity on a global scale.

Even within the United States, the conflation of militant labor with Indigenous savagery extended beyond Indigenous Americans to Indigenous peoples in general. For example, a piece by the artist Rodney Thomson, ca. 1913, depicted a giant inciting anarchism, with a wise Uncle Sam looking down with concern on a meeting of the Industrial Workers of the World. In the meeting, a man with long hair, fedora, and an unkempt beard held an "IWW Meeting" sign. Next to and above him, perhaps on a soap box like those on which IWW orators often delivered speeches, stood an IWW organizer with long hair and beard breathing fire out onto the crowd of gullible workingmen who listened intently to the organizer. A giant bellows labeled "Class Hatred" is attached to the back of the organizer's head, furnishing the air to blow the fire out of his mouth. Controlling the bellows was a giant "God of Barbarism" depicted in a way whites in the era would have recognized as an Aboriginal Australian. He squatted on a hill behind the IWW orator intently operating the bellows, using the IWW orator as a tool to blow the flames of class hatred onto the crowd of poor and ignorant workingmen. He had dark skin, wore thick, long hair tied back, a scraggly beard, a fur skirt for clothing, large hoop earrings, and wrist and arm bands, one labeled "Barbarism." In this way, Thomson associated the radical labor movement with white notions of Indigeneity in order to depict it as primitive and barbarous. Thomson's work appeared in mainstream magazines such as *Puck*, *Life*, and *Vanity Fair*. His fame as an artist came from two kinds of work: antilabor cartoons and romanticized illustrations of the Western US "frontier," especially pictures of wild animals, hardy settlers, and Native people.

Thomson, like Hay, was artistically inspired by a combination of antilabor and settler colonizer sentiment.[92]

## Breadwinners and Mormons

Within this cultural context, outraged by both Little Bighorn and the railroad uprisings, John Hay wrote his novel *The Breadwinners*, an anti-labor-movement narrative with an Indian War backdrop. The protagonist of the novel was an educated middle-aged gentleman, property owner, businessman, and local civic leader named Arthur Farnham. The story takes place in a young, thriving midwestern city called Buffland, based on Hay's city Cleveland. Farnham lives on Buffland's wealthiest and most beautiful street, Algonquin Avenue, which was based on Hay's actual residence on Cleveland's elite Euclid Avenue. Farnham exemplified the bourgeois notion of civilized manliness. He was a wealthy, white, prominent citizen: genteel, a property owner, and a local leader who served on boards but whose character was forged through frontier violence and hardship. He came from a "life of toil and danger in the wide desolation of the West."[93]

Prior to his life as a prominent citizen of Buffland, Farnham served as a cavalry captain, perhaps in the Seventh Cavalry, fighting "savages" on the frontier. He had sacrificed much in service to the Republic, including his wife, who died on the prairie, in the hot sun during a forced march across the plains. He married her not for love, but because "She was the only unmarried white woman within a hundred miles."[94] In moments of quiet in the luxury and comfort of Algonquin Avenue, he waxed nostalgic for the "wild chaos" of the West, "the scent of sage brush," and "the tingling cold of the Black Hills."[95]

His longing for frontier adventure would not go unfulfilled for very long, however, as he would soon have the role of heroic Indian killer thrust on him once again as Buffland came under attack from a new breed of American savage, the foreign proletarian. A gang of immigrant union toughs called the Breadwinners stirred up the naïve, gullible Buffland working class to carry out a general strike. They were "ruffians with theories in their heads and revolvers in their hands" and "seemed of the lower class of laboring men."[96] Breadwinners rampaged across Buffland murdering and looting, and the state was too weak to stop them. Farnham sprang into action, forming an extralegal capitalist paramilitary organization made up of veterans such as himself, and by force of arms they rescued the mayor, repelled the Breadwinners' assault on Algonquin Avenue, and quelled the strike.

Hay based Farnham to some extent on himself, all the way down to Farnham's city, street, and home. Hay never served as a cavalry officer, but his older brother Augustus Leonard Hay, whom John Hay idolized, did, which likely contributed to Hay's strong affinity for frontier US Army cavalrymen. In the settler colonizer tradition of "playing Indian," John Hay referred to his brother as "the chief of my tribe, in birth as well as in mind and character."[97] Like Farnham, Hay epitomized the role of the civilized gentleman, and Hay fancied himself likewise to be a son of the frontier, forged into a man through pioneer grit. Hay's friend and biographer Thayer described Hay as "Born the son of a frontier doctor in a small dwelling on the edge of the Western wilderness."[98] To emphasize Hay's familial roots as a "true American," Thayer wrote that Hay's earliest ancestors in America included a man named John who as a child was "patted on the head by General Washington" and a man named Adam who "probably did his fair share of Indian fighting."[99] Being a US American meant being connected to a tradition of Indian killing.

Hay was born in Salem, Indiana, but grew up in western Illinois, in the town of Warsaw and in Pike County, at the edge of white US American "civilization." Warsaw's origin was rooted in the Indian killer Major Zachary Taylor's military campaigns to eliminate Native nations from their hunting grounds along the Des Moines rapids on the Mississippi River so that white fur traders and farmers could settle in the area. White settlers later applied the violent tactics of extermination and expulsion to drive Mormon settlers out of Missouri and Illinois. Though US Mormons in the present day have earned a reputation for being a "hyperwhite" and ultra-conservative social group, in the 1830s-40s, US society vilified and racially othered Mormons as an "un-American," sexually deviant, and "tribal" people forging alliances with Indians to overthrow the United States.[100]

Mormons fled to Illinois after white settlers employing a combination of formal state violence and vigilante terror expelled them from Ohio and Missouri. Though Mormons were white settler colonizers themselves—in truth they were simultaneously refugees and settler colonizers—dominant white settler society viewed them with suspicion and hostility.[101] Among other alleged Mormon outrages, false rumors circulated in Missouri that Mormons were encouraging enslaved Black people to rise up and conspiring with Indians to organize an insurrection against the United States. White property-owning Missourians demanded Mormon scalps, and settler militias raided Mormon settlements, destroyed Mormon property, sexually violated Mormon women and girls, and murdered Mormon children and adults. After some Mormons retaliated, Missouri Governor Lilburn W. Boggs issued his infamous "Extermination Order," officially known as Missouri Executive Order 44, which declared open season on Mormons. Boggs wrote to the commander of the state militia, "The Mormons must be treated as enemies, and must be exterminated or driven from the state if necessary for the public peace—their outrages are beyond all description."[102] Historian Paul Reeve argues that Missourians applied the white settler logic of Indian extermination to Mormons, pitting "red against white and savagery against civilization, with Mormons on the wrong side of both."[103]

104    CHAPTER 4

Mormons fled to the banks of the Mississippi River in western Illinois and formed a settlement they named Nauvoo—an old Hebrew word for "beautiful place"—which by 1844 had swelled to a population of about twelve thousand, briefly making it the largest city in Illinois, at the time more populous than Chicago and Springfield.[104] It was located in the same county, Hancock, as John Hay's hometown of Warsaw. The white settlers of western Illinois initially welcomed Mormons as refugees fleeing religious persecution, but as Nauvoo grew significantly in population, and in political and economic power, conflict between Mormons and non-Mormons burgeoned. Surrounding communities grew increasingly inflamed with anti-Mormon sentiment.

During John Hay's childhood in the 1840s, his town of Warsaw was the center of anti-Mormonism in Illinois. The town's mainstream Whig-affiliated newspaper, the *Warsaw Signal*, regularly printed anti-Mormon propaganda, hyperbolically referring to Mormons as "the ruthless, lawless, ruffian band of MORMON MOBOCRATS."[105] In that same extra edition, the *Signal* explicitly called for citizens to form a vigilante mob to murder the Mormon's prophet, Joseph Smith:

> War and extermination is inevitable! Citizens ARISE, ONE and ALL!!!—Can you stand by, and suffer such INFERNAL DEVILS!! to ROB men of their property and RIGHTS, without avenging them. We have no time for comment, every man will make his own. LET IT BE MADE WITH POWDER AND BALL!!![106]

This call to action was in response to Joseph Smith ordering the destruction of the *Nauvoo Expositor* printing press. The printing press incident was the last straw on top of a long list of grievances the non-Mormons of Hancock County held against the Mormons. The *Nauvoo Expositor* was a new newspaper in the Mormon town of Nauvoo. Its first issue reported that Joseph Smith was practicing polygamy, which was true, but was something Smith was trying to keep secret, even from members of his church. It also reported that Smith was planning on creating a theocracy with himself as monarch. Smith, as mayor of Nauvoo, responded by declaring the newspaper a public nuisance and ordered the town marshal to destroy the printing press. The destruction of the printing press, and consequent uproar in Hancock County, led to Illinois state officials arresting Smith for inciting to riot and treason and detaining him in the Carthage, Illinois, jail. Smith never got a chance to face the charges in court, as a mob of some two hundred anti-Mormons, with faces painted black, raided the jail and murdered Joseph Smith and his brother Hyrum while Joseph awaited trial.[107]

That the mob attacked Smith and his associates in jail as they awaited trial highlights the fact that the notion of the lynch mob as something that arose in the absence of formal state authority was more a settler-colonial myth than

The Guns of 1877     105

reality. Lynch mobs often acted, with state complicity, in times and places where formal state authority was firmly in place. Vigilantism was a complement to, rather than a substitute for, state violence. By arresting and detaining the targets of vigilante mobs, and then allowing mobs to take custody—through either active participation with the mob or silent complicity—official state agents often facilitated vigilante violence.[108] As historian Monica Muñoz Martinez observes, "vigilantism was in fact practiced in places where criminal justice systems were well established" and "law enforcement officers facilitated the conditions for making prisoners vulnerable to mob violence and even participated in lynchings."[109] There were, however, cases such as the 1877 uprisings, rebellions of enslaved people, and Indigenous resistance, where the state, though not absent, was indeed out of breath, overwhelmed by power from below, and relied on vigilantism to augment state power. In Smith's case, the vigilantes did not form to augment state power, rather, they formed because they believed the judicial system was overrun by Mormons and "Jack Mormons" and would rule in Smith's favor. The vigilantes conceived of themselves as "good citizens" saving the state from a Mormon takeover.[110]

The anti-Mormon violence did not cease with the assassination of Joseph Smith. Anti-Mormon vigilante squads continued attacking Mormons with the goal of expelling them from the region. Just as John Hay was turning six years old, his small town of Warsaw served as a staging ground from which armed anti-Mormon vigilantes organized what they called a "great wolf hunt," in which "the wolves to be hunted were the Mormons and Jack Mormons."[111] This is the society and culture in which John Hay spent his formative years.

In his 1869 piece "The Mormon Prophet's Tragedy," in which a thirty-one-year-old Hay reflected back on those Warsaw days, it is clear that Hay absorbed the anti-Mormon and provigilante sentiment of the society he grew up in. "It is impossible to deny," wrote Hay, "that the Mormons were bad neighbors." He called Joseph Smith an "evil genius" and referred to anti-Mormon mobs as "volunteer companies." Hay described Nauvoo as a refuge for the criminal class. While "thieves and vagrants" were punished and expelled from respectable towns such as Warsaw, they "were in Nauvoo patronized and protected" by the Mormon-controlled local court. Nauvoo was a place where undesirables could find asylum. "For years, scarcely a criminal had been brought out of Nauvoo. The evil was growing every day less endurable." Hay likened the Mormons to the vilified Irish, saying that the Mormon vote "was invariably cast for the Democratic ticket, as is the Fenian vote today. And like the Fenian vote, it had a demoralizing influence on both parties." By voting as a bloc, "the Mormons ruled the county."[112]

Hay's perception of Nauvoo as a refuge for "undesirables" and the criminalized was not entirely without basis. Four months before his assassination, Joseph Smith released a public statement outlining his views on government policy.

106    CHAPTER 4

Smith argued that, with the exception of the crime of murder, prisons should be abolished:

> Petition your state legislatures to pardon every convict in their several penitentiaries: blessing them as they go, and saying to them in the name of the Lord, go thy way and sin no more. . . . Rigor and seclusion will never do as much to reform the propensities of man, as reason and friendship. Murder only can claim confinement or death. Let the penitentiaries be turned into seminaries of learning, where intelligence, like the angels of heaven, would banish such fragments of barbarism: Imprisonment for debt is a meaner practice than the savage tolerates with all his ferocity. "Amor vincit omnia." Love conquers all.[113]

Smith also argued for the state to "Abolish the practice in the army and navy of trying men by court martial for desertion."[114]

In that same statement, Smith argued for the abolition of slavery: "Petition also, ye goodly inhabitants of the slave states, your legislators to abolish slavery by the year 1850, or now, and save the abolitionist from reproach and ruin, infamy and shame."[115] Though the Church would later, under the leadership of Brigham Young, institute virulently anti-Black policies banning Black people from the priesthood and the temple and discouraging interracial marriage, the church under Joseph Smith ordained Black men, such as Q. Walker Lewis and Elijah Abel, to the priesthood. Lewis was a radical abolitionist who, in 1926, cofounded the Massachusetts General Colored Association, an all-Black abolitionist organization that later merged with William Lloyd Garrison's New England Anti-Slavery Society.[116] The presence of people such as Lewis among the Mormons is part of why "respectable" white society viewed Mormon settlements as harboring "undesirables" and part of why false rumors spread about Joseph Smith conspiring to incite slave rebellions.[117]

In previous years, Smith had unsuccessfully attempted to institute a collectivist economic model he called the United Order, based on his understanding of the early Christians who, according to the New Testament, "had all things common; And sold their possessions and goods, and parted them to all men, as every man had need."[118] Smith's Book of Mormon equated righteousness with economic equality and a society without social distinctions: "And they had all things common among them: therefore there were not rich and poor, bond and free, but they were all made free, and partakers of the heavenly gift." The Book of Mormon associated wickedness with class society, describing the beginning of the process of a people becoming wicked as a shift away from collectivism: "And from that time forth they did have their goods and their substance no more common among them. And they began to be divided into classes."[119] In his statement on government policy, Smith argued for "more equality through

The Guns of 1877     107

the cities, towns and country" and "less distinction among the people" so that "the neighbor from any state, or from any country, of whatever color, clime or tongue, could rejoice when he put his foot on the sacred soil of freedom."[120] To men such as John Hay, who equated civilization with private property, such ideas were associated with savagery.

For Hay, the vigilante mob was the hero of the story. Because the Mormons had so much influence over the courts of Hancock County, "The Smiths were sure of a speedy trial and acquittal." Smith, explained Hay, was drunk with power and grew increasingly lawless but always managed to slip out of trouble with the law because Mormon juries and Jack Mormon sheriffs and judges always sided with Smith. "There was only one way of getting out of the groove. The *Deus ex machina*, who alone could settle matters, was the mob." At a public meeting in Warsaw, the citizens unanimously "*Resolved*, that we will forthwith proceed to Nauvoo and exterminate the city and its people." According to Hay, every Warsaw man, with only a few exceptions, took off to put an end to the Mormon problem once and for all. His childhood impression was that "the men were all gone." Instead of going to Nauvoo, they turned toward Carthage, where Smith was in jail. "In the mind of any anti-Mormon, there was nothing more criminal in the shooting of Smith than in the slaying of a wolf or panther." After the assassination of Joseph and Hyrum Smith, the *Warsaw Signal* defended the vigilante mob as "the executioners of justice." Hay ended his piece by likening the expelled Mormons to Indians being pushed westward—"Tribes and religions cannot travel against the sun"—and comparing Joseph Smith's successor Brigham Young to the "Oriental despot" of white imagination: "there was not in all the slavish East a despot more absolute than he when at last he started, with his wives and his servants and his cattle, to lead his people into the vast tolerant wilderness."[121] From his upbringing in Warsaw, Illinois, John Hay learned that in civilization's ongoing struggle against savagery, the vigilante mob was civilization's *Deus ex machina*. The men of Warsaw defended civilization from Mormons just as the men of Algonquin Avenue would defend it from Breadwinners.

## The Gatling Guns of Euclid Avenue

In the United States the line between state violence and extra-legal vigilantism, or "lynch law," has historically been quite blurry, and often non-existent. In dominant US discourse, vigilantism was not a departure from law and order, but was something that "good citizens" engaged in to uphold law and order—a certain kind of racial, gender, and economic order—in times and places official state authority was, either in reality or in the imagination of vigilantes and their supporters, too weak to do so. In a classic piece, Black radical sociologist Oliver Cromwell Cox wrote that lynch law is "in the whip hand of the ruling class," meaning it is a tool or a weapon that the dominant class wields to preserve the status quo.[122] Rather than being composed of alienated poor whites, "the mob," wrote Cox, is often made up of the most socially, economically, and politically enfranchised members of white society: "people who have been carefully indoctrinated in the primary social institutions of the region" to conceive of their victims "as extra-legal, extra-democratic objects, without rights which the white men are bound to respect."[123]

Contrary to being an "uncivilized" departure from US American values and traditions, vigilante violence is written into the structure of the United States. As Roxanne Dunbar-Ortiz demonstrates in her book *Loaded: A Disarming History of the Second Amendment*, rather than being about armed citizens keeping the government in check—as many gun-rights advocates in the present day erroneously believe—the Second Amendment enshrined previously existing laws and customs white settlers designed for the purpose of controlling Black people, enslaved and free, and for waging total war on Indigenous nations to make the land available to white property owners. The Indian Wars were not waged by US Army regulars alone but also by armed civilian white settlers acting extralegally as individuals or self-organized settler militias—which were separate from official state-regulated militias. The Second Amendment, and the many preexisting laws and customs on which its crafters modeled it, recognized settler vigilantism and paramilitary violence as the patriotic cutting edge of US nation building through the intertwined structures of slavery and settler colonialism. Armed white citizens put down Black insurrections, captured and punished escaped enslaved people, controlled Black movement, and exterminated Indigenous people where the formal forces of the state lacked capacity.[124]

As urban proletarian rebellion in 1877 rose to a level beyond what the state had the capacity to contain, well-heeled property-owning white citizens were alarmed and turned to the US American settler tradition of extralegal vigilante violence in defense of existing structures of racial and class dominance. In the aftermath of the strike, John Hay and his wealthy industrialist father-in-law Amasa Stone, along with other members of Cleveland "high society," formed two complementary, private, right-wing—in that they were explicitly ant-socialist in their aims—paramilitary units: a cavalry unit called the First City Troop, or FCT, and an artillery unit called the Gatling Gun Battery, or GGB. One reason that the formal city and state militias were ineffective against the railroad strikers is that they were made up of working-class men who sympathized and fraternized with the strikers. The FCT and GGB, in contrast, were composed of members of the local bourgeoisie: they were, in the words of sociologist Larry Isaac, "paramilitary capitalist elites."[125]

According to Isaac's study of the social composition of Gilded Age capitalist militias, "Approximately two-thirds of the GGB and FCT members had their homes or family estates located in the exclusive 'Millionaire's Row' segment of Euclid Avenue," and the rest of the members lived in the wealthy Euclid neighborhood area either just north of Millionaire's Row on Superior Avenue or just south on Prospect Avenue. Isaac's study also shows that, in addition to being neighbors, most of the initiators of the GGB and FCT were members of the Cleveland Board of Trade, which was an association of Cleveland's leading business owners. "High society Cleveland, located within the Euclid corridor, was a tightly knit community organized by all the bonds of social class—commerce (overlapping directorships and co-ownerships in finance and industry), neighborhood (mostly Euclid Avenue), social clubs, civic associations, churches, and social functions (parties, balls, and banquets)."[126] It was a united, class-conscious bourgeoisie composed of men who, despite any conflicts, competition, or that rivalries existed among them, shared a common anxiety about organized rebellion from below. They were keenly aware that they, the men of property, were vastly outnumbered by propertyless toilers who had little to lose and everything to gain through subaltern insurgency. Perhaps that is why the bourgeoisie's weapon of choice was the Gatling gun, a postbellum weapon designed to give the few the ability to mow down the many.

The Gatling gun was primarily a weapon of colonialism and empire. With only two men operating it, a single 1865 model Gatling gun could fire 350 rounds per minute, and later models could fire some 400 rounds. John Hay's *deus ex machina* saving civilization from savagery now truly was a "god from the machine," and a terrible god it was. The US Army officially added Gatling guns to its arsenal in 1866. The army placed Gatling guns in its frontier forts and used them to great military success in campaigns against Indigenous people resisting colonialism on the Great Plains and in the Southwest and Northwest. Later, the United States deployed Gatling detachments against native Hawaiians and with US forces invading Cuba and the Philippines. The celebrated Civil War Union Army hero Colonel Nelson Miles brought Gatling detachments with him during his genocidal campaigns against Kiowa, Comanche, Cheyenne, and Arapaho peoples in 1874–75. During the 1877 railroad strikes, US Army units in the Pacific Northwest used Gatling Guns against Nez Percé and Palouse people.[127]

The Canadian state took notice and hired a US Gatling gunner, a Connecticut National Guard lieutenant named Arthur Howard, to introduce the Gatling gun to the Canadian army during the Métis Rebellion in 1885. Howard gained a reputation as an Indian fighter from his prior service in the First Cavalry Regiment, a unit that was famous for killing Indigenous people in Oregon, Idaho Territory, California, Nevada, New Mexico, Oklahoma, and Arizona and especially for its pursuit of the Apache anticolonial resistance fighters led by Cochise. For his and his Gatling gun's role in crushing the Métis uprising, Howard earned the nickname "Gat," which he proudly went by for the rest of his life. The British empire, seeing the US success with the Gatling gun against Indigenous North American peoples, deployed Gatling detachments against the peoples of the Gold Coast during its Ashanti Empire "expedition" in 1873–74, and then with the British Army of South Africa: a campaign for which the empire commissioned US American "Gat" Howard to train and lead a machine-gun unit.[128]

John Hay, Amasa Stone, and their Cleveland "high society" neighbors were among the first to see this modern Indian-killing machine as a weapon for controlling the urban proletariat. It became a standard strike-breaking weapon over the next few decades after the uprisings of 1877. The state—both its formal and its extralegal agents—deployed the Gatling gun for two primary purposes: ridding the frontier of Indigenous peoples and controlling the urban proletariat. Historian of the Gatling gun Julia Keller writes,

> In the United States, the deployment of Gatling guns by strike breakers at a labor riot, or by soldiers in the West against the native population, or by policemen at the barest hint of the formation of a mob, was a chilling demonstration of the iron rule of the dominant classes. Gatling guns were routinely wheeled out to make a highly theatrical but inarguable point about who was really in charge. "In the early stages of an acute outbreak of anarchy, a Gatling gun, or if the case be severe, two, is the sovereign remedy," lectured an 1886 editorial in the *New York Times*, in the wake of the deadly labor unrest in Chicago's Haymarket Square. In the battle of the ordinary working stiff versus the wealthy and powerful, the Gatling gun was very much regarded as the mascot of the latter.[129]

The Gatling gun, and later its more deadly and easier-to-operate successor the machine gun, became the weapon of choice for strike breakers. The Baldwin-Felts Detective Agency, a mercenary outfit that worked for the Rockefeller family, built an armored car—armored with Rockefeller Steel—with a machine gun mounted to it. They called it the "Death Special."[130] Mercenaries driving the Death Special patrolled Rockefeller's West Virginia coalfields and killed miners during a strike. Shortly thereafter, Baldwin-Felts agents hired by Rockefeller deployed the Death Special against striking miners and their families during the tragic Ludlow Massacre. This mercenary violence was in addition to the National Guardsmen—who received two paychecks, one from the US government and one from Rockefeller—who fired machine guns at miners and their wives and children at Ludlow. That kind of indiscriminate and dehumanizing mowing down of human bodies was a form of violence reserved for Indigenous anticolonialists and insurgent proletarians. In both cases, it was for the same purpose, the protection of the private property and profits of the white man.[131]

Within Euclid neighborhood society were a number of Arthur Farnham types: refined wealthy gentlemen who formerly served as US military officers in both the Civil War and the Indian Wars. This included men such as General James Barnett, Brigadier General Edward Meyer, Colonel William Harris, Major William Goodspeed, and Captain Charles Bolton. Being mostly from the upper echelon of the officer corps, these men had the contacts and the social capital to acquire enough military-grade weapons to fill the FCT and GGB private armory, which was also located on Euclid Avenue. Former US Army officers with experience in Civil War and, more important, Indian War tactics became the first leaders in the new antisocialist paramilitary organizations.[132]

The FCT and GGB exemplify the blurriness of the line between state violence and vigilante violence in US history. Most early FCT and GGB activity consisted of weekly drills, marches, and other public events. Through public displays of their strength, such as in drills and marches with their Gatling guns on display, the local bourgeoisie served notice to the Cleveland working class that were the workers to ever attempt something like the railroad strike again, they would not be met by sympathetic amateur local militiamen, but by a well-funded, independent capitalist paramilitary armed with the most advanced Indian-killing weaponry available. Even though the unit acquired weapons through clandestine channels and had its own command structure independent of formal state authority, the state did not see this independent paramilitary activity as illegal or as a threat. These vigilantes were the city's "leading citizens" protecting the social order. Ten years after the FCT's and GGB's founding, the state made them into a single formal unit of the Ohio National Guard: the First Cleveland Cavalry, or Troop A, and later the 107th Cavalry Regiment, but nicknamed and popularly known as the Black Horse Troop.[133]

The Black Horse Troop served as a force for both industrial control and frontier control. During the Cleveland Streetcar Strike of 1899, the unit was called into action on behalf of the Cleveland Electric Railway Company. Black Horse cavalrymen protected scabs crossing the picket lines and ensured that the streetcars kept running during the strike. The state called Troop A into service to crush another streetcar strike in Columbus in 1910. In 1908, during the Black Patch Tobacco Wars, the state sent the unit to southern Ohio to protect the interests of the large industrial monopoly, the American Tobacco Company. During a border dispute in 1916, the Black Horse Troop deployed to the Texas frontier to patrol the US-Mexico borderlands on horseback.[134]

At the time the Black Horse Troop was patrolling the border, Texas Rangers and white supremacist vigilantes were in the midst of a decades-long ethnic cleansing project to rid the region of Mexican and Indigenous people in the interests of white landowners. Monica Muñoz Martinez writes, "Vigilante violence on the border had a state building function. It both directed the public to act with force to sustain hierarchies of race and class and complemented the brutal methods of law enforcement in this period. . . . State racial terror and

112    CHAPTER 4

vigilantism were linked."[135] Mexican anarchist Ricardo Flores Magón—of mostly Indigenous descent and from a Mazatec community in Oaxaca—briefly worked in Texas as a farm laborer and dishwasher during this era of racial terror. In the Mexican anarchist newspaper *Regeneración*, Magón deliberately took the very language the US bourgeoisie used to vilify Mexicans, Indigenous people, and anarchists and turned it against the forces of white settler colonialism to describe the plight of Mexicans in Texas:

> Mexicans are not admitted to hotels, restaurants, and other public establishments in Texas. The public schools close their doors to children of our race. North American semi-savages take target practice on Mexicans. How many men of our race have died because a white-skinned savage decided to prove his ability with firearms by shooting at us?[136]

On "the savage plains of Texas," continued Magón, a "mob of white savages" viciously targeted a young Mexican man named Antonio Rodríguez, who was not tried in court for any crime, but was nonetheless "tied to a post by a horde of white North Americans and burned alive."[137] For Magón, the plains were only "savage" because wealthy white settlers—what he called "the North American plutocracy"—took possession of them.[138] Settlers "cut down our forests, in order that they exploit for their own sole benefit the riches of the Mexican lands and seas, and in order that they function as authorities, in almost every case more brutal than native authorities."[139] This was the economic and racial order the Black Horse troop deployed to Texas to uphold.

The famed bandmaster John Philip Sousa (1854–1932) greatly admired Troop A and wrote his popular march "The Black Horse Troop" in their honor. Sousa's band debuted the song in Cleveland's Public Auditorium in 1925. An eleven-year-old Frederick Fennell (1914–2004), who would grow up to become an internationally famous conductor, was in attendance. Fennell looked back on that event as a formative experience, a concert unlike any he had ever seen. As the Sousa band began to play the song, members of the Black Horse Troop rode their horses onto the stage and stood behind the band "to the tumultuous cheering of all."[140] According to Fennell, "The March King [Sousa] enjoyed a long relationship with the men and horses of Cleveland's Ohio National Guard, known as Troop A."[141] In the present day, "The Black Horse Troop" remains a staple in the repertoires of US military bands, as well as high school and university marching bands throughout the United States, though likely few, if any, are aware of the Black Horse Troop's origin as a right-wing paramilitary vigilante squad.

Cultural representation and counterinsurgency policy have always been intertwined in white American settler culture and politics. As historian Gary Nash wrote in his classic *Red, White, and Black*, early European settler representations of Indigenous North American nations were a prelude and justification for ex-

The Guns of 1877     113

termination policies: "The image of the Indian as a savage beast was therefore a way of predicting the future, preparing for it, and justifying what one would do, even before one caused it to happen."[142] In *Gunfighter Nation*, Richard Slotkin observes a similar relationship between Cold War–era Hollywood westerns and US counterinsurgency policy in Vietnam: "Movie and policy address similar ideological concerns and use the same mythological language, the same ideologically loaded images of heroism and savagery, the same narrow and essentially racist views of non-White peoples and cultures, the same hope that all problems can be solved by a burst of action and a spectacular display of massive yet miraculously selective firepower."[143] The same can be said of nineteenth- and early-twentieth-century adventure novels and undoubtedly applies to Hay's novel, *The Breadwinners*.

## The Wars in the West

John Hay's narrative of Indian killers turning their guns on an insurgent proletariat accompanied and idealized a reality of Indian killers turning their guns on an insurgent proletariat. The mobilization of Arthur Farnham's fictional anti-Breadwinner militia paired with the mobilization of the Euclid neighborhood antisocialist paramilitary exemplifies that not only did the discourse and mythological structure of Indian killing become the discourse and mythological structure of proletarian social control, but the tactics of frontier control became the tactics of proletarian control. As Slotkin writes, "The Indian analogy partly determined the kind of policy that could be conceived for dealing with the labor problem."[144] From 1877 onward, the mercilessly violent language of Indigenous elimination became the language of capitalist control over labor, and the tactics of Indigenous elimination became the tactics for quelling labor revolt.

Reportedly, in response to striking railroad workers' demand for bread, Pennsylvania Railroad President Thomas Scott infamously said, "Give them the rifle diet for a few days and see how they like that kind of bread." It is unclear whether Scott actually said those words; as journalist Janny Scott—Thomas Scott's great-granddaughter—correctly observes, the only known records of him saying those words are hearsay.[145] Nevertheless, regardless of whether Scott actually said it or was merely rumored to have said it, such a sentiment was well in line with the sentiments that representatives of the capitalist class are actually on record as uttering and, more important, well in line with the policies that Scott's class and the state employed against the strikers. Chicago's leading ruling-class paper, the *Chicago Tribune*, responded to railroad workers' demand for a living wage with commentary such as "The world owes these classes rather extermination than a livelihood. The 'world' will be better off in the degree that such wretches cease to exist."[146] As the working-class organizer and anarchist Albert Parsons—who was a Chicago labor leader during the 1877 strike—said in court during the Haymarket Trial in October 1886,

> Was it not Tom Scott who first said, "Give them a rifle diet?" Was it not the [Chicago] *Tribune* which first said, "Give them strychnine?" And they [the capitalists] have done it. Since that time they have administered a rifle diet; they have administered strychnine."[147]

Parsons understood the relationship between bourgeois rhetoric and state policy.

Characterizing the strikers as Indigenous savages threatening civilization itself implied that the state must deal with strikers with the same "grasping, unyielding, relentless and deadly" force with which it exterminated Indigenous insurgents.[148] As the strike spread, even New York's relatively labor-friendly liberal mainstream newspaper *The Sun*, which was headed by Charles Dana—a former abolitionist and participant in the Fourierist-socialist Brook Farm utopian project—engaged in "rifle diet" rhetoric against the strikers. Calling it an "Insurrectionary Strike," *The Sun* asked, "Is this novel, startling, and unparalleled trouble to be settled by concession and conciliation, or by force and bloodshed?"[149] It offered the latter as the answer to the question. *The Sun* criticized West Virginia's governor for being too lenient with the strikers in the beginning: "If the Governor of West Virginia had been a man of force and decision, the railroad riots would very probably have ended at Martinsburg, where they began."[150] Instead of firing blanks as a warning to the strikers when the work stoppage began, argued *The Sun*, he should have ordered his troops to kill the workers with live rounds.

The liberal reasoning was that dealing with workers in this "most prompt and decisive way is the most merciful" because it prevents the strike from spreading and thereby eliminates the need for any further violence.[151] The conservative *Chicago Tribune* agreed fully with the first half of the sentiment: "A little powder, used to teach the dangerous classes a needful lesson, is well burned, provided there are bullets in front of it. We have no faith in blank cartridges, or in muskets pointed upward."[152] Unlike *The Sun*, the *Chicago Tribune* was not interested in what was "most merciful," only in what was most effective. For Chicago's leading paper, the less merciful, the better.

Ohio's highest-circulation newspaper, the *Cleveland Leader*—which was born of a merger of a few abolitionist newspapers in the 1850s—likewise called for the state to kill striking workers. During the height of the strikes, it ran front-page headlines such as "THE BAYONET—It Has a Soothing Effect upon the Railroad Outlaws."[153] Though the *Cleveland Leader* was antislavery, Republican-affiliated, and opposed to the expansion of slavery into the western territories, it also served as an organ of the conspiracy-theorist, anti-Catholic, anti-immigrant Know-Nothing movement. White antislavery sentiment was not necessarily rooted in a commitment to human equality or justice. As dominant US institutions increasingly characterized labor as a mass of foreign, racialized outsiders, Ohio's most influential newspaper sided unequivocally with capital.

The bourgeoisie's paper of choice, the *New York Tribune*—for which John Hay was an assistant editor and lead editorial writer—was undisguisedly blunt in its calls for the state to mass-slaughter strikers. "Napoleon was right," declared the *Tribune*, "It is always a blunder as well as a crime to exasperate a mob without exterminating it."[154] The state, according to the *Tribune*, was duty-bound to kill disobedient workers in the name of Civilization: "Government has no right to spare lives in restoring that authority without which civilized society cannot exist."[155] It was not enough to employ the minimum amount of force necessary to end the railroad "insurrection," but the state must "make the results so costly and so terrible to those who have arranged it that no other like it shall ever be attempted in this country."[156] Hay's *Tribune* justified its calls for the extermination of "insurrectionary" workers the same way white America justified Indian extermination: vilification and dehumanization of them as enemies of civilization. It animalized rebellious proletarians as "ravenous plundering creatures who gather at every scene of disorder as jackals gather about a carcass."[157] This was not a mere labor dispute, it was "a revolt against all laws of trade, all government, all order, and all the conditions that make civilized society possible."[158] This, according to the most widely read newspaper in the United States at the time.[159]

Hay's *New York Tribune* had no sympathy for proletarian suffering during the economic downturn. Yes, conceded the *Tribune*, it is true that the large surplus population of unemployed people caused by economic crisis created a situation in which capital had all the leverage over labor, but that did not mean workers should organize for higher wages. On the contrary, it meant that workers should be grateful for any job under any conditions. "If seventy-five cents a day is 'starvation wages,'" scoffed the *Tribune*, "nothing a day is more so."[160] A regularly occurring argument in the editorial pages of the *Tribune* during July and August of 1877 was that the union organizer with his socialist and anarchist theories, not the capitalist, was the real enemy of labor.

The mouthpiece of capital identified two major reasons for the state's inability to quickly contain the "spread of the contagion."[161] The first reason was that the working-class composition of the state militias caused militiamen to sympathize with, rather than mercilessly crush, the strikers. When ordered to fire on strikers, militiamen would purposely aim high to miss the target and, worse, they fraternized with strikers and in some cases joined the strike. In Pittsburgh, complained the *Tribune*, where the strikers were most militant and caused the most property destruction against the railroad companies, "The Pittsburgh home guards fraternized with the mob," and the militia company at nearby Altoona refused to even take up arms.[162] Only in New York City was

116    CHAPTER 4

the state militia strong and disciplined enough "to keep the dangerous classes in perfect subjection."[163] By late July, the bourgeoisie concluded that "The state militia seems to be for the most part of no value."[164]

The second reason was that the professional army units most capable of carrying out the will of the capitalists, the most willing to mercilessly crush the strikers with overwhelming force, were already stretched too thin with the project of Indigenous genocide. We expect the army to take care of the "labor problem" for us, editorialized the *Tribune*, "Yet that little Army has to patrol the Rio Grande, garrison a long chain of forts of the Western Plains, overawe the treacherous tribes in New Mexico, prevent the return of Sitting Bull to the Yellowstone Valley, fight with [Chief] Joseph in Idaho, and now repress domestic violence in five states."[165] For the bourgeoisie, the issue was not that the state needed to pull troops away from the project of Indigenous extermination, but rather the nation needed to vastly increase the size and scope of the state's repressive apparatus and significantly increase funding and material support to professional military and police organizations. "The most important development resulting from the great strike," said Hay's *Tribune*, "is the amazing exhibition it has made of the weakness of our governments."[166]

In the meantime, in the absence of a strong repressive state apparatus, the wealthy turned to the authority of "Judge Lynch." Vigilantes representing capitalist interests deputized themselves as state agents, just like the white settlers in the "Old West" adventure tales, who "in the absence of legitimate authority and regular organizations," visited "a swift and terrible retribution" on the "Anarchists and desperadoes," to restore "the beautiful spirit of order and progress" from the "chaos and confusion of blood."[167] Cities' "leading citizens" formed vigilance committees as a defense against "the Communistic element."[168] "San Francisco depends on its vigilance committee," reported the *Tribune*, "Chicago and St. Louis are defended by extemporized organizations of the citizens" and "Louisville suspends business in order that the inhabitants may take up arms."[169] The governor of Ohio, it reported, "invites the people" to engage in anticommunist vigilantism "in every town and village of the state."[170] The propertied class in Zanesville, Ohio, did just that, forming a vigilance committee made up of what *The Sun* called "about a thousand of our best citizens."[171] On July 25, at 3:40 p.m., reported *The Sun*, "The vigilance committee are assisting the police, who are picking up the leaders of the mob rapidly."[172] Here it is clear that in respectable white society, right-wing vigilantes were not considered to be mobs, but workers on strike were "the mob." The vigilantes, though extralegal, were considered by respectable society to be agents of the state, "assisting the police." Vigilantes were "our best citizens."

The capitalist class ultimately suppressed the railroad uprising the same way it suppressed Indigenous resistance, through the deadly force of a combina-

The Guns of 1877     117

tion of formal state forces—mainly army infantry—artillery, cavalry regiments, police, and informal extralegal paramilitarism, all of which scholars ought to recognize as state violence. US Army regulars, police, and right-wing vigilantes all acted as state agents and did so in coordination with each other. In the eyes of the propertied class, the "railroad war" was an Indian war and would be won the same way. The coverage in John Hay's *Tribune* of the state's suppression of the strikes was in some cases indistinguishable from its coverage of the Indian Wars, and the conflation was more than rhetorical. The ideology underlying them was identical and beyond rhetoric and ideology; in some cases, the real-world state action to suppress the two was indistinguishable. Again, this is not to suggest that the radical working-class left became the "new Indians" or that anticommunism replaced Indian hating but to say that settler colonialism is such a formative component in the structure of the United States that internal state repression in defense of the white man's property developed along colonialist counterinsurgency lines.

The *Tribune's* July 27, 1877, front-page news sharply exemplifies the point. Its left-most column reported on "Indian Outrages in Dakota."[173] After Custer's defeat at the Greasy Grass the previous summer, the US Army responded by deploying several units armed with Gatling guns, including Civil War hero Nelson Miles's Fifth Infantry Regiment, deep into Cheyenne and Lakota territory to wage total war on Indigenous nations in the region. Upon arriving, Colonel Miles's regiment established Fort Keogh, named for Myles Keogh of the "Myles Keogh's Horse" myth: demonstrating that the army conceived of this deployment as revenge for Custer's Last Stand. Through overwhelming military force, the United States dispossessed Lakota, Cheyenne, and Arapaho peoples of their lands, confining them to reservations, and transferring the land into the hands of white property owners, who quickly moved in to establish private ranches. The United States formally annexed the land with what it called the "Agreement of 1877," which Congress enacted in late February 1877. In the eyes of the United States, this settled the so-called Great Sioux War, but many displaced Plains groups never agreed to the US terms and did not see an "agreement" forced at the point of a Gatling gun as valid.[174]

As proletarian insurgents burned down railroad company property in industrial centers such as Pittsburgh and Chicago, Lakota and Cheyenne people burned down white ranchers' newly established property in the Black Hills region.[175] Indigenous insurgents refused to be expelled from their lands or contained on reservations, opting instead to expropriate livestock and hay from the landowners who established ranches in Lakota and Cheyenne territory and burn down the ranch houses. They were Indigenous people defending their lands from an ongoing settler colonizer invasion intent on eliminating Indigenous existence, but the *Tribune* characterized them as the "savage" invaders: "THE COUNTRY

118    CHAPTER 4

Ravaged by Savages," ran the subheadline.[176] It reported "outrages by the savages, who seem to have broken away from the Agencies [meaning the US Indian agents overseeing the reservations] in large numbers," and, said the *Tribune* in the classic genocidal language of animalization and disease, "are infesting the country in all directions."[177] It continued, "Nearly every ranche [*sic*] along the Red Water and in Spearfish Valley has been devastated."[178] The article reported on the disappearance of one army unit in the region, led by a Lieutenant Lemley, and augmented by a dozen civilian settler vigilantes, which reflects the fact that Indigenous extermination in the region was being carried out by formal and extralegal forces working together to protect the white man's property interests.

This is precisely the approach the state took to quelling the labor revolt, as reflected in the rightmost column of that same *Tribune* page. Its description of the state suppressing the uprising in Chicago, where labor organizers Albert and Lucy Parsons were involved in strike support work, read the same as its descriptions of Indian War battles: "Riots in the West," read the headline, with the subtitle "a savage mob is charged by police and troops, and persistently reforms—heavy firing upon them at night."[179] More than two thousand working-class men and boys "showed savage bravado and seemed fearless of death itself" as three hundred police charged them.[180] It was John Hay's version of Custer's Last Stand—"Three Hundred to Three Thousand!"—playing out in the streets of Chicago, where "the White man meets the Red."[181] Only this time, Custer would emerge victorious.

The agents of state violence would not be tempered by the fact that children were in the crowd. General Sherman's previously mentioned remarks that during an assault on savages, "the soldiers can not pause to distinguish between male and female, or even discriminate as to age," seemed to apply to the state's efforts against proletarian insurgency.[182] A US Army cavalry unit led by Colonel Agramont "came up immediately, and in conjunction with the police made a deadly onslaught," reportedly killing twelve strikers and wounding 150. This cavalry charge temporarily scattered "the savage mob," but they soon reformed, and "a gang" put another train out of commission on Twentieth Street. This excerpt is particularly instructive:

> The 2d regiment was sent to the scene of the battle, as also the Mounted Police, and the Veteran Force of Chicago [vigilantes who were Civil War and Indian War veterans]. The artillery was also sent. At 11:40 a.m. cannon-firing was heard at the corner of Sixteenth and Halstead [present-day Halsted] sts., where the mob had collected, and it is reported that the regulars opened fire with grape and cannister, and that the slaughter is terrible.[183]

Here it describes the coordinated deadly action of police, US Army regulars, and extralegal vigilantes against strikers to protect railroad company property.

The Guns of 1877    119

Grape and canister artillery ammunition was designed to indiscriminately kill and maim enemy personnel en masse.

Throughout the day, more US Army units arrived in Chicago, two companies of the Twenty-Second Infantry, followed by four more companies of the Twenty-Second and six companies of the Ninth Infantry. The *Tribune's* 4:00 p.m. report said, "the number of casualties reported is large" and "a large crowd of police and mounted vigilantes are conducting prisoners to the station." The reporting again demonstrates that vigilantes were part of the repressive state apparatus. After hours of being fired on by soldiers, police, and vigilantes, some strikers fired back. "Many shots are being fired by the rabble, and serious trouble is anticipated." The 6:30 p.m. edition reported that the fighting "has been continuous and bloody." Even with the aid of vigilantes, arresting strikers was difficult. "Hardly a man was taken to the Station House without a rush being made to release him, and a consequent interchange of shots. . . . The police begin to complain that they are being shot and stoned down in that vicinity."[184]

Rumors circulated that a gang of workers from the stockyards in solidarity with the railroad strikers were on their way, armed with the tools of their trade—butcher knives and gambrel sticks—to "clean out every policeman on Halstead-st." More right-wing vigilante gangs, euphemistically called "societies for protection," formed in response to such rumors and prepared "for a lively campaign" against the strikers at nightfall. The 9:40 p.m. edition reported that there was "heavy firing" in the Halsted Street Viaduct vicinity and that army artillery and cavalry regiments were on the scene. "A volley of perhaps 100 [artillery] rounds has just been fired."[185] On the front page of the leading newspaper in the United States, readers could see that whether it be Dakota or Chicago, the country was "ravaged by savages" and that it was all part of the same war of Civilization versus Savagery.

## Conclusion

The year 1877 was a turning point for John Hay's class. Reflecting on the lessons of the railroad uprisings, the ruling class determined that, from then on, an Indian War counterinsurgency strategy would be the approach for dealing with the labor movement. Exemplifying this turning point was the Chicago Citizens' Association—an association of Chicago's wealthiest business and church leaders. In the aftermath of 1877, writes Carolyn Ashbaugh, the Citizens' Association purchased a Gatling gun and donated it to the city to use for proletarian control. The state established military armories in major US cities "to house soldiers for putting down insurrection, and legislatures passed conspiracy laws aimed directly at workers."[186] As long as John Hay's class was in power, there would be no Paris Commune on US soil.

# 5

## Republicans and Anarchists

### The Civil War, Reconstruction, and the Nadir

In the United States, 1877 was as much a turning point for the labor move-ment as it was for the capitalist class. Albert and Lucy Parsons are an instructive example of how labor politics shifted, as they were on the cutting edge of that shift. The Parsonses came to Chicago as refugees from Texas racial terror. They had been involved in Radical Republican politics, working for Black political enfranchisement during the Reconstruction era. Being an interracial couple involved in Reconstruction politics made them a target of the first Ku Klux Klan, which was active in several towns in Texas in the era. Albert Parsons learned that white supremacist vigilantes could not be debated or reasoned with and could be defeated only through the force of organized community self-defense. Four days before his execution for alleged involvement with the Haymarket bombing, while sitting in Cook County Jail "Dungeon No. 7," Parsons thought back on those days, and wrote,

> In nearly every neighborhood there was usually a gang of desperados, who, as kuklux [sic], made life a terror to the defenseless blacks. In some instances these gangs took to the highway and began to depredate upon the whites. Such gangs usually became emboldened with their easy terrorization at first, until in sheer desperation the peaceably-disposed portion of the community would combine, and in a frenzy kill them or drive them off.[1]

In 1868, at the age of twenty, Albert Parsons founded and edited a short-lived Reconstruction newspaper called the *Spectator* and, over the next three years, in addition to working as a traveling correspondent for the *Houston Daily Tele-graph*, served in various Republican positions, appointed and elected, including as a reading secretary of the Texas State Senate in 1871.

Here some discussion is warranted of the fact that Albert Parsons served as a soldier in the Confederacy during the Civil War. Most writers who have discussed Parsons mention this fact but leave out the context of his service to the Confederacy. Albert Parsons's mother died when he was a baby and his father died when Albert was five. Albert's eldest brother William Henry Parsons, who was twenty-two years older than Albert, became his legal guardian. William Henry Parsons was a white Texas "frontier" settler and an enslaver. He participated in the US invasion of Mexico as a soldier under the command of the Indian-killer General Zachary Taylor. After the war, he settled in Texas and became a newspaper owner and editor. In 1860, he founded the Waco weekly the *South West*, which was a prosecession, proslavery, "states' rights" paper. When Texas seceded to become part of the Confederate States of America, Albert was a child. His older brothers left to lead Confederate military units in the war. His brother, Richard Parsons, served as an infantry captain at Sabine Pass, Texas, by the Sabine River, which was the border between Texas and Louisiana, and his eldest brother and guardian William served as a colonel commanding the cavalry outposts on the west bank of the Mississippi river from Helena, Arkansas, to the mouth of the Red River in Louisiana.[2]

William left Albert in the care of family friend Willard Richardson, who was a leader of the secession movement in Texas. Richardson was the owner of the *Daily News* in Galveston, which was the most profitable, highest-circulation paper in antebellum Texas. Albert had already been working for Richardson's paper, apprenticed from around age eleven as a "printer's devil" and a paper boy. Richardson ran the paper for the express purpose of opposing abolition and advocating for the expansion of the slave trade. In the lead-up to the 1860 election, he had his newspaper network distribute a campaign sheet titled "The Crisis!," which used states'-rights rhetoric to encourage voters to elect proslavery candidates. After Lincoln won the election, Richardson, referring to Republicans as "Black Republicans," began to openly push for secession.[3] The men who were the boy Albert Parsons's immediate examples and mentors were settler colonizers, enslavers, and leaders in the Southern secession movement.[4]

As an adult looking back, Parsons remembered that, as a child, he was so indoctrinated by the adults in his life and the primary white supremacist institutions of the region that "I wanted to enlist in the Rebel army and join Gen. Lee in Virginia," but his guardian Willard Richardson would not allow it "on account of my age and size."[5] When a local Confederate militia called the Lone Star Grays came around in early 1861 looking for volunteers, the thirteen-year-old boy jumped at the chance to be like his older brothers and took French leave of Richardson's home to fight for the ideals Texas white settler society had instilled in him.[6] He set sail into the Gulf of Mexico on a steamship with the Lone Star Grays to assist in the surrender of US Army General David E.

122    CHAPTER 5

Twiggs, who had switched sides and turned over his entire command—including armaments and installations—to the Confederacy and was rewarded with a commission as major general by the Confederate States for his treachery. After that short mission, and in spite of receiving "an ear-pulling" from Richardson upon returning, the child Albert ran away again to find his brothers, first to work as a powder monkey for the cannoneers in an infantry company at Sabine Pass, where his brother Captain Richard Parsons was in command, and then to the Mississippi River to join Texas's Twelfth Cavalry Regiment—also known as Parsons's Mounted Volunteers—under his eldest brother Colonel William Henry Parsons's command. William assigned Albert to a company called the McInoly Scouts, during which time Albert participated in the battles of the Curtis, Canby, and Banks campaigns.[7]

Because Albert Parsons was, even by Confederate standards, an underage child at the time he joined the Confederate military, it is highly questionable that his Confederate service should in any way be used by historians to characterize his thinking or the kind of person he was. By present-day standards of international law, as defined by article 77.2 of the Additional Protocols to the 1949 Geneva Conventions, the 1989 United Nations Convention on the Rights of the Child, and the 2002 Rome Statute of the International Criminal Court, Albert Parsons was a child soldier, and enlisting him to serve in the military would have been a war crime. In light of who his mentors and guardians were, and the virulently white supremacist settler-enslaver society that raised him, it is remarkable that, by his late teens and into his early twenties, Albert Parsons had fully abandoned Confederate ideology, became a Radical Republican Reconstructionist dedicated to Black political enfranchisement, urged the acceptance of the terms of surrender, publicly supported the Thirteenth, Fourteenth, and Fifteenth Amendments to the US Constitution, and worked in open opposition to the white society of his childhood. In his early twenties, Parsons was actively involved in Reconstruction politics, serving several roles to support Republican political campaigns and even serving as a secretary in the Texas state senate during Reconstruction. He did not give much explanation for this seemingly abrupt change beyond "I was strongly influenced in taking this step out of respect and love for the memory of dear old 'Aunt Easter,' then dead, and formerly a slave and house-servant of my brother's family, she having been my constant associate and practically raised me, with great kindness and a mother's love."[8]

His work after embracing Reconstruction politics put him in direct conflict with the dominant white settler society he grew up in: "I was hated and scorned by the whites."[9] His former white friends turned against him: "I soon found myself completely ostracized . . . and during the political campaigns was not permitted shelter and lodging in a white man's house."[10] White Texas society ostracized Parsons, but Black communities were welcoming. He participated in Black public meetings in courthouses at county seats, in which Black people organized and discussed Reconstruction politics. Parsons mused that these meetings "had an effect upon the whites similar to a red rag in the face of a wild bull."[11] It was through this work—with Black American Reconstructionists rather than with European-born anarchists and socialists—that Parsons learned his first lessons in political economy and social movement organizing. Retrospectively, Parsons called the Republican Party a "labor party" in that it was, in his understanding at the time, dedicated to the political enfranchisement of the Black proletariat.[12] Chicago would change his mind about that.

It was also during this time in Reconstruction politics that Parsons met his wife Lucy, a formerly enslaved Black young woman who claimed Mexican and Indigenous American ancestry.[13] Lucy Parsons appeared by many accounts to be racially ambiguous. Historian Jacqueline Jones has uncovered the fact that Lucy Parsons was born Lucia in Virginia to a seventeen-year-old Black mother named Charlotte who was enslaved by the physician Thomas J. Taliaferro. It is unknown who Lucia's father was. Jones suggests that Lucia's father was likely her enslaver Taliaferro or another white man.[14] The prevalence of sexual violence against Black women and girls at the hands of white enslavers makes Jones's theory anything but far-fetched. Lucy Parsons publicly shared little about her origins but claimed that "There is not a drop of Caucasian blood in my veins."[15] She maintained throughout her life that her father was of Creek and Mexican descent. If her biological father was an enslaver and rapist, it is conceivable that Parsons would refuse to acknowledge him as her father and manufacture a story of someone else as her father. We must also consider that young Lucia's mother and enslaver may not have told her the truth about who her father was. It is possible that she did not know or that others lied to her. It is also conceivable that Lucia's father was exactly who she claimed he was. With the lack of conclusive evidence, all suggestions who Lucia's father was are speculation.

Interracial marriage was legal in Texas only for a short period of time during Reconstruction, and, as Jacqueline Jones writes, "the couple took advantage of this window of opportunity to marry legally in a state dominated by white supremacists."[16] The white nationalists soon after took back control of the state and reinstituted laws forbidding marriage across the color line. White Texas society branded Albert a "miscegenationist." Thirteen years after the Parsonses left Texas, the *Waco Daily Examiner* still referred to him as "beast Parsons," the "Miscegenationist" and "Moral Outlaw, For Whom the Gallows Waits."[17] Of Lucy Parsons, it said, "She is of Mexican and Indian origin. . . . She has often said that the ambition of her life is to fire the engine that shall run the guillotine to cut off the heads of capitalists."[18] Here Waco's mainstream white newspaper

124    CHAPTER 5

characterized the leading anarchists of Chicago in racial terms: as a "miscegenationist beast" and a bloodthirsty Mexican-Indian.

That same page also reported that Cincinnati, Ohio, city employees on strike for the eight-hour day would be reinforced by six hundred socialists armed with rifles and dynamite bombs, and that the Haymarket bomb was manufactured in Cincinnati: none of which was true other than that city employees struck for the eight-hour day. It reported that Cincinnati was prepared to give the "Red Demons a Red-Hot Reception" by right-wing vigilante groups it euphemistically called "safety organizations," special police trained in counterinsurgency tactics, and several Ohio National Guard units armed with "two field [artillery] pieces and nine Gatling guns."[19] Of all this news, the leading headline was that the anarchist "scorpions" led by the "miscegenationist beast" Parsons—with his "sneaking snarl" and his ferocious Indian wife—were in hiding.[20]

During Parsons's term as a secretary in the Texas State Senate, Texas's Reconstruction governor Edmund Jackson Davis—a white Southerner who opposed the Confederacy and served as a general in the Union Army—commissioned Parsons as a colonel in the state militia, to lead a unit of twenty-five men to protect Black voters at the polls in a local election in Belton, the county seat of Bell County, Texas. Parsons remembered that mission as "a most warlike and dangerous undertaking."[21] White property-owning Texans knew that Black people voting in large numbers meant that Radical Republican Reconstructionists would win a majority of seats in some districts, and white supremacist vigilantes were determined to unleash a campaign of racial terror to prevent that from happening. Parsons wrote of his mission to protect the polls: "the blacks had no rights which (as Justice Taney had said) the whites should respect. But at the muzzle of revolvers I protected the poor blacks in the exercise of their elective franchise."[22] Parsons knew from the preceding three years dealing with "kuklux" gangs that it was futile to appeal to the morality or reason of white nationalists. The only strategy for dealing with them was to organize more force than they did and overpower them.

Overpowering them was possible as long as the federal government was invested in Reconstruction, but federal commitment to Black enfranchisement was short-lived. Through racial terror campaigns waged by right-wing paramilitary groups, who mass-lynched Black children and adults and mass-raped Black women and girls, white Texans demoralized and defeated the Radical Republicans to reestablish white rule in the state. White supremacists targeted both Black people and white Radical Republicans. Parsons wrote that by entering Republican politics, "I incurred thereby the hate and contumely of many of my former army comrades, neighbors, and the Ku Klux Klan" and "I was regarded a political heretic and traitor by many of my former associates."[23] While Albert

Parsons downplayed the amount of violence white Texans inflicted upon him, he lived in constant danger.

During his time as a Radical Republican, whites targeted Parsons with acts of violence and threats of lynching and, in one instance, bashed him in the temple with a piece of a broken iron cogwheel. The latter incident occurred after a Black man named Sheppard "Shep" Mullens—one of the leaders of Black Reconstruction in Texas—was elected to the Texas House of Representatives. The election of Black legislators greatly angered former Texas state legislator and white supremacist John Thompson Flint. Flint formerly served in the Texas state legislature as a representative of Belton, Bell County, Texas—the very district in which Albert Parsons's militia would later protect Black voters at the polls. Flint was a leading member of the local bourgeoisie: an attorney, founder of the Flint and Chamberlin Bank in Waco, president of the Waco and Northwestern Railroad Company and Waco Tap Railroad Company, and a member of the Board of Trustees for Waco University.[24] Flint saw the election of men such as Shep Mullens as a threat to the domination of the white bourgeoisie. He blamed Black election victories on Republicans such as Albert Parsons, who mobilized and protected Black voters. At Black Reconstruction events, Parsons gave speeches in which he encouraged Black people to vote for Black candidates: "I told them . . . they could work for themselves, and vote for themselves."[25] Upon seeing Parsons in a hallway, Flint upbraided Parsons "for aiding the election of a 'nigger.'"[26] In Parsons's words, "he suddenly drew back and struck me in the temple with the iron, making a cut of two inches, from which rushed a stream of blood that drenched my clothing."[27] Flint suffered no legal repercussions.[28]

There is little record of what Lucy Parsons experienced during this period; neither she nor Albert spoke of it publicly or in any existing private correspondence. In the area of Texas in which she lived during that period, several instances occurred of Ku Klux Klan gangs assaulting, robbing, and murdering Black children and adults with impunity, and especially targeting Black women and girls with brutal acts of sexual violence. Lucy Parsons spoke very little of her past or personal experiences, but she did say that she witnessed atrocities white supremacist vigilantes committed in the South, and she wrote with intense anger against Southern white racial violence. She was a strong proponent not only of Black armed self-defense but also of Black armed revenge on white lynch mobs. She was particularly passionate in her denunciations of white supremacist attacks on Black women and girls:

> Women are stripped to the skin in the presence of leering, white-skinned, black-hearted brutes and lashed into insensibility and strangled to death from the limbs of trees. A girl child of fifteen years was lynched recently by these brutal bullies. . . . John Brown's body lies moldering in the grave. But will

his spirit lie there moldering too? Brutes, inhuman monsters—you heartless brutes—you whom nature forms by molding you in it, deceive not yourselves by thinking that another John Brown will not arise.[29]

Parsons did not believe in white saviors, however, nor did she believe in appealing to the morality of white people: "The white race furnished us one John Brown; the next must come from our own race."[30]

More than half a century before Malcolm X and Kwame Ture ever gave a speech, Lucy Parsons argued that whites would never respect Black people as the result of appeals to white morality, but that power, not moral suasion, was the basis of respect. Black people, said Parsons, would gain the respect of white society when Black communities were strong and organized enough to make white oppressors dread them, and not before that. "For the torch of the incendiary, which has been known to show murderers and tyrants the danger line, beyond which they may not venture with impunity, cannot be wrested from you."[31] After attending what she described as a "meeting of colored citizens" in Chicago, on March 27, 1886, in protest against lynchings, she was impressed that Black people were shifting away from appeals to Republican politicians, who had abandoned Reconstruction, toward community self-help and militant collective self-defense. White lynch mobs, she wrote, "are not only sowing the wind which they will reap in the whirlwind, but the flame which they will reap in the conflagration" and then, quoting one of the speakers at the meeting, she wrote, "Prepare for the crisis. God helps those who help themselves."[32] She was not wrong. In many cases during the Nadir and later, Black armed community self-defense became the dominant and most effective strategy—in contrast with moral suasion, legalism, or electoralism—to combat extralegal racial violence.[33]

As transnational poet Warsan Shire writes, the most common survival strategy for people who live in "the mouth of a shark" or "the barrel of a gun" is "to quicken your legs": that is to say, migration.[34] Though Albert Parsons, in his role as a Radical Republican, took part in armed action against white vigilantes, ultimately the forces of white reaction outnumbered and overwhelmed the forces of Reconstruction in Texas. Like millions of others in the crosshairs of Southern white vigilantes, Albert and Lucy Parsons "quickened their legs" north to join the ranks of the urban industrial working class. They arrived in Chicago in the winter of 1873–74. In Chicago's migrant and refugee working-class neighborhoods, writes Ashbaugh, "Lucy would no longer have to fear rape by the Klan at every moment. She would have room to develop her own potential as a crusader for human rights."[35] The North, however, was no bastion of equality. They arrived just as the Panic of 1873 was ushering in the Long Depression. They were out of the mouth of a shark and into the jaws of a lion.

Republicans and Anarchists     127

## Chicago

The Parsonses arrived in Chicago at a time of heightened class antagonism and mass working-class protest. Chicago's working class lived and worked in dangerous and unhealthy conditions. Infant mortality was high, and half of the children in Chicago's highest-density ward did not survive to the age of five.[36] Historian Jacqueline Jones writes of that moment that "out of a working population of 112,000, an estimated 25,000 had recently lost their jobs, causing untold misery among some 125,000 family members in a city of 400,000."[37] For the working class, hours were long, wages low, housing substandard, neighborhoods unsanitary and overcrowded, and disease rampant, and the only social safety net was private charity.

The most prominent members of Chicago's bourgeoisie—industrialists such as railroad magnate George Pullman, major manufacturers Nathaniel Kellogg Fairbank and J. McGregor Adams, real-estate developer Wirt Dexter, clothing company owner Henry W. King, and the founder of Chicago's premier department store Marshall Field—were board members of the Relief and Aid Society.[38] After the Great Fire of 1871, the city government appointed the Relief and Aid Society to be the city's official relief organization. It remained a private organization but received public funds, which it dispensed only to those it deemed the "worthy poor." Because of the antimigrant sentiments of some board members, such as J. McGregor Adams, it is not surprising that only a small minority of the city's poor were deemed "worthy."[39] Controversy erupted over board members funneling millions of dollars of Relief and Aid Society funds into their own companies. The winter that Albert and Lucy Parsons arrived in Chicago, some ten thousand working-class Chicagoans gathered at City Hall to protest the actions of the Relief and Aid Society.[40]

They were out of the frying pan of the white vigilante's race war and into the fire of the white industrialist's class war. For Lucy Parsons, both these things were thoroughly intertwined. She often wrote and spoke of the working-class struggle against "wage slavery" as the continuation of the Black struggle against chattel slavery.

> The overseer's whip is now fully supplanted by the lash of hunger! And the auction block by the chain-gang and convict cell! The same land which you once tilled as a chattel slave you still till as a wage slave, and in the same cabin which you then entered at eve not knowing but what you would be sold from wife and little ones before the morrow's setting sun, you now enter with dread lest you will be slain by the assassin hand of those who once would simply have sold you if they did not like you.[41]

In recent years, leading prison reformers, prison abolitionists, and scholars have begun exploring the idea that many elements and functions of enslavement continued, after the passage of the Thirteenth Amendment, through the criminal justice system.[42] Lucy Parsons, herself formerly enslaved and heavily targeted by the criminal justice system throughout her life, made the connection as early as 1886, as she describes in the passage just quoted. For Lucy Parsons, Reconstruction was not complete until capitalism was abolished. She did not see her new life in the proletarian struggle as a shift away from Reconstruction politics, but as a continuation of Reconstruction. Three decades later, when she became editor of a pro-IWW anarchist newspaper, she named it *The Liberator*, after the old abolitionist newspaper of the same name, consciously linking the struggle against wage slavery with the struggle against chattel slavery.[43]

Albert Parsons likewise saw the working-class struggle he came upon in Chicago as a continuation of what he understood Reconstruction was about. His first impression of Chicago's wealthy elite was that they were of the same type as Texas's class of white wealthy former enslavers who opposed Reconstruction. He compared the defenders of Chicago's Relief and Aid Society to the defenders of white supremacy in Texas:

> I also discovered a great similarity between the abuse heaped upon these poor people [who criticized and made demands upon Chicago's Relief and Aid Society] by the organs of the rich and the actions of the late southern slaveholders in Texas toward the newly enfranchised slaves, whom they accused of wanting to make their former masters "divide" by giving them "forty acres and a mule," and it satisfied me there was a great fundamental wrong at work in society and in existing social and industrial arrangements.[44]

This understanding led him away from the Republicans toward the labor movement.

Albert Parsons's allegiance was to an evolving set of ideals, not to any organization or party, and so, when the Republicans abandoned Reconstruction, he abandoned the Republicans. Chicago Republicans stood for a set of values and policies very different from those of the Texas Radical Republicans Parsons previously associated with. In the industrial cities of the North, the Republican Party was not the Reconstruction party of the Black proletariat but rather the party of the white bourgeoisie, of the George Pullmans of the city. The people who carried on in the spirit of the emancipation struggle, as Parsons understood it, and whose ideals were most aligned with his, were the social democrats and the workingmen's organizations. As the Republicans moved right, Albert and Lucy Parsons moved left. While Albert Parsons's political affiliations changed several times throughout his life, as a fully formed adult, he was quite clear about

Republicans and Anarchists    129

which side he was on: "My enemies in the southern states consisted of those who oppressed the black slave. My enemies in the North are among those who would perpetuate the slavery of the wage workers."[45]

The Parsonses found acceptance in the multiethnic, multilingual, working-class area of Larrabee Street and North Avenue, "an area of basement sweatshops, German beer gardens and community gathering places, and refugees from Bismarck's anti-socialist laws."[46] It was a socially conscious, politically active, internationalist, working-class community abuzz with social movement organizing. Having years of newspaper printing and layout experience under his belt, he joined Typographical Union No. 16, through which he was hired to work temporarily as a compositor for the *Inter-Ocean* and then permanently for the *Chicago Times*. Because of his years of participation in the Black Reconstruction movement, Albert Parsons arrived in Chicago already an experienced and skilled organizer, writer, and orator. He quickly became a leading figure of Chicago's labor movement. He joined the Social-Democratic Party of America, which, in 1876, merged into the Workingmen's Party of the United States and two years later changed its name to the Socialistic Labor Party. In 1876, he also joined the Knights of Labor, and, by the spring of 1877, the Knights had formed Assembly 400, the first Chicago Knights of Labor local in Chicago, with Albert Parsons as its local delegate. He was the Workingmen's Party nominee for several elections at the local and state levels, for offices such as alderman, county clerk, and governor.[47]

Prior to and during the summer of 1877's Great Railroad uprisings, Albert Parsons was not a revolutionist, but a democratic-socialist reformist. During the height of the strikes in Chicago, he advised workers not to resort to militant direct-action tactics, "but go to the polls, elect good men to make good laws, and thus bring about good times."[48] The week prior to the state's final deadly military crackdown on railroad strikers in Chicago, Parsons, in his role as a Workingmen's Party representative, addressed a mass meeting of some thirty thousand workers assembled on Market Street. He argued, in line with the Workingmen's Party program, that the means of production, transportation, communication, and exchange should be taken out of the hands of private enterprise and socialized. He attempted to pacify the strikers, telling them that the way to achieve this was not through disruptive strikes but by joining the Workingmen's Party and helping to get Workingmen's Party candidates elected to office.[49]

He would soon come to believe that the electoral road to socialism was a dead end and that it was folly to attempt to temper the revolutionary inclinations of the rank and file of the working class. But, at that point in his political development, Parsons was still operating somewhat from a Reconstruction and social democrat playbook that emphasized social change through the official channels of the state's nominally democratic institutions. Despite the fact that he played a pacifying role in the strike, he faced reprisal from the state and his employer simply for being involved at all.

The morning after his Market Street speech, Albert Parsons showed up for work at the *Chicago Times* to find he was no longer an employee: "I was discharged and blacklisted by this paper for addressing the meeting that night."[50] A few hours later, two armed plainclothes police officers found Parsons at the office of the German-language organ of the Workingmen's Party, the *Arbeiter-Zeitung* and escorted him to the City Hall building. According to Parsons's account, they brought him to a room filled with police officers and then to what they called "the Mayor's room" to meet with Police Superintendent Michael Hickey, who, after making Parsons wait awhile, entered the room with an entourage of about thirty men in civilian clothes. "I knew none of them," Parsons later wrote, "but I seemed to be known by them all." Superintendent Hickey questioned and browbeat Parsons as other men in the room commented, "Hang him!" "Lynch him!" "Lock him up!" and the like. Hickey asked Parsons why he didn't "know better than to come up here from Texas and incite the working people to insurrection." Parsons was surprised to learn that these men viewed him as a leader of the strike. From Parsons's point of view, the strike was happening largely *in spite of* the leadership of the Workingmen's Party, not *because* of it. Workingmen's Party leaders such as himself were out of breath trying to keep up with and control the insurrection, not leading it.[51]

According to Parsons's account, the meeting ended with Superintendent Hickey taking Parsons by the arm, leading him to the door, and stopping before shoving him out the door to say,

> Parsons, your life is in danger. I advise you to leave the city at once. Beware. Everything you say or do is made known to me. I have men on your track who shadow you. Do you know you are liable to be assassinated any moment on the street? . . . Why, those Board of Trade men [an association of Chicago's wealthiest business leaders] would as leave hang you to a lamp-post as not. . . . Take warning.[52]

Albert Parsons escaped the constant threat of lynching by Texas white vigilantes only to have the head of Chicago's police force threaten him with extrajudicial execution on behalf of Chicago's leading industrialists.

The threats against his life did not end at City Hall. Having been fired that morning from his job at the *Chicago Times*, Parsons walked that evening to the office of the *Chicago Tribune*, to see whether some of his colleagues and fellow members of the Typographical Union who worked on the fifth floor at the *Tribune*'s composing room might be able to find him employment on the night shift. The chairman of the executive board of the Typographical Union, a Mr. Manion, had some sway over hiring decisions, and he worked that shift. Around

8:00 p.m., as Parsons and Manion chatted about the hot topic of the day—the railroad strike—three armed men, unknown to the composing-room workers, approached Parsons from behind and, taking hold of him, began pushing and shoving him toward the door.

> They cursed me between their teeth, and, opening the door, began to lead me down-stairs. As we started down one of them put a pistol to my head and said: "I've a mind to blow your brains out." Another said: "Shut up or we'll dash you, out the window upon the pavements below." Reaching the bottom of the five flights of stairs, they paused and said, "Now go. If you ever put your face in this building again you'll be arrested and locked up."[53]

Parsons found that for about two years after the railroad strikes, "I was black-listed and unable to find employment in the city, and my family suffered for the necessaries of life."[54]

Over the next week, Parsons witnessed the lengths to which the state would go on behalf of the captains of industry to suppress and control the urban proletariat. He witnessed police, soldiers, and right-wing vigilantes working together to kill and maim strikers and bystanders. At one nonviolent mass meeting of some three thousand workers on Market Street, Parsons witnessed the following incident: "Over 100 policemen charged upon this peaceable mass-meeting, firing their pistols and clubbing right and left." The police imposed repressive measures against not only railroad workers, but trade unions in general:

> The printers, the iron-molders, and other trades unions which had held regular monthly or weekly meetings of their unions for years past, when they came to their hall doors now for that purpose, found policemen standing there, the doors barred, and the members told that all meetings had been prohibited by the Chief of Police. All mass-meetings, union meetings of any character were broken up by the police, and at one place (Twelfth Street Turner Hall), where the Furniture-Workers' Union had met to confer with their employers about the eight-hour system and wages, the police broke down the doors, forcibly entered, and clubbed and fired upon the men as they struggled pell-mell to escape from the building, killing one workman and wounding many others.[55]

The following day, as Parsons recollected, the Illinois National Guard First Regiment fired on a crowd "of several thousand men, women, and children, killing several persons, none of whom were ever on a strike, at Sixteenth street viaduct."[56]

For Albert and Lucy Parsons, the events of 1877 were a disillusioning and radicalizing experience. They learned that the legal and extralegal violence of the white supremacist South was not peculiar to the South but that it was a feature of the US system of class dominance even in the progressive North. They learned that the US ruling class would stop at nothing to maintain that system. Both Albert and Lucy Parsons marked 1877 as a turning point in their thinking, away from reformism toward revolutionary unionism and anarchism. Any belief they had in US political institutions as vehicles for progressive reform was mowed down by the Gatling guns of 1877.[57]

They were not alone in their disillusionment but representative of a larger shift in working-class politics. The year 1877 unmasked the state, demystifying the class structure of US society and the naked violence on which that structure rested. For example, the famous labor agitator Mary Harris Jones—popularly known as Mother Jones—remembered 1877 as an awakening and "the beginning of America's industrial life." In her autobiography, Mother Jones ended her discussion of the 1877 strikes writing that

> Hand in hand with the growth of factories and the expansion of railroads, with the accumulation of capital and the rise of banks, came anti-labor legislation. Came strikes. Came violence. Came the belief in the hearts and minds of the workers that legislatures but carry out the will of the industrialists.[58]

Historian Sam Mitrani observes that, during the strikes of 1877, in the eyes of the working-class public, "the police appeared most starkly as little more than hired thugs of the city's businessmen."[59]

In the aftermath of 1877, in response to the indiscriminate violence that police, soldiers, and vigilantes unleashed on the city's working class, proletarian militias proliferated. Having shed the belief that state institutions would protect them, working-class men increasingly joined armed self-defense organizations. Notable examples were the Irish Labor Guard, the Jaeger Verein (hunter's club), and the Bohemian Sharpshooters, but the largest and most dangerous in the eyes of the wealthy was the German socialist-anarchist-organized Lehr und Wehr Verein (Education and Defense Society).[60] German migrant workers in Chicago founded the Lehr und Wehr Verein in 1875 with only thirty members but, after the violence of 1877, its numbers exploded to somewhere between six hundred and fifteen hundred participants.[61] Albert Parsons, being one of the leading propagandists of Chicago's radical left, became somewhat of an unofficial spokesperson for the Lehr und Wehr Verein. In an 1880 issue of the *Arbeiter-Zeitung*, Parsons wrote, "The underlying idea for the formation of the Armed Organization [*sic*] of the proletarians of Chicago has been to give battle to the present system of industry oppressing the workman."[62]

Albert Parsons's comrade and, later, fellow Haymarket martyr August Spies, who became a leader in the Lehr und Wehr Verein, remembered 1877 as the catalyst that led him to join the organization:

> The events of that year [1877], the brute force with which the whining and confiding wage-slaves were met on all sides impressed upon me the neces-

Republicans and Anarchists    133

sity of *like* resistance. The latter required organization. Shortly afterwards I joined the "Lehr and Wehr Verein," an armed organization of the workingmen, numbering about 1,500 well drilled members.[63]

Of this escalation of labor militancy, Albert Parsons wrote,

> These representatives of the moneyed aristocracy advised the use of police clubs, and militia bayonets, and Gatling guns to suppress strikers and put down discontented laborers struggling for better pay—shorter work-hours. The millionaires and their representatives on the pulpit and rostrum avowed their intention to use force to quell their dissatisfied laborers. The execution of these threats; the breaking up of meetings, arrest and imprisonment of labor "leaders;" the use of club, pistol, and bayonet upon strikers; even to the advice to throw hand-grenades (dynamite) among them—these acts of violence and brutality led many workingmen to consider the necessity of self-defense of their person and their rights. Accordingly, workingmen's military organizations sprang up all over the country. So formidable did this plan of organization promise to become that the capitalistic Legislature of Illinois in 1878, acting under orders from millionaire manufacturers and railway corporations, passed a law disarming the wage-workers.[64]

The law Parsons referred to was actually an 1879 militia act passed by the Illinois legislature that banned private militias from operating in the state without permission from the governor. Illinois legislators crafted this law specifically to put an end to socialist militias.[65]

In the present day, the militia movement and Second Amendment fanaticism are largely the domain of the right wing, but in the Gilded Age United States, the conservative establishment pushed for gun control laws against the threat of an armed insurgent left. It was the radical left of the labor movement that used Second Amendment rhetoric to defend gun rights. On the day Illinois's militia act went into effect, July 1, 1879, a company of the Lehr und Wehr Verein and a company of the Bohemian Sharpshooters marched fully armed in military formation through the streets of Chicago as an open challenge to the Illinois law, on Second Amendment grounds. Police arrested the leaders who then challenged the constitutionality of the charges in court. The US Supreme Court eventually took on the case in *Presser v. Illinois*, siding with the state of Illinois against the socialist militiamen. Herman Presser, the Socialistic Labor Party member who commanded the Lehr und Wehr Verein company during the July 1 march was fined $10.[66] This episode presaged the events of seven decades later when the National Rifle Association and conservatives such as California Governor Ronald Reagan would push for a series of strict gun control laws, such as the Mulford Act, that lawmakers crafted in reaction to the Black Panther Party for Self-Defense's bold armed protests on statehouse steps. Historically, US

134    CHAPTER 5

conservatives are quite willing to regulate firearms as long as those regulations target groups who challenge the capitalist white power structure of the United States. As Dunbar-Ortiz argues, the Second Amendment was never for groups like the Lehr und Wehr Verein and the Black Panthers but was always about "frontier" control and white nationalism.[67]

## The International Working People's Association

The escalation of organized labor militancy after 1877 accompanied a leftward shift in labor politics in general, with Albert and Lucy Parsons on the cutting edge of that shift. They became founding members and key organizers of the International Working People's Association (IWPA), or Black International. The IWPA was the first mass anarchist communist organization in the United States, and many key labor organizers in the eight-hour movement were IWPA members. All eight Haymarket defendants were IWPA members. Organizers intended the IWPA to be a branch of the Anarchist International founded at the London Congress in 1881, which was an attempt by working-class radicals and political refugees to rebuild the defunct International Workingmen's Association along anarchist lines. The international never coalesced, so the IWPA stood as its own independent organization. Albert and Lucy Parsons attended the founding congress of the organization at a secret location near Pittsburgh in 1883. Out of this congress came the document the "Pittsburgh Manifesto" outlining the organization's platform. The principal authors of the manifesto were Albert Parsons, his comrade August Spies, and the newly arrived famous anarchist refugee Johann Most, who had recently been released from London's Clerkenwell House of Detention.[68]

The German Johann Most was banned from nearly every country in Europe for his incendiary propaganda. He spent a year and a half in Clerkenwell as punishment for an article he wrote in his newspaper *Freiheit* in which he praised the *Narodnaya Volya* (People's Will) for assassinating Czar Alexander II of Russia. He stepped off of the steamship *Wisconsin* in New York City on a frozen morning in December 1882 to a scene of some forty German socialist men waiting to welcome him, each wearing a scarlet ribbon on his lapel, one holding a red flag, and a throng of reporters, pencils and notepads in hand, eagerly waiting to bombard him with questions. He gave them all the show they wanted. With the enthusiasm of a religious zealot, he announced, "I shall, in this city and around this country, denounce the persecution of socialists and spread the truth of socialism. . . . I'm more radical than ever. . . . Violence is justified against tyranny and tyrants. If society must be organized, communism is the way."[69]

Prior to 1877, characters like Johann Most were shunned by the US labor movement, shunned by leaders such as Albert Parsons, but in this new era in which naked capitalist violence flowed down the social hierarchy in abundance, in which major media outlets openly called for state agents to mercilessly slaughter strikers en masse, Most's message of sending that violence back up the social hierarchy now easily found sympathetic ears. Albert Parsons, who, five years earlier, called on workers to vote instead of strike, was now working alongside Europe's most infamous propagandist of revolutionary violence drafting a platform for an anarchist communist organization.

By 1886, the IWPA grew to five thousand members in the United States, three times the size of the Socialistic Labor Party.[70] The influence of Johann Most notwithstanding, in practice, the IWPA concentrated on labor organizing rather than revolutionary violence, though it did not shun the latter. Through mass working-class organizing in the labor movement, the anarchists had an influence far greater than their numbers. Historian Alan Dawley writes that Chicago anarchists of the IWPA organized cigarmakers, cabinetmakers, and metalworkers, among others, into unions and brought those unions into a new Chicago Central Labor Union, which overshadowed the more politically moderate Amalgamated Trades and Labor Assembly. "They believed in unionism as both the means to the future socialist society and the living example of what a truly cooperative commonwealth would be like. In this they anticipated syndicalist philosophy and the revolutionary unionism of the Industrial Workers of the World."[71]

The IWPA's six stated objectives, as outlined in its Pittsburgh Manifesto, were

First: —Destruction of the existing class rule, by all means, i.e., by energetic, relentless, revolutionary and international action.
Second: —Establishment of a free society based upon co-operative organization of production.
Third: —Free exchange of equivalent products by and between the productive organizations without commerce and profit mongering.
Fourth: —Organization of education on a secular, scientific and equal basis for both sexes.
Fifth: —Equal rights for all without distinction to sex or race.
Sixth: —Regulation of all public affairs by free contracts between the autonomous (independent) communes and associations, resting on a federalistic basis.[72]

Though the IWPA faded away in the 1890s, anarchism exerted a powerful influence in the US labor movement for decades. Historian Kenyon Zimmer writes, "Anarchism would be the dominant radical ideology among Jewish immigrants until the mid-1890s, among ethnic Russian and Asian immigrants until the 1920s, and among Spanish, Mexican, and Italian immigrants into the 1930s."[73]

The radical labor movement in the United States was not unique in its anarchist influence but was aligned with a larger global trend in revolutionary

136    CHAPTER 5

left politics. In *Under Three Flags*, Benedict Anderson observes that, from the early 1880s until the rise of the Soviet Union, anarchism "was the dominant element in the self-consciously internationalist radical Left."[74] The anarchist shift in the United States was part of a larger global movement—or loose network of movements—from below in response to the colossal intertwined forces of global capital and colonialism.

Albert Parsons became an editor for the IWPA's main English-language organ *The Alarm*: a lively newspaper in which appeared some of the most incendiary articles to emerge from the labor movement in the United States before or since. *The Alarm* was not an ordinary labor newspaper, it was a subaltern war cry against the United States and "Christian civilization" itself. As both a labor and a socialist newspaper, it was unique for its time in that it had its finger on the pulse of the discontent of the era to a degree most English-language labor and even anarchist papers did not, making bold, caustic assaults on US institutions in ways that linked capitalist exploitation with colonialism, white supremacy, and empire.

In one editorial, Albert Parsons railed against the commissioner of the US Office of Indian Affairs Hiram Price. Price (1814–1901) was part of the wave of white settlers who displaced the Sauk, Meskwaki, Ho-Chunk, and Dakota peoples from the Louisiana Purchase territory of Iowa in the 1830s–1850s. He settled in Iowa two years before the federal government granted it statehood and quickly rose to become one of Iowa's leading capitalists. He served as president of the State Bank of Iowa and then as president of the First National Bank of Davenport. He was elected on the Republican ticket to the US House of Representatives and served in Congress on the Committee on Pacific Railroads until the end of his term in 1869, after which railroad industry magnates rewarded him for serving their interests by making him president of the Davenport and St. Paul Railroad Company. Price exemplified the anarchists' contention that lawmakers do not merely serve the interests of the capitalists but that lawmakers *are* the capitalists: that business leaders and government leaders are all part of the same ruling class. As Marx and Engels wrote in their 1848 *Manifesto*, "The executive of the modern State is but a committee for managing the common affairs of the whole bourgeoisie."[75] After a term as Davenport and St. Paul president, Price returned to serve two more terms in the US Congress. He was then appointed by US President James A. Garfield to serve as commissioner of Indian Affairs from 1881 to 1885, during which time he laid the groundwork for the 1887 Dawes Act, of which he was an active supporter.[76]

Price saw the Dawes Act as a way to quell Indigenous resistance, "giving these simple people pruning hooks instead of spears, and plowshares instead of swords."[77] He viewed Indigenous people as dangerous alcoholics with a "savage taste for scalping enemies" and other "evil tendencies."[78] While Price did not agree with the aphorism, popularly attributed to General Sheridan, that "the only good Indian is a dead Indian," he told his fellow reformers, "a dead Indian is less dangerous to the community than a drunken Indian, and might therefore be preferred. A drunken white man is a curse to himself, his family, and community, but a drunken Indian, in addition to all these, is an intensified condensation of savage brutality."[79]

Such was the rhetoric of the Fifth Annual Lake Mohonk Conference. From 1883 to 1916, white humanitarian reformers and government agents who considered themselves "friends of the Indian" met annually at the beautiful Mohonk Mountain House resort on the shore of Lake Mohonk, New York, to solve the "Indian problem." Conference participants included liberal organizations such as the Indian Rights Association in Philadelphia, the Women's National Indian Association (also in Philadelphia), the Boston Indian Citizenship Committee, the Board of Indian Commissioners, Quakers, Unitarians, and wealthy philanthropists who funded the fashionable white liberal cause of Indian assimilation.[80]

At the 1884 Lake Mohonk Conference, famed ethnologist Alice Fletcher argued against Massachusetts Senator Henry Dawes over the "Coke Bill," which called for communal tribal title, rather than individual allotment, of Indian reservation lands. Fletcher, of Harvard's prestigious Peabody Museum and the abusive Carlisle Indian Boarding School, argued that communal title to land by Native nations was wrong on principle and that "The only way out for the Indian is right out into our civilization."[81] Fletcher impressed Dawes so much that he brought her on to help him write and implement the Dawes Act three years later. At that same 1884 conference, the progressive reformers passed several resolutions, including "That the organization of the Indians in tribes is, and has been, one of the most serious hindrances to the advancement of the Indian toward civilization, and that every effort should be made to secure the disintegration of all tribal organizations; that to accomplish this result the Government should . . . cease to recognize the Indians as political bodies or organized tribes," that "our conviction has been strengthened as to the importance of taking Indian youth from the reservations to be trained in industrial schools placed among communities of white citizens," and that the law should treat Indians as individual US citizens rather than members of sovereign Indigenous nations.[82]

Price, like the other "enlightened" reformers of the Mohonk Conference, saw the role of the state being to whiten Indians by civilizing the Indianness out of them, by providing Indians with the resources to live according to the economy and religion of the white man. Price lectured his fellow reformers, including the philanthropists with the checkbooks, "To civilize and Christianize wild savages is not the work of a day, but of a lifetime. It requires time, patience, courage, labor, and money."[83] Indians were "wards of the nation," in "the transition state" from "the gloom of barbarism to the light of civilization."[84] The goal

138    CHAPTER 5

of these reformers was to assist in the process of making Indians cease to be Indians, to become US Americans: in short, genocide by assimilation, inasmuch as genocide is about erasing the existence of a people as a people. Absent from discussions at Lake Mohonk were any sentiments about respecting Indigenous nationhood. These enlightened reformers and liberal Christians agreed with the most hardline conservatives that the existence of Indigenous nations stood in the way of US civilization but differed in offering assimilation as a humane alternative to extermination.

Albert Parsons saw both solutions to the so-called "Indian problem" as monstrous injustice. Commissioner Hiram Price's 1884 report to the US Secretary of the Interior called for, among other things, an increase in federal funding for police and courts overseeing Native groups, a larger appropriation for individual farm allotments to break up communally held tribal land, more support to Indian boarding schools, stricter measures to stop the sale of firearms to Native people—again showing who exactly the Second Amendment applied to—and a pay raise for US Indian agents. Price cheerfully reported that, under his leadership, programs aimed at "civilizing" the Indians were working:

> More Indians are living in houses and fewer in tepees than there were one year ago. More are cultivating the soil and fewer following the chase than when I made my last annual report. There are more in the carpenter, blacksmith, and other mechanical shops, trying to earn an honest living, and fewer at the war dance, scalp dance, and sun dance than in October, 1883. There are also several hundred more Indian children in industrial, agricultural, and mechanical schools fitting themselves to become useful, intelligent citizens, than there were twelve months since. During the same period many Indians . . . are making praiseworthy efforts to take their places among the independent agriculturalists of the country. Taken altogether . . . it is fair to presume that, with the aid of such industrial, agricultural, and mechanical schools as are now being carried on, the Indian will be able to care for himself, and be no longer a burden but a help to the Government.[85]

Parsons scoffed at such talk.

In *The Alarm*, he wrote a seething response to Commissioner Price's report. "What a commentary the above report is upon our boasted civilization. What a jargon of meaningless assertions." *Civilization*, argued Parsons, was nothing more than a white euphemism for extermination. The Indian was being "'civilized' out of existence and exterminated from the continent by the demon of 'personal property.'" Indigenous North Americans "were betrayed, then kidnapped and sold into slavery by the early settlers of the Atlantic coast." Parsons called Manifest Destiny "the surveyor's chain reaching ocean to ocean." With this chain, and the weapon of law in the hands of white settlers, Indigenous peoples were "driven from the soil, disinherited, robbed and murdered by the piracy of capitalism." Sardonically playing on the kind of language that abounded at Lake Mohonk conferences, Parsons wrote that dispossessed Native peoples were now left to become "the 'national wards' of their profit-mongering civilizers."[86]

For Parsons, the savages of the story were the white settlers—which included his own ancestors—with their notions of private property. "Under the Aegis of 'mine and thine,' barbarism became so cruelly refined that man prospers best and only when he exterminates his fellow man." Indigenous peoples, as Parsons saw the situation, were rightly involved in "a ceaseless struggle of more than three centuries" against the colonizers' system of private property. There was no "Indian problem," there was a white property problem. The program of turning communal tribal lands into private allotments was designed to subject and dispossess an insurgent population, since the "personal ownership" touted by progressive so-called "friends of the Indian," wrote Parsons, "requires masters and slaves." At the time Parsons wrote that, the state was intensely, unambiguously engaged in the genocidal project of containing, expelling, exterminating, and assimilating Indigenous peoples. The fact that many Indigenous peoples did not vanish is not because the state and other white settler forces were not intent on making it so, but because Indigenous peoples resisted genocide and continue to resist.[87]

While the IWPA—made up overwhelmingly of urban working-class European refugees and migrants—was not directly involved with Indigenous resistance, IWPA members followed the news of Indigenous struggle intently and publicly expressed sympathy with Indigenous struggle and support for Indigenous autonomy. For example, when the Métis people rose up in armed rebellion to defend their and other Indigenous groups' autonomy and land rights, declaring independence from the British Empire in early 1885, the anarchists put *The Alarm* to work raising public sympathy for the Métis cause: "They [the Métis] are struggling to retain their homes, of which the statute laws and the chicanery of modern capitalism seeks to dispossess them. May their trusted rifles and steady aim make the robbers bite the dust."[88] Such rhetoric in the pages of *The Alarm* certainly did not challenge the US ruling establishment's conflation of anarchists with insurgent Indigenous groups.

By November of that year, with the aid of the previously-mentioned US American Gatling gun specialist and professional Indian killer Arthur "Gat" Howard, the Canadian state mercilessly drowned the Métis Rebellion in blood.[89] Canadian officials hanged Métis leader Louis Riel. The IWPA held a memorial meeting in Chicago to honor Riel. IWPA organizers, including Albert Parsons, Samuel Fielden, and August Spies, praised Riel, characterizing him as a man of their ilk, a revolutionary, "a martyr to human freedom," slain by the "social order."[90] As previously mentioned, Europe's leading criminologist Cesare Lombroso would agree that they were of the same ilk, classifying Riel, Paris com-

140    CHAPTER 5

munards, and anarchists as the same "criminal type."[91] Two years later, Parsons and Spies met the same fate as Riel, hanged by the state and memorialized as martyrs by revolutionary leftists.

The connections between the Chicago anarchists and Riel did not end there. After Riel's execution, Riel's secretary, William Henry Jackson—a white man who joined the Métis cause and changed his name to the Métis designation Honoré Joseph Jaxon—escaped his Canadian captors and fled to the United States on foot, where he eventually found his way to the anarchist movement in Chicago. Jaxon coordinated a successful carpenter's strike for the eight-hour day in 1886, using guerilla tactics, which he adapted from the Métis struggle, against scabs. The main obstruction to the success of the strike was that there were several "ten-hour scabs" who continued to work for smaller contractors around the city and undermine the strike. Plainclothes detectives posing as workers attended union meetings and fed information to police to ensure the scabs were well protected from any union action against them. Jaxon neutralized the police and scabs by having union leaders give out false information at union meetings to misdirect police to the wrong worksites and then deployed small squads to multiple worksites in different parts of the city to simultaneously attack scabs—with fists and slingshots, not guns—in short hit-and-run assaults. Jaxon's committee coordinated these attacks irregularly in quick, simultaneous bursts in different locations so the police were unable to react fast enough to stop them. After six weeks of this, the smaller contractors, no longer able to effectively use scabs, acceded to the carpenters' eight-hour demand.[92]

Historian Steven Sapolsky writes that, after the success of that strike, "union-sponsored organized violence became common in Chicago. This was the legacy of the Riel Rebellion for the Chicago labor movement: Long after its goals were forgotten, its 'shotgun policy' lived on."[93] Jaxon also became involved with the cause of the Haymarket defense, concerned that the Haymarket defendants would end up like Riel. He visited the Haymarket defendants in jail and tried to convince Albert Parsons to beg the state for clemency. Parsons maintained that he was innocent of the charges and therefore should not have to beg the state for anything. Jaxon told Parsons, "It is better to live and continue to fight for freedom than it is to die before you are free."[94] Having seen so many of his Métis friends killed by the state, Jaxon did not want his new anarchist friends to likewise become martyrs.[95]

## A Christmas Story

Of all the anarchists who wrote articles for *The Alarm*, it was Lucy Parsons who held the distinction of launching the most provocative attacks on the white man's "civilization." In the Christmas 1885 issue, she told a sardonic tale, "A

Republicans and Anarchists    141

Christmas Story," that began with a civilized Christian missionary shipwrecked on a "barbarous isle." The Indigenous heathens of the isle helped the missionary in his time of distress, and, in return for their kindness, the missionary proposed "to carry a few of them back with him to his own country that he may show them the benefits of a Christian civilization in order that the benighted barbarian may return to his own country and become a missionary in the cause of Christian civilization and good government." And so, a group of the heathens traveled across the mighty ocean with their new white savior to become civilized and then returned to the isle as missionaries themselves to save the rest of their people. Throughout the story, Lucy Parsons used tongue-in-cheek language to mock the kinds of sentiments expressed by liberal "friends of the Indian" at their Lake Mohonk Conferences.[96]

Upon returning, the new missionaries gathered their people to tell them of their experience visiting Christian civilization. The missionaries told them of a great continent "where nature seemed to always smile." There were beautiful seabirds called steamships and horses of steel called locomotives that could cross over the entire continent, even over mountains, without ever tiring: time and space annihilated under the onward strides of steam power. There were enormous structures, magnificent cities in which people in the costliest raiment traveled about with ease through avenues of wealth and marts of trade: "they were in fact the sole possessors of the earth and all it contained and lived but to enjoy. In our admiration we exclaimed, 'Mighty is the Christian Civilization! Great is their government!'" Upon hearing this fantastic description, the heathens in the audience shouted, "Let's emigrate."[97]

"Hold on, comrades, hear us through," said the missionaries. They continued telling of the great sights they saw of Christian civilization's arts, sciences, and industry, of marble halls and banquet boards, of lovely women wearing precious jewels, whose "fair faces fairly beamed with contentment, ease and happiness." Parsons possibly had Chicago's Board of Trade or Citizens' Association events in mind as she wrote the description. "Mighty is the Christian Civilization," replied the audience. The civilized people held a banquet in which they drank sparkling wine and made toasts: "Happy, contented and prosperous are our people under the benign influence of a wisely managed and Christian Government." The scene was abruptly disturbed by an apparition. "That apparition was the wretchedest of women. And from her cavernous eyes, pale flashes seemed to rise, as when the northern skies gleamed in December. And like the water's flow under December snow came a dull voice of woe from the heart's chamber":

'Ladies and gentlemen, Christian people,' said she, 'while at your banqueting board will you hear the prayer of the widow, the cry of the orphan? Without, the blinding snow falls thick and fast. Three months ago this day I, for the fifth time, became a mother, and on that very day I was made a widow and they were orphaned by my poor husband being crushed to a shapeless mass among the machinery in that man's factory (pointing to the proposer of the last toast) and I swear to you that twice these twelve hours past we have been without a morsel of food or a bit of fuel, and I am afraid to return to my wretched hovel for fear they have already perished from cold and hunger. Oh! In God's name hear their cries if not mine!'

Then emerged "an officious person all done up in a large blue coat with brass buttons"—a policeman—to silence the woman. "Didn't the Christians say anything?" the audience asked the missionaries. This fictional poor woman was based on reality. Many children of Chicago's poor did perish from cold and hunger in winter, and workers did indeed die in factories full of dangerous machinery with few safety regulations.[98]

From at least as early as the late 1870s, Lucy Parsons exhibited a special disdain for Chicago's class of wealthy white women who had servants, poor women, doing all the housework and childcare. So much of the dehumanization and unreasonable demands that domestic workers dealt with came from the "mistress of the house." Parsons characterized such privileged women as cruel and oblivious to the realities working women faced.[99] That disdain came out in Parsons's description of the Christian ladies' responses to the plea of the poor widow: "Pshaw! Such management, as to let such a creature make her way into the banqueting hall, and especially when strangers are present." Another lady, "of very matronly appearance," complained, "Oh! Did you hear the language she used about becoming a mother? Just as though we care how many brats she had or when they were born."[100] Lucy Parsons, herself an economically insecure mother by this point, with a husband who was blacklisted, was well acquainted with the callousness the wealthy white progressive ladies of Chicago displayed for economically insecure mothers and their children.

To come up with the words for the Christian gentlemen's responses to the poor widow, Lucy Parsons, a sharp-witted political satirist, pulled language straight from the editorial pages of the *Chicago Tribune*. One gentleman said, "Those fancied grievances from the improvident lower classes, in venting their supposed wrongs and annoying decent people, is becoming altogether too frequent. We must have the military well practiced in 'street riot drill,' and equipped so as to be ready to quell the first manifestation of an attempt on their part to force a recognition of the 'justness' of 'righting their alleged wrongs.'" To make it obvious that those cruel words against the widow came from the *Chicago Tribune*, the next gentleman responded, "Yes, yes, you are right. We have been reading the *Tribune*'s appeal to businessmen after the Thanksgiving Day street riot drill, and I have myself been soliciting contributions from among the propertied classes, with no small success."[101]

Republicans and Anarchists  143

With the widow removed, the evening returned to its pleasant atmosphere, and the people resumed their praises of the "prosperity and hospitality of a Christian people." Upon leaving from that event, the heathens learning to become civilized saw more of the "brass-buttoned fellows" arresting young women, sex workers, for soliciting on the street. The young women plead with the officers not to arrest them as they were in a desperate situation: one woman's aged mother was without "food or fuel," another said that her landlord served notice that he would evict her and her children if she does not pay rent by tomorrow. The heathens turned to their would-be guide for some explanation of the meaning of this, and he informed them that in Christian countries we turn such immoral nuisances over to the authorities to be dealt with. "In fact, that is mainly why we have our government for, the taking charge of the lower classes."[102]

The hypocrisy of respectable US society criminalizing and vilifying sex workers was a common theme for anarchist women writers and orators in the era. Anarchist women knew that more working-class women than society cared to admit at some point relied on sex work to make ends meet, and that more well-heeled Christian gentlemen than society cared to admit solicited sex workers. Emma Goldman wrote that "our industrial system leaves most women no alternative except prostitution."[103] The Philadelphia anarchist writer and orator Voltairine de Cleyre wrote that "Women considering themselves very pure and moral, will sneer at the street-walker, yet admit to their homes the very men who victimized the street-walker."[104] Lucy Parsons saw it as deeply evil to criminalize a poor woman for sex work, to brand her "immoral" and "impure," while the landlord who evicts her and her children in the middle of winter is considered a law-abiding, upright citizen in the eyes of both the church and the state.

Lucy Parsons also used this story to criticize the hypocrisy of the Church. The missionaries continued their description of Christian civilization to the heathens of the isle:

> When the Sabbath bells pealed out calling these Christians to their gorgeous temples to worship their gods, we, too, were escorted to one of them, and introduced to the minister in charge as some "heathen who had been induced to come among us to learn the habits of a God-fearing people, that they might learn the ways of the Christian, in order that they might return to their own land and become missionaries." The minister very sanctimoniously declared that "we are faithful followers of the meek and lowly Jesus, who had nowhere to lay his head," then mounted his gorgeous pulpit and took for his text words to this effect: "That it was as difficult for a rich man to enter the kingdom of heaven as for a camel to go through the eye of a needle, unless they were very generous to the poor," and when the contribution box was passed around it was very generously remembered.

The way the guide spoke about the heathens to the minister was quite similar to how progressive "friends of the Indian," such as ministers, reformers, and Indian boarding school proponents spoke about the Native people in their programs.[105]

After a few weeks in Christian civilization, the heathens explored the city to find a new sight: monstrous buildings from which emerged masses of worn-out, shabbily dressed, stressed, unhealthy-looking people hurrying to and fro as though their lives depended on it. In this "struggling mass of hurrying humanity we could see little children of tender age looking as over-worked as those more mature in years." As the heathens tried to figure out why these people looked "so different from those whom we had seen at church and at the banquet," their guide signaled to them not to think too much on it. Those people were "only the working class; the lower element in our society." The heathens were confused. If those were the working people, then are they the ones who built these magnificent buildings? Yes, the guide answered them, but we "superintend" them. So, if these workers built all of this, then surely they own all of this, reasoned the heathens. The guide tried to explain: "Well, you see, it is very difficult for the heathen to understand the political economy of a Christian civilization." He explained the wage system to them, and what a blessing the wage system was to these workers, "for if they were not so employed by us they could not obtain the comforts of life they now enjoy." This further confused the heathens, as it did not seem that the workers enjoyed any comforts of life. They asked their guide, Are these workers satisfied with this arrangement? They submit to this? "No," he answered, "not always," but, when necessary, "we deal with them summarily." An answer that helped the heathens understand why there were so many of those men wearing the blue coats with brass buttons around.[106]

At this point, the audience on the isle hearing this story asked, "What do you think of the Christian government and their boasted civilization?" Here Lucy Parsons wrote with her characteristically blunt anarchist voice: their government "is simply organized fraud and oppression." If the people really are so content with this system, then why do they need police everywhere to maintain it? In their religion "they are hypocrites." In their "economical or industrial system they are robbers, fleecing old and young alike, and under the shadow of their altars they keep great engines of destruction that they may send their enemies to hell wholesale." One of the heathens made a proposal: "I move that we send missionaries among them at once, not to teach them how to die, but how to live; not to be soul-savers but body-savers. Teach them how not to make criminals of the people by overwork and poverty that their ministers may have a job praying them out of hell!" Another heathen seconded the motion. "Send missionaries at once!"[107]

Like the anarchist Ricardo Flores Magón, with his previously mentioned denunciations of "white-skinned savages" and the "North American Plutocracy," and like Albert Parsons, with his denunciations of the Anglo-settlers of North America, Lucy Parsons used the anarchist press to turn the discourse of "civilization versus savagery" on its head.[108] If anyone was a savage who needed to be exterminated or saved, it was the wealthy white property owner. In an editorial, "Our Civilization: Is it Worth Saving?," she asked the working class, "When will you tire of such a civilization and declare in words, the bitterness of which shall not be mistaken, 'Away with a civilization that thus degrades me; it is not worth the saving?'"[109] In her "Christmas Story," her heathens decided to send missionaries to save the Christians from civilization, but, in reality, she preferred a more militant approach to the "white property problem."[110]

## Subverting Ruling Class Narratives

US industrial centers were sites of open class war waged by the rich against the poor. In Lucy Parsons's reasoning, if the owners of industry were going to answer our demands for bread by feeding us a diet of lead, then we will answer in kind. If they can have their *New York Tribune* and *Chicago Tribune*, then we the workers will have our *Alarm* and *Arbeiter-Zeitung*. If they can have their Citizen's Associations, police, army units, and vigilante squads, then we will have our IWPA, unions, and workers' militias. If the rich man's soldiers can shoot us and stab us with their bayonets—as they did to quarry workers on strike on May 4, 1885—then we can "lay in wait on the steps of the palaces of the rich and stab or shoot their owners as they come out."[111] If they can unleash their Gatling guns and artillery pieces on us, then we will unleash our dynamite and homemade explosives on them. If, in the words of the *Chicago Tribune*, "The world owes these classes rather extermination than a livelihood," and the world "will be better off in the degree that such wretches cease to exist," then, responded Lucy Parsons, let us so-called wretches "kill them without mercy, and let it be a war of extermination and without pity." An anarchist but still a reconstructionist at heart formed in the war against the Confederacy, she added, "Let us devastate the avenues where the wealthy live as Sheridan devastated the beautiful valley of the Shenandoah."[112]

The class-war rhetoric, from above and below, distanced the anarchist movement from the safety of whiteness. Lucy Parsons often gave conflicting and false information about her racial and ethnic background, but she was quite happy to be distanced from whiteness and civilization. To a Chicago *Inter-Ocean* reporter who assumed from her appearance that she had one-eighth white ancestry—a paper that previously vilified her as "a very determined looking negress," her children as "anarchist sucklings," and her husband as "dynamite-eating Parsons"—she proudly said, "there is not a drop of Caucasian blood in my veins."[113] In respectable white society's discourse of civilization versus savagery, she publicly aligned

146    CHAPTER 5

herself always with the "savages" resisting colonization: "When the conquering hosts of Cortez moved upon Mexico, my mother's ancestors were there to repel the invader; so that I represent the genuine American."[114] Although Lucy Parsons changed the presentation of her racial and ethnic identity according to her situation, it was always an anticolonial identity. Similarly, the IWPA anarchist August Spies introduced himself to the US American public with the words

> "Barbarians, savages, illiterate, ignorant anarchists from Central Europe, men who cannot comprehend the spirit of our free American institutions,"—of these I am one.[115]

As Lauren Basson observes, "Parsons and other anarchists generally adapted conventional discourses to serve very different purposes from those for which they were originally intended."[116] This certainly was the case with the anarchists' subversion of the discourse of civilization versus savagery.

The US workingmen's movement's orientation changed significantly after the battles of 1877. This new working *people's* movement leadership called for nothing short of social revolution, and, to the dismay of moderate workingmen's movement leaders such as Terrence Powderly, the anarchists were increasingly popular. The IWPA leaders of Chicago would regularly hold lakefront meetings on the shore of Lake Michigan on Sunday afternoons as an anarchist alternative to church, during which IWPA organizers gave speeches railing against US institutions and the very foundations of the United States political and economic system. Lucy and Albert Parsons were regular crowd favorites. Despite the constant negative coverage in the capitalist press, which vilified, racialized, and animalized the anarchists, crowds of one to five thousand people regularly showed up at the Sunday afternoon gatherings.[117] Chicago resident Mary Harris Jones, who would later become known as Mother Jones, was not an anarchist but regularly attended the lakefront meetings. She remembered of the period that "From then on the people of Chicago seemed incapable of discussing a purely economic question without getting excited about anarchism."[118]

Jones, who would later become an influential labor organizer and agitator in her own right, thought the anarchists were over the top, but she recognized how skilled they were as organizers, orators, and propagandists in channeling the working-class discontent of the era. She remembered Christmas day, 1885, when the anarchists led a procession of "hundreds of poverty stricken people in rags and tatters, in thin clothes, in wretched shoes" along "fashionable Prairie Avenue before the mansions of the rich, before their employers, carrying the black flag." Jones "thought the parade an insane move on the part of the anarchists, as it only served to make feeling more bitter." The idea as the anarchists saw it was that if poor people, because of poverty, were unable to have a pleasant Christmas day, their bosses should not be able to have a pleasant Christmas day either.[119]

Republicans and Anarchists    147

Jones thought such actions would lead only to more state repression against the working class. She was not wrong but, for the anarchists, bringing social contradictions to the fore of public consciousness required confrontation. Otherwise, it was too easy for the privileged to ignore poverty and injustice. It was the classic point of tension on the left, which continues into the present day, of the politics of respectability versus the politics of disruption and confrontation. Mother Jones herself, as much as she disagreed with the anarchists' approach, would later in life employ confrontational, militant, and impolite tactics in the labor struggle. She absorbed some of the spirit of those lakefront Sundays. Despite her distaste for the anarchists, she recognized that the discontent they channeled was valid, the social and political injustices they railed against were real, and that class war existed: "The working people on one side—hungry, cold, jobless, fighting gunmen and police clubs with bare hands. On the other side the employers, knowing neither hunger nor cold, supported by newspapers, by the police, by all the power of the great state itself."[120] For poor people in such a situation, the anarchists' arguments did not require much convincing. Poverty and the policeman's club likely did more to radicalize people than *The Alarm*. What the IWPA and *The Alarm* did was tap into, amplify, and channel the subaltern suffering and discontent that already existed.

With anarchism becoming a major force in the labor movement, the specter of the Paris Commune, which was a staple of bourgeois invectives against the 1877 strikes, became a common point of comparison the US press employed to contextualize anarchists in the following decades. Papers often compared Lucy Parsons to Louise Michel of the Communards. For example, the *Inter-Ocean* began a story on Parsons with the sentence "Anarchists in Paris have a Louise Michel; anarchists in Chicago their Lucy Parsons."[121] Though the press compared Parsons to Michel as a way to sensationalize and demonize her as a threat to US institutions, Parsons took the frequent comparison as a badge of honor. "A strong character like Louise Michel," wrote Parsons, "looms up like a pillar of light or a star of hope, and the wary reformer sees it and takes fresh courage to struggle on in the surging ocean of humanity."[122] Ruling-class men such as John Hay saw Louise Michel as a "crazy creature" who threatened the institutions on which civilization rested, and Lucy Parsons was delighted to be perceived as a woman of the same caliber.[123]

## Conclusion: "Refinement! Civilization!"

Ironically, John Hay and Albert Parsons had more in common than either man likely realized. Both staked their claims to Americanness on a frontier and colonial past. Hay was "Born the son of a frontier doctor in a small dwelling on the edge of the Western wilderness."[124] Parsons grew up "on a range" on the

"Texas frontier, while the buffalo, antelope, and Indian were in that region" and then "in the valley of the Brazos River," where, wrote Parsons, "My frontier life had accustomed me to the use of the rifle and the pistol, to hunting and riding, and in these matters I was considered quite an expert."[125] Both claimed ancestral connections to heroes of the US American Revolution. Hay boasted of one ancestor named John who as a child was "patted on the head by General Washington" and another named Adam who "probably did his fair share of Indian fighting."[126] Parsons boasted of an ancestor who served "with Gen. George Washington at the battles of Brandywine, Monmouth, and Valley Forge," an ancestor who "was an officer in the Revolution of 1776," and another who "was wounded at the battle of Bunker Hill."[127] Both Hay and Parsons were committed Republicans during Reconstruction, and both were outspoken proponents of Black political enfranchisement during that period.

As the state abandoned the project of Reconstruction, the two men's paths diverged substantially. When the Republican Party abandoned Reconstruction, Parsons held on, zealously, to the spirit of Reconstruction and its promise of social equality, while Hay took the more politically expedient route of staying within the mainstream of respectable white society. Even in this divergence, however, they mirrored each other. Both men stood out as leaders among their peers. Both became newspaper editors and editorialists, driven to write forcefully about the most politically charged issues of the day: Hay from above and Parsons from below. Both men experienced 1877 as a turning point in US labor and management relations. Both described 1877 as a disillusioning experience, changing their ideas of the nature of US industrial society and the role of the state. Both men, in the aftermath of 1877, became associated with militias: Hay an explicitly capitalist militia composed of and for the urban bourgeoisie, and Parsons an explicitly socialist militia composed of and for the urban proletariat.

Prior to their divergence, both men were well connected with and part of the ownership class, Hay in the North and Parsons in the South. Parsons, had he taken the path of least resistance and remained within the mainstream of bourgeois white society, could well have ended up a successful property owner, major newspaper owner and editor, or successful businessman in Texas like his brothers—or even could have become a successful Republican politician in Illinois. He came close at least twice to defeating establishment candidates in Chicago and did so running on a third-party ticket. Had he decided to remain a figure in Republican politics instead of going the Workingmen's Party route, it is conceivable that he could have been quite successful as a politician. Perhaps he even could have ended up as one of the well-dressed men participating in Chicago Board of Trade and Citizens' Association banquets discussing the most efficient methods of managing the lower classes.

Parsons's life demonstrates that, for white settlers, commitment to the intertwined systems of white supremacy, capitalism, and colonialism was a choice, and that people could choose other paths. His life also demonstrates the limits of such choices. That white society ostracized, targeted with vigilante violence, blacklisted, surveilled, imprisoned, and ultimately hanged Parsons shows the lengths—both legal and extralegal—to which dominant US institutions and white society would go to enforce white allegiance to US structures of inequality. Parsons was able to escape the Klansman's noose, but the policeman, prosecutor, judge, and executioner succeeded where the Klansman failed. In Abraham Lincoln's mass execution of Dakota freedom fighters, in the Texas white vigilantes' lynchings, and in the Haymarket executions, civilization was not represented by heroic Perseus slaying monsters, or by marble statues of Caesar, but by the hangman's noose. From cell 29 of what Albert Parsons called "Cook County Bastille," he sent a small wooden tugboat he whittled to his comrade Justus Schwab—whose Lower East Side saloon served as a popular social center for New York City anarchists—to raffle for the benefit of Parsons's wife and children. "Also," wrote Parsons,

> I send you a hangman's noose which is emblematic of our capitalistic, Christian civilization. The rope is official—the kind which it is proposed to strangle myself and comrades with. The knot was tied by myself, and is the regulation style. I give it to you as a memento of our time.[128]

On the morning of his execution, Parsons continued to subvert the discourse of civilization: "Well, my dear old comrade, the fatal hour draws near. Caesar kept me awake till late at night with the noise (music) of hammer and saw, erecting his throne, my scaffold. Refinement! Civilization!" scoffed Parsons, "Magnanimous Caesar! Alas, goodbye! Hail the social revolution! Salutations to all."[129] Anarchists of Chicago, like so many others who found themselves on the wrong side of the US war of "civilization versus savagery," were killed by civilization.

# 6

# The Respectable Mob

Though Illinois Governor John Altgeld later pardoned the remaining Haymarket defendants and denounced the Haymarket trial as a travesty of justice—with great damage to his political career—anticommunist state repression intensified over the following decades. Altgeld's pardon did not give the United States any moment of redemption. On the contrary, the US bourgeoisie and their media organs took the moment to reassert US American values. Major newspapers denounced Altgeld as "un-American," a "foreigner," and an "anarchist" with not "a drop of true American blood in his veins." Historian Paul Avrich wrote that "The pardon made Altgeld for a long time one of the most reviled men in America." Theodore Roosevelt vilified Altgeld as "a friend of the lawless classes." White crowds lynched Altgeld in effigy. Church leaders denounced him in sermons. The respectable ruling-class establishment feverishly worked to reassure the public that hanging the anarchists was the right thing to do and that there was no cause to lose faith in the police or the courts.[1]

Historians should resist the patriotic urge to find happy endings in US history, in which cooler heads prevail, progress marches forth, and justice is eventually realized. Altgeld's pardon was less indicative of the direction US leaders would take than the anti-anarchist reaction to the pardon. Cooler heads did not prevail. Police did not become less violent or less dishonest. Courts did not become less cruel or less unjust in their treatment of the poor. Police, courts, jails, and prisons continued to be wielded by the bourgeoisie as weapons with which to keep the working class in subjection. Repression increased, with episode after episode of state violence against labor. One of many possible instructive examples is San Diego 1912.

From January through late May of 1912, San Diego police and vigilantes collaborated in a violent campaign of repression and terror against the Industrial

Workers of the World. The line between state violence and mob violence blurred as the police and vigilantes worked together to silence radical labor voices and rid San Diego of "undesirables." The police killed IWW members Michael Hoey and Joseph Mikolasek. Other victims were "disappeared" by the mob. The police also killed a baby when they fired a high-power water hose indiscriminately into a crowd at an IWW street meeting.[2] Vigilantes kidnapped and tortured more than three hundred IWW members and sympathizers. In some cases, the police delivered the IWW members they "arrested" directly to the vigilantes rather than jail.

Scholars have, correctly, studied this episode as part of the history of the struggle for free speech and as capitalist repression of the labor movement. It certainly was those things, but it was also much more. This chapter argues three intertwined points: (1) The San Diego Citizen's Committee, which organized the vigilantes, may accurately be referred to as a lynch mob—that "lynching" is the proper term to describe San Diego's 1912 brutality. (2) This terrorism took place not only within the framework of capitalist repression, but also the racist, imperialist, and colonialist framework of the "taming of the Wild West." (3) These scenes of carnivalesque cruelty took the form of gender violence and sexual violence. The mob violence of San Diego, 1912, was not a departure from US American law and order but an expression of it, in defense of the very things that make up the foundations of US politics and culture—capitalism, white supremacy, and imperialism—and all three of these pillars are entwined with patriarchal gender notions.

In 1986, Joan Scott published her classic article "Gender: A Useful Category of Historical Analysis."[3] Scholars have since shown that beyond being a significant category of analysis in and of itself, gender—particularly in modern colonialist-imperialist states—is a category deeply intertwined with capitalism, white supremacy, and imperialism.[4] Indigenous feminist scholars in particular have shown that, under colonialism, state violence and gender violence are often one in the same.[5] San Diego 1912 is one of several striking examples demonstrating that the violence on which capitalism, white supremacy, and imperialism are based can and should be studied as gender violence.

## An Ordinance Prohibiting Public Speaking or Singing

On January 8, 1912, the San Diego City Council passed Ordinance 4623. It was "An Ordinance Prohibiting Public Speaking or Singing within Certain Boundaries."[6] It read, in part, "It shall be unlawful for any person to address any assemblage, meeting or gathering of persons or hold or conduct any public meeting or make or deliver any public speech, lecture or discourse or sing any song or songs, or take part in any public debate or discussion in or upon any public street or alley within that certain district in the city of San Diego."[7] In short, it outlawed street speaking in the most congested section of the city's downtown district. The city council passed it in response to a petition signed by one hundred of San Diego's most prominent property owners, businessmen, and professionals: "Gentlemen: We, the undersigned citizens and property owners, respectfully petition your honorable body to pass certain laws and ordinances to prohibit street speaking (said street speaking being considered by us a nuisance and a detriment to the public welfare of this our city)."[8] These businessmen and property owners were specifically anxiety-ridden about the IWW—who used soapbox oratory, rowdy music, and homespun poetry as tools to educate, organize, and mobilize working-class people.

The IWW—or "Wobblies"—had already faced similar anti–free speech laws in many cities, such as Missoula, Montana, and Spokane, Washington. The IWW had some success in defeating these laws through prolonged campaigns of nonviolent civil disobedience. The main tactic was "jail stuffing." Wobblies defied antispeech ordinances en masse, forcing authorities to arrest them by the hundreds. They overwhelmed the courts and jails, embarrassed city officials, and attracted unwanted attention to the city from progressive reformers and liberal newspapers. Eventually city officials would decide that antispeech ordinances were more trouble than they were worth and that they were helping the IWW's cause more than hindering it. Cities would decide to strike down, or at least cease enforcing, antispeech laws.[9]

San Diego proved to be different. According to the anarchist Emma Goldman—who was violently expelled from the city by vigilantes and police on two separate occasions—San Diego was different "because the city is isolated and consists largely of wealthy real estate people, retired bankers and army men."[10] San Diego's property owners, businessmen, church leaders, retired military officers, and mainstream conservative newspapers were well aware of IWW free-speech victories in other cities, and they were determined that San Diego would not follow suit. The general consensus among the "respectable" men of San Diego was that other cities had been too soft on leftists, too afraid to resort to terrorism—both state terror and extralegal terror. The *San Diego Union* newspaper wrote, "Possibly if the word shall go out that San Diego is not a healthy place for Anarchists their brethren elsewhere will abandon their intention of coming here to defy the law" and "Let us make it so hot a place that there will be no room on our streets for an anarchist; no place for a red flag."[11]

The first day Ordinance 4623 went into effect, February 8, 1912, the police arrested forty-one Wobblies for street speaking. The Wobblies, many of whom were veterans of free-speech battles in other cities, were well prepared for the arrests. They brought in Wobblies from all over the US West as reinforcements.

The Respectable Mob     153

No matter how many street speakers the police arrested, the Wobblies always had more to step up and take their place. On February 13, the San Diego City Council passed a "move-on" ordinance that gave police the right to break up any IWW assembly in any part of the city, which was to go into effect on March 28. The police broke up meetings and shut down IWW meeting places. Still, the IWW continued to agitate. The jails were so full that the city had to start sending Wobblies to jails in other cities. So many Wobblies defied the speech ordinance that the city hired and deputized civilians and Pinkerton Guards to reinforce the police. Some city officials and leading citizens appealed to the US Justice Department for federal help in defeating the IWW.[12]

Most odious, San Diego's privileged class formed a citizen's committee, which was a lynch mob that operated with the full support and cooperation of Police Superintendent John Sehon and Police Chief Keno Wilson. Chief Wilson was known to the public as a hardy, no-nonsense, "Old West" horseback lawman who, when a young man, sold a horse to William "Buffalo Bill" Cody himself. He cultivated a reputation for being the type of man who was "taming" the "Wild West."[13] The police and the citizen's committee worked together, inside and outside the law, toward the same goal of "restoring order," that order being capitalism, white supremacy, and patriarchy—all of which they perceived as threatened by the presence of what they called the "Industrial Anarchists of the World."[14]

## Lynching and the Status Quo

The vigilante San Diego Citizen's Committee leaders publicly warned that any Wobblies or sympathizers heading into San Diego to support the free-speech fight would "be met by 'Judge Lynch.'"[15] *The Call* wrote, "No attempt is made to conceal the fact that lynchings will follow."[16] Lynching is rarely the random lashing out of isolated groups of alienated people. Lynch mobs in the early-twentieth-century United States were usually organized by the most enfranchised members of the community. Rather than being a departure from law, order, and social control, in practice, lynching was a weapon of a certain type of social order. Black radical sociologist Oliver Cromwell Cox's classic 1945 article "Lynching and the Status Quo" still stands as the most insightful and useful exposition on lynching.[17]

Cox challenges the notion of lynching as merely the spontaneous, passionate violence of an angry crowd. He argued that lynching is a *social institution* that serves racial, national, political, and class interests. He saw lynching as a weapon not only of white supremacy, but also of capitalism. He called lynching "the whip hand of the ruling class," which operated in the interest of the status quo.[18] Cox's imagery is particularly apt for describing San Diego's violence, in

154    CHAPTER 6

which many vigilantes used horsewhips as their torture instrument of choice. A former San Diego park commissioner even called for a "horsewhip vigilance committee" to literally drive the "hordes of Independent Workers of the World" out of San Diego.[19]

Cox defined lynching as "an act of homicidal aggression committed by one people against another through mob action for the purpose of suppressing either some tendency in the latter to rise from an accommodated position of subordination or for subjugating them further to some lower social status."[20] More simply, lynching is about enforcing conformity to the social hierarchy. The provigilante *Evening Tribune* exemplified the psychology of the lynch mob: "The E-Street agitators [meaning the IWW street speakers] have defied the majority sentiment of this community and if they suffer unpleasant or even unjust consequences they have nobody to blame but themselves."[21]

Cox was careful to distinguish between lynching and any mob action. Lynching is a specific type of mobbing, directed not only against an individual, but against a whole people or class. It is violence of a dominant group against a subjugated group. It is not the same as "race rioting." Lynching is organized and it is one-sided. A lynch mob does not fight against an opposing mob. The violence is strikingly asymmetrical.

Lynching, according to Cox, is a natural outgrowth of systems of oppression and privilege. He challenged the notion that lynchings are illegal. On paper they may be illegal, he said, but in practice they are committed with the open approval and even participation of police, judges, and lawmakers. Of San Diego's "citizen's committee," Emma Goldman wrote in a letter to a friend, "The mob as bloodthirsty and infuriated, surrounded the jail because it knew that it was backed by the police."[22] Throughout the entire episode, the *San Diego Union* and the *Evening Tribune*, which were San Diego's mainstream conservative newspapers, regularly praised the vigilantes as defenders of peace and order who rose to the call of the community when "the legal machinery to meet the emergency was lacking."[23]

Lynchings are not isolated acts of passion committed by social outsiders but are mainstream rituals of violence that serve dominant hierarchies and are carried out or supported by members of mainstream, respectable white society. "The mob," writes Cox, "is composed of people who have been carefully indoctrinated in the primary institutions of the region" to conceive of their victims "as extra-legal, extra-democratic objects, without rights which the white men are bound to respect."[24] Lynch mobs include sheriffs, mayors, and prosecuting attorneys. In the case of San Diego: the Chamber of Commerce, the Merchants' Association, the San Diego Builders Exchange, and the San Diego Realty Board all adopted resolutions sustaining and commending the citizen's committee and the police department. The *San Diego Union* pointed to these endorsements

The Respectable Mob    155

as proof that the vigilantes were on the side of law and order.[25] According to *The Call*, a San Francisco ruling-class newspaper, the vigilantes in San Diego were helping the police "maintain peace," cause the "law to be respected," and "clean" the city of "the lawless element."[26] It was the classic colonialist language of cleansing and removing. There are many, said *The Call*, "who believe that the services of the vigilantes are required to maintain these peaceful conditions."[27] In the ruling-class discourse, the victims of the vigilantes were the lawless mob.

The leaders of the vigilantes were the city's leading citizens: economically well off, well dressed, well educated, well known in the community, and well respected. Ben Reitman, who was tortured and sexually assaulted by the vigilantes, described them as "Christian gentlemen."[28] In Reitman's words, it "was a typical respectable mob, made up of retired bankers, retired army officers, real estate men, lawyers, doctors, businessmen, and saloon keepers."[29] Reitman wanted the public to know that these cruelties were not committed by backward extremists, but by fully bona fide members of the local bourgeoisie: "Most of the active vigilantes own an automobile and property."[30] A lynch mob numbering in the thousands surrounded the hotel Emma Goldman was staying in. She described them contemptuously as "good Christians" and "patriots."[31] Like Reitman, Goldman noted that many of the lynchers owned automobiles. The women were "fashionably-dressed" and the men carried US flags.[32] They sang "The Star-Spangled Banner" as they entered the hotel lobby before threatening the hotel manager with death if he did not "Turn over the two damned anarchists."[33]

Some of the leaders and most active vigilantes of the citizen's committee were John M. Porter, of Porter and Forbes Real Estate; Walter P. Moore, assistant superintendent of streets; Amy Johnson (a man), of the Southern Title and Trust Company; Francis Bierman, reporter for the *San Diego Union*; John Mason Dodge (known publicly as "Jack" Dodge), theater manager, former blackface actor, former county clerk, former city treasurer, former mining and realestate agent, and first "Exalted Ruler" of the San Diego Elks Lodge; Clark Braly, wealthy rancher and former park commissioner; George Fishburn, president of the Marine National Bank of San Diego; Carl Ferris, of Ferris and Ferris Drug Store; R. J. Walsh, owner of R. J. Walsh Real Estate Company; W. Litzenberg, of Homeland Real Estate Company; and many more of San Diego's wealthiest and most influential citizens: in short, the local bourgeoisie.[34] The anarchist journal *Mother Earth* sardonically referred to them as "God-fearing, desirable American citizens," in contrast to the newspapers' referring to Wobblies and anarchists as foreign "undesirables."[35]

One of Cox's important insights was that lynching is as much about enforcing conformity to a certain kind of social order within the dominant group as it is about enforcing the conformity of the subjugated group. This insight was further strengthened by later lynching studies such as James Inverarity's classic

156    CHAPTER 6

1976 "Populism and Lynching in Louisiana."[36] Inverarity applied sociologist Kai Erikson's theory of "boundary crisis" to the phenomenon of lynching in the United States. Erikson's hypothesis was that the disruption of solidarity—the disruption of group conformity to the established social order—what he called a "boundary crisis"—produces a sudden and dramatic increase in repressive justice or extralegal forms of boundary control. Inverarity applied Erikson's theory to explain the epidemic of lynching in Louisiana in the 1890s.

A boundary crisis ensued in Louisiana at the time with the rise of the Populist Movement. White identity politics united white southerners who would otherwise be divided by their opposing class interests—large plantation owners, small farmers, and landless workers—under the Democratic Party as a "solid South." Populism threatened the solid South in the 1890s by building solidarity between poor white and Black farmers and by forming coalitions with the Republican Party. By the end of the 1890s, this boundary crisis had largely been resolved. Populism collapsed, white supremacy was reaffirmed, and the solid South was restored on the basis of white nationalism. Inverarity showed that lynching was central to why this happened. He used statistical analysis to show that repressive justice in the form of lynching intensified most in times and places in which the boundary crisis caused by the Populist revolt was highest. Collective ritualized violence of whites against Blacks functioned to rebuild white solidarity in places where white solidarity had been weakened by class-based populism. The white ruling class used the manufactured threat of Black domination of whites as a catalyst for the recoalescence of the solid South. Lynching served to enforce cross-class white solidarity just as much as it served to keep Black people submissive.[37]

In the case of southern California in 1912, it was not the Populists, but the IWW who created the boundary crisis. While the wealthy elite and the conservative labor unions both preached "harmony between capital and labor," meaning working-class obedience to ruling-class institutions, the IWW preached anticapitalist revolution. The preamble to the IWW Constitution explicitly aimed to break up the white cross-class alliance:

> The working class and the employing class have nothing in common. . . . Between these classes a struggle must go on until the workers of the world organize as a class, take possession of the earth and the machinery of production, and abolish the wage system. . . . Instead of the conservative motto, "A fair day's wage for a fair day's work," we must inscribe on our banner the revolutionary watchword, "Abolition of the wage system." It is the historic mission of the working class to do away with capitalism.[38]

The IWW aimed to replace racial, ethnic, religious, and national solidarities with transnational working-class solidarity. Wobbly organizer Elizabeth Gurley Flynn recalled an IWW campaign to organize the multiracial labor force in Grabow, Louisiana. Her accomplice, "Big" Bill Haywood, insisted that the workers ignore Jim Crow laws and customs. "Negro and white workers sat together wherever they pleased, in all parts of the hall, at the mass meeting and at their convention."[39]

In San Diego, there was the obvious boundary crisis of class solidarity replacing racial, national, ethnic, and religious solidarities, and there was an additional boundary crisis created by the speech ordinance. Some middle- and upper-class San Diegans who were otherwise repulsed by the IWW's anticapitalist politics and uncouth style were even more outraged by the speech ordinance and the vigilante violence, which was an affront to what they understood US ideals to be. The mainstream liberal newspapers, which represented that category of people, criticized the vigilantes and expressed sympathy for—but not agreement with—the IWW free-speech fighters. The terrorism of the vigilantes served to enforce both working-class conformity to capitalism, and middle- and upper-class conformity to the conservative social order.

Vigilantes targeted the liberal press and liberal lawyers. The mob violently silenced any paper that criticized the speech ordinance, police brutality, or vigilantism. Any lawyer who defended the victims of the police or vigilantes was targeted by both. Through the use of repression and terrorism, the police and vigilantes enforced rigid boundaries for expression and association. The citizen's committee ordered local printing presses to cease printing the liberal *San Diego Herald* and the *Labor Leader*. They destroyed presses that refused to comply. The police arrested anyone they found selling newspapers sympathetic to the IWW. Political cartoonist A. S. Hermetet, whose work lampooned the San Diego police, was attacked by Police Chief Wilson. Wilson used his rifle butt to split open Hermetet's head and break his right arm.[40]

Some newspaper editors received nighttime "visits" from vigilantes. For example, on April 5, vigilantes kidnapped the *Herald* editor Abram Sauer from his home. They drove him out of town, beat him badly, put a noose around his neck, and ordered him, under threat of lynching, never to return to San Diego or identify them. He did return, and immediately set about printing an issue that identified the mob as merchants, bankers, church members, bartenders, members of the Chamber of Commerce, the real-estate board, the mainstream press, public utilities, and members of the grand jury. While the issue was printing, some thirty vigilantes broke in, stopped the printing, and destroyed the galleys.[41]

Lawyers faced similar pressure. Marcus Robbins and Fred Moore, attorneys defending the Wobblies, "received notice" from the vigilantes to leave town.[42] Another IWW attorney, Earnest E. Kirk, was arrested for "conspiracy" to violate Ordinance 4623. Because he helped arrange a speaking engagement for Emma Goldman, the vigilante mob threatened him with death: "We know you, Kirk,

158 CHAPTER 6

and it's the rope for you. We'll kill you, you s__ of a b____."[43] To emphasize the impunity with which the vigilantes operated: They made this threat in broad daylight in front of a large crowd that included police. Kirk identified the men threatening him as J. M. Porter, Walter P. Moore, and Amy Johnson, who are listed previously in this chapter as vigilante leaders.[44]

The mob organized to enforce the conformity of the working class by silencing, expelling, or killing radical agitators. It worked to enforce the conformity of the middle and upper class by silencing liberal journalists, newspaper editors, and lawyers with violence and the threat of lynching. And, finally, the mob worked to enforce the conformity of members of the mob itself. For example, when Emma Goldman and Ben Reitman returned to San Diego one year after they had been violently expelled, they were again attacked by the same vigilantes and police. The members of the vigilante mob wore US flag pins to demonstrate their patriotism. When one man in the crowd declined to allow an organizer to pin a flag on him, the others beat him down to the ground until the police broke it up. Lynching is not only about keeping a subjugated group in a submissive state, it is about whipping all of society into place within a rigid, conservative ideological framework.[45]

## Civilization versus Savagery

The terrorism in 1912 San Diego occurred under the cultural and political framework of "the taming of the Wild West." In the late-nineteenth- and early-twentieth-century United States, "Old West" novels were widely distributed and read. For the most part, they were tales of civilization—represented by manly white men—subduing and triumphing over savagery—represented by wild terrain, ferocious animals, and dark-skinned wild people. If these manly white men sometimes resorted to extralegal violence, it was only in the interest of expanding the blessings of civilization. As mentioned in chapter 2, *Thrilling Adventures among the Early Settlers*, for example, opened by praising lynch mobs as enforcers of peace, law, and order:

> In the absence of legitimate authority and regular organizations, lynch law usurps its place, and ofttimes visits a swift and terrible retribution upon the offenders. Anarchists and desperadoes are either exterminated or driven farther west, and the beautiful spirit of order and progress emerges from the chaos of confusion and blood.[46]

The civilizing mission was one of extermination and expulsion. This was precisely the type of cultural narrative that defined the San Diego vigilantes as heroic defenders of order, in spite of the fact that they were an extralegal body that broke several laws. It was also the type of cultural narrative that gave power to the idea that Wobblies and anarchists were savages without rights, even when they operated well within the constitutional rights of speech and assembly.

"Old West" novels and similar cultural expressions were not conceived or consumed in a vacuum. They were the product of the larger forces of US settler colonialism and imperialism. The United States was born as a violent, expansionist, settler colonialist state. In the decade-and-a-half prior to the San Diego violence, the US military, government officials, and businessmen used coercion abroad to establish US control over Hawaii, Cuba, the Philippines, Puerto Rico, and Guam, while simultaneously continuing genocidal anti-Indian policies domestically—such as land dispossession and "Kill the Indian, Save the Man" programs. At the time of the San Diego episode, the US government and leading industrialists were involved in the Panama Canal project, and several military units were deployed from San Diego to enforce US control of the Panama Canal Zone. All this activity—be it settler colonialism on the "frontier," imperialism abroad, or repression of anarchists at home—was justified by its proponents through the discourse of "civilization versus savagery." Overseas imperialism and domestic repression of radical anticapitalists were an extension of the Indian Wars.[47]

Imperialism and colonialism manifest themselves in the local social realm in several ways, most visibly in nativism, jingoism, flag-fetishism, the glorification of the military, and the creation and demonization of the enemy alien through racialization and animalization. The anti-anarchist terrorist campaign of San Diego in 1912 contained all these ingredients in abundance. The conservative newspapers emphasized the racial otherness of the IWW. *The Call* made it a point to note that one of the IWW leaders in San Diego was "negro agitator" George Washington Woodbey.[48] The front page of the *San Diego Weekly Union* reported a "horde" of Wobblies en route to San Diego: "It is now claimed that the band contains many more Mexicans than at first reported, in fact, Mexicans are in the majority. Tobo, the leader, is a half-breed."[49] As the vigilantes inflicted physical torture on Ben Reitman, they berated him in racist and nativist terms: "Why did you come here, you dago, you ignorant foreigner? We don't want you here. This is our town."[50]

From January through May 1912, the *San Diego Union* and the *Evening Tribune* frequently used the words "hordes," "undesirables," and "vagrants" in referring to the Wobblies. The IWW was a "horde of degenerate foreigners."[51] The situation was "the anarchist problem" and "the anarchist menace." Wobblies were "lawless nomads"—a term whites used to describe Indigenous groups—and "wretches" for whom there should be "no maudlin sympathy."[52] In defense of police brutality and mob violence, the *San Diego Union* said, "The conditions created by the horde of anarchists who had swarmed the city could have been remedied only by some such drastic measures as were taken."[53] Emma Goldman and Ben Reitman were "the human vulperine and her wolfmate."[54]

The police, vigilantes, and their supporters spoke of the Wobblies as though they were foreign invaders. The *Evening Tribune* referred to the IWW as "a lot of European agitators who have scarcely learned to speak the English language intelligibly, who read Karl Marx and Jean Jacques Rousseau only in the original."[55] The *San Diego Union* reported that Police Chief Wilson "has announced that he will henceforth cope with the situation on the theory that San Diego is being invaded by a stream of lawless and anarchistic men."[56] Conservatives complained that immigration policies were too lax to protect the United States from the foreign invaders: "No one knows how many gun men and dynamiters we have let into this country, but the number is appalling, and it is going to cost huge sums of money and many good lives before this dangerous element is rounded up and deported."[57] The lack of tough immigration restrictions, they argued, allowed "an undesirable, degenerate element" to "come in by the shipload, and when it arrives it is against our government, ready and ripe for revolution and destruction."[58] This type of rhetoric inspired xenophobia, repression, and violence. Emma Goldman and Elizabeth Gurley Flynn accused the *San Diego Union* and the *Evening Tribune* of being just as responsible for the terrorism as the police and vigilantes.[59]

The newspapers were full of calls for the deportation of the free-speech agitators:

> Alien anarchists can be deported. . . . They publicly assail the United States, the nation's flag, and everything that patriotic Americans respect. With rare exception these men are aliens and subject to deportation on the strength of their public utterances.[60]

Christian ministers likewise advocated deportation. In a sermon titled "The Red Flag and the Stars and Stripes," Reverend Willard Brown Thorp of San Diego's First Congregational Church asserted that "There is no room in this country" for people who fly the red flag: "It would be entirely within the rights of our nation to deprive them of citizenship and deport them from its borders."[61]

Thorp's sermon was in response to an IWW May Day parade, in which marchers carried red flags, but no US flags. The San Diego establishment was in an uproar of manufactured outrage about "the recent insults heaped upon the stars and stripes."[62] Reverend W. E. Crabtree of the Central Christian Church gave a sermon in which he preached that "Our glorious ensign was born in wartime . . . and woe betide the man who insults it . . . [for] there is absolutely no room anywhere along the line for insult for our beloved and intimate flag."[63] In response to the "reviling" and "insulting" of the flag by a "lawless element"

The Respectable Mob      161

in the community, the local Knights of Columbus—a name colonialist to the core—suggested a patriotic demonstration in support of the US flag.[64] The *San Diego Union* said that the "worthless loafers" who fly the red flag "should be arrested and given a job on a chain gang."[65] A few weeks earlier, the *San Diego Union* had interviewed military veterans about the importance of respect for the flag. The veterans praised the vigilantes and called for more violence with such statements as "All honor to the citizens who have been and are guarding the line and turning back the spoilers and anarchists" and "I feel sure that there are at least ten thousand good citizens here in San Diego who would gladly respond to a call to tear the red flag from its last place in the city and destroy it utterly."[66]

This type of aggressive flag-fetishism, a direct product of US imperialism, was more than mere rhetoric. Police disrupted the funeral of Michael Hoey, a sixty-three-year-old IWW free-speech fight veteran who was murdered by San Diego police. When a fellow worker draped a red flag over the coffin, the police moved in and arrested him. The IWW paper, the *Industrial Worker*, reacted, saying, "Thus the grave of the aged is desecrated by the ghouls who were the direct cause of his death."[67] Even worse, the citizens committee rounded up IWW members at gunpoint and forced them to endure brutal, and sometimes deadly, "flag-kissing ceremonies."[68]

"Flag-kissing ceremonies" were organized rituals of patriotic cruelty. The citizens committee kidnapped IWW members and sympathizers, took them away from the city and into the desert, and tortured them. Sometimes the vigilantes took their victims directly from the city jail, with the full cooperation of the jail authorities.[69] The vigilantes forced their victims to kiss and salute the US flag, sing "The Star-Spangled Banner," and march away from the city. Sometimes the ceremony involved a gauntlet, in which as many as a hundred vigilantes would line up in two parallel lines, facing each other, holding horsewhips, wagon wheel spokes, ax handles, and broken whiskey bottles. They forced their victims to "run the gauntlet," meaning walk between the two lines while the vigilantes took turns beating them mercilessly. Wobblies left these ceremonies with broken bones, deep cuts, and severe bruises. They were left in the desert with no food or water and sometimes with no clothes. Some Wobblies were "disappeared." The *Industrial Worker* reported that "a number of men have been disappeared and no trace of them can be found."[70]

The *Evening Tribune* reveled in the tortures inflicted on those it derogatorily referred to as the "Industrial Anarchists of the World":

> It was a happy thought, this compulsory obeisance and abnegation in the presence of the American flag by a gang of impudent hoboes, most of them of foreign birth or extraction, who had for weeks been denouncing the flag, the government and all authority, defying the police and the law, and inflicting

upon an otherwise peaceful community annoyance and outrage. [This lynch mob will] go far towards crushing out the law-defying, disloyal, anarchistic groups of discontent that seem to have fastened upon the body politic largely by reason of the lax enforcement of inadequate immigration laws.[71]

According to the mainstream conservative discourse, the lynch mob was protecting civilization from an invasion of savages.

## The Other Half Is Not Printable

Emma Goldman and her lover and tour manager Ben Reitman entered the scene on the afternoon of May 14, 1912.[72] A lynch mob of thousands, led by the citizens committee, waited at the train station to "welcome" Goldman and Reitman to San Diego. The mob subjected the two radicals to what Goldman called "the horrors of hell."[73] After the traumatic experience, Goldman immediately set to work raising public condemnation against the outrages. One of the first places she turned to was the *Denver Post*, as it had recently published three articles by her, and Denver had been a very welcoming city to her on the tour. She wrote an account of her San Diego experience, which she assured *Denver Post* editor Fred Bonfils was not only free of exaggeration but in fact, "does not give half the side of the occurrence. The other half is not printable."[74]

Many other descriptions of the vigilante violence against Wobblies and anarchists likewise left the impression that much of what happened was unspeakable. Elizabeth Gurley Flynn wrote of IWW men taken out of prison by vigilantes, assaulted with guns and clubs, and then tortured "indescribably."[75] There was a category of violence "too horrible to mention." The *Industrial Worker* reported on the "Vigilance Committee" kidnapping eighty-four socialists and Wobblies, tying them to trees, horsewhipping them, "and otherwise brutally treating them."[76] This leads to the question, What is the "otherwise," the "indescribable," the "unprintable" other half? The evidence points to sexual violence.

Indigenous feminist scholarship teaches us that sexual and gender violence are features of the interconnected systems of racism, colonialism, capitalism, and imperialism: that under colonialist states, sexual and gender violence uphold state power.[77] The organized, collective violence of San Diego in 1912, which was committed very explicitly in defense of these interconnected systems, was sexual violence. It was heavily shaped by the dominant gender politics of the era.

This was an era under the Comstock Act of 1873, which prohibited "obscene" material. Open discussion of sex was dangerous enough, and those who dared engage the topic—such as Moses Harman, Voltairine de Cleyre, and Emma Goldman—faced legal and social persecution for it.[78] Sexual violence was an even more taboo topic, especially when men were the victims of that violence.

Notions of manliness had everything to do with why the violence assumed the form that it did, as well as why so much of that violence was "unprintable" and "indescribable." It was an era of white male hyperanxiety as rapid urbanization, mass migration, industrialization, Black mobility, and feminism destabilized the old conservative order. Influential white men worried that "overcivilization" was making the "American race"—meaning white men—soft, and that the nation was losing its manliness. Men founded boxing and "outdoors" clubs to develop the "barbarian virtues." Prize fighting, which had previously been "lowbrow," became popular with "respectable" society. Lieutenant General Robert Stephenson Smyth Baden-Powell, 1st Baron Baden-Powell, founded the Boy Scouts in 1910 as a paramilitary organization to make white boys into virile men. General Baden-Powell was a British military officer involved with the colonization of India and South Africa. He felt that many of the soldiers under his command were lacking in manliness. He wrote *Scouting for Boys* in 1908 to teach boys to be manly and soon after formed the Boy Scouts. Theodore Roosevelt agreed heartily with Baden-Powell and became a strong proponent of Boy Scouting in the United States.[79]

Anarchists and Wobblies were not immune from dominant notions of manliness, but they were critical of the cult of violent masculinity in relation to militarism and imperialism: for example, the IWW called Boy Scouts "embryonic assassins."[80] The IWW nevertheless used the rhetoric of manliness to mobilize Wobblies to go to San Diego to aid in the free-speech fight. The day that the move-on ordinance went into effect, the IWW newspaper called for "100 More Men to Go to San Diego! Are You a Man?"[81]

Tragically, under the dominant gender ideology, to be sexually assaulted was to have one's manhood destroyed. Psychologically, it was far worse than other forms of abuse. Wobblies could publicly admit to being kidnapped, beaten, and tortured but not to being sexually assaulted. Ben Reitman was deeply affected by the sexual assault he endured. He was embarrassed, he considered himself a coward for not being able to stop it from happening, and he lost his sexual desire. In speeches he referred to himself as a coward. Emma Goldman was saddened by his reaction and embarrassed by his openness to the public about it. In a letter to Reitman, she pleaded with him:

> I hope Hobo dear that if you ever face another S.D. [San Diego] you may not have to herald your action as cowardly, or at least if you feel it to be such, that you will keep it to yourself. It certainly cannot be indifferent to the woman, who loves a man, especially the woman who has all her life faced persecution to hear that man shout from the house tops, he is a coward. It's a million more times painful than to have the rest of the world say so.[82]

164     CHAPTER 6

Most victims of the mob did keep it to themselves, telling of being kidnapped, tortured, and "otherwise" harmed.

For insight into what the white propertied class's dominant notions of manliness were in the era—and particularly the kinds of gender notions that shaped a highly patriotic, militaristic society that was economically, politically, and socially invested in imperialism, such as existed in San Diego in 1912—consider Baden-Powell's 1908 handbook, *Scouting for Boys*. The handbook was popular among whites in Britain and the United States as a guide to teach young men and boys what it meant to be manly. It taught patriotism, loyalty to empire, violence, and white supremacy. It had a section about tracking "Red Indians," who it claimed "had been raiding and murdering whites" for no apparent reason.[83] It taught white boys how to shoot a man:

> Shooting at a fixed target is only a step towards shooting at a moving one like a man. . . . Aim first at the man, then moving the muzzle a little faster than he is moving, and fire while moving it when it is pointing at where he will be a second or two later, and the bullet will just get there at the same time as he does and will hit him.[84]

This advice was immediately followed by a section titled "Helping Police," which is exactly what the San Diego vigilantes claimed to be doing.[85]

Manliness was proven and expressed through violence, particularly violence against the savage "other." One of the founders of the Boy Scouts of America, Colonel Theodore Roosevelt, proved his manliness by invading Cuba on horseback, bravely charging at the "dark savage hordes" like the supposed Indian fighters of old.[86] The police and vigilantes proved their manliness by defeating the invading anarchist "hordes of undesirables." It was all part of the same project of cleansing and removing.

San Diego's mob violence was collective sexualized violence. In that era of white male status anxiety, carnivalesque acts of cruelty against racialized or animalized others were a disturbingly common way for respectable white men to assert manliness. This carnivalesque cruelty often included sexualized and even homoerotic elements. For example, lynchings, which were in part manifestations of bourgeois white male status anxiety and irrational fear of black masculinity, often included genital mutilation and sodomization. The point of this for the white male tormentor was to assert dominance over that which he felt threatened his dominance and to do so by destroying his victim's manliness through public sexual humiliation.[87]

Sexual humiliation was a significant element of the San Diego mob's violence. The vigilantes, the newspapers, and the victims were silent about the sexual nature of the violence, with the exception of Ben Reitman. It is through Reitman's

The Respectable Mob    165

accounts that we get a glimpse of the "indescribable" and "unprintable" half of the story. Reitman was far more open about issues of sex and sexuality than the general public. Dealing with the "unspeakable" aspects of human interaction was how Reitman made his living. He was a venereal disease doctor who served sex workers, migrant laborers, and homeless people. His unabashed sexual openness was too much even for many in the anarchist movement, who considered him to be rude, irresponsible, and unrefined. Emma Goldman's love for Reitman is the only reason why the anarchists tolerated him. Though he thought of himself as a coward for not being "manly" enough to stop the vigilantes or get violent revenge on them, he was the only person with the courage to talk publicly about the "unspeakable" things that the vigilantes did. Despite whatever character faults Reitman may have had, bringing the truth about sexual violence out of secrecy and into the light of day was a deeply courageous act, in defiance of the patriarchal conventions of the era.

Reitman wanted the public to know that what happened to him was not an isolated incident, but that it was typical of how the vigilantes had behaved throughout the episode. "In relating my experience I want our readers to know that that which was done to me was done in a measure to 300 other men, mostly members of the I.W.W."[88] Reitman began by talking the same way others did, "They tortured and humiliated me in the most unspeakable manner," but unlike others, he explained exactly what an "unspeakable manner" entailed.[89]

After dark, the vigilantes kidnapped Reitman at gunpoint, took him directly past a uniformed policeman who did nothing to stop them, threw him in a waiting automobile, and, in his words, "began to torture me hysterically calling me the vilest names."[90] One of the men urinated on him while the others held him down. They drove him to a ranch about twenty miles outside the city. During the drive they inflicted all kinds of punishments on him. He wrote, "I wish I could describe the terror of that twenty-mile ride in the beautiful California moonlight."[91] They pinched his stomach and bit his arms. They punched, kicked, cursed, and beat him. They put their fingers in his eyes and nose, and subjected him to "every cruel, diabolical, malicious torture that a God-fearing respectable businessman is capable of conceiving."[92] As they threatened him with death, they told him, "We've got the law and the police on our side," which was true.[93] They forced him to sing "The Star-Spangled Banner."

When the vigilantes arrived with Reitman at the destination, they parked next to another car that was also full of vigilantes. According to Reitman, there were fourteen vigilantes in total. They turned on the car lights making a "sickly stage light."[94] They threw him on the ground and formed a ring around him. They tore his clothes off, and as he lay naked on the ground, they kicked and beat him. They forced him to kiss the US flag. With a lit cigar they burned the letters I-W-W on his buttocks. They poured hot tar all over his head and body and rubbed sagebrush on him in place of feathers. One man twisted Reitman's testicles. Another man sodomized Reitman with a cane. They gave him back his underwear, vest, some—but not all—of his money, and his railroad ticket, and told him to leave and never return to San Diego. Finally, they compelled Reitman to "run the gauntlet" so they might leave him with some parting blows and forced him to make a patriotic speech. They pointed him in a direction to march away. He walked into the darkness, not knowing where he was going until the sun came up and he found a sign pointing to the nearest railroad station, which was in Escondido.[95]

In the following days, several newspapers carried the story of Reitman's treatment, but they left out the sexual violence. They reported on Reitman being tarred and feathered, beaten, and forced to kiss the flag, but the most there was about sexual violence were "Dr. Reitman had an experience that cannot wholly be told in print," and "Besides burning him, they subjected him to shameful indignities."[96] Dr. Reitman, on the other hand, wanted the public to know about the depravity of the supposedly respectable men of society. At public meetings, to raise awareness about the San Diego situation, Reitman spoke openly about what happened to him. He even pulled his pants down to expose the burns on his buttocks to audiences to prove that he was not making it up. This openness shocked audiences and embarrassed Emma Goldman, who wished her partner would act in a more dignified manner.[97]

That Reitman was targeted by the mob much more aggressively than was Goldman was itself a very gendered phenomenon. When the two were together, the mob shouted specifically for Reitman, in spite of the fact that it was Emma Goldman, not Reitman, who was the great anarchist propagandist, orator, organizer, and agitator. When the two returned to San Diego one year later, they were again met by a mob shouting for Reitman.[98] Reitman's contribution to the anarchist movement was that he arranged Emma Goldman's speaking engagements. It was Goldman who was the "dangerous anarchist." Reitman, however, was the man in the relationship—both the romantic relationship and the business relationship. It was his job to control "his" woman. Instead of controlling her, he assisted her in touring the country to speak about free love, contraception, anarchism, and communism and give talks with titles such as "Sex, the Great Element of Creative Life." The United States establishment was—and still is in many ways—a patriarchal society, which is why the mob held Reitman responsible for Goldman's politics.

Nevertheless, the mob also targeted Emma Goldman, in ways clearly shaped by gender and sexual politics. When Goldman arrived in town, the San Diego mob greeted her with hooting, catcalls, and threats of sexual violence. The main headline on the front page of the *San Diego Sun* was "Emma Goldman In; Hooted by Crowd; Can't Get a Hall."[99] The liberal San Francisco *Bulletin*

The Respectable Mob     167

reported that "A gang of rowdies and boys . . . shouted threats, catcalls, and insulting remarks to the woman orator" and "the police did nothing to check the disturbance."[100] One woman who cheered for Emma Goldman "was roughly handled" by men in the crowd.[101] Goldman and Reitman were able to sneak from the train to the bus that was waiting to drive them to the Grant Hotel, where they had arranged to stay. When the crowd realized what had happened, they chased after the bus in their own cars, shouting threats at the driver to stop and "Give up that anarchist."[102] According to Goldman's account, even upper-class women joined in the threats of sexual violence: "We will strip her naked; we will tear out her guts," and, added Goldman, "Many other things were said by those 'cultured' women which could not be repeated in public."[103]

The bravery of the Grant Hotel bus driver and the hotel manager in hiding Goldman from the mob, in the face of death threats, was likely the only reason that the vigilantes did not get their hands on her. Late that night, she snuck to the train station but was again chased by a mob of vigilantes threatening her with sexual violence. They chased her on foot as she ran to get on the train. A train worker lifted her up onto the train and locked the door, but the train was not leaving for another eight minutes, and so Goldman sat there for eight minutes while the vigilantes banged on the doors and windows, shouting threats at Goldman. She wrote of it:

> [Those were] the most terrible, the most hideous eight minutes of my life. There were the good Christian, law-abiding respectable citizens, and the howl they raised, the language they used, the efforts they made to break into the train, are beyond description, beyond anything that the most depraved human beings could be capable of.[104]

After several failed attempts to seize Goldman, and several threats of bodily mutilation and sexual violence against her, the vigilantes claimed that their gentlemanly sense of chivalry—another form of patriarchy—is why they did not physically harm her. "Emma Goldman's sex is the only thing that saved her from similar treatment" [in reference to Reitman's].[105]

Goldman and Reitman returned to San Diego one year later but were again met by a mob organized by the same citizens committee and again were expelled under similar conditions. The capitalist establishment gloated, in gendered language, about San Diego's toughness in the face of the anarchist invaders: "The shrew is tamed."[106] In reality, Goldman was far from tamed. She left San Diego for the second time determined to return and give the speech she had planned on giving in 1912. She finally succeeded two years later. She returned to San Diego on June 20, 1915, this time with her anarchist comrade Alexander Berkman. She gave three lectures at the Fraternal Brotherhood Hall. In the morning, she delivered the talk that she was prevented from giving in 1912: a lecture on

168    CHAPTER 6

Henrik Ibsen's play *An Enemy of the People*. In the afternoon, she gave a talk titled "Nietzsche and the War" and, in the evening, she gave a presentation to raise awareness and support for Margaret Sanger, who had been arrested earlier in the year under the Comstock laws for distributing birth-control information.[107] Radicals and progressives in San Diego saw Goldman's lectures as the triumph of the free-speech movement that the Wobblies started in 1912.[108]

## Conclusion

Nevertheless, historians should resist the urge to find a happy ending in this story. In the years following that brief triumph, the United States entered the World War I, which became the pretext for an extraordinary wave of repression that specifically targeted Wobblies and anarchists. Scenes similar to those of San Diego in 1912 played out nationwide. There were several other IWW members who were lynched by patriotic white mobs over the following years, for example, the 1917 lynching of Frank Little in Butte, Montana, and the 1919 lynching of Wesley Everest in Centralia, Washington. Indeed, the three main racialized non-Black migrant groups to be victims of white lynch mobs in the United States—Italians, Mexicans, and Jews—were also three of the most well-represented groups in the US anarchist movement. Many anarchists and Wobblies, including Emma Goldman and Alexander Berkman, were deported by increasingly aggressive US border control and Justice Department authorities.

The anarchists in 1912 understood well that the outrage of San Diego did not merely represent the local peculiarities of San Diego. It was not simply about one corrupt police chief, one conservative media outlet, or a few right-wing extremists. Lynch law was not a departure from what the United States stood for; it was an expression of it. Judge Lynch and Uncle Sam were the same person, just wearing different outfits. Ben Reitman heard the anarchists claim as much for years, but it took his San Diego experience for him to really understand it. Writing of San Diego, Reitman bitterly reflected that:

> Twenty-five years ago I was thrilled when I took part in a chorus which sang "Oh, the Star Spangled Banner, long may it wave." Now when I hear those songs I want to weep; to me they are hollow mockery—covering all the sins and crimes of a cowardly nation. I was taught to loathe my native flag, not by Anarchists, or by ignorant foreigners, but by law-abiding, respectable businessmen.[109]

State violence and vigilante violence were part of the same system: in the words of Alexander Berkman, "a regime of terroristic oppression against every opponent of existing conditions."[110]

Feminist scholar bell hooks once wrote, "I often use the phrase 'imperialist white-supremacist capitalist patriarchy' to describe the interlocking political systems that are the foundation of our nation's politics."[111] San Diego 1912 is a clear example of the appropriateness of such a phrase. The terrorism of San Diego—whether it was state terror or vigilante terror—was simultaneously an expression of all those interlocking systems. It was imperialist violence in the form of jingoism and nativism. It was white supremacist violence in the obvious form of racism. It was capitalist violence, directed down the social hierarchy by the rich against the poor, in defense of private property. It was patriarchal violence, deeply shaped by the era's gender and sexual politics. It was colonialist violence, committed by property-owning white men who conceived of their actions as a defense of civilization. None of these categories of violence operates independently. If to be radical is to strike problems at the roots, then the first task of radical resistance is to find and expose the roots. It is in episodes such as San Diego 1912 that US institutions show their true colors and the foundations of US culture and politics are most exposed.

# 7

# Aliens and Mobs

On December 20, 1919, the US House of Representatives met for its final congress of the year before adjourning for the Christmas holiday. The House chaplain, Universalist minister Henry Noble Couden—a respected war hero who lost his sight from wounds acquired in battle during the Civil War—opened the meeting with a Christmas prayer:

> Father in heaven, our hearts go out to Thee in gratitude and unfeigned love for Thine own best gift to the world, crystallized in the life, character, and message of the Christ; and we would join with the millions of Christians in the heavenly anthem sung by the angels on the plains of Bethlehem two thousand years ago: Glory to God in the highest, and on earth peace, good will toward men.[1]

With that out of the way, the pious Christian congressmen set to the work of the day, mainly the criminalization and deportation of socialistic Jews. The names Emma Goldman and Alexander Berkman in particular came up several times throughout the day's proceedings.[2]

Lawmakers conceived of and enacted anarchist expulsion and deportation within a larger social context of anticommunist and white nationalist mob violence, which was entwined with, and an extension of, US settler colonialism. In enacting and implementing anarchist expulsion, lawmakers simply made what white mobs were already doing unofficially and extralegally as the official project of formal state agencies. White settler vigilante groups were the cutting edge of US policy. As Theodore Roosevelt wrote in 1886—as previously discussed—it is not the formal forces of the state, but the "armed settler, whose presence announces the permanent dominion of the white man."[3] Much of the work of US lawmakers has been to formally institutionalize white settler mob violence. For example, what are law enforcement and border control agencies if not the institutionalization of the slave patrols and right-wing settler "frontier" paramilitary groups that preceded them? The House and the Senate's push to ban anarchists such as Goldman and Berkman must be understood as a continuation of the anticommunist violence of white settler mobs that preceded the official policies. In fact, some of the groups that anticommunist US lawmakers in 1919 and 1920 cited as their constituents, such as the American Legion and the Benevolent Protective Order of Elks, were the very groups that made up the membership of murderous anticommunist mobs. US settler colonialism always was, and remains, a white nationalist project of elimination. In the decades of this study's focus, deportation increasingly became a key weapon of that project.

## Anarchist Exclusion

As the House of Representatives met before Christmas 1918 to discuss anarchist exclusion, the two Jewish anarchists—Goldman and Berkman—and 247 other Russian-born "alien undesirables" had been rounded up by J. Edgar Hoover's Radical Division of the Justice Department and were scheduled to be deported the following day.[4] According to the *New York Tribune*, 200 of the 249 "reds" were "members of the Union of Russian Workers" who were "rounded up in Chicago, New York, Youngstown, Pittsburgh, Boston, Bridgeport [CT], New London [CT], Hartford, Buffalo, Baltimore, Detroit, Akron, St. Louis, Kansas City, Seattle, and other cities."[5] Despite the fact that "alien anarchists" were already scheduled for deportation, and there was already in force a 1918 anti-anarchist federal law—the Alien Act—members of the House vigorously discussed crafting a stronger bill designed to ban and deport anarchists and Wobblies from the United States for good.

During the discussion on the "Deportation of Alien Anarchists" bill, US congressmen explicitly pitted anarchists and Wobblies against whiteness. Arkansas Representative Thaddeus Horatius Caraway—who would later work to ban Black people from serving in the army and navy, and who introduced bills to racially segregate Washington, DC, transportation and housing—complained that though his state did not have many "aliens" living in it, "many negroes" were "being agitated and incited to crime by this organization of I.W.W." His was a historical example of the "outside agitator" trope that agents of capitalism and the state continue to use in the present to delegitimize Black rebellion. Black people engaging in political and economic organizing were, in Caraway's explanation, "victims of the [IWW] agitators from outside of the borders of the state," as though working-class Black people in Arkansas could not possibly have had any grievances of their own.[6]

In his characteristic slow, southern drawl, Tennessee Congressman Ewin Lamar Davis railed against Emma Goldman and Jewish socialist politician Victor Berger—who was elected on the socialist ticket to represent a Milwaukee district in that very Congress but was denied his seat by the House after the state charged Berger with violating the Espionage Act for his antiwar politics. Justifying the House's refusal to abide by the election results, Davis said, "We already know that he is unfit to sit with us, and should immediately expel him by resolution. Those who voted for him are not worthy to be represented." Not only should Berger be banned from serving in the office he was elected to, argued Davis, but "he should be denaturalized and deported." Contrasting the people of his district with the "unworthy" and "foreign" voters of Milwaukee, Davis boasted,

> I am proud of the fact that I have the honor to represent a district in which there are but few aliens, and, so far as I am aware, no anarchists, Bolshevists, I. W. W.'s, or other similar radicals. We are not afflicted with that sort of cattle. My constituents are almost altogether of pioneer American stock—pure Anglo-Saxon. . . . They have no patience whatever with the Victor Bergers, the Emma Goldmans, the Alexander Berkmans, or the W. Z. Fosters.[7] They do not see any reason whatever why we should temporize with anarchy, bolshevism, I.W.W.ism, communism, syndicalism, or any other radicalism. As generous in spirit and as kind-hearted as they are, they do not think there is any room anywhere within the broad confines of our country for any set of men imbued with such pernicious and un-American doctrines. I am in thorough accord with their views.[8]

Here Davis used the common US euphemism for settler colonizer—"pioneer"—to describe his constituents, and he posed a racial category, "pure Anglo-Saxon," as the antithesis of communism. Not only did he racialize anarchists, communists, and Wobblies, but he animalized them as "cattle." The choice of language was reminiscent of the 1917 Bisbee Deportation, in which law enforcement officers and right-wing vigilantes loaded nearly 1,300 striking mine workers—members and supporters of the heavily Mexican and Indigenous IWW Local 800—into actual cattle cars provided by the El Paso and Southwestern Railroad.[9]

As Congressman Davis drawled on, Hoover and his Department of Justice agents were busy preparing "alien anarchists" to be transported like cattle from their cages to a tugboat that would take them to the *USAT Buford* for deportation. Hoover was just beginning his career as a communist hunter, intent on eliminating Jewish and other "foreign" anarchists such as Ethel Bernstein, Dora Lipkin, Alexander Berkman, and Emma Goldman from the United States. Of the latter two, Hoover wrote, in a memo to the Department of Justice, "Emma

Goldman and Alexander Berkman are, beyond doubt, two of the most dangerous anarchists in this country and if permitted to return to the community will result in undue harm."[10] So intent was Hoover on the deportation of Goldman and Berkman that he joined them on the 4 a.m. trip in subfreezing, windy weather on the tugboat that transported them and the other migrant anarchists across the New York Harbor to the "Soviet Ark" *USAT Buford*.

The twenty-four-year-old Justice Department prosecutor Hoover tauntingly said to the fifty-year-old Goldman, "Haven't I given you a square deal, Miss Goldman?" She replied, "Oh, I suppose you've given me as square a deal as you could. We shouldn't expect from any person something beyond his capacity." It was Goldman's way of telling Hoover that he was nothing special, just another cog performing his function in the larger system. Hoover afterward complained that the anarchists were not respectful toward him, but instead were "very cocky," and "full of sarcasm for the Department of Justice and immigration agents." Hoover began his career hunting "foreign" anarchists and ended his career hunting Black communists, such as Angela Davis, whom he added to his "Ten Most Wanted" list. At his death in 1972, his FBI agents were escalating their activities to destroy the Black Panther Party and the American Indian Movement. To Hoover, whether he was going after Wobblies, anarchists, Black radicals, or the American Indian Movement, it was all the same war of the United States against "reds."[11]

The *Buford* was not the beginning or end but just one episode in an era of mass deportations and anticommunist secret policing as the state turned its project of cleansing and removing increasingly inward. The Department of State promised that there would be more "Soviet Arks" to follow.[12] The *Buford* was the only ship the state chartered specifically for transporting "anarchist" deportees, but the state continued the deportations, in smaller batches, on passenger ships, which carried deportees and regular paying customers. For example, two years later the United States deported Eastern European Jewish migrant anarchists Mollie Steimer, Samuel Lipman, Hyman Lachowsky, and Jacob Abrams, among others, on the SS *Estonia* bound for Soviet Russia. Many of these anarchists never settled anywhere, remaining always on the move, supporting the social movements, uprisings, revolutions, and antifascist resistance struggles of the following decades, everywhere criminalized, and always enemies of the state wherever they went, including Soviet Russia. As Alexander Berkman put it in 1916, "an anarchist knows that he has no country."[13] Goldman spent her final days in Toronto, Canada, Berkman in Nice, France, and Molly Steimer, along with several other stateless "reds" of the era, lived her last days in Cuernavaca, Mexico.[14]

The "Soviet Ark" was one of the highest profile mass deportations in US history, but was relatively small in scale compared to some of the lesser-known mass deportation episodes of the era against Mexican and Indigenous anarchists, socialists, and Wobblies, which are what set the stage for the "Soviet Ark." For example, two and a half years before the *Buford* set sail was the aforementioned Bisbee Deportation, which local law enforcement and patriotic vigilantes carried out in service to the Phelps Dodge Corporation. Here it is important to distinguish between international deportation as expulsion from a nation-state, and internal "deportation" as forced expulsion from a local community. The Bisbee Deportation along with other comparable "deportation" episodes—such as the 1886 expulsion of Chinese workers from Seattle, and the 1917 expulsion of working-class Black families from East St. Louis—fall into the latter category.

The whites who carried out these violent, murderous expulsions—which included white members of the Knights of Labor in the Seattle case and of the American Federation of Labor (which Wobblies derided as the *A.F. of Hell*) in the East St. Louis case—drew from the already-existing framework of Indian removal. Both types of deportation—forced expulsion from the borders of the United States and forced expulsion from a local community or region within the borders of the United States, are forms of removal and ethnic cleansing which the state and vigilantes carried out within a settler colonial framework, inasmuch as—discussed in earlier chapters—"elimination is an organizing principle of settler-colonial society."[15]

## The East St. Louis Pogrom

In July 1917, white mobs carried out the East St. Louis Pogrom, which historians sometimes inaccurately refer to as a race riot. White mobs, which included white women, violently expelled some six thousand working-class Black people from East St. Louis, Illinois, and sadistically murdered some two hundred mostly working-class Black people of all ages in the process. The pogrom was orchestrated by white businessmen and AFL leaders who felt their white power threatened by the increasing political and economic power of the city's Black residents.[16] Unlike the IWW, the AFL at the time, rather than being a broad working-class organization, was an extremely racist and anticommunist organization that drew color and gender lines. It mainly represented the top layer of the relatively well paid white male skilled sector of the trades, barring the majority of the working class from membership. In late May, the secretary of the AFL-affiliated Central Trades and Labor Union of East St. Louis, Edward Mason, called a meeting not to discuss how to unite and empower the working class, of which Black workers were a part, but how to take drastic action to stop the migration of Black people to the city and to "devise a way to get rid of a certain portion of those already here."[17] In other words, ethnic cleansing to reestablish white supremacy. Armed whites systematically went from house to house in

Aliens and Mobs     175

Black neighborhoods setting houses on fire and murdering and torturing Black people of all ages. Before the dust had settled, the National Association for the Advancement of Colored People (NAACP) sent W.E.B. Du Bois and Martha Gruening to East St. Louis to investigate. Du Bois and Gruening collaborated on a detailed report, which was published in the September 1917 issue of the NAACP's monthly magazine, *The Crisis*.[18]

Gruening also wrote a condensed version of the report—with some of her own editorializing added—for the August 1917 issue of the anarchist journal *Mother Earth*. In April of that same year, Klan sympathizer US President Woodrow Wilson gave his famous speech to Congress in which he declared, "The world must be made safe for Democracy." With those words in mind, Gruening, who, along with Emma Goldman, was an antimilitarist and a member of the No-Conscription League, retorted in *Mother Earth*,

> East St. Louis is an example of that democracy we are to spread over the world—the democracy of caste and race oppression, of unspeakable cruelty and intolerance, of hideous injustices. . . . I have seen this democracy at close range, and I know what it means. That is why I want the world made unsafe for it.[19]

Gruening and *Mother Earth* were strong supporters of the labor movement but had nothing but harsh words for the AFL, which they saw not as part of the labor movement but as "loyal n.-hating Americans" and therefore enemies of the workers of the world.[20] In investigating the violence, Du Bois and Gruening found that many acts of anti-Black homicidal violence during the pogrom were committed by groups of white women against Black women and Black children. They wrote, "The violence was confined not only to men. Women were in many cases the aggressors and always ready to instigate and abet."[21] In the pages of *The Crisis* and *Mother Earth*, they described in gruesome detail, cruel acts of murder, torture, and mutilation white women and men committed against Black babies, children, and adults. The kinds of acts Du Bois and Gruening described white women and men committing in East St. Louis read very similar to Helen Hunt Jackson's previously mentioned report of the 1864 Sand Creek Massacre, including the taking of body parts as trophies. In both cases, the purpose of the violence was the same: elimination of a people through extermination and expulsion.[22]

## The Bisbee Deportation

Nine days after the East St. Louis Massacre, legal and extralegal white settler forces in Arizona carried out the Bisbee Deportation. In the preceding months, Mexican and Indigenous organizers who were simultaneously members of the

IWW and the anarchist revolutionary organization Partido Liberal Mexicano (PLM) were actively organizing in mining camps across the Southwest. Outsiders nicknamed PLM members Magonistas after the anarchist-communist Ricardo Flores Magón, who was the editor of the PLM's main propaganda organ, *Regeneración*. Historian Devra Anne Weber points out that the overlap between the membership of the IWW and the PLM in the Southwest was so great that local sheriffs used the terms "Magonistas" and "Mexican IWW" as synonyms.[23]

Indigenous anarchists in particular were key to organizing poor and working-class people in the region because they had the cultural and language skills to connect workers and poor communities across racial, ethnic, national, and linguistic lines. Mayo anarchist Fernando Palomares, for example, could speak his native language Yoeme as well as Spanish and English. At first he organized in mining camps among Mayo and Yaqui workers, but soon became a leading organizer in the multiethnic, multilingual IWW/PLM on both sides of the US-Mexico border. Another example is Camilo Jiménez, a Cocopah anarchist and agricultural laborer who likewise organized militant struggles on both sides of the US-Mexico border, and who likewise was a leader in both the PLM and the IWW. A key organizer of the 1917 mine workers' strike in Bisbee, Arizona, was Rosendo Dorame, possibly of Opata descent, and also an organizer in both the IWW and the PLM.[24]

Indigenous anarchists were not only in the US-Mexico border regions but organized throughout Central and South America, "from Mexico to Argentina, and from Francisco Zalacosta in the Chalco to Facón Grande in Patagonia." In the classic study *El anarquismo en America latina*, the Argentine philosopher and historian Ángel Cappelletti observed that because of the resemblance of "the anarchist doctrine of self-managed collectivism" to some Indigenous groups' ways of life in Central and South America, "anarchism took root much more deeply and extensively among Indigenous workers than did Marxism, perhaps with the exception of Chile."[25] As touched on in earlier chapters, the visible presence of Indigenous people, Mexicans, and "half-breeds" in the radical labor and anarchist movements was seized on by anticommunists to characterize radical labor and anarchists as "savages" who threatened "civilization."

In Arizona, white settlers dealt with these Wobblies and "Magonistas" the same way they dealt with Indigenous and Mexican borderland groups in general, with a campaign of vigilante violence and ultimately expulsion at gunpoint. In June 1917, when Rosendo Dorame's IWW Local 800 called for a strike, 85 percent of all mineworkers in the entire town of Bisbee, some three thousand workers, joined the strike. The county sheriff, Harry Wheeler, led the charge to break the strike. Wheeler was a veteran of the First Cavalry in the Spanish-American War and afterward became captain of the settler militia, the Arizona Rangers, which acted mainly as an anti-Mexican, anti-Indigenous, and antilabor

Aliens and Mobs   177

death squad on behalf of mining companies owned by US businessmen on both sides of the border.[26]

When the Wobblies went on strike in Bisbee, Sheriff Wheeler dealt with it the only way he knew how: he called for a posse of settler vigilantes. Wheeler illegally deputized 2,200 settlers from the region, who then violently rounded up the strikers and their supporters into a baseball field. The vigilantes forced 1,286 Wobblies and suspected Wobblies at gunpoint to board manure-filled cattle cars—the operation was conducted with such haste that the settlers unloaded the cattle and then loaded the striking workers without cleaning the cars in between—with no water, in July Arizona heat near 100 degrees Fahrenheit. Despite the fact that the operation of kidnapping people en masse at gunpoint and shipping them away in subhuman conditions with no due process was entirely illegal according to state and federal law, no state or local officials, or vigilantes, faced any prosecution or legal accountability whatsoever. US Attorney General A. Mitchell Palmer sided with the vigilantes and used Bisbee as an example for why the state needed stronger anti-anarchist laws, arguing that the good settlers of Arizona would not have had to resort to vigilante violence and kidnapping if federal law enforcement had greater repressive power. Two years later, when Congressman Davis referred to Wobblies, anarchists, and communists as "cattle," it was not mere rhetoric, but reflected the reality of US "frontier" violence and how white settler society treated racialized working-class rebels.[27]

## Settler Death Squads and the Lynching of Frank Little

On August 1, 1917, while the dust was still settling from the East St. Louis pogrom and the Bisbee Deportation, a mob of antiunion thugs abducted labor organizer Frank Little in Butte, Montana, tortured him, and then hanged him from a railroad trestle. The white settler mob, aided by the police, lynched Frank Little as part of the local business elite's campaign to crush a major miners' strike. In committing this heinous act, the mob drew heavily on Montana's white settler mythology to give meaning and justification to their violence.

Frank Little was a union organizer and an antimilitarist who believed that part of the role of the union was to keep workers out of the capitalists' wars. He organized mine, lumber, and oil field workers in the US West. At the time of his assassination, he sat on the IWW executive board. He played a significant role in making the IWW not just a labor organization but a working-class antiwar and anti-imperialist organization. He went to Butte to help organize poor copper miners who—after a major mine fire that killed nearly two hundred workers—were striking against their employer, the Anaconda Copper Company, the largest copper-mining company in the world at the time, which was important to the war effort.

The antiunion death squad fractured Little's skull with a rifle butt and tied him to the back of a car to drag him on the street, scraping the skin off his kneecaps. They pinned a note to his thigh. It contained the numbers "3-7-77," which was the signature of a settler death squad called the Montana Vigilantes. Montana settler vigilantes had been using the numbers 3-7-77 since 1879 as a message to "undesirables" to leave town or die. It is a mystery what the numbers referred to—though there are several theories—but it is not a mystery that the numbers meant banishment. Since 1879, as part of Montana's white settler lynch-law culture, when the white settlers of a town such as Helena, Virginia City, or Butte wanted to banish an "undesirable," they left a message that said, "3-7-77." If that person remained in town, vigilantes killed the person.[28]

In the case of Frank Little and the IWW, the white settlers of the region drew from what they understood to be "Old West" settler tactics of "frontier" social control to a modern union-busting effort. This again raises Shelley Streeby's and Michael Denning's argument that "frontier" myths were related to class conflict and that the figure of the western outlaw in popular culture was a figure of class conflict.[29] Only this was not a popular dime novel but an event played out in reality. When internal state and capitalist repression are understood as being shaped by the larger framework of US settler colonization and empire, as this study argues they should be, then it becomes clearer why murderous white men protecting the interests of the US military and the world's largest copper company inserted themselves into the role of "hardy white men taming the Wild West." In the words of the previously mentioned popular adventure book *Thrilling Adventures among the Early Settlers*, on the frontier, lynch law was a necessary and heroic part of establishing civilization: "Anarchists and desperadoes are either exterminated or driven farther west, and the beautiful spirit of order and progress emerges from the chaos of confusion and blood."[30]

Little claimed to be, and was believed by the public to be, "half-Indian"—although, as Botkin's book shows, he was at most a fraction of that.[31] Little's actual ancestry aside—and note that the notion of blood quantum is itself extremely problematic, rooted in white supremacy and colonialism—the public perception of Little as "half Indian" likely made him more lynchable in the eyes of his murderers by marking him as less than white and therefore out of place and less than American. By using 3-7-77 to make themselves out to be Montana vigilantes, the members of the lynch mob presented themselves as Old West frontier heroes protecting civilization from a supposed "wild Indian" or dangerous desperado. Frank Little's lynched body was itself a message to other labor organizers. The 3-7-77 note pinned to Little's corpse also carried the words "Others take notice!

Aliens and Mobs    179

first and last warning!" and what appeared to be the initials of six other union leaders. This 3-7-77 showed the intent to banish the IWW from Montana.

The striking migrant laborers sent a message of their own back to the vigilantes by making Frank Little's funeral procession the largest public event in Butte history. Ten thousand workers lined the procession route to pay respects, while the procession of 3,500 workers, labor organizers and agitators, and friends and family of Little solemnly passed through. In an act of defiance against the region's settler vigilantes and wealthy businessmen, they buried Little in Butte's local Mountain View Cemetery in a prominently marked grave with an epitaph that read "Slain by capitalist interests for organizing and inspiring his fellow men." The grave with that epitaph remains there to this day. Though there was ample evidence to connect Anaconda company thugs, Pinkertons, and members of local law enforcement, including Butte's head detective, to the lynching, state authorities did not officially question, apprehend, or prosecute anyone for the murder. Federal authorities, however, continued to persecute Frank Little's family members with raids, arrests, and indictments under the 1918 Sedition Act.[32]

## The Vigilante Code

Montana's white settler culture continues to celebrate the symbol "3-7-77" as something to be proud of. In fact, the high-profile lynching of Frank Little contributed to Montana's "frontier" mythology. In 1920, with vigilantism and "3-7-77" fresh in the public mind from the lynching of Little, state officials—in an effort to boost tourism to the state by capitalizing on Montana's image as the "Wild West"—changed the names of its routes from Butte to Yellowstone National Park to "The Vigilante Trail." They marked the route with circular red, white, and blue signs that said, "Vigilante Trail," and the numbers "3-7-77" written across the middle. The state advertised it with tourist promotions that said things such as "Follow the Vigilante Trail that winds like a snail through the playgrounds of the West."[33] Montana state tourism authorities continue to promote this mythology, with its current website, which includes the "3-7-77" logo, encouraging tourists to visit the Vigilante Trail:

> The Vigilante Trail . . . provides a corridor for Montana tourists from Butte to West Yellowstone. The trail was marked with the vigilante code, 3-7-77, on bright signs to ensure that visitors would not lose their way. This code served as a warning for frontier ruffians and criminals to leave the area immediately—or else. The trail cuts through the heart of Southwest Montana, taking travelers along the road that was frequented by so many of the early Montana settlers. Rich in territorial history, outdoor recreational opportunities, and genuine Montana hospitality, a trip along the Vigilante Trail will provide a memorable experience for all visitors.[34]

180    CHAPTER 7

Quite a contrast from the reality of the lynching of Frank Little and the murderous anti-union, anticommunist intent of "3-7-77."

This "Vigilante code" currently appears on the flight suit patches of the Montana Air National Guard, whose 120th Air Lift Wing goes by the name "Vigilantes," also written on the patch. Wearing their "3-7-77" patches, the Montana "Vigilantes" took part in the United States' invasion of Afghanistan—Operation Enduring Freedom—and the invasion of Iraq—Operation Iraqi Freedom. More recently they were involved in Operation Spartan Shield in the Middle East.[35] The Montana Army National Guard 1–189th General Support Aviation Battalion likewise has "3-7-77" on its battalion logo, and likewise nicknames itself "Vigilantes." The 1–189th likewise took part in Operation Spartan Shield as part of a task force called "Task Force Vigilante."[36] These kinds of units are an example of how US Empire continues to draw on settler "frontier" mythology—the notion of "taming the Wild West"—to imbue its militarism with meaning.

The Montana Highway Patrol currently has "3-7-77" as part of its official logo. Montana troopers proudly wear these "3-7-77" patches on their uniforms, acknowledging, however unwittingly, that the police developed in part from "frontier" lynch mobs, and that the police perform the same function in society as the death squad that murdered Frank Little: protecting the property of the wealthy, keeping the poor in line, and upholding the capitalist order.[37] State troopers wearing the "vigilante code" on their uniforms exemplify the blurriness of the line between official state violence and extralegal right-wing vigilante violence. Both police violence and right-wing vigilante violence serve a "cleansing" and removing function: "cleaning up the streets" to protect "civilization," eliminating or containing groups that threaten or stand outside of the aims of the white supremacist capitalist social order.

## "Praying for the Enactment of Legislation"

The US Senate began its first meeting of 1920 discussing the need for stronger anti-anarchist laws. Among the opening announcements of the January 5 meeting was a message from the House of Representatives informing the Senate that the House had passed bill H.R. 11224, for which the House requested the concurrence of the Senate. It was a bill to strengthen the 1918 Alien Act, which they described as "An act to exclude and expel from the United States aliens who are members of the anarchistic and similar classes."[38] It was not just congressmen and law enforcers calling for the banishment of "reds" from the body politic, but 1920 began with a slew of white men's fraternal, civic, and business associations calling for the elimination of anarchists, Wobblies, and communists from the United States. The previous summer, the conservative, whites-only men's organization the Benevolent Protective Order of Elks unanimously adopted

Aliens and Mobs    181

a "Flag Day Resolution" to ban and oppose anyone "who openly, or covertly, directly or indirectly, gives aid, comfort or support to the doctrines, practices or purposes of the Bolsheviki, Anarchists, the I.W.W., or kindred organizations, or who does not give undivided allegiance to our Flag."[39] Now, organizations such as the Elks were pressuring the Senate to turn such resolutions into federal law, notwithstanding the fact that such resolutions already were federal law through the 1903 and 1918 Immigration Acts.

After the message from the House about H.R. 11224, Senators from various states submitted to their colleagues on the Senate floor petitions from various respectable white men's organizations urging Congress to pass laws to increase state repression against militant labor, anarchists, and other socialists. Senator Charles Curtis of Kansas—who would later serve as vice president to Herbert Hoover—began the spectacle. The men of Elks Lodge No. 586 of Concordia, Kansas, were "praying for the enactment of legislation providing for the suppression of anarchy and the deportation of undesirable aliens." The Booster Club of Garnett, Kansas, was "praying for the enactment of legislation for the prevention and punishment of extreme radicalism." The Coffeyville, Kansas, post of the Grand Army of the Republic—a fraternal organization of US Civil War veterans—likewise was "praying for the enactment of legislation providing for the suppression of anarchism and the deportation of undesirable aliens." The identical language in many of the petitions suggests that they were part of a coordinated anticommunist effort.[40]

It was appropriate that Charles Curtis lead the Senate's charge against communism. He was also a leader of the US theft of Indigenous lands and the dissolution of Indigenous governments. His career was more tragic in that Curtis, who went by the nickname "Indian Charlie," was a member of the Kaw nation and grew up on a Kaw reservation speaking Kansa and French before he learned English. He was the first Indigenous person to serve as US vice president, and one of the first to serve in the House and Senate.[41] Curtis's political career is a reminder that firsts are not always a step toward progress and that assimilation and representation within the system are not the same thing as freedom, justice, and liberation for colonized peoples. Indeed, firsts sometimes occur because the "first" has demonstrated to the ruling class that they are willing to be tokenized and willing to betray their own people for career advancement.

In 1873, when the federal government, at the behest of white landowners, expelled the Kaw from Kansas to relocate them to Indian territory in what is now Oklahoma, Curtis did not move with his people but went to Topeka to be raised by his white grandparents and assimilate into white society. As he got involved in politics, he favored the passage of the Dawes Act of 1887 and supported separating Indigenous children from their parents and placing them in boarding schools designed to "kill the Indian and save the man." Two years after the passage of the Dawes Act, Curtis was elected by the white settlers of

Kansas to represent them in the US House of Representatives. There he became a member of the House's Committee on Indian Affairs, where he set to work drafting the Curtis Act, which extended the power of the Dawes Act to what the state called the "Five Civilized Tribes" of Oklahoma. His policies dissolved several tribal governments, including his own Kaw Nation, and further opened Indigenous lands to white settlers.[42] By 1920, this US politician who led the charge to dispossess Native peoples of their lands and cultures was now leading the charge to expel anarchists and other "undesirable aliens" from the United States. Curtis's efforts to liquidate Indigenous nations and expel anarchists were part of the same project: the permanent dominion of the capitalist class.

Other senators submitted petitions similar to those of Curtis's constituents. An association of leading North Dakota business owners, the Larimore Commercial Club, who were worried that "civilization and organized society is threatened by sedition and anarchy," urged Congress to take away workers' "right to combine to strike" and to declare labor unions "to be unlawful." The statement of Elks Lodge No. 1089 of Minot, North Dakota, read, in part,

> That we view with deep concern the spread of disloyalty and seditious sentiments promulgated by syndicalists, I.W.W.'s, and Bolsheviki. That we believe that the time has arrived when Americans should assert themselves and drive from their shores all disloyal agents, and adequately punish those who betray their country by disloyal acts. We hereby call upon the United States Congress to immediately enact a law providing for the summary deportation of every alien in the country who is an enemy of this Government. That the law should further provide for the immediate cancellation of the citizenship papers of any naturalized citizen affiliated with and lending aid and comfort to such enemy aliens. That we believe no person should be permitted to issue or circulate any writing or pamphlet which has for its apparent object the undermining of American institutions or the inciting of rebellion.[43]

The Minot Elks made it a point to include that their lodge consisted of "800 loyal American citizens." The Huntington, West Virginia, post of the right-wing military veterans' group, the American Legion, was "praying for the enactment of legislation for the suppression of anarchism." Other American Legion posts in other states did likewise, such as the Glastonbury, Connecticut, branch, whose members were "praying for the enactment of legislation providing for the suppression of anarchy and the deportation of undesirable aliens."[44]

## The American Legion and the Lynching of Wesley Everest

Some of the groups that had the ears of US senators consisted of the very people who made up the membership of anticommunist lynch mobs in the era. The American Legion, for example, was extremely aggressive in enforcing

Aliens and Mobs    183

patriotism and violently suppressing the left in several states. The American Legion was formed in March 1919 by Theodore Roosevelt's eldest son Theodore Roosevelt Jr., a Harvard-educated investment banker who at the time was serving as an officer in the American Expeditionary Force. He would later become a US colonial official, serving terms as governor-general of the Philippines and governor of Puerto Rico, among other high-level positions in US politics and business. The junior Roosevelt and other AEF officers, concerned about low troop morale, which they attributed in part to the spread of anarchist, communist, and other antimilitarist ideas within the enlisted ranks, decided to form the American Legion to oppose the left and enforce "Americanism." Over the following two decades the Legionnaires acted not only as a lobbyist group for veterans but as right-wing vigilante thugs for the bourgeoisie.[45]

Four months before the founding of the American Legion, on the day of the signing of the armistice between the Allies and Germany, a right-wing mob in service to lumber companies burned down an IWW hall in Centralia, Washington, and beat several lumber workers affiliated with the IWW. The Wobblies rebuilt their hall by Armistice Day, November 11, 1919, one year later, and again were actively organizing lumber workers in the region. The American Legion decided to celebrate Armistice Day 1919 by attacking the new union hall to violently expel the "American Bolsheviki"—what the Legionnaires called the Wobblies—from Centralia. According to IWW journalist, artist, poet, and organizer Ralph Chaplin, "the affair was the outgrowth of a struggle between the lumber trust and its employees—between Organized Capital and Organized Labor."[46]

The Legion's plan was that their Armistice Day Parade would end by attacking and destroying the IWW hall. Wobblies, many of whom were also veterans, got wind of the plan and decided to defend the hall. When the parade neared the hall, Legionnaires charged, carrying rifles, handguns, and coils of rope, suggesting they intended to lynch Wobblies. Wobblies fired on the Legionnaires in self-defense, killing the leader of the mob—the Legion post commander, former army officer, and virulent anticommunist Warren Grimm—and two others and wounding nearly a dozen more. The mob outnumbered and outgunned the Wobblies, overrunning the hall and forcing the Wobblies to run for their lives. The police aided the mob by capturing and arresting several of the fleeing Wobblies. Other Wobblies were captured by the mob and delivered to the local jail, where police then tortured the Wobblies in jail cells. While some Legionnaires continued to pursue their victims, others moved the furniture from the hall into the street and burned it in a large bonfire. A group of Legionnaires cornered Wesley Everest—an IWW member, lumber worker, and draftee who served much of his time during the war in military prison for refusing to salute the flag. Everest fired at the mob in self-defense, killing one, but he was taken down by the others, who beat him all over his head and body with rifle butts.

184    CHAPTER 7

They dragged his bruised and bloodied body through the street and delivered him to the jail where the other Wobblies were being tortured by police officers.

Later that night, the police returned Everest to the mob, who then hanged and shot him at the Mellen Street Bridge, over the Chehalis River. Ralph Chaplin's account says that the mob also castrated Everest. The police report says nothing about castration, but the police were hardly an impartial or trustworthy party in the matter, and there was no autopsy. The local coroner was a leader of the Armistice Day Parade and, according to the Wobblies, was a member of the mob. The full extent of the mob's violence against Everest remains unknown beyond the facts that they beat, hanged, and shot him. After the mob dropped his dead body in the river, the police retrieved the body and returned it to the jail, displaying it, with the noose still around Everest's neck, to the jailed Wobblies to terrorize them. Seven Wobblies were sentenced to prison terms ranging from twenty-five to forty years for firing at Legionnaires, but the state did not arrest or charge even a single member of the lynch mob. To the US ruling class, the Legionnaires were the victims and heroes of the story. The city government erected a bronze statue to honor the four members of the lynch mob whom the Wobblies killed in self-defense. On Armistice Day, November 11, 1922, US President Warren G. Harding gave a formal tribute to the American Legion lynch mob members who died in the episode, as though they died in a glorious battle for US American freedom. The following two decades were filled with incidents of American Legion vigilantes attacking leftists to, in the words of the Preamble to the legion's constitution, "foster and perpetuate a 100 percent Americanism."[47]

As a bleak coincidence, November 11, the date that the mob lynched Wesley Everest, is also the date in 1887 when agents of the state hanged the Haymarket martyrs in an act that anarchists and socialists referred to at the time as a "legal lynching."[48] It is also the date in 1831 when white vigilantes and agents of the state hanged, flayed, and beheaded Black freedom fighter Nat Turner and executed or tortured some 120 enslaved Black people whom whites suspected of being Nat Turner's comrades. While mainstream US society treats November 11 as an official federal holiday reserved for honoring veterans of the US military, anarchists see it as a date on which the alliance between the state, capital, and murderous reactionaries has been abundantly displayed. Rather than celebrating militarism, anarchists and other revolutionary socialists treat November 11 as a day to remember martyrs of the social revolution: Nat Turner, Louis Lingg, Albert Parsons, August Spies, George Engel, Adolph Fischer, Wesley Everest, and all the freedom fighters whose lives were stolen by state and vigilante violence.[49]

Groups like the American Legion had a chilling effect, as even the threat of the Legion served to enforce an anticommunist social order. For example, in November 1936, former syndicalist Samuel Hammersmark, who at the time was

Aliens and Mobs    185

the Communist Party's candidate for Illinois governor, had to cancel his talk in Urbana at the University of Illinois at the last minute when American Legion members showed up to attack him and harass the students who invited him. In a letter to the university's newspaper the *Daily Illini*, one witness described the Legionnaires as a "self-appointed, hyper-patriotic group of citizens" who were "obviously intolerant and itching for trouble" and had "all the self-assurance of gang courage." When it became clear that Hammersmark was not there, the Legionnaires cornered three or four young undergraduates and berated them:

> You ought to be ashamed of yourselves for being radical. If you don't like this country, why don't you go back to Russia? Here we the taxpayers give you this grand institution, the University of Illinois, and this is the way you show your appreciation. In 10 years you'll be ashamed of yourself for advocating communism.

After the ordeal, one of the students remarked, "It's a good thing the speaker didn't show up. They'd have strung him up to a tree."[50]

## Woodrow Wilson and the Klan

Warren G. Harding—who celebrated and honored Centralia's patriotic lynch mob—was not the first or the last US president to approve of right-wing vigilante mobs. US presidential support for extralegal right-wing violence is a US American tradition that goes back to the early settler militias and slave patrols whose members established "the permanent dominion of the white man."[51] Andrew Jackson was "an unabashed lyncher, as revealed in his own letters and in reports about his unceremonious 1818 hanging of two "hostile" Indian chiefs without trial and his brisk court-martial and hanging of two British subjects who had aided and led Indians in war against Americans."[52] US President Trump's infamous "very fine people" comments about the murderous Charlottesville white nationalists were very much an echo of Woodrow Wilson's apologism for the Ku Klux Klan: apologism that was saturated with settler colonial logic.[53] Wilson was the head of state who oversaw the Justice Department during the first Red Scare period.

Indeed, much of the antileft and white supremacist rhetoric of more recent years was articulated more than a century ago by Wilson in his supportive words for the Klan. It is well known that Wilson held a special White House screening of the film *The Birth of a Nation*, which glorified the Klan and anti-Black lynching and contributed to the rise of the second Ku Klux Klan in reality. It is less well known that Wilson held and articulated pro-Klan sympathies for decades prior to that screening. Before entering politics, Wilson educated the sons of the wealthy at the elite Princeton University, during which time he published volumes of histories of the United States, histories that glorified the Confederacy,

186    CHAPTER 7

romanticized the enslavement of African people, and defended the Ku Klux Klan. The Wilson pro-Klan quote that infamously appeared on an intertitle in *The Birth of a Nation*—"The white men were roused by a mere instinct of self-preservation until at last there had sprung into existence a great Ku Klux Klan, a veritable empire of the South, to protect the Southern country"—was a slightly modified quote from one of Wilson's academic works, his *History of the American People*.[54] Wilson's vile anti-Black and segregationist policies are an example of the politics of the extralegal white mob being formalized into law.

Wilson characterized Klansmen—along with members of other racist right-wing death squads that formed to overthrow the progress of Reconstruction, such as the Knights of the White Camellia, the Pale Faces, the Constitutional Union Guards, and the White Brotherhood—as misunderstood saviors of the South. He referred to them as "knights errant" serving "to protect their people from indignities and wrongs" that resulted from the supposed "dominance of the Negroes in the South." White vigilantes' function was to reestablish white settler control of the region through a campaign of expulsion, just as the armed settlers who originally established white control of the South had done: "It became the chief object of the night-riding comrades to silence or drive from the country the principal mischief-makers of the reconstruction regime, whether white or black." It was a project of cleansing, removing, expulsion, elimination: in short, settler colonialism. In Wilson's narrative, a classic example of the language of settler colonialism, white vigilantes were heroes riding around on horseback to save civilization from Reconstructionists who were "like a predatory horde" intent on destroying organized society.[55]

The early Klan and similar right-wing death squads specifically targeted teachers: a crime against humanity that Woodrow Wilson defended. Wilson referred to teachers during Reconstruction with the term "adventurers," which was a term that functioned the same way the term "outside agitators" does in the present. According to Wilson, Reconstructionist teachers were "adventurers" who indoctrinated children with "lessons of self-assertion against the whites." Teachers "train their pupils to be aggressive Republican politicians and mischief makers between the races."[56] Compare this to much later right-wing antiteacher rhetoric, exemplified by conservative politicians manufacturing and then campaigning on white fears of a nebulous monster called Critical Race Theory and "far left indoctrination" in schools.[57]

Wilson characterized the Klan as victimized whites who were forced by circumstances to extralegal activity. These supposed good white men, the "real leaders" of the South, were "alienated" because Black men, "ignorant negroes" in Wilson's language, incited by "adventurers," voted supposed corrupt outsiders into office. How often even into the present does the dominant narrative in the United States attribute the heinous behavior of white nationalists, and even racist mass shooters to white men and boys being "alienated." These "real

Aliens and Mobs    187

leaders," as in the white men to whom political power rightly belonged, had no choice but to act as "a force outside the government" to "defend the constitution of the United States."[58] This was the exact logic that many of the Capitol rioters used to justify their actions on January 6, 2021, that they were defending the Constitution: heroes saving the United States from outsiders taking over and corrupting its institutions. In fact, some of these white rioters, who were military veterans, were captured on video reciting their oath to "defend the Constitution from all enemies foreign and domestic" just before they breached the Capitol.[59]

Wilson described the early Klan as mere "pranksters" whose lighthearted "zest" was all in good fun. They were not malicious terrorists, but simply young men engaging in inside jokes and "innocent mischief." Wilson described the Klansmen as clever young "lads" having some fun with the supposed irrationality of Black people. The "extravagant prank and mummery" of these delightful Klansmen, explained Wilson, "threw the negroes into a very ecstasy of panic." Wilson described Black fear of white vigilantes as "comic fear," as these Klansmen meant no harm; it was all just an inside joke.[60] These supposed inside jokes grew into very real campaigns of ethnic cleansing, including mass murder, lynching, and sexual violence as tactics of reestablishing white supremacy against the progress of Reconstruction. That history should serve as a warning in the present day against taking the far-right's "it's just a joke" justifications for their malicious attempts to "trigger the left" at face value.

Like the American Legion, the Klan functioned as an extralegal gang of thugs for the local bourgeoisie for upholding the white supremacist capitalist order. In the early 1920s, at the height of the second Ku Klux Klan's influence, both the Klan and the American Legion mobilized to defend organized capital against the threat of organized labor. They targeted the IWW for its radical politics and racial and religious otherness. Both the Klan and the Legion viewed anarchists, socialists, and Wobblies as "un-American." One example of police, Klansmen, and Legionnaires working together to protect capitalism and the state occurred in June 1923, in Port Arthur, Texas. Port Arthur police arrested, detained, and beat three IWW members who were organizing marine transport workers in the area. Police then released the Wobblies into the hands of vigilantes who further brutalized the Wobblies. Rumors spread among the local white bourgeoisie that twenty thousand multiracial Wobblies from all over the country were going to invade Port Arthur to take revenge on the city for its treatment of its members. Though the rumors were not true, the local police, the Ku Klux Klan, and the American Legion all prepared for an armed response to protect capital from the specter of communism. In this case, no IWW invasion materialized, but the fact that the police, the Klan, and the American Legion were all on the same side, ready to kill members of a labor union, illuminates the historical relationship between official state law enforcers and extralegal anticommunist–white supremacist death squads.[61]

The relationship between the police and the Ku Klux Klan continued in following years. One of many possible examples was the Los Angeles Police Department's and the Ku Klux Klan's violent campaigns from 1922–23 to crush the militant IWW Marine Transport Workers Industrial Union, San Pedro Local 510. After enduring months of police and extralegal harassment and violence, including raids on their meetings and headquarters by police and Klansmen, some three thousand port workers in San Pedro walked off the job not only to demand higher wages and better working conditions but also to protest the police and white nationalist thugs who continually assaulted union members and to demand the release of Wobblies imprisoned under anti-anarchist laws. The strike effectively shut down the port, immobilizing ninety ships in the Los Angeles harbor. City officials responded as San Diego did in 1912, by banning IWW street meetings, making mass arrests of Wobblies and their supporters—including jailing the famous author Upton Sinclair—and through murderous extralegal white mob violence that continued for months. A year after the strike, the Ku Klux Klan again raided the IWW hall with murderous intent. They tortured some Wobblies by tarring and feathering them, among other cruelties. The Klansmen hospitalized a young girl named May Sundstedt after severely scalding her by shoving her into a pot of boiling water. They brutally beat the girl's mother, who died two months later. Through this kind of violence, the cops and the Klan worked hand in hand to restore white supremacist capitalist order.[62]

Wobblies learned from experience, just as Albert Parsons learned in Texas decades earlier, that the only way to defeat the Klan was by organizing community self-defense capable of overpowering the white nationalists. In February 1924, in Greenville, Maine, about forty Klansmen marched to a boardinghouse where lumber workers organizing an IWW branch were staying and ordered the Wobblies to leave town or be forced out by the Klan. Rather than leave town, the 175 IWW members organized armed patrols to walk the streets in the area in the freezing Maine winter weather to keep the Klan out. IWW organizer Bob Pease told the local press, "We are going to stick, and if the Klan starts anything, the I.W.W. will finish it. The slave drivers, the Great Northern Paper Company and Hollingsworth and Whitney people do not want us here, but we are too strong for them." Peas further described the Klan in Greenville as company thugs working for the lumber interests.[63] The Wobblies recognized that murderous white supremacist gangs such as the Klan were not alienated extremists but were a feature of the capitalist order in the United States. Klansmen served the interests of the local ruling class.

The Klan carried out their ethnic cleansing and racial terror campaigns all within a pervasive settler logic of "this is ours." As Wilson argued, these "alienated" white men were the "real leaders" of the South. This same logic was on full display in Charlottesville on August 11 and 12, 2017, when economically and

Aliens and Mobs    189

politically enfranchised white nationalists, mostly young white men, marched with torches chanting, "You will not replace us!" the "us" being white men who were supposedly the "real leaders," and the "you" referring to nonwhite groups, Indigenous people, immigrants, Muslims, Jews, LGBTQ people, "the radical left," and anyone who existed in opposition to white power. This settler logic was again on full display in the January 6, 2021, "Save America" mob, who confidently told the Capitol police to get out of the way because "This is our house!" and "It belongs to us!"[64] Indigenous feminist scholar Aileen-Moreton Robinson observes in *The White Possessive* that, in settler colonizer logic, the state itself is white property.[65] A white mob, enraged that "their country" is being overrun by outsiders, engaging in extralegal violence to "save America," claiming the center of US lawmaking to be their own is settler logic to the core. Such logic was entwined with anticommunism and anti-anarchism.

## Conclusion

In incident after incident of white settler mob violence, the Justice Department and federal lawmakers sympathized with the white mob rather than with the victims of the white mob. Rather than crafting legislation to criminalize white settler mob violence, lawmakers institutionalized the violence, so that what white mobs did first on an extralegal level became what the formal forces of the state would do in an official capacity. The pattern persists throughout US history. In this sense, the white settler lynch mob was the cutting edge of US policy for internal social control. When the House and Senate met in late 1919 and early 1920 to create—or more accurately, expand and strengthen—a legal basis for anarchist exclusion and deportation, they were conforming to that pattern. When US senators pointed to their constituents "praying for the enactment of legislation providing for the suppression of anarchy," they were pointing to the very groups—such as the American Legion, the Elks, and so on—who made up the membership of the patriotic "respectable mobs" of the previous years. The anticommunist units that operated under the authority of men such as President Woodrow Wilson, US Attorney General A. Mitchell Palmer, and head of the Radical Division J. Edgar Hoover were the state formalizing the right-wing death squads that murdered people such as Frank Little, Wesley Everest, and others in the "Wild West." What settler thugs such as Sheriff Wheeler deployed an extralegal posse to achieve on a regional level, the Justice Department and immigration authorities would deploy formal federal agents to achieve on a national level. This is one of the many ways that frontier settler colonial violence was built into the structure of the United States on a formal, institutional level for internal social control.

# Conclusion
## "The Problem of the Proletariat and the Colonial Problem"

The white nationalism, antileft repression, border violence, and antimigrant cruelty of more recent years are not a departure from US American values, but an expression of the United States' own violent settler colonial history.[1] Anticommunism, which includes anti-anarchism, is part of the structure of the United States. In the US context, as this study has argued, settler colonialism significantly influenced the development of anticommunism. The relationship sheds light on why so much of the language of US anticommunism is the language of US settler nationalism and vice versa and why US anticommunist policy historically looks like colonial counterinsurgency. It is why US leaders described Indigenous groups they intended to eliminate as communists in the 1850s and why they later described anarchists, other socialists, and proletarian insurgents in general, as Indians. More important, it explains why the policies, tactics, and weapons the state employed against Indigenous and proletarian insurgency were so similar.

Aimé Césaire wrote that the ascendance of the bourgeoisie gave rise to two major problems: "the problem of the proletariat and the colonial problem."[2] So much of this book has been the violent story of agents of US capitalism and the state attempting to deal with these two problems and doing so as though the two problems were one in the same. Another way of saying this is that the way the United States dealt with the "problem of the proletariat" was deeply informed and shaped by how it dealt with the "colonial problem."

This study is one important piece of the story but is far from exhaustive. Much remains to be said, much remains to be expanded on, and much remains to be studied. For example, these two problems, which are at their root problems of capitalism and the state, underly the formation of the national security state. The US history of secret policing, border policing, and political policing, and the formation and development of state agencies that carry out these functions—such as the Federal Bureau of Investigation, the Secret Service, the Central Intelligence Agency, the US marshals, Immigration and Customs Enforcement, and Customs and Border Protection—are directly rooted in this larger history of the intertwined forces of settler colonialism and anticommunism. It is not new information that the FBI originated as an antiunion, anarchist-hunting secret police force, but what warrants more study is how in forming as an anti-anarchist, anticommunist, and antiunion agency it further adapted and institutionalized already existing settler colonizer ideology, strategies, and approaches for external expansion to internal social control. This is one of many possible avenues for further research to which this study points.

Another avenue ripe for more exploration to which this study points is the relationship between US settler colonialism-imperialism and policing. It is not only in major uprisings—such as Ferguson in 2014–15, Baltimore in 2015, Standing Rock in 2016–17, Minneapolis, Seattle, Portland in 2020, and so on—that militarized police apply counterinsurgency strategies developed for outward invasions and occupations to domestic social control.[3] Counterinsurgency is not present in US policing only during extraordinary moments but is part of everyday policing. Police adapting the tactics, ideology, weapons, equipment, and approaches of outward US military invasions and occupations to local domestic control is so common that sociologists have a term for it: *imperial feedback.*[4] As this work has argued, the approach of the United States to controlling and containing its racialized migrant working class is rooted in settler colonial ideology and practices. Centering the framework of US settler colonization and imperialism offers much more that historians of US labor and working-class history can develop toward contextualizing and understanding policing in the United States.

In addition to its implications for the field of labor and working-class history, this history has important implications for the labor movement. The intertwined history of US settler colonialism, capitalism, and US repression of working-class struggles suggests that to be effective beyond small gains that leave the overall system intact, the labor movement must be infused with anticolonial consciousness. Tragically, far too many leaders in the mainstream "respectable" labor movement in the United States have allied themselves with ruling-class interests: with the interests of settler colonial land theft, border violence, imperialist war, and the carceral state. They have, in the name of good jobs, flown the stars and stripes and misled workers to support policies and projects that increase injustice, inequality, and human suffering in the world. AFL-CIO President Richard Trumka's shameful statement of support for the Dakota Access Pipeline in 2016, in the face of a historic, global, pan-Indigenous movement fighting to stop the pipeline from being built, is a classic example of the lack of anticolonial consciousness and solidarity among the leadership of the mainstream labor movement.[5]

American Federation of Teachers president Randi Weingarten's opposition to the Palestinian Boycott, Divestment, and Sanctions movement (BDS)—even as the union's rank-and-file increasingly supports BDS—is another classic example.[6] BDS is a global picket line in solidarity with an Indigenous people struggling against settler colonialism, apartheid, and military occupation, an occupation heavily bolstered by US military, economic, and political support. US labor leaders who oppose BDS are scabs. Too many leaders of the mainstream labor movement in the United States have forgotten the labor movement's radical roots and its internationalist history: a history of opposing militarism, white supremacy, capitalism, and imperialism and a history of solidarity with anticolonial struggle. What might the labor movement look like, and what threat might it pose to the intertwined systems of inequality on which capitalism and the state rest, if it had a greater historical understanding of how settler colonialism is foundational to the economic and political systems that keep poor and working-class people in a position of subjection?

Of course, the labor movement in the United States has never been any one thing. It has always contained both emancipatory and reactionary elements. In more recent years, as much as there have been out-of-touch, overpaid union brass misleading workers, and ignorant union locals waving US flags and singing the national anthem, there have been glimmers of hope: wildcat strikes in "right to work" states, union electricians, carpenters, plumbers, and other union members in the trades donating their skills to support the camp at Standing Rock to oppose the DAPL, dockworkers in the ILWU shutting down ports in support of the George Floyd uprisings, union locals in the trades—many of whose members are racialized migrants themselves—refusing to work on border walls, and multiracial and gender diverse workers self-organizing, without consulting established union brass, in industries long ignored by petrified institutionalized labor, such as Amazon warehouse workers, Starbucks workers, fast-food workers, and sex workers, among others. These are a few of many examples that point not to inevitabilities, but to possibilities of a working-class movement ready to fight not simply for small gains in individual workplaces but for radical structural change. The more this movement allies itself with anticolonial and anticapitalist struggle within the United States and across borders, the more of a threat to the system it will become. Understanding the historical connections between settler colonialism, white supremacy, capitalism, and internal proletarian control will be an important component of such a project.

Another possible avenue of further research is the role of the state itself in producing violent extralegal far-right extremists. The many military veterans, law enforcement, and former law enforcement officers involved in extralegal right-wing extremist groups and neo-Nazis who are former employees of the Department of Homeland Security and the like are not a new phenomenon and are not a departure from what the United States has been. The extralegal right-wing vigilante mob with connections to official state agencies is a feature of US settler colonialism. John Hay knew it. Theodore Roosevelt knew that it was not only the formal forces of the state, but "the armed settler whose presence announces the dominion, the permanent dominion, of the white man." Now that we are in an era in which far-right, antileftist, majority-white mobs are again—if they ever ceased to be—part of the political landscape, it is useful to contextualize them not in a framework of European fascism, as many observers do, but in a framework of US settler colonialism and to see them not primarily as a system-oppositional force—though there may be some system-oppositional elements at least on the surface—but as an informal, extralegal arm of capitalist and state power.

The US Senate's failure to convict Trump is indicative that the post-Trump United States was not on a path of redemption or democracy, and the failure of the United States to dismantle its concentration-camp infrastructure and border-control apparatus is even more indicative. While working-class migrant-led mass social movements called for the abolition of ICE and the abolition of migrant detention, the United States under Joe Biden expanded its detention, imprisonment, and deportation system.[7] While working-class Black and Indigenous-led social movements called for the disempowerment and defunding of the police, and the reallocation of resources away from law enforcement and incarceration toward housing, jobs, mental health services, health care, childcare, and education, Joe Biden ran on a platform of "increasing funding to the police" and chose a pro-police former prosecutor with a "tough on crime" reputation as his running mate.[8] While working-class leftists called for bold, sweeping policy changes for dealing with the economic crisis, environmental crisis, and global pandemic, Biden promised wealthy donors in Manhattan's five-star luxury Carlyle Hotel that he would not "demonize" the wealthy, and that if elected "nothing would fundamentally change" in the class structure.[9] While an Indigenous-led movement mobilized to protect land, water, and sacred sites, candidate Joe Biden promised the resource extraction industry, "I will not ban fracking. Period."[10] While Black-led and Indigenous-led organizers and activists defaced and toppled patriotic monuments to settler colonialism and slavery and burned down symbols of police power, Joe Biden told voters that "anarchists and arsonists should be prosecuted."[11] When the Biden administration recognized the unelected figurehead and right-wing failed-coup leader Juan Guaido as the leader of Venezuela, it signaled what was already obvious, that the administration would continue to pursue an anticommunist foreign policy.[12] US immigration law continues to bar alien anarchists and communists from naturalization.[13]

The purpose of pointing out these examples is not to vilify the Trump or Biden administration as *uniquely* evil. On the contrary, both represent business as usual in the United States. It is to show that, even with very different administrations in office—and indeed, a Democratic administration is very different from a Republican administration—there is a lot of continuity in policies concerning border policing, internal policing, and outward imperialism. That certain policy orientations and projects continue and expand regardless of which politician or party is in office suggests that they are built deeply into the structure of the United States. As this study has argued, such policies and projects are rooted in the violent settler colonial history of the United States. Undoing these violent, authoritarian, and cruel systems and policies will require reckoning with that history and its implications. Substantive structural change will require dispensing with patriotism, whether it be of conservative, progressive, or even state socialist varieties. There can be no socialism on stolen land, no equality under a US flag, no "liberty and justice for all" under capitalism and the state.

While specific policies adopted depend on which politicians are in office and which parties hold the most sway at any given moment, the underlying settler colonial structure remains, so that different parties and politicians simply have different methods of achieving the same ends.[14] For example, in the period of this study's focus, roughly the 1840s–1920s, so-called progressives and conservatives agreed that the continued existence of Indigenous peoples on lands that white settlers coveted was "the Indian problem." They agreed that Indigenous groups should be eliminated. More conservative politicians were content to achieve their elimination through outright mass extermination carried out by the military and extralegal settler death squads. Supposedly humane progressives saw such policy as barbaric and instead pushed for policies of cultural genocide designed to "break up the tribal mass" by privatizing Indigenous lands and abusing Indigenous children at "kill the Indian, save the man" boarding schools run by white do-gooders. Both approaches—conservative and progressive—were deeply racist and genocidal.

On the question of "border security," contemporary "tough talking" Republicans seem to be itching to solve the problem of overcrowded migrant detention facilities with state-funded, for-profit, privatized concentration camps/prisons, and in some cases even mass extermination, while mainstream Democrats would solve it by building more "humane" detention facilities—in some cases also run by publicly funded private corporations—to increase the state's capacity to contain and expel "undesirables." Both support a heavily militarized border and pouring federal funds into border policing and surveillance technologies.

The human notion that racialized, poor, and working-class people should have freedom of movement and should not be criminalized for seeking sanctuary is beyond reason for both. Federal agencies such as CBP and ICE act as gangs of reactionary thugs regardless which party is in power. Both parties accept the underlying violent settler logic of "border security."

Conservative and liberal alike view social uprising "from below" with fear and consistently favor police and private property over justice. Conservatives talk tough, and push for ham-fisted, overblown responses by mobilizing violent local, state, and federal law enforcers to crush what they view as "radical left" uprisings with vulgar force. The more sophisticated of the liberals move to gain control over people's movements from below and discipline them under the milquetoast leadership of liberal nonprofits and Democratic politicians who channel movements away from radical demands and toward election campaigns and exercises in futility such as "writing letters to your congressperson." Both approaches aim to restore capitalist order and uphold the existing underlying systems and hierarchies. Trump deploying his Border Control Tactical units to assault people he and several other Republicans haphazardly labeled "anarchists," "terrorists," and "antifa" in response to the uprisings of 2020 exemplifies the thuggish conservative approach. Exemplifying the more sophisticated liberal approach were leading Democrats in Congress responding to the George Floyd uprisings by wearing kente cloth scarves and kneeling on the marble floor of Emancipation Hall in the US Capitol for a moment of silence for George Floyd, then rising to unveil "reforms" that increased funding to the police and increased the power, size, and scope of law enforcement. Both approaches were expressions of the same underlying structure, and both functioned to "restore order."

There is no happy ending. There is no redemption for the United States. Any hope—not for the United States but for humanity—lies in social movements and cultures that reject the logic of the state and organize and exist outside and against the system: with the very people the state developed its anticommunist ideology and practices to contain, control, ban, expel, and eliminate: the very people the state vilifies, marginalizes, and criminalizes as dirt, disease, animals, wild savages, mischief makers, stateless hordes, criminals, terrorists, outside agitators, ignorant foreigners "who cannot comprehend the spirit of our free American institutions," indeed, *anticolonialists, abolitionists, communists,* and *anarchists.*

# Notes

## Author's Note on Terminology

1. Some of many possible examples: Peter Kropotkin, *Memoirs of a Revolutionist* (Montreal: Black Rose, 1989); Emma Goldman, *Living My Life*, 2 vols. (New York: Dover, 1970); Alexander Berkman, *Prison Memoirs of an Anarchist* (Pittsburgh, PA: Frontier, 1970); M. P. T. Acharya and Ole Birk Laursen, eds., *We Are Anarchists: Essays on Anarchism, Pacifism, and the Indian Independence Movement, 1923–1953* (Chico, CA: AK Press, 2019); Daniel Guérin, *No Gods No Masters: An Anthology of Anarchism* (Oakland, CA: AK Press, 2005); Davide Turcato, ed., *The Method of Freedom: An Errico Malatesta Reader* (Oakland, CA: AK Press, 2014); Davide Turcato, ed., *The Complete Works of Errico Malatesta*, vols. 3 and 4 (Oakland, CA: AK Press, 2016, 2019); Candace Falk, Barry Pateman, and Jessica Moran, eds., *Emma Goldman: A Documentary History of the American Years*, vols. 1 and 2 (Urbana: University of Illinois Press, 2008); Candace Falk and Barry Pateman, eds., *Emma Goldman: A Documentary History of the American Years*, vol. 3 (Berkeley: University of California Press, 2012); Peter Glassgold, ed., *Anarchy! An Anthology of Emma Goldman's Mother Earth* (Washington, DC: Counterpoint, 2001); Alexander Berkman, ed., *The Blast: Complete Collection of the Incendiary San Francisco Bi-monthly Anarchist Newspaper Edited by Alexander Berkman from 1916–1917 That Gave Voice to the Worldwide Anarchist Movement* (Edinburgh, Scotland: AK Press, 2005); Chaz Bufe and Mitchell Cowen Verter, eds., *Dreams of Freedom: A Ricardo Flores Magón Reader* (Oakland, CA: AK Press, 2005); Gale Ahrens, ed., *Lucy Parsons: Freedom, Equality and Solidarity, Writings and Speeches, 1878–1937* (Chicago: Charles H. Kerr, 2004); Praxedis G. Guerrero, *I Am Action: Literary and Combat Articles, Thoughts, and Revolutionary Chronicles*, trans. Javier Sethness-Castro (Chico, CA: AK Press, 2018); Alexander Berkman, ed., *The Selected Works of Voltairine de Cleyre: Poems, Essays, Sketches, and Stories, 1885–1911* (Chico, CA: AK Press, 2016).

2. Some of many possible examples: Jesse Cohn, *Underground Passages: Anarchist Resistance Culture, 1848–2011* (Oakland, CA: AK Press, 2014); Mark Bray, *The Anarchist*

*Inquisition: Assassins, Activists, and Martyrs in Spain and France* (Ithaca, NY: Cornell University Press, 2022); Antonio Senta, *Luigi Galleani: The Most Dangerous Anarchist in America* (Chico, CA: AK Press, 2019); Mark Leier, *Bakunin: The Revolutionary Passion* (New York: St. Martin's Press, 2006); Ángel J. Cappelletti, *Anarchism in Latin America*, trans. Gabriel Palmer-Fernández (Chico, CA: AK Press, 2017); Kenyon Zimmer, *Immigrants against the State: Yiddish and Italian Anarchism in America* (Urbana: University of Illinois Press, 2015); Jennifer Guglielmo, *Living the Revolution: Italian Women's Resistance and Radicalism in New York City, 1880–1945* (Chapel Hill: University of North Carolina Press, 2010); Tom Goyens, *Beer and Revolution: The German Anarchist Movement in New York City, 1880–1914* (Urbana: University of Illinois Press, 2007); Steven Hirsch and Lucien van der Walt, eds., *Anarchism and Syndicalism in the Colonial and Postcolonial World, 1870–1940: The Praxis of National Liberation, Internationalism, and Social Revolution* (Leiden, Neth.: Brill, 2010).

3. Friedrich Engels, *The Origin of the Family, Private Property and the State* (Chicago: Charles H. Kerr, 1902), 211–12. First published in 1884 in Hottingen-Zurich, Switz.

4. Pierre Kropotkine, *La Conquête du pain*, 2nd ed. (Paris: Tresse and Stock, 1892), 31. My translation.

5. Robert Graham, *We Do Not Fear Anarchy, We Invoke It: The First International and the Origins of the Anarchist Movement* (Oakland, CA: AK Press, 2015).

## Introduction

1. Some of many possible examples: M. J. Heale, *American Anticommunism: Combating the Enemy Within, 1830–1970* (Baltimore: Johns Hopkins University Press, 1990); Robert J. Goldstein, *Political Repression in Modern America: From 1870 to 1976* (Urbana: University of Illinois Press, 2001); Regin Schmidt, *Red Scare: FBI and the Origins of Anticommunism in the United States, 1919–1943* (Copenhagen, Denmark: Museum Tusculanum Press, 2000); Frank J. Donner, *Protectors of Privilege: Red Squads and Political Repression in Urban America* (Berkeley: University of California Press, 1990); Frank J. Donner, *The Age of Surveillance: The Aims and Methods of America's Political Intelligence System* (New York: Knopf, 1980); Kenneth D. Ackerman, *Young J. Edgar: Hoover and the Red Scare, 1919–1920* (Falls Church, VA: Viral History Press, 2011); Rhodri Jeffreys-Jones, *The FBI: A History* (New Haven, CT: Yale University Press, 2007); Bud Schultz and Ruth Schultz, *It Did Happen Here: Recollections of Political Repression* (Berkeley: University of California Press, 1989); Theodore Kornweibel Jr., *Seeing Red: Federal Campaigns against Black Militancy, 1919–1925* (Bloomington: Indiana University Press, 1998); Joel Kovel, *Red Hunting in the Promised Land: Anticommunism and the Making of America* (London: Cassell, 1997); Richard M. Fried, *Nightmare in Red: The McCarthy Era in Perspective* (New York: Oxford University Press, 1990); Paul Avrich, *The Haymarket Tragedy* (Princeton, NJ: Princeton University Press, 1984).

2. On empire and mythological structure, see Edward Said, *Culture and Imperialism* (New York: Vintage, 1993); Philip J. Deloria, *Playing Indian* (New Haven, CT: Yale University Press, 1998); Roy Harvey Pearce, *Savagism and Civilization: A Study of the Indian and the American Mind* (Berkeley: University of California Press, 1988); Greg Grandin,

*The End of the Myth: From the Frontier to the Border Wall in the Mind of America* (New York: Metropolitan, 2019); Richard Drinnon, *Facing West: The Metaphysics of Indian-Hating and Empire-Building* (Norman: University of Oklahoma Press, 1997); Michael Rogin, *Ronald Reagan the Movie: And Other Episodes in Political Demonology* (Berkeley: University of California Press, 1988); Richard Slotkin, *Gunfighter Nation: The Myth of the Frontier in Twentieth-Century America* (New York: Harper Perennial, 1993); Steven Salaita, "'Playing Indian' and the US Colonial Imagination," *University of Minnesota Press Blog* (blog), March 16, 2017, https://uminnpressblog.com/2017/03/16/playing-indian-and-the-us-colonial-imagination/; Ward Churchill, *Fantasies of the Master Race: Literature, Cinema, and the Colonization of American Indians* (San Francisco: City Lights, 1998).

3. Vincent Brown, *Tacky's Revolt: The Story of an Atlantic Slave War* (Cambridge, MA: Harvard University Press, 2020); Gerald Horne, *The Apocalypse of Settler Colonialism: The Roots of Slavery, White Supremacy, and Capitalism in Seventeenth-Century North America and the Caribbean* (New York: Monthly Review Press, 2018); Gerald Horne, *The Dawning of the Apocalypse: The Roots of Slavery, White Supremacy, Settler Colonialism, and Capitalism in the Long Sixteenth Century* (New York: Monthly Review Press, 2020); Roxanne Dunbar-Ortiz, *An Indigenous Peoples' History of the United States* (Boston: Beacon Press, 2015); Walter Rodney, *How Europe Underdeveloped Africa* (New York: Verso, 2018).

4. US Declaration of Independence.

5. Dunbar-Ortiz, *Indigenous Peoples' History*, 3.

6. Max M. Edling, *A Revolution in Favor of Government: Origins of the U.S. Constitution and the Making of the American State* (Oxford: Oxford University Press, 2003); Max M. Edling, *A Hercules in the Cradle: War, Money, and the American State, 1783–1867* (Chicago: University of Chicago Press, 2014).

7. Roxanne Dunbar-Ortiz, *Loaded: A Disarming History of the Second Amendment* (San Francisco, CA: City Lights, 2018), 39.

8. Merritt Roe Smith, ed., *Military Enterprise and Technological Change: Perspectives on the American Experience* (Cambridge, MA: MIT Press, 1985).

9. Horne, *Apocalypse of Settler Colonialism*; Horne, *Dawning of the Apocalypse*.

10. Walter Johnson, *The Broken Heart of America: St. Louis and the Violent History of the United States* (New York: Basic Books, 2020), 9–10.

11. Ranajit Guha, *Elementary Aspects of Peasant Insurgency in Colonial India* (Durham, NC: Duke University Press, 1999), 4.

12. Some notable exceptions are Dongyoun Hwang, *Anarchism in Korea: Independence, Transnationalism, and the Question of National Development 1919–1984* (Albany, NY: SUNY Press, 2016); Arif Dirlik, *Anarchism in the Chinese Revolution* (Berkeley: University of California Press, 1991); Benedict Anderson, *Under Three Flags: Anarchism and the Anti-colonial Imagination* (London: Verso, 2007); Hirsch and van der Walt, *Anarchism and Syndicalism*; Maia Ramnath, *Haj to Utopia: How the Ghadar Movement Charted Global Radicalism and Attempted to Overthrow the British Empire* (Berkeley: University of California Press, 2011); Maia Ramnath, *Decolonizing Anarchism: An Anti-authoritarian History of India's Liberation Struggle* (Oakland, CA: AK Press, 2011); John M. Hart, *Anarchism and the Mexican Working Class, 1860–1931* (Austin: University of

Texas Press, 1978); Kirwin R. Shaffer, *Black Flag Boricuas: Anarchism, Antiauthoritarianism, and the Left in Puerto Rico, 1897–1921* (Urbana: University of Illinois Press, 2013).

13. Here again there are some notable exceptions such as those mentioned in note 12.

14. Annie Karni and Maggie Haberman, "At Mt. Rushmore and the White House, Trump Updates 'American Carnage' Message for 2020," *New York Times*, July 4, 2020, https://www.nytimes.com/2020/07/04/us/politics/trump-mt-rushmore.html; Dalton Walker, "Black Hills Treaty Defender Faces Felony Charges," *Indian Country Today*, July 6, 2020, https://indiancountrytoday.com/news/black-hills-treaty-defender-faces-felony-charges-UIcevFnGqUKdRfDckw7qWw. One of the arrested treaty defenders, Nick Tilson of the Oglala Lakota, said to the press, "We made it clear that the president of the United States wasn't welcome in our territory without the prior consent of our people and our tribal leaders."

15. Patrick Wolfe, "Settler Colonialism and the Elimination of the Native," *Journal of Genocide Research* 8, no. 4 (2006): 387–409.

16. Some examples: Dunbar-Ortiz, *Indigenous Peoples' History*; Horne, *Apocalypse of Settler Colonialism*; Horne, *Dawning of the Apocalypse*; Steven Salaita, *Inter/Nationalism: Decolonizing Native America and Palestine* (Minneapolis: University of Minnesota Press, 2016); Kelly Lytle Hernández, *City of Inmates: Conquest, Rebellion, and the Rise of Human Caging in Los Angeles, 1771–1965* (Chapel Hill: University of North Carolina Press, 2017); Nick Estes, *Our History Is the Future: Standing Rock versus the Dakota Access Pipeline, and the Long Tradition of Indigenous Resistance* (London: Verso, 2019); Nick Estes et al., *Red Nation Rising: From Bordertown Violence to Native Liberation* (Oakland, CA: PM Press, 2021); Harsha Walia, *Undoing Border Imperialism* (Oakland, CA: AK Press/Institute for Anarchist Studies, 2013); Harsha Walia, *Border and Rule: Global Migration, Capitalism, and the Rise of Racist Nationalism* (Chicago: Haymarket, 2021).

17. For example, Julian Go, "The Imperial Origins of American Policing: Militarization and Imperial Feedback in the Early 20th Century," *American Journal of Sociology* 125, no. 5 (2020): 1193–254.

18. "Concentrating Troops," *New York Tribune*, July 27, 1877, 1; "Incidents in Washington," *New York Tribune*, July 27, 1877, 1.

19. "Concentrating Troops"; "Incidents in Washington."

20. "Concentrating Troops"; "Incidents in Washington."

## Chapter 1. Class, Race, Gender, and Empire

1. Concerning the politics of gender, race, and class influencing US leaders' decisions to go to war, see Kristin L. Hoganson, *Fighting for American Manhood: How Gender Politics Provoked the Spanish-American and Philippine-American Wars* (New Haven, CT: Yale University Press, 1998); Matthew Frye Jacobson, *Barbarian Virtues: The United States Encounters Foreign Peoples at Home and Abroad, 1876–1917* (New York: Hill and Wang, 2000); Gail Bederman, *Manliness and Civilization: A Cultural History of Gender and Race in the United States, 1880–1917* (Chicago: University of Chicago Press, 1995).

2. Chuck Morse, "African Anarchism: Interview with Sam Mbah," *Perspectives on*

*Anarchist Theory* (Spring 1999): 9; Sam Mbah and I. E. Igariwey, *African Anarchism: The History of a Movement* (Tucson, AZ: See Sharp Press, 1997).

3. Lorenzo Kom'boa Ervin, *Anarchism and the Black Revolution* (New York: Horse and Goat Peoples' Affinity Group, 1979).

4. Ruth Wilson Gilmore, "Abolition Geography and the Problem of Innocence," in *Futures of Black Radicalism*, ed. Gaye Theresa Johnson and Alex Lubin (New York: Verso, 2017), 225.

5. Cedric Robinson, *Black Marxism: The Making of the Black Radical Tradition* (Chapel Hill: University of North Carolina Press, 2000); Robin D. G. Kelley, "What Did Cedric Robinson Mean by Racial Capitalism?" *Boston Review*, January 12, 2017, http://bostonreview .net/race/robin-d-g-kelley-what-did-cedric-robinson-mean-racial-capitalism.

6. Cedric Robinson, quoted in H. L. T. Quan, "Geniuses of Resistance: Feminist Consciousness and the Black Radical Tradition," *Race and Class* 47, no. 2 (2005): 47.

7. Frantz Fanon, *The Wretched of the Earth* (New York: Grove, 2004), 5.

8. Charisse Burden-Stelly, "Constructing Deportable Subjectivity: Antiforeignness, Antiradicalism, and Antiblackness during the McCarthyist Structure of Feeling," *Souls* 19, no. 3 (2017): 342–58; Charisse Burden-Stelly, "Modern U.S. Racial Capitalism: Some Theoretical Insights," *Monthly Review*, July 1, 2020, https://monthlyreview.org/ 2020/07/01/modern-u-s-racial-capitalism/; "Radicalism and Sedition among the Negroes, As Reflected in Their Publications," *New York Times*, November 23, 1919.

9. "Radicalism and Sedition."

10. "Negro Workers: The A.F. of L. or I.W.W.," *The Messenger*, July 1919.

11. "Why Negroes Should Join the I.W.W.," *The Messenger*, July 1919.

12. Ibid.

13. Heather Cox Richardson, *The Death of Reconstruction: Race, Labor, and Politics in the Post–Civil War North, 1865–1901* (Cambridge, MA: Harvard University Press, 2001), 89.

14. This conflation of Black freedom struggles with communist reds intent on destroying America became a staple in US anti-communist ideology and state policy. On this, see Gerald Horne, *Black Liberation/Red Scare: Ben Davis and the Communist Party* (Newark: University of Delaware Press, 1994).

15. Richardson, *Death of Reconstruction*.

16. William Jay, *The Life of John Jay with Selections from His Correspondence and Miscellaneous Papers*, vol. 1 (New York: J and J Harper, 1833), 70.

17. Sven Beckert, *The Monied Metropolis: New York City and the Consolidation of the American Bourgeoisie, 1850–1896* (Cambridge: Cambridge University Press, 2001).

18. Dick Gaughan, *Handful of Earth* (Edinburgh, Scotland: Topic Records, 1981).

19. Emma Goldman to Stella Ballantine, August 2, 1919, quoted in Kathy Ferguson, *Emma Goldman: Political Thinking in the Streets* (Lanham, MD: Rowman and Littlefield, 2011), 212.

20. Matthew Frye Jacobson, *Whiteness of a Different Color: European Immigrants and the Alchemy of Race* (Cambridge, MA: Harvard University Press, 1998), 95.

21. David Roediger, *Working toward Whiteness: How America's Immigrants Became*

*White: The Strange Journey from Ellis Island to the Suburbs* (New York: Basic Books, 2005).

22. Noel Ignatiev, *How the Irish Became White* (New York: Routledge, 1995), 3.

23. *Irish Times*, March 23, 1992

24. "Irish Give Key to City to Panthers as Symbol," *New York Times*, March 3, 1970, 31.

25. Jennifer Guglielmo, *Living the Revolution: Italian Women's Resistance and Radicalism in New York City, 1880–1945*, 236.

26. Kenyon Zimmer, *Immigrants against the State: Yiddish and Italian Anarchism in America* (Urbana: University of Illinois Press, 2015) 73–75.

27. Salvatore Salerno, "I delitti della razza blanca (crimes of the white race): Italian Anarchists' Racial Discourse as Crime," in *Are Italians White?: How Race Is Made in America*, ed. Jennifer Guglielmo and Salvatore Salerno (New York: Routledge, 2003), 121.

28. Zimmer, *Immigrants against the State*; Guglielmo, *Living the Revolution*; Ferguson, *Emma Goldman*.

29. Emily C. Brown, *Har Dayal: Hindu Revolutionary and Rationalist* (Tucson: University of Arizona Press, 1975), 133.

30. Alexander Berkman, *The Blast*, February 19, 1916, 4–5.

31. Kanno Sugako, "Reflections on the Way to the Gallows," 1911, in Mikiso Hane, *Reflections on the Way to the Gallows: Rebel Women in Prewar Japan* (Berkeley: University of California Press, 1988), 66.

32. Alexander Berkman, *What Is Anarchism?* (Edinburgh, Scotland: AK Press, 2003), 203.

33. Guglielmo, *Living the Revolution*, 217.

34. Ibid., 201–7.

35. Robert Blauner, "Internal Colonialism and Ghetto Revolt," *Social Problems* 16, no. 4 (1969): 393–408; Robert Blauner, *Racial Oppression in America* (New York: Harper and Row, 1972).

36. Christina Heatherton, "University of Radicalism: Ricardo Flores Magón and Leavenworth Penitentiary," *American Quarterly* 66, no. 3 (September 2014): 557–81; Ramnath, *Haj to Utopia*; Shaffer, *Black Flag Boricuas*; Peter Cole, *Wobblies on the Waterfront: Interracial Unionism in Progressive-Era Philadelphia* (Urbana: University of Illinois Press, 2007); Peter Cole, *Ben Fletcher: The Life and Times of a Black Wobbly* (Chicago: Charles H. Kerr, 2006); Peter Cole, David Struthers, and Kenyon Zimmer, eds., *Wobblies of the World: A Global History of the IWW* (London: Pluto, 2017); Zimmer, *Immigrants against the State*; Kenyon Zimmer and Cristina Salinas, eds., *Deportation in the Americas: Histories of Exclusion and Resistance* (College Station: Texas A and M University Press, 2018).

37. Brown, *Har Dayal*, 112–17; Mark Bray and Robert H. Haworth, eds., *Anarchist Education and the Modern School: A Francisco Ferrer Reader* (Oakland, CA: PM Press, 2019); Paul Avrich, *The Modern School Movement: Anarchism and Education in the United States* (Oakland, CA: AK Press, 2006); Ramnath, *Haj to Utopia*; Ramnath, *Decolonizing Anarchism: An Antiauthoritarian History of India's Liberation Struggle* (Oakland, CA: AK Press, 2011); Zimmer, *Immigrants against the State*, 105–6.

38. Brown, *Har Dayal*, 112–17; Ramnath, *Decolonizing Anarchism*; Ramnath, *Haj to Utopia*; Richard Drinnon, *Rebel in Paradise: A Biography of Emma Goldman* (Boston: Beacon, 1961), 206–9.

39. E. J. Hobsbawm, *Revolutionaries: Contemporary Essays* (London: Weidenfeld and Nicolson, 1973), 61–62.

40. Ángel J. Cappelletti, *Anarchism in Latin America* (Oakland, CA: AK Press, 2017); John M. Hart, *Anarchism and the Mexican Working Class, 1860–1931* (Austin: University of Texas Press, 1978); David Porter, *Eyes to the South : French Anarchists and Algeria* (Oakland, CA: AK Press, 2011); Hwang, *Anarchism in Korea*; Hirsch and van der Walt, *Anarchism and Syndicalism*; Ramnath, *Haj to Utopia*; Maia Ramnath, *Decolonizing Anarchism*; Shaffer, *Black Flag Boricua*; Cole et al., *Wobblies of the World*; Anderson, *Under Three Flags*; John Crump, *Hatta Shuzo and Pure Anarchism in Interwar Japan* (New York: St. Martin's, 1993); Dirlik, *Anarchism in the Chinese Revolution*; Kenyon Zimmer, "Haymarket and the Rise of Syndicalism," in *The Palgrave Handbook of Anarchism*, ed. Carl Levy and Matthew S. Adams (London: Palgrave Macmillan, 2019).

41. Anderson, *Under Three Flags*, 2.

42. Benedict Anderson, in Hirsch and van der Walt, *Anarchism and Syndicalism*, xvii.

43. Cole, *Wobblies on the Waterfront*; Cole, *Ben Fletcher*; Cole et al., *Wobblies of the World*; Hirsch and van der Walt, *Anarchism and Syndicalism*.

44. Mohammed Elnaiem, "Interview: The League of Revolutionary Black Workers," *JSTOR Daily*, July 9, 2020, https://daily.jstor.org/league-revolutionary-black-workers/?f bclid=IwAR1aRffYEnWepCBFGAjh_NaqgpZhpmTovv28ahtKJqLlG0G4SCd3gDOc9L0.

45. Jeff Shantz, "Bows and Arrows: Indigenous Workers, IWW Local 526, and Syndicalism on the Vancouver Docks," *Libcom*, February 17, 2021, https://libcom. org/history/bows-arrows-indigenous-workers-iww-local-526-syndicalism-vancouver -docks?fbclid=IwAR3CacAIBz0DPbkGMueKT_qwAH0vImjt6lGy0CwDQYxzullIJ7N FoOOUih4. Rolf Knight, *Indians at Work: An Informal History of Native Indian Labour in British Columbia, 1858–1930* (Vancouver, BC: New Star, 1978); Chris Roine, "The Squamish Aboriginal Economy, 1860–1940" (Burnaby, Simon Fraser University, 1996); Andrew Parnaby, *Citizen Docker: Making a New Deal on the Vancouver Waterfront 1919–1939* (Toronto: University of Toronto Press, 2008); James P. Delgado, *Waterfront: The Illustrated Maritime History of Greater Vancouver* (Vancouver, BC: Stanton Atkins and Dosil, 2010); Harold Deppiesse, Ben Swankey, and International Longshoremen's and Warehousemen's Union Local 500 Pensioners, *Man along the Shore! : The Story of the Vancouver Waterfront as Told by Longshoremen Themselves, 1860's-1975* (Vancouver, BC: ILWU Local 500 Pensioners, 1975).

46. Cappelletti, *Anarchism in Latin America*; Devra Anne Weber, "'Different Plans': Indigenous Pasts, the Partido Liberal Mexicano, and Questions about Reframing Binational Social Movements of the Twentieth Century," *Social Justice* 42, nos. 3–4 (142) (2015): 10–28; Devra Anne Weber, "Keeping Community, Challenging Boundaries: Indigenous Migrants, Internationalist Workers and Mexican Revolutionaries, 1900–1920," in *Mexico and Mexicans in the History and Culture of the United States*, by John Tutino (Austin: University of Texas Press, 2012), 208–35; Devra Anne Weber, "Wobblies of the

Notes to Chapter 1     203

Partido Liberal Mexicano: Reenvisioning Internationalist and Transnational Movements through Mexican Lenses," *Pacific Historical Review* 85, no. 2 (2016): 188–226.

47. Walter Rodney, "Race and Class in Guyanese Politics" (lecture, Columbia University, New York, 1978); Sina Rahmani, "Walter Rodney on Race and Class in Guyanese Politics (1978)," *The East Is a Podcast*, February 24, 2019, https://eastisapodcast.libsyn.com/walter-rodney-on-race-and-class-in-guyanese-politics-1978.

48. Rodney, "Race and Class."

49. Guglielmo, *Living the Revolution*, 106.

50. Roediger, *Working toward Whiteness*, 77.

51. Erik S. McDuffie, *Sojourning for Freedom: Black Women, American Communism, and the Making of Black Left Feminism* (Durham, NC: Duke University Press, 2011); Aileen Moreton-Robinson, *Talkin' Up to the White Woman: Aboriginal Women and Feminism* (Queensland, Australia: University of Queensland Press, 2000); Aileen Moreton-Robinson, *The White Possessive: Property, Power, and Indigenous Sovereignty* (Minneapolis: University of Minnesota Press, 2015); Leanne Betasamosake Simpson, *As We Have Always Done: Indigenous Freedom through Radical Resistance* (Minneapolis: University of Minnesota Press, 2017); Joanne Barker, ed., *Critically Sovereign: Indigenous Gender, Sexuality, and Feminist Studies* (Durham, NC: Duke University Press, 2017).

52. Claudia Jones, *An End to the Neglect of the Problems of the Negro Woman!* (New York: National Women's Commission, CPUSA, 1949), 3–4.

53. Ibid.

54. Barbara Smith, ed., *Home Girls: A Black Feminist Anthology* (New Brunswick, NJ: Rutgers University Press, 2000), 267–68.

55. Smith, *Home Girls*, xvi.

56. Moreton-Robinson, *White Possessive*.

57. Pierre-Joseph Proudhon, *What Is Property? An Inquiry into the Principle of Right and of Government*, trans. Benjamin R. Tucker (New York: Dover, 1970). First published in French in 1840.

58. For discussion of the relationship between property and theft, see Robert Nichols, *Theft Is Property!: Dispossession and Critical Theory* (Durham, NC: Duke University Press, 2020).

59. Robin D. G. Kelley, "Lucy Parsons," in *Black Women in America*, vol. 2 (New York: Carlson, 1993), 909–10; Carolyn Ashbaugh, *Lucy Parsons: American Revolutionary* (Chicago: Charles H. Kerr, 1976); Gale Ahrens, ed., *Lucy Parsons: Freedom, Equality, and Solidarity, Writings and Speeches, 1878–1937* (Chicago: Charles H. Kerr, 2004).

60. Nayan Shah, *Stranger Intimacy: Contesting Race, Sexuality, and the Law in the North American West* (Berkeley: University of California Press, 2011).

61. Brown, *Har Dayal*, 115.

62. Margaret Marsh, *Anarchist Women, 1870–1920* (Philadelphia: Temple University Press, 1981); Candace Serena Falk, *Love, Anarchy, and Emma Goldman*, rev. ed. (New Brunswick, NJ: Rutgers University Press, 1990); Drinnon, *Rebel in Paradise*; A. J. Brigati, ed., *The Voltairine de Cleyre Reader* (Oakland, CA: AK Press, 2004); Sharon Presley and Crispin Sartwell, eds., *Exquisite Rebel: The Essays of Voltairine de Cleyre* (New York: SUNY Press, 2005). For more on Comstock laws, see Amy Werbel, *Lust on Trial:*

*Censorship and the Rise of American Obscenity in the Age of Anthony Comstock* (New York: Columbia University Press, 2018); Leslie J. Reagan, *When Abortion Was a Crime: Women, Medicine, and Law in the United States, 1867–1973* (Oakland, CA: University of California Press, 2022).

63. Alexander Berkman, *Prison Memoirs of an Anarchist* (Pittsburgh, PA: Frontier Press, 1970); Falk, *Love, Anarchy, and Emma Goldman*, 1990.

64. Sarah Deer, *The Beginning and End of Rape: Confronting Sexual Violence in Native America* (Minneapolis: University of Minnesota Press, 2015), xv.

65. Dian Million, *Therapeutic Nations: Healing in an Age of Indigenous Human Rights* (Tucson: University of Arizona Press, 2013).

66. A few examples: Kim Anderson, *A Recognition of Being: Reconstructing Native Womanhood*, 2nd ed. (Toronto: Women's Press, 2016); Jennifer Nez Denetdale, "Securing Navajo National Boundaries: War, Patriotism, Tradition, and the Dine Marriage Act of 2005," *Wicazo Sa Review* 24, no. 2 (Fall 2009): 131–48; Audra Simpson, "The State Is a Man: Theresa Spence, Loretta Saunders and the Gender of Settler Sovereignty," *Theory and Event* 19, no. 4 (2016).

67. Deepa Kumar, *Islamophobia and the Politics of Empire* (Chicago: Haymarket, 2012).

68. Omar Waraich, "Malala, Obama, Socialism: Nobel Laureate's Political Views Are Complex," *Al Jazeera America*, December 23, 2014, http://america.aljazeera.com/articles/2014/12/23/-hold-malala-obamasocialismnobellaureatespoliticalviewscomplex.html.

69. Oliver C. Cox, "Lynching and the Status Quo," *Journal of Negro Education* 14, no. 4 (Autumn 1945): 576–88.

## Chapter 2. "Civilization" versus "Savagery"

1. Paul Avrich, *The Haymarket Tragedy* (Princeton, NJ: Princeton University Press, 1984); Jeremy Brecher, *Strike!*, rev. ed. (Oakland, CA: PM Press, 2014); Frank Donner, *Protectors of Privilege: Red Squads and Police Repression in Urban America* (Berkeley: University of California Press, 1990); Melvyn Dubofsky, *We Shall Be All: A History of the Industrial Workers of the World* (Chicago: Quadrangle, 1969); Fried, *Nightmare in Red*); Goldstein, *Political Repression*); Heale, *American Anticommunism*); Nell Irvin Painter, *Standing at Armageddon: The United States, 1877–1919* (New York: W. W. Norton, 1987); Richard Slotkin, *The Fatal Environment: The Myth of the Frontier in the Age of Industrialization, 1800–1890* (Norman: University of Oklahoma Press, 1985); Tim Weiner, *Enemies: A History of the FBI* (New York: Random House, 2012); Kristian Williams, *Our Enemies in Blue: Police and Power in America*, 3rd ed. (Oakland, CA: AK Press, 2015).

2. Peter Adams, *The Bowery Boys: Street Corner Radicals and the Politics of Rebellion* (Westport, CT: Praeger, 2005); Heale, *American Anticommunism*.

3. Shelley Streeby, *American Sensations: Class, Empire, and the Production of Popular Culture* (Berkeley: University of California Press, 2002).

4. Adams, *Bowery Boys*.

5. *Congressional Globe*, 30th Cong., 1st sess. 656 (1848).

6. Ibid.

7. Thanks to Matt Stoller for tipping me off about mid-nineteenth-century anticommunism in the *Congressional Record*.

8. *Congressional Globe*, 30th Cong., 1st sess. 906 (1848).

9. Ibid.

10. Ibid.

11. Jack K. Bauer, *Zachary Taylor: Soldier, Planter, Statesman of the Old Southwest* (Baton Rouge: Louisiana State University Press, 1985).

12. *House Documents, Otherwise Publ. as Executive Documents*, 31st Congress, 2d Session, Vol. 1, Washington, DC: Printed for the US House of Representatives, 1850, 80.

13. Ibid.

14. Ibid., 81.

15. *Proceedings of the Third Annual Meeting of the Lake Mohonk Conference of Friends of the Indian* (Philadelphia: Sherman, 1886), 43.

16. *House Documents, Otherwise Publ. as Executive Documents*, 31st Congress, 2d Session, Vol. 1, 1850 (Washington, DC: n.p., printed for the US House of Representatives), 109–10.

17. Ibid., 107.

18. Ibid.

19. *Collections of the Minnesota Historical Society*, vol. 10, pt. I (St. Paul: Minnesota Historical Society, 1905).

20. John Locke, *Two Treatises on Civil Government* (London: George Routledge and Sons, 1884). Locke is further discussed in chapter 4. See chapter 4, notes 1–3.

21. Alexander Ramsey, *Message of Governor Ramsey to the Legislature of Minnesota: Delivered at the Extra Session, September 9, 1862* (St. Paul, MN: Wm. R. Marshall, 1862).

22. Gary Clayton Anderson, *Kinsmen of Another Kind: Dakota-White Relations in the Upper Mississippi Valley, 1650–1862* (St. Paul: Minnesota Historical Society Press, 1984); Gary Clayton Anderson, *Little Crow: Spokesman for the Sioux* (St. Paul: Minnesota Historical Society Press, 1986); Gary Clayton Anderson and Alan R. Woolworth, eds., *Through Dakota Eyes: Narrative Accounts of the Minnesota Indian War of 1862* (St. Paul: Minnesota Historical Society Press, 1988); Waziyatawin Angela Wilson, *Remember This!: Dakota Decolonization and the Eli Taylor Narratives*, trans. Wahpetunwin Carolynn Schommer (Lincoln: University of Nebraska Press, 2005); Waziyatawin Angela Wilson, ed., *In the Footsteps of Our Ancestors: The Dakota Commemorative Marches of the 21st Century* (St. Paul, MN: Living Justice, 2006).

23. Jacqueline Jones, *Goddess of Anarchy: The Life and Times of Lucy Parsons, American Radical* (New York: Basic Books, 2017); Ashbaugh, *Lucy Parsons*; Ahrens, *Lucy Parsons*.

24. Franklin Rosemont, "Anarchists and the Wild West," in *Haymarket Scrapbook* (Chicago: Charles H. Kerr, 1986), 101.

25. Michael J. Schaack, *Anarchy and Anarchists: A History of the Red Terror and the Social Revolution in America and Europe; Communism, Socialism, and Nihilism in Doctrine and Deed; the Chicago Haymarket Conspiracy, and the Detection and Trial of the Conspirators.* (Chicago: F. J. Schulte, 1889), 117.

26. Ibid.

27. Ibid., 118–19.

28. Ibid., 370.

29. Ibid., 126.

30. "Anarchy's Den: Emma Goldman, Its Queen, Rules with a Nod the Savage Reds," *New York World*, July 28, 1892; Candace Falk, Barry Pateman, and Jessica Moran, *Emma Goldman: A Documentary History of the American Years*, vol. 1, *Made for America, 1890–1901* (Urbana: University of Illinois Press, 2003).

31. "Anarchy's Den"; The phrase "broader chested than Sullivan" refers to the 1882–92 world heavyweight boxing champion and white supremacist who raised the color bar in the newly popular sport of gloved boxing, John L. Sullivan.

32. "Anarchy's Den."

33. Warren Wildwood, *Thrilling Adventures among the Early Settlers* (Philadelphia: J. Edwin Potter, 1890).

34. Ibid., 347–48.

35. Ibid., 176–81.

36. Ibid., 5–6. It is important to note that in reality, vigilante violence often functioned where formal state authority was not at all lacking. White supremacist vigilantes often removed their victims from jails, with state complicity. Vigilantism was not a stand-in for formal state violence but often functioned in addition to and in coordination with the formal forces of the state. The notion that vigilantes acted to preserve order in the absence of state authority is a myth that functioned to legitimize and idealize white supremacist mob violence.

37. Streeby, *American Sensations*, 253; Michael Denning, *Mechanic Accents: Dime Novels and Working-Class Culture in America* (London: Verso, 1998).

38. John Joseph Flinn and John Elbert Wilkie, *History of the Chicago Police* (Chicago: Chicago Police Book Fund, 1887), 11.

39. Flinn and Wilkie, *History of the Chicago Police*, 9.

40. Ann Durkin Keating, *Rising Up from Indian Country: The Battle of Fort Dearborn and the Birth of Chicago* (Chicago: University of Chicago Press, 2012), 238.

41. Dunbar-Ortiz, *Indigenous Peoples' History*, 86.

42. John Grenier, *The First Way of War: American War Making on the Frontier, 1607–1814* (Cambridge: Cambridge University Press, 2005), 5.

43. Grenier, *First Way of War*; Keating, *Rising Up*; Dunbar-Ortiz, *Indigenous Peoples' History*.

44. Keating, *Rising Up*, 5.

45. Keating, *Rising Up*; Grenier, *First Way of War*; Dunbar-Ortiz, *Indigenous Peoples' History*.

46. Flinn and Wilkie, *History of the Chicago Police*, 443.

47. Keating, *Rising Up*.

48. Robert W. Rydell, *All the World's a Fair: Visions of Empire at American International Expositions, 1876–1916* (Chicago: University of Chicago Press, 1984); Daniel E. Bender, *American Abyss: Savagery and Civilization in the Age of Industry* (Ithaca. NY: Cornell University Press, 2009); Jacobson, *Barbarian Virtues*; Bederman, *Manliness and Civilization*; James Gilbert, *Perfect Cities: Chicago's Utopias of 1893* (Chicago: University of Chicago Press, 1991).

49. *An act to provide for celebrating the four hundredth anniversary of the discovery of America by Christopher Columbus, by holding an international exposition of arts, industries, manufactures, and products of the soil, mine, and sea in the city of Chicago, in the state of Illinois*, H.R. 9710, 52nd Congress, 1st sess., August 5, 1892.

50. Virginia C. Meredith, "Woman's Part at the World's Fair," *Review of Reviews* 7, June 1893, 417.

51. Bender, *American Abyss*, 28.

52. Bender, *American Abyss*, 51–52.

53. The original celebrated *bon mot* was "The only good Indians I ever saw were dead." Officers present, impressed by the phrase, passed it along until it morphed into the genocidal aphorism "The only good Indian is a dead Indian" (Edward S. Ellis, *The History of Our Country from the Discovery of America to the Present Time* [Los Angeles: Sanderson Whitten, 1900], 1483; Dee Brown, *Bury My Heart at Wounded Knee: An Indian History of the American West* [New York: Henry Holt, 1970], 170–72).

54. Keating, *Rising Up*, 239–40.

55. Attendees are listed in Chicago Historical Society, *Ceremonies at the Unveiling of the Bronze Memorial Group of the Chicago Massacre of 1812* (Chicago: Blakely and Rogers, 1893), 3–5.

56. Ibid., 7.

57. Ibid., 17.

58. 59. 60. Flinn and Wilkie, *History of the Chicago Police*, 6.

61. Ibid., 359.

62. Ibid., 14–15.

63. This settler colonizer notion of policing remains firmly in place into the present, as evidenced by the police metaphor the "thin blue line," which symbolizes law enforcement's justification of itself as the barrier standing between civilization and savagery, or order and chaos. For further discussion of the thin blue line metaphor, see James Lasley, *Los Angeles Police Department Meltdown: The Fall of the Professional-Reform Model of Policing* (Boca Raton, FL: Taylor and Francis, 2012), 5–7; Jeff Sharlett, "A Flag for Trump's America," *Harper's Magazine*, July 2018, 60–61.

64. Bender, *American Abyss*; Jacobson, *Barbarian Virtues*; Hoganson, *Fighting for American Manhood*; Glenda Elizabeth Gilmore, *Gender and Jim Crow: Women and the Politics of White Supremacy in North Carolina, 1896–1920* (Chapel Hill: University of North Carolina Press, 1996); John F. Kasson, *Houdini, Tarzan, and the Perfect Man: The White Male Body and the Challenge of Modernity in America* (New York: Hill and Wang, 2001); Amy S. Greenberg, *Manifest Manhood and the Antebellum American Empire* (Cambridge: Cambridge University Press, 2005); Bederman, *Manliness and Civilization*; Richard Slotkin, *The Fatal Environment: The Myth of the Frontier in the Age of Industrialization, 1800–1890* (Norman: University of Oklahoma Press, 1985).

65. Schaack, *Anarchy and Anarchists*, 207.

66. Ibid., 207–8.

67. Carolyn J. Eichner, *Surmounting the Barricades: Women in the Paris Commune* (Bloomington: Indiana University Press, 2004).

68. Hay to Amasa Stone, March 11, 1883, in John Hay, *Letters of John Hay and Extracts from Diary*, vol. 2 (New York: Gordian, 1969), 83.

69. Peter Kropotkin, *Direct Struggle against Capital: A Peter Kropotkin Anthology*, ed. Iain McKay (Oakland, CA: AK Press, 2014), 83; Robert Graham, *We Do Not Fear Anarchy, We Invoke It: The First International and the Origins of the Anarchist Movement*, ISBN: 978-1-84935-211-6, in the public domain, https://theanarchistlibrary.org/library/robert-graham-we-do-not-fear-anarchy-we-invoke-it#toc9, 244.

70. Louise Michel, *The Red Virgin: Memoirs of Louise Michel*, ed. Bullitt Lowry and Elizabeth Ellington Gunter (Tuscaloosa: University of Alabama Press, 1981), 162; Graham, *We Do Not Fear Anarchy, We Invoke It: The First International and the Origins of the Anarchist Movement*.

71. Genesis 3:1–13 (King James version).

72. "Women Anarchists Have Become the Terror of World's Police," *Rochester Democrat and Chronicle*, March 15, 1908.

73. *Los Angeles Times*, March 15, 1908.

74. Ibid.

75. Ibid.

76. Ibid.

77. "The Communists in Chicago," *New York Tribune*, July 28, 1877, 1.

78. Cesare Lombroso and William Ferrero, *The Female Offender* (New York: D. Appleton, 1903), 288.

79. Jan Lewis, *The Pursuit of Happiness: Family and Values in Jefferson's Virginia* (Cambridge: Cambridge University Press, 1983); Barbara Welter, "The Cult of True Womanhood: 1820–1860," *American Quarterly* 18, no. 2 (Summer 1966): 151–74.

80. Linda K. Kerber, "Separate Spheres, Female Worlds, Woman's Place: The Rhetoric of Women's History," *Journal of American History* 75, no. 1 (June 1988): 9–39.

81. European "enlightenment" philosophers developed the "stages of history" narrative directly in response to North American Indigenous critiques of private property. This is discussed more in depth in David Graeber and David Wengrow, *The Dawn of Everything: A New History of Humanity* (New York: Farrar, Straus, and Giroux, 2021).

82. Rosemarie Zagarri, "Morals, Manners, and the Republican Mother," *American Quarterly* 44, no. 2 (June 1992): 201.

83. Louise Michel Newman, *White Women's Rights: The Racial Origins of Feminism in the United States* (New York: Oxford University Press, 1999); Manuela Thurner, "'Better Citizens without the Ballot': American AntiSuffrage Women and Their Rationale during the Progressive Era," *Journal of Women's History* 5, no. 1 (Spring 1993): 33–60.

84. Emma Goldman, *Anarchism and Other Essays*, 2nd ed. (New York: Mother Earth, 1911), 203.

85. Daniel Gookin, *Historical Collections of the Indians in New England: Of Their Several Nations, Numbers, Customs, Manners, Religion and Government, before the English Planted There* (Boston: Belknap and Hall, 1792), 9.

86. Pearce, *Savagism and Civilization*, 103.

87. "The Modern Medusa," *Punch* 105, December 1893, 270–71.

88. Ibid.

89. Ibid., 270.

90. Ibid.

91. Some of many possible examples: Sarah Deer, *The Beginning and End of Rape: Confronting Sexual Violence in Native America* (Minneapolis: University of Minnesota Press, 2015); Anderson, *Recognition of Being*; Denetdale, "Securing Navajo National Boundaries"; Simpson, "The State Is a Man."

92. Million, *Therapeutic Nations*.

93. Oscar Neebe, "Address of Oscar Neebe," in *The Chicago Martyrs: The Famous Speeches of the Eight Anarchists in Judge Gary's Court and Altgeld's Reasons for Pardoning* (San Francisco: Free Society, 1899), 22.

94. Neebe, "Address of Oscar Neebe," 22; The term "misogynoir" was coined by Black feminist scholar Moya Bailey for the specific kind of misogyny directed against Black women. See her article "New Terms of Resistance: A Response to Zenzele Isoke," *Souls* 15, no. 4 (2013): 341–43.

95. Ashbaugh, *Lucy Parsons*, 135–36.

96. "San Diegans Assail Emma Goldman: Her Manager Is Tarred, Feathered and Burned by Vigilantes," *Bulletin*, May 15, 1912, 1.

97. "Emma Goldman in; Hooted by Crowd; Can't Get a Hall," *San Diego Sun*, May 14, 1912, 1.

98. "Emma Goldman and Ben Reitman Tell of San Diego Experience," *Industrial Worker*, June 6, 1912, 4.

99. Ibid.

100. Candace Falk, *Love, Anarchy, and Emma Goldman*, rev. ed. (New Brunswick, NJ: Rutgers University Press, 1990); Drinnon, *Rebel in Paradise*; Roger Bruns, *The Damndest Radical: The Life and World of Ben Reitman, Chicago's Celebrated Social Reformer, Hobo King, and Whorehouse Physician* (Urbana: University of Illinois Press, 1987).

101. The shooting was reported in several US newspapers: *Daily Evening Bulletin* (San Francisco), January 25, 1888; *Daily Inter-Ocean* (Chicago), January 25, 1888; *Milwaukee Journal*, January 25, 1888.

102. Michel, *Red Virgin*; Edith Thomas, *Louise Michel* (Montreal: Black Rose, 2009).

103. Ross Winn, "Voltairine de Cleyre," *Winn's Firebrand*, January 1903.

104. A. J. Brigati, ed., *The Voltairine de Cleyre Reader* (Oakland, CA: AK Press, 2004), ix.

105. Berkman, *Selected Works of Voltairine de Cleyre*, 204.

106. For a short introduction to the vast amount of classical anarchist writing on carceral systems, see Anthony J. Nocella II, Mark Seis, and Jeff Shantz, eds., *Classic Writings in Anarchist Criminology: A Historical Dismantling of Punishment and Domination* (Chico, CA: AK Press, 2020).

107. David Hurst Thomas, *Skull Wars: Kennewick Man, Archaeology, and the Battle for Native American Identity* (New York: Basic Books, 2000); Ann Fabian, *The Skull Collectors: Race, Science, and America's Unburied Dead* (Chicago: University of Chicago Press, 2010); Stephen Jay Gould, *The Mismeasure of Man*, rev. ed. (New York: W. W. Norton,

1996); Andrew Zimmerman, *Anthropology and Antihumanism in Imperial Germany* (Chicago: University of Chicago Press, 2001).

108. "Character in Unconventional People: A Pair of Anarchists," *Phrenological Journal of Science and Health* 99 (February 1895): 88–92; Falk et al., *Emma Goldman*, 1: 215.

109. "Character in Unconventional People"; Falk et al., *Emma Goldman*, 1: 216.

110. "Emma Goldman Comes to Preach 'Anarchism' to I.W.W.'s: Female Agitator Full of Sympathy for Mexican Insurrectos," *Fresno Morning Republican*, May 14, 1911; Falk et al., *Emma Goldman*, 1: 315.

111. "Anarchy's Den: Emma Goldman, Its Queen, Rules with a Nod the Savage Reds"; Falk et al., *Emma Goldman*, 1: 112.

112. Wolfe, "Settler Colonialism," 388.

113. "Lucy Parsons Is Mild," *Sunday Inter-Ocean*, August 12, 1900.

114. Cesare Lombroso, *Criminal Man* (New York: G. P. Putnam's Sons, 1911).

115. Kenyon Zimmer, "Positively Stateless: Marcus Graham, the Ferrero-Sallitto Case, and Anarchist Challenges to Race and Deportation," in *The Rising Tide of Color: Race, State Violence, and Radical Movements across the Pacific*, ed. Moon-Ho Jung (Seattle: University of Washington Press, 2014), 132.

116. Cesare Lombroso, *L'Homme criminel: atlas*, 2nd ed., vol. 2 (Paris: Ancienne Librairie Germer Baillière, 1895), plates 49–50.

117. Cesare Lombroso, "Illustrative Studies in Criminal Anthropology," 3, "The Physiognomy of the Anarchists," *Monist* 1, no. 3 (April 1891): 338.

118. Wayne Morrison, *Criminology, Civilisation and the New World Order* (New York: Routledge, 2006); Alejandro Forero, "Old and New Discourses: The Role of Positivist Criminology in the Criminalization of Anarchism" 1, no. 2 (December 2017): 178–99.

119. Lombroso, *Criminal Man* (New York: G. P. Putnam's Sons, 1911), xii.

120. Lombroso, "Illustrative Studies," 338.

121. Ibid., 338–39.

122. Ibid.," 341.

123. J. Langdon Down, "Observations on an Ethnic Classification of Idiots," *Clinical Lecture Reports of the London Hospital* 3 (1866): 260.

124. Murray K. Simpson, "From Savage to Citizen: Education, Colonialism and Idiocy," *British Journal of Sociology of Education* 28, no. 5 (September 1, 2007): 561–74; Morrison, *Criminology, Civilisation and the New World Order*.

125. Michael Schwab, "A Convicted Anarchist's Reply to Professor Lombroso," *Monist* 1, no. 4 (July 1891): 520–24.

126. Gould, *Mismeasure of Man*, 125–26.

127. Cesare Lombroso, "L'Anarchie et ses héros," in *Documents d'études sociales sur l'anarchie* (Lyon, Fr.: A. H. Storck, 1897), 119–41. English translation at https://www.marxists.org/subject/anarchism/lombroso.htm.

128. Lombroso, "Illustrative Studies," 340.

129. Ibid., 340.

130. 57th Cong., 2nd sess., 1214 (1903).

131. "Anarchist Turner Tells of His Fight," *New York Times*, March 14, 1904.

132. Paul Avrich, *Anarchist Portraits* (Princeton, NJ: Princeton University Press, 1988); Julia Rose Kraut, "Global Anti-anarchism: The Origins of Ideological Deportation and the Suppression of Expression," *Journal of Global Legal Studies* 19, no. 1 (Winter 2012): 169–93.

133. Kraut, "Global Anti-anarchism," 170.

134. Avrich, *Anarchist Portraits*; Kraut, "Global Anti-anarchism."

135. Thomas, *Skull Wars*, 57.

136. Ibid.

137. Fabian, *Skull Collectors*; Thomas, *Skull Wars*; Ari Kelman, *A Misplaced Massacre: Struggling over the Memory of Sand Creek* (Cambridge, MA: Harvard University Press, 2013); Zimmerman, *Anthropology and Antihumanism*.

138. Lombroso, "Illustrative Studies."

139. Lombroso, "Anarchie."

140. Gabriel Tarde, *La Criminalité comparée*, 4th ed. (Paris: Ancienne Librairie Germer Baillière, 1898), 27.

## Chapter 3. Cleansing the Republic

1. "Various Items," *Army Navy Journal* 40, no. 48 (August 1, 1903): 1211.

2. *Annual Reports of the War Department for the Fiscal Year Ended June 30, 1902*, vol. 9 (Washington, DC: Government Printing Office, 1902), 173.

3. Emma Goldman, *Living My Life* (New York: Dover, 1970), 1: 425–29.

4. Ibid.

5. *Mob Work: Anarchists in Grand Rapids*, 4 vols. (Grand Rapids, MI: Sprout Distro, 2014); "Buwalda Declares He's No Anarchist," *San Francisco Call*, May 15, 1908. All Goldman quotes in this paragraph are from Goldman, *Living My Life*, 1: 425–29.

6. Goldman, *Anarchism and Other Essays*, 139–40.

7. "Buwalda Declares He's No Anarchist."

8. Theodore Roosevelt to Army Judge Advocate General, June 24, 1908, in Falk et al., *Emma Goldman*, 2: 337.

9. Goldman, *Living My Life*, 1: 448–49.

10. "Emma Goldman and Reitman in Trouble," *Los Angeles Herald*, January 16, 1909, 3.

11. Ferguson, *Emma Goldman*, 228.

12. Ibid., 227.

13. *Mexico Weekly Ledger*, June 24, 1886, 1.

14. "Execution of Anarchists," *Washington Post*, February 25, 1908.

15. Quoted in Robert J. Goldstein, "The Anarchist Scare of 1908: A Sign of Tensions in the Progressive Era," *American Studies* 15, no. 2 (Fall 1974): 61.

16. "The Growth of Anarchy," *Washington Post*, March 4, 1908.

17. James Green, *Death in the Haymarket: A Story of Chicago, The First Labor Movement and the Bombing That Divided Gilded Age America* (New York: Pantheon, 2006), 201.

18. For discussion of the origins of European- and Anglo-American racial thought

and the roots of white supremacy, see Robinson, *Black Marxism: The Making of the Black Radical Tradition*; Horne, *Dawning of the Apocalypse*; Horne, *Apocalypse of Settler Colonialism*.

19. John Toland, *Adolf Hitler: The Definitive Biography* (New York: Anchor, 1992), 702.

It must be mentioned here that the Boers, though briefly targeted by British imperialism, were brutal colonizers themselves who became the leaders of an apartheid state.

20. Adolf Hitler, quoted in Carroll P. Kakel III, *The American West and the Nazi East: A Comparative and Interpretive Perspective* (New York: Palgrave Macmillan, 2011), 1.

21. James Q. Whitman, *Hitler's American Model: The United States and the Making of Nazi Race Law* (Princeton, NJ: Princeton University Press, 2017).

22. David E. Stannard, *American Holocaust: The Conquest of the New World* (New York: Oxford University Press, 1992), x.

23. Congressman William Vaile, "Deportation of Anarchist Aliens: Extension of Remarks of Hon. William N. Vaile, Rep.," *Congressional Record* (January 5, 1920), in *The Emma Goldman Papers: A Microfilm Edition*, ed. Candace Falk, Ronald J. Zboray, and Daniel A. Cornford (Alexandria, VA: Chadwyck-Healey, 1990), reel 65; Ferguson, *Emma Goldman*, 228.

24. Ferguson, *Emma Goldman*, 227–28. For a fuller treatment of the *Buford* deportees, see Kenyon Zimmer, "The Voyage of the *Buford*: Political Deportations and the Making of America's First Red Scare," in *Deportation in the Americas: Histories of Exclusion and Resistance*, ed. Kenyon Zimmer and Cristina Salinas (College Station: Texas A&M University Press, 2018).

25. Aimé Césaire, *Discourse on Colonialism*, trans. Joan Pinkham (New York: Monthly Review Press, 2000), 36.

26. Zak Cope, *Divided World Divided Class: Global Political Economy and the Stratification of Labour under Capitalism* (Montreal: Kersplebedeb, 2012), 294.

27. "Vaile, William Newell (1876–1927)," in *Biographical Directory of the United States Congress, 1774–Present*, http://bioguide.congress.gov/scripts/biodisplay.pl?index=V000004.

28. "Soviet Ark Lands Its Reds in Finland," *New York Times*, January 18, 1920.

29. Mark Grueter, "Anarchism and the Working Class: The Union of Russian Workers in the North American Labor Movement." PhD diss., Simon Fraser University, Burnaby, BC, 2018, https://summit.sfu.ca/item/18580; Zimmer, *Immigrants against the State*, 116–18; Tim Weiner, *Enemies: A History of the FBI* (New York: Random House, 2012).

30. Jonathan Kinghorn, *The Atlantic Transport Line, 1881–1931: A History with Details on All Ships* (Jefferson, NC: McFarland, 2012); Jeffrey Ostler, *The Plains Sioux and U.S. Colonialism from Lewis and Clark to Wounded Knee* (Cambridge: Cambridge University Press, 2004); Paul N. Beck, *The First Sioux War: The Grattan Fight and Blue Water Creek, 1854–1856* (Lanham, MD: University Press of America, 2004); R. Eli Paul, *Blue Water Creek and the First Sioux War, 1854–1856* (Norman: University of Oklahoma Press, 2004); Robert M. Utley, *Frontiersmen in Blue: The United States Army and the Indian, 1848–1865* (Lincoln: University of Nebraska Press, 1967); Clifford L. Swanson, *The Sixth United States Infantry Regiment, 1855 to Reconstruction* (Jefferson, NC: McFarland, 2001).

31. "Contract for Newport News," *Richmond Dispatch*, May 25, 1900.

32. Kinghorn, *Atlantic Transport Line*; NavSource Online: USAT *Buford*, Civilian Identification Numbered Ships Photo Archive, http://www.navsource.org/archives/12/173818.htm, accessed September 26, 2019.

33. Marion Meade, *Buster Keaton: Cut to the Chase, a Biography* (New York: Da Capo, 1997).

34. Donald Crisp and Buster Keaton, dirs., *The Navigator* (Metro-Goldwyn, 1924).

35. Theodore Roosevelt to G. Stanley Hall, 1899, in Jacobson, *Barbarian Virtues*, 3.

36. Crisp and Keaton, *The Navigator*.

37. Joan Potter, *African American Firsts: Famous, Little-Known and Unsung Triumphs of Blacks in America* (New York: Dafina, 2009), 73–74.

38. Crisp and Keaton, *The Navigator*.

39. For further cultural analysis of *Birth of a Nation* and the politics of white "manliness," see Melvyn Stokes, *D. W. Griffith's the Birth of a Nation: A History of "the Most Controversial Motion Picture of All Time"* (Oxford: Oxford University Press, 2007); Ava DuVernay, *13th* (Kandoo Films, 2016); Bederman, *Manliness and Civilization*.

40. Crisp and Keaton, *The Navigator*.

41. Ibid.

42. Library of Congress, National Film Preservation Board, https://www.loc.gov/programs/national-film-preservation-board/film-registry/frequently-asked-questions/, accessed September 24, 2019.

43. Ruben Kimmelman, "'Jurassic Park,' 'The Shining,' and 23 Other Movies Added to National Film Registry," NPR, December 12, 2018, https://www.npr.org/2018/12/12/675384976/jurassic-park-the-shining-and-23-other-movies-added-to-national-film-registry.

44. "For the National Defense," *Washington Post*, January 27, 1920, quoted in Ferguson, *Emma Goldman*, 228.

45. Mary Douglas, *Purity and Danger: An Analysis of Concepts of Pollution and Taboo* (New York: Routledge, 2003 [first published in 1966]).

46. For a discussion of William James's anarchist sympathies, see Andrew Fiala, "Political Skepticism and Anarchist Themes in the American Tradition," *European Journal of Pragmatism and American Philosophy* 5, no. 2 (2013): 90–104.

47. William James, as quoted in Douglas, *Purity and Danger*, 165.

48. Douglas, *Purity and Danger*, 36.

49. Ibid., 37.

50. "Indian Outrages in Dakota," *New York Tribune*, July 27, 1877.

51. Horne, *Apocalypse of Settler Colonialism*, 65.

52. *The Moderate Cavalier, or, The Soldiers Description of Ireland and of the Country Disease, with receipts for the same* (Cork: n.p., 1675; attributed to William Mercer), quoted in Katie Kane, "Nits Make Lice: Drogheda, Sand Creek, and the Poetics of Colonial Extermination," *Cultural Critique* no. 42 (Spring 1999): 84.

53. Kane, "Nits Make Lice," 84.

54. In addition to Horne, for a discussion of the influence of English colonial practices against the Irish on Anglo-American settler colonialism, see Nicholas P. Canny,

"The Ideology of English Colonization: From Ireland to America," *William and Mary Quarterly* 30, no. 4 (1973): 575–98.

55. Theodore Roosevelt, *Oliver Cromwell* (New York: Charles Scribner's Sons, 1900), 1.

56. Horne, *Apocalypse of Settler Colonialism*, 65.

57. Theodore Roosevelt, *The Winning of the West*, part 1, *The Spread of English-Speaking Peoples* (New York: Current Literature Publishing, 1905), 28–30.

58. There is no written copy of the speech itself. One of Chivington's men, S. E. Browne, quoted Chivington's speech in his sworn testimony before the US Senate in 1867 during the congressional investigation of the Sand Creek Massacre (Kane, "Nits Make Lice," 83).

59. For a discussion of Chivington and his collaborator and political ally John Evans, see Alexander Saxton, *The Rise and Fall of the White Republic: Class Politics and Mass Culture in Nineteenth-Century America* (London: Verso, 1990).

60. Helen Hunt Jackson, *A Century of Dishonor: A Sketch of the United States Government's Dealings with Some of the Indian Tribes* (New York: Harper and Brothers, 1881); Kane, "Nits Make Lice"; Dunbar-Ortiz, *Indigenous Peoples' History*, 2014; Kelman, *Misplaced Massacre*.

61. Jackson, *Century of Dishonor*, 345.

62. Ibid., 344.

63. Ibid., 344–45.

64. Ibid., 345.

65. Quoted in Kane, "Nits Make Lice," 83.

66. Jackson, *Century of Dishonor*, 345.

67. Ibid.; Kelman, *Misplaced Massacre*; Dunbar-Ortiz, *Indigenous Peoples' History*; Kane, "Nits Make Lice."

68. *History of Caldwell and Livingston Counties, Missouri* (St. Louis: National Historical Company, 1886), 149. Also discussed and quoted in W. Paul Reeve, *Religion of a Different Color: Race and the Mormon Struggle for Whiteness* (Oxford: Oxford University Press, 2015), 53.

69. James E. Quinlan, *Tom Quick: The Indian Slayer, and the Pioneers of Minisink and Wawarsink* (Monticello, NY: De Voe and Quinlan, 1851), 32.

70. Quinlan, *Tom Quick*, 32–33.

71. Ibid., 33; also discussed in Reeve, *Religion of a Different Color*, 53–54.

72. Tom Quick tales are also discussed in Reeve, *Religion of a Different Color*.

73. Kane, "Nits Make Lice," 81–82. The original phrase attributed to Sheridan was "The only good Indians I ever saw were dead." See ch. 2, n. 53.

74. Mary Crow Dog and Richard Erdoes, *Lakota Woman* (New York: Grove, 1990), 5; quoted in Kane, "Nits Make Lice," 81.

75. Crow Dog and Erdoes, *Lakota Woman*.

76. "Execution of Anarchists," *Washington Post*, February 25, 1908, 6.

77. "The Growth of Anarchy," *Washington Post*, March 4, 1908, 6.

78. Schaack, *Anarchy and Anarchists*, 25.

Notes to Chapter 3     215

79. Ibid., 26.

80. Carl Sandburg, *Always the Young Strangers* (New York: Harcourt, Brace, 1952), 132–33.

81. Upton Sinclair, *American Outpost: A Book of Reminiscences* (New York: Farrar and Rinehart, 1932), 142.

82. Paul Avrich, *Anarchist Voices: An Oral History of Anarchism in America* (Princeton, NJ: Princeton University Press, 1995), 18–19.

83. Paul Avrich, *Anarchist Voices: An Oral History of Anarchism in America* (Princeton, NJ: Princeton University Press, 1995), 18–19.

84. Theodore Roosevelt, *The Works of Theodore Roosevelt* (New York: Co-Operative Publication Society, ca. 1900), 1: 45.

85. "Angiolillo Died Bravely," *New York Times*, August 22, 1897.

86. Nunzio Pernicone and Fraser M. Ottanelli, *Assassins against the Old Order: Italian Anarchist Violence in Fin de Siècle Europe* (Urbana: University of Illinois Press, 2018); Richard Bach Jensen, *The Battle against Anarchist Terrorism: An International History, 1878–1934* (Cambridge: Cambridge University Press, 2014); Mary S. Barton, "The Global War on Anarchism: The United States and International Anarchist Terrorism, 1898–1904," *Diplomatic History* 39, no. 2 (2015): 303–31; Anderson, *Under Three Flags*; Frederic Trautmann, *The Voice of Terror: A Biography of Johann Most* (Westport, CT: Greenwood Press, 1980).

87. Martin Clark, *Modern Italy, 1871 to the Present*, 3rd ed. (New York: Routledge, 2014), 127.

88. Eric Rauchway, *Murdering McKinley: The Making of Theodore Roosevelt's America* (New York: Hill and Wang, 2003), 102.

89. Hoganson, *Fighting for American Manhood*; Rydell, *All the World's a Fair*; Bender, *American Abyss*; Jacobson, *Barbarian Virtues*; Anderson, *Under Three Flags* .

90. Turcato, *The Method of Freedom*(Oakland, CA: AK Press, 2014); Turcato, *The Complete Works of Errico Malatesta, vol. 3, "A Long and Patient Work": The Anarchist Socialism of L'Agitazione, 1897–98* (Chico, CA: AK Press, 2017); Turcato, *Complete Works of Malatesta, vol. 4, Towards Anarchy: Malatesta in America, 1899–1900* (Chico, CA: AK Press, 2019) ; Graham, *We Do Not Fear Anarchy*; Cappelletti, *Anarchism in Latin America*; Anderson, *Under Three Flags*.

91. "Malatesta," *Cleveland Press*, September 13, 1901.

92. Voltairine de Cleyre, "McKinley's Assassination from the Anarchist Standpoint," in Brigati, *Voltairine de Cleyre Reader*, 175. Emphasis in original.

93. Emma Goldman, "The Tragedy at Buffalo," *Free Society* 7, no. 33 (October 6, 1901): 1; reproduced in Falk et al., *Emma Goldman*, 1: 476.

94. Moon-Ho Jung, *Subversive Histories: Race, National Security, and Empire across the Pacific* (New York: CUNY Graduate Center, February 19, 2013), video, 63 min., https://pcp .gc.cuny.edu/2013/03/video-moon-ho-jung-subversive-histories/.

95. Jung, *Subversive Histories*; Eric Rauchway, *Murdering McKinley: The Making of Theodore Roosevelt's America* (New York: Hill and Wang, 2003); Daryl Rasuli, "James B. Parker Revisited" (Buffalo: State University of New York at Buffalo Digital Collections, 2001), https://digital.lib.buffalo.edu/items/show/91880; Kachun Mitch, "'Big Jim' Parker

and the Assassination of William McKinley: Patriotism, Nativism, Anarchism, and the Struggle for African American Citizenship," *Journal of the Gilded Age and Progressive Era* 9, no. 1 (January 2010): 93–116.

96. Theodore Roosevelt, *Message of the President of the United States, Fifty-Seventh Congress,* 1st sess. (Washington, DC: Government Printing Office, 1901), 3.

97. Ibid., 5.

98. Theodore Roosevelt, *Message of the President of the United States, Fifty-Seventh Congress,* 1st sess. (Washington, DC: Government Printing Office, 1901).

99. Trautmann, *Voice of Terror,* 215.

100. *Statesboro News,* September 27, 1901, quoted in Amy Louise Wood, *Lynching and Spectacle: Witnessing Racial Violence in America, 1890–1940* (Chapel Hill: University of North Carolina Press, 2009), 134.

101. Jung, "Subversive Histories."

102. Cox, "Lynching and the Status Quo"; Michael J. Pfeifer, ed., *Lynching beyond Dixie: American Mob Violence outside the South* (Urbana: University of Illinois Press, 2013); Wood, *Lynching and Spectacle.* The term "Nadir," first used by historian Rayford Logan, is one that some scholars use to describe the period from the end of Reconstruction to the early 1920s, when lynching and other forms of white supremacist extralegal mob violence were at their height, and US race relations were at their nadir, or lowest point.

103. Wood, *Lynching and Spectacle,* 132.

104. Jill Jonnes, *Empires of Light: Edison, Tesla, Westinghouse, and the Race to Electrify the World* (New York: Random House, 2003); Craig Brandon, *The Electric Chair: An Unnatural American History* (Jefferson, NC: McFarland, 1999); Mark Essig, *Edison and the Electric Chair: A Story of Light and Death* (New York: Walker, 2003).

105. Wood, *Lynching and Spectacle,* 293n46.

106. *Statesboro News,* September 27, 1901, discussed in Wood, 134.

107. Roosevelt, *Message of the President.*

108. Theodore Roosevelt to Henry Cabot Lodge, September 9, 1901, in *Theodore Roosevelt: Letters and Speeches* (New York: Penguin, 2004), 237–38.

109. George Frisbie Hoar, *Autobiography of Seventy Years* (New York: Charles Scribner's Sons, 1903); Roger Daniels, *Coming to America: A History of Immigration and Ethnicity in American Life,* 2nd ed. (New York: Perennial, 2002). For more on Hoar, see George Frisbie Hoar Papers, Massachusetts Historical Society, https://www.masshist .org/collection-guides/view/fa0298.

110. "Shall We Have a Penal Colony?: The Question of National Importance Looked At from Several Viewpoints," *Our Day* 21, no. 1 (January 1902): 9; "An Island for the Anarchists," *Literary Digest,* December 1901, 796–97.

111. Barton, "The Global War on Anarchism: The United States and International Anarchist Terrorism, 1898–1904"; Goldstein, "The Anarchist Scare of 1908: A Sign of Tensions in the Progressive Era."

112. Roosevelt, *Message of the President.*

113. Hoganson, *Fighting for American Manhood*; Bederman, *Manliness and Civilization*; Sarah Watts, *Rough Rider in the White House: Theodore Roosevelt and the Politics of Desire* (Chicago: University of Chicago Press, 2003).

Notes to Chapter 3    217

114. Theodore Roosevelt, *Thomas Hart Benton*, 4th ed. (Boston: Houghton, Mifflin, 1889, 211–12.

115. Roosevelt, *Thomas Hart Benton*, 214–16.

116. Quoted in Hermann Hagedorn, *Roosevelt in the Bad Lands* (Boston: Houghton Mifflin, 1921), 355.

117. Roosevelt, *Thomas Hart Benton*, 216.

118. Quote in Hagedorn, *Roosevelt in the Bad Lands*, 355.

119. Theodore Roosevelt, *Ranch Life and the Hunting-Trail* (New York: Century, 1888), 107.

120. Greg Grandin, *The End of the Myth: From the Frontier to the Border Wall in the Mind of America* (New York: Metropolitan, 2019), 6.

121. Mark Lause, *The Great Cowboy Strike: Bullets, Ballots and Class Conflicts in the American West* (New York: Verso, 2017).

122. Kelly Lytle Hernández, *City of Inmates: Conquest, Rebellion, and the Rise of Human Caging in Los Angeles, 1771–1965* (Chapel Hill: University of North Carolina Press, 2017).

123. Roosevelt, *Thomas Hart Benton*, 218.

124. Quoted in Henry F. Pringle, *Theodore Roosevelt: A Biography* (New York: Harcourt, Brace, 1931), 110–11; see also Paul Avrich, *The Haymarket Tragedy* (Princeton, NJ: Princeton University Press, 1984), 218.

125. Roosevelt, *Ranch Life*, 109.

126. Richard Drinnon, "'My Men Shoot Well': Theodore Roosevelt and the Urban Frontier," in *Haymarket Scrapbook* (Chicago: Charles H. Kerr, 1986), 130.

127. "A Dead Anarchist," *Ohio Democrat*, August 7, 1886.

128. Avrich, *Haymarket Tragedy*, 238. From Canada, Schnaubelt traveled to England, and then, at the invitation of Errico Malatesta, he took a steamer to Buenos Aires. Malatesta, who was wanted by authorities all over Europe for his anarchist and anticolonial organizing—including forming a group in 1882 to fight against the British in the Anglo-Egyptian War—escaped to Argentina in 1885, where he became involved in forming a militant bakers' union in Buenos Aires. To this day, pastries in Buenos Aires have anarchist names such as *bolas de fraile* (friar's balls), *cañoncitos* (little cannons), *bombas* (bombs), and *libritos* (little books), the last of which are pastries folded into layers to resemble anarchist pamphlets. The origin of these pastry names and styles is the union of anarchist bakers that Malatesta helped organize in the 1880s (Rebecca Treon, "The Surprising Origin of Argentina's Brazen Pastry Names," BBC, November 2, 2017, http://www.bbc.com/travel/story/20171101-the-surprising-origin-of-argentinas-brazen-pastry-names.

129. "How Can They Be Kept Out?," *The Sun* (New York), May 9, 1886.

130. Robert C. Nesbit, *The History of Wisconsin*, vol. 3, *Urbanization and Industrialization, 1873–1893* (Madison: State Historical Society of Wisconsin, 1985).

131. "How Can They Be Kept Out?"

132. Ibid.

133. Slotkin, *Gunfighter Nation*, 91–92.

## Chapter 4. The Guns of 1877

1. Anthony Pagden, "The Struggle for Legitimacy and the Image of Empire in the Atlantic to c. 1700," in *The Origins of Empire: British Overseas Enterprise to the Close of the Seventeenth Century*, ed. Nicholas Canny, vol. 1 in *The Oxford History of the British Empire* (Oxford: Oxford University Press, 1998), 43.

2. John Locke, *Two Treatises on Civil Government* (London: George Routledge and Sons, 1884), 206, 204.

3. For further discussion of Locke and the relationship between private property, dispossession, and anti-Indigeneity, see Robert Nichols, *Theft Is Property! Dispossession and Critical Theory* (Durham, NC: Duke University Press, 2020).

4. Quoted in David Roediger and Elizabeth Esch, *The Production of Difference: Race and the Management of Labor in US History* (New York: Oxford University Press, 2012), 28.

5. Quoted in ibid., 28–29.

6. Quoted in ibid., 55.

7. *House Documents, Otherwise Publ. as Executive Documents*. 13th Congress, 2nd sess. –49th Congress, 1st sess., October 21, 1850, 80.

8. Larry Isaac, "To Counter 'The Very Devil' and More: The Making of Independent Capitalist Militia in the Gilded Age," *American Journal of Sociology* 108, no. 2 (September 2002): 353–405.

9. Scott Dalrymple, "John Hay's Revenge: Anti-labor Novels, 1880–1905," *Business and Economic History* 28, no. 1 (Fall 1999): 133–42.

10. The Columbian Senate refused to ratify Hay-Herrán selling the Canal Zone to the United States, and so the United States gave economic and military aid to a French businessman invested in the canal, Philippe-Jean Bunau-Varilla, to orchestrate the Panamanian Revolution and turn over control of the Canal Zone to the United States. It is a pre–Cold War example of the United States engaging in a proxy war for private business interests (Julie Greene, *The Canal Builders: Making America's Empire at the Panama Canal* [New York: Penguin Press, 2009]).

11. William Roscoe Thayer, *Life and Letters of John Hay* (Boston: Houghton Mifflin, 1915), 1: 424.

12. Ibid.

13. Ibid.

14. Drinnon, *Facing West*, 259.

15. Here one can see that the US military practice of "playing Indian" by giving military vehicles, equipment, and weapons Indigenous North American names-e.g., Apache helicopter, Blackhawk helicopter, Tomahawk missile, etc.—which goes back directly to genocidal nineteenth-century US Army campaigns. For further discussion of this practice and its meaning, see Salaita, "Playing Indian."

16. Evan S. Connell, *Son of the Morning Star* (New York: North Point, 1984), 142.

17. https://biodiversity.ku.edu/exhibits/comanche.

18. John Hay, *The Complete Poetical Works of John Hay* (Boston: Houghton Mifflin, 1916), 77.

19. Hay to Reid, quoted in Kenton J. Clymer, *John Hay: The Gentleman as Diplomat* (Ann Arbor: University of Michigan Press, 1975), 232n; Drinnon, *Facing West*, 261.

20. Clymer, *John Hay*, 232n; Drinnon, *Facing West*, 261.

21. For more on Whitelaw Reid and Helen Hunt Jackson, see Royal Cortissoz, *The Life of Whitelaw Reid*, 2 vols. (New York: Charles Scribner's Sons, 1921); Kate Phillips, *Helen Hunt Jackson: A Literary Life* (Berkeley: University of California Press, 2003); Jackson, *Century of Dishonor*.

22. Thayer, *Life and Letters of John Hay*, 2: 14.

23. The slogan was coined in 1840 by the French social theorist Pierre-Joseph Proudhon, who said, "La propriété, c'est le vol!" Proudhon was highly influential in the early communist, anarchist, and workingmen's movements in Europe. By the era when John Hay was attacking anarchists and labor unions, anarchists had moved away from much of Proudhon's thinking but retained the "property is theft" slogan (Pierre-Joseph Proudhon, *Qu'est-ce que la propriété? ou Recherche sur le principe du droit et du gouvernement* [Paris: Brocard, 1840], 2).

24. Ned Blackhawk, *Violence over the Land: Indians and Empires in the Early American West* (Cambridge, MA: Harvard University Press, 2006); Aileen Moreton-Robinson, *The White Possessive: Property, Power, and Indigenous Sovereignty* (Minneapolis: University of Minnesota Press, 2015).

25. Sven Beckert, *The Monied Metropolis: New York City and the Consolidation of the American Bourgeoisie, 1850–1869* (Cambridge: Cambridge University Press, 2001), 149.

26. Richard White, *Railroaded: The Transcontinentals and the Making of Modern America* (New York: W. W. Norton, 2011), 25.

27. Dunbar-Ortiz, *Indigenous Peoples' History*, 144.

28. Sherman to Grant, May 28, 1867, quoted in Michael Fellman, *Citizen Sherman: A Life of William Tecumseh Sherman* (Lawrence: University Press of Kansas, 1997), 264; Dunbar-Ortiz, *Indigenous Peoples' History*, 145.

29. Sherman to Herbert A. Preston, April 17, 1873, quoted in John F. Marszalek, *Sherman: A Soldier's Passion for Order* (New York: Free Press, 1992), 379; Dunbar-Ortiz, *Indigenous Peoples' History*, 145.

30. Dunbar-Ortiz, *Indigenous Peoples' History*, 144–46; Robert M. Utley, *Cavalier in Buckskin: George Armstrong Custer and the Western Military Frontier* (Norman: University of Oklahoma Press, 2001), 57–103.

31. Philip S. Foner, *The Great Labor Uprising of 1877*, 7th ed. (New York: Pathfinder, 2008); David O. Stowell, ed., *The Great Strikes of 1877* (Urbana: University of Illinois Press, 2008); Brecher, *Strike!*; White, *Railroaded*; Josh Shelton, "Pages from US Labor History: The Great Railroad Strike of 1877," *In Defense of Marxism* (blog), November 10, 2003, http://www.marxist.com/great-railroad-strike1877.htm.

32. Workingmen's Party of Illinois, "Declaration of Independence," 1876, quoted in Howard Zinn, *A People's History of the United States: 1492–Present* (New York: Harper Collins, 2003), 245.

33. "Labor Raising Its Voice," *The Sun* (New York), July 27, 1877.

34. Ibid.

35. Ibid.

36. Isaac, "To Counter 'The Very Devil,'" 363.

37. Stowell, *Great Strikes of 1877*; Foner, *Great Labor Uprising of 1877*; Brecher, *Strike!*; White, *Railroaded.*

38. Selig Perlman and Ira B. Cross, "The Anti-Chinese Agitation in California," in *History of Labor in the United States* (New York: Macmillan, 1921), 2: 254.

39. Ibid., 252–68.

40. On the settler colonial roots of white identity politics, see Horne, *Apocalypse of Settler Colonialism.*

41. "Labor Raising Its Voice."

42. *The Labor Standard* (New York), Aug. 11, 1877, quoted in Philip S. Foner, *History of the Labor Movement in the United States: From Colonial Times to the Founding of the American Federation of Labor* (New York: International, 1947), 469.

43. David T. Burbank, *Reign of the Rabble: The St. Louis General Strike of 1877* (New York: Augustus M. Kelley, 1966), 2; also quoted in Zinn, *People's History of the United States*, 250.

44. "St. Louis Communism," *Chicago Tribune*, July 29, 1877.

45. *New York Times*, May 31, 1871.

46. Quoted in Burbank, *Reign of the Rabble*, 178.

47. "On the Baltimore and Ohio," *New York Tribune*, July 23, 1877.

48. Hay to Amasa Stone, August 23, 1877, in Thayer, *Life and Letters of John Hay*, 2: 5.

49. Thayer, *Life and Letters of John Hay*, 2: 6.

50. For US views of the Paris Commune, see Samuel Bernstein, "The Impact of the Paris Commune in the United States," *Massachusetts Review* 12, no. 3 (Summer 1971): 435–46.

51. Thayer, *Life and Letters of John Hay*, 2: 6.

52. Ibid.

53. Hay to Amasa Stone, July 24, 1877, in Thayer, *Life and Letters of John Hay*, 2: 2.

54. Thayer, *Life and Letters of John Hay*, 1: 421.

55. Ibid.

56. Ibid.

57. James Ford Rhodes, *History of the United States from Hayes to McKinley, 1877–1896* (New York: Macmillan, 1919), 46.

58. James Ford Rhodes, *History of the United States from the Compromise of 1850 to the Final Restoration of Home Rule at the South in 1877* (New York: Macmillan, 1910), 6: 35. Rhodes's interpretation of US history was rightly criticized by Black intellectuals in the era, such as John R. Lynch, "Some Historical Errors of James Ford Rhodes," *Journal of Negro History* 2, no. 4 (October 1917): 345–68.

59. "Trades-Unionism vs. the Government," *New York Tribune*, July 25, 1877.

60. "On the Baltimore and Ohio."

61. "The Commune in the United States," *New York Tribune*, July 25, 1877.

62. "The Strikers' Sympathy," *New York Tribune*, July 26, 1877.

63. Ibid.

64. "Commune in the United States."

Notes to Chapter 4     221

65. Ibid.

66. "Capital and Labor," *New York Tribune*, July 28, 1877.

67. Hay to Amasa Stone, July 24, 1877, in Thayer, *Life and Letters of John Hay*, 2: 2.

68. Hay to Stone, July 25, 1877, Thayer, *Life and Letters of John Hay*, 2: 3.

69. Ibid.

70. *Missouri Republican*, July 27, 1877, quoted in David Roediger, *Towards the Abolition of Whiteness: Essays on Race, Politics, and Working Class History* (New York: Verso, 1994), 88.

71. "Railroad War," *Harper's Weekly*, August 18, 1877, 640–41; also discussed in Slotkin, *Fatal Environment*, 480–81.

72. Slotkin, *Fatal Environment*, 478.

73. "Railroad War," 640–41.

74. *New York Tribune*, July 20, 1877.

75. Slotkin, *Fatal Environment*, 477–98.

76. "Railroad Strike," *New York Tribune*, July 25, 1877; Slotkin, *Fatal Environment*, 481.

77. *The War Correspondence of the "Daily News," 1877: With a Connecting Narrative Forming a Continuous History of the War between Russia and Turkey: Including the Letters of Mr. Archibald Forbes, Mr. J. A. MacGahan and Many Other Special Correspondents in Europe and Asia*, 3rd ed. (London: Macmillan, 1878), 333.

78. Ibid., 334; for discussion of the role and activities of Kurdish units in the Russo-Turkish War, see James J. Reid, *Crisis of the Ottoman Empire: Prelude to Collapse 1839–1878* (Stuttgart: Franz Steiner, 2000), 154–62.

79. "The News This Morning," *New York Tribune*, July 28, 1877.

80. Ibid.

81. Ibid.

82. Ibid.

83. "Consequences of Trades Unionism," *New York Tribune*, July 28, 1877.

84. "Time's Waxworks," *Punch*, December 31, 1881.

85. The romanticized image of Ravachol persists into the twenty-first century. For example, the character Claude Ravache in the popular 2011 Hollywood film *Sherlock Holmes: A Game of Shadows*, was based on Ravachol. The film was directed by Guy Ritchie, produced by Warner Bros.

86. Mitchell Abidor, ed., *Death to Bourgeois Society: The Propagandists of the Deed* (Oakland, CA: PM Press, 2015). Quote is from "The Guillotine's Sure Work; Details of the Execution of Vaillant, the Anarchist," *New York Times*, February 6, 1894.

87. Lombroso, "L'Anarchie," 133."

88. Ibid.

89. Osvaldo Bayer, *The Rebellion in Patagonia* (Chico, CA: AK Press, 2016); Osvaldo Bayer, *The Anarchist Expropriators: Buenaventura Durruti and Argentina's Working-Class Robin Hoods* (Oakland, CA: AK Press, 2015); Ryan C. Edwards, *A Carceral Ecology: Ushuaia and the History of Landscape and Punishment in Argentina* (Oakland, CA: University of California Press, 2022); Daniel Nugent, *Spent Cartridges of Revolution: An Anthropological History of Namiquipa, Chihuahua* (Chicago: University of Chicago

Press, 1993); Ana María Alonso, *Thread of Blood Colonialism, Revolution, and Gender on Mexico's Northern Frontier* (Tucson: University of Arizona Press, 1995).

90. Bayer, *Rebellion in Patagonia*.

91. *El soldado argentino*, January 15, 1922, as discussed and quoted in Bayer, *Rebellion in Patagonia*, 371–72.

92. Rodney Thomson, original lithograph (untitled) depicting an I.W.W. meeting (Kalamazoo, MI: G. H. Lockwood, ca. 1913), https://www.vialibri.net/years/books/98408076/9999-iww-thomson-rodney-original-lithograph-untitled-depicting-an-iww.

93. John Hay, *The Breadwinners* (New York: Harper and Brothers, 1883).

94. Ibid., 51.

95. Ibid., 8.

96. Ibid., 166–68.

97. Hay to Theodore Roosevelt, November 16, 1904, in Thayer, *Life and Letters of John Hay*, 1: 15.

98. Thayer, *Life and Letters of John Hay*, 1: 2.

99. Ibid., 1: 3.

100. Reeve, *Religion of a Different Color*.

101. In settling in the Great Basin, Mormons dispossessed and expelled Ute, Goshute, Paiute, and Shoshone peoples (Ned Blackhawk, *Violence over the Land: Indians and Empires in the Early American West* [Cambridge, MA: Harvard University Press, 2006]).

102. Governor Lilburn W. Boggs to General John B. Clark, October 27, 1838, in *Document Containing the Correspondence, Orders, &C. in Relation to the Disturbances with the Mormons; and the Evidence Given before the Hon. Austin A. King, Judge of the Fifth Judicial Circuit of the State of Missouri, at the Courthouse in Richmond, in a Criminal Court of Inquiry, Begun November 12, 1838, on the Trial of Joseph Smith, Jr. and Others, for High Treason and Other Crimes against the State* (Fayette, MO: Boon's Lick *Democrat*, 1841), 61.

103. Reeve, *Religion of a Different Color*, 69.

104. Susan Easton Black, "How Large Was the Population of Nauvoo?," BYU Studies 35, no. 2 (1995): 91–94.

105. *Warsaw Signal*, extra edition, June 11, 1844.

106. Ibid.

107. D. Michael Quinn, *The Mormon Hierarchy: Origins of Power* (Salt Lake City, UT: Signature, 1994); Richard Lyman Bushman, *Joseph Smith: Rough Stone Rolling* (New York: Vintage, 2007); Reeve, *Religion of a Different Color*.

108. This remains true into the present era as antimigrant US vigilante groups have detained, kidnapped, and terrorized migrants, in some cases with the active coordination of, and in other cases with the silent complicity of, US Customs and Border Patrol agents.

109. Monica Muñoz Martinez, *The Injustice Never Leaves You: Anti-Mexican Violence in Texas* (Cambridge, MA: Harvard University Press, 2018), 6.

110. Bushman, *Joseph Smith*; Reeve, *Religion of a Different Color*; Quinn, *Mormon Hierarchy*.

The term *Jack Mormons* as it was used in the 1840s referred to Mormon sympathizers,

Notes to Chapter 4     223

or non-Mormons who were friendly to Mormons. In the present day, it is slang within Mormon communities to refer to members of the Church who have a lax attitude toward the Church's rules.

111. Thomas Ford, *A History of Illinois, from Its Commencement as a State in 1818 to 1847. Containing a Full Account of the Black Hawk War, the Rise, Progress, and Fall of Mormonism, the Alton and Lovejoy Riots, and Other Important and Interesting Events* (Chicago: S. C. Griggs, 1854), 364.

112. John Hay, "The Mormon Prophet's Tragedy," *Atlantic Monthly*, December 1869, 672.

113. Joseph Smith, *General Smith's Views of the Powers and Policy of the Government of the United States* (Nauvoo, IL: John Taylor, 1844), 9.

114. Ibid.

115. Ibid.

116. Connell O'Donovan, "The Mormon Priesthood Ban and Elder Q. Walker Lewis: 'An Example for His More Whiter Brethren to Follow,'" *John Whitmer Historical Association Journal* 26 (2006): 48–100.

117. Bushman, *Joseph Smith*; Reeve, *Religion of a Different Color*.

118. Acts 2:44–45 (King James Version).

119. Book of Mormon, 4 Nephi 1:3, 25, 26.

120. Smith, *General Smith's Views*.

121. Hay, "Mormon Prophet's Tragedy," 673–78. The irony is that in being expelled and pushed further west, Mormons became what Roosevelt termed "the vanguard of the white advance," expelling Indigenous peoples from the Great Basin and expanding the reach of US empire.

122. Oliver C. Cox, "Lynching and the Status Quo," *Journal of Negro Education* 14, no. 4, (Autumn 1945): 581.

123. Ibid., 580.

124. Dunbar-Ortiz, *Loaded*.

125. Isaac, "To Counter 'The Very Devil,'" 382.

126. Ibid., 382–84.

127. Julia Keller, *Mr. Gatling's Terrible Marvel: The Gun That Changed Everything and the Misunderstood Genius Who Invented It* (New York: Viking, 2008); Philip Stigger, "Reconsideration of the Role of the Gatling Gun in the Ashanti Campaign of 1873/4," *Journal for the Society for Army Historical Research* 70, no. 284 (Winter 1992): 271–73; P. G. Smith, "Great Guns!," *Military History* 35, no. 4 (November 2018): 64–71.

128. Keller, *Mr. Gatling's Terrible Marvel*; Stigger, "Reconsideration of the Role of the Gatling Gun"; Smith, "Great Guns!"

129. Keller, *Mr. Gatling's Terrible Marvel*, 9.

130. Zeese Papanikolas, *Buried Unsung: Louis Tikas and the Ludlow Massacre* (Lincoln: University of Nebraska Press, 1982).

131. "Charges Murder by Union," *New York Times*, February 13, 1914; Scott Martelle, *Blood Passion: The Ludlow Massacre and Class War in the American West* (New Brunswick, NJ: Rutgers University Press, 2007); Anthony Roland DeStefanis, "Guarding

Capital: Soldier Strikebreakers on the Long Road to the Ludlow Massacre," PhD diss., College of William and Mary, 2004.

132. Isaac, "To Counter 'The Very Devil.'"

133. Ibid.; Alfred Mewett, *A Brief History of Troop A, 107th Regiment of Cavalry, Ohio National Guard, The Black Horse Troop, for Many Years Knows as The First City Troop of Cleveland* (Cleveland, OH: Veterans' Association, 1923); Western Reserve Historical Society, Cleveland Military Units Records, 1877–1964, box 1, 1–3; box 17, 1–7; box 18, 1–7; box 19, 1–6; box 20, 1–20, http://catalog.wrhs.org/collections/view?docId=ead/MS3000 .xml.

134. Mewett, *Brief History of Troop A*; Western Reserve Historical Society, Cleveland Military Units Records.

135. Muñoz Martinez, *The Injustice Never Leaves You*, 6–7.

136. *Regeneración*, November 12, 1910, in *Dreams of Freedom: A Ricardo Flores Magón Reader* ed. Chaz Bufe and Mitchell Verter (Oakland, CA: AK Press 2005), 199.

137. Ibid., 200.

138. Ibid.

139. Ibid., 199–200.

140. Frederick Fennell, ed., *The Black Horse Troop* (Van Nuys, CA: Alfred, 2001), 1.

141. Ibid.

142. Gary B. Nash, *Red, White, and Black: The Peoples of Early America*, 2nd ed. (Upper Saddle River, NJ: Prentice Hall, 1982), 39.

143. Slotkin, *Gunfighter Nation*, 486.

144. Ibid., 481.

145. Janny Scott, *The Beneficiary: Fortune, Misfortune, and the Story of My Father* (New York: Riverhead, 2019), 65–67.

146. "To Whom Does the World Owe a Living?," *Chicago Tribune*, July 29, 1877.

147. *The Chicago Martyrs: The Famous Speeches of the Eight Anarchists in Judge Gary's Court and Altgeld's Reasons for Pardoning Fielden, Neebe and Schwab* (San Francisco: Free Society, 1899), 77.

148. Flinn and Wilkie, *History of the Chicago Police*, 9.

149. "The Insurrectionary Strike," *The Sun* (New York), July 25, 1877.

150. "Reflections," *The Sun* (New York), July 25, 1877.

151. Ibid.

152. "The Dangerous Classes," *Chicago Tribune*, July 29, 1877.

153. *Cleveland Leader*, July 20, 1877.

154. "Law Must Be Vindicated," *New York Tribune*, July 24, 1877.

155. Ibid.

156. Ibid.

157. Ibid.

158. Ibid.

159. John Taliaferro, *All the Great Prizes: The Life of John Hay, from Lincoln to Roosevelt* (New York: Simon and Schuster, 2013), 131.

160. "Conspiring against the Laborer," *New York Tribune*, July 24, 1877.

Notes to Chapter 4    225

161. "The War against Railroads," *New York Tribune*, July 24, 1877.

162. "News This Morning," *New York Tribune*, July 24, 1877.

163. "Our Governments," *New York Tribune*, July 28, 1877.

164. Ibid.

165. "News This Morning," *New York Tribune*, July 23, 1877.

166. "Our Governments."

167. Wildwood, *Thrilling Adventures*, 5–6.

168. "Our Governments."

169. Ibid.

170. Ibid.

171. "Zanesville Aroused," *The Sun* (New York), July 25, 1877.

172. Ibid.

173. "Indian Outrages in Dakota," *New York Tribune*, July 27, 1877,

174. Jerome A. Greene, ed., *Lakota and Cheyenne: Indian Views of the Great Sioux War, 1876–1877* (Norman: University of Oklahoma Press, 1994); Jerome A. Greene, *Yellowstone Command: Colonel Nelson A. Miles and the Great Sioux War, 1876–1877* (Norman: University of Oklahoma Press, 2006); Ernie LaPointe, *Sitting Bull: His Life and Legacy* (Salt Lake City: Gibbs Smith, 2009).

175. For discussion on how the building of the railroads affected Indigenous nations, see Manu Karuka, *Empire's Tracks: Indigenous Nations, Chinese Workers, and the Transcontinental Railroad* (Oakland: University of California Press, 2019).

176. "Indian Outrages in Dakota."

177. Ibid.

178. Ibid.

179. "Riots in the West," *New York Tribune*, July 27, 1877.

180. Ibid.

181. Hay, *Complete Poetical Works*, 77.

182. Sherman to Herbert A. Preston, April 17, 1873, quoted in Marszalek, *Sherman*, 379; Dunbar-Ortiz, *Indigenous Peoples' History*, 145.

183. "Riots in the West."

184. Ibid.

185. Ibid.

186. Ashbaugh, *Lucy Parsons*, 25.


## Chapter 5. Republicans and Anarchists

1. Albert Parsons to George Schilling, November 7, 1887, in Lucy E. Parsons, ed., *Life of Albert R. Parsons, with Brief History of the Labor Movement in America* (Chicago: Lucy E. Parsons, 1889), 218.

2. John Q. Anderson, *Campaigning with Parsons' Texas Cavalry Brigade, CSA* (Hillsboro, TX: Hill Junior College Press, 1967); Anne J. Bailey, *Between the Enemy and Texas: Parsons's Texas Cavalry in the Civil War* (Fort Worth: Texas Christian University Press, 1988); B. P. Gallaway, *The Ragged Rebel: A Common Soldier in W. H. Parsons' Texas Cavalry, 1861–1865* (Austin: University of Texas Press, 1988); Parsons' Texas Cavalry Brigade

Association, *A Brief and Condensed History of Parsons' Texas Cavalry Brigade* (Waxahachie, Texas: Flemister, 1892); Edward T. Cotham, *Sabine Pass: The Confederacy's Thermopylae* (Austin: University of Texas Press, 2004); Parsons, *Life of Albert R. Parsons*; Anne J. Bailey, "Parsons, William Henry," *Handbook of Texas Online*, http://www.tshaonline.org/handbook/online/articles/fpa43.

3. Willard Richardson to George Ware Fulton, February 2, 1861, in A. Ray Stephens, "Letter from the Texas Secession Convention, 1861: Willard Richardson to George Ware Fulton," *Southern Historical Quarterly* 65, no. 3 (January 1962): 395–96.

4. Parsons, *Life of Albert R. Parsons*; Sam Hanna Acheson, *35,000 Days in Texas: A History of the Dallas News and Its Forbears* (New York: Macmillan, 1938); George Louis Crocket, *Two Centuries in East Texas: A History of San Augustine County and Surrounding Territory, from 1685 to the Present Time* (Dallas: Southwest, 1932); Marilyn McAdams Sibley, *Lone Stars and State Gazettes: Texas Newspapers before the Civil War* (College Station: Texas A&M University Press, 1983); Stephens, "Letter from the Texas Secession Convention"; Randolph Lewis, "Richardson, Willard," *Handbook of Texas Online*, http://www.tshaonline.org/handbook/online/articles/fri13.

5. Parsons, *Life of Albert R. Parsons*, 8.

6. Historian Jacqueline Jones places Albert Parsons's birthdate in 1845 rather than 1848. Jones's reason for this claim is that an 1850 census worker who interviewed Parsons's father recorded Albert's birth year as 1845. Albert and those close to him claimed he was born in 1848, and in his own autobiography, the ages he gives at which he was at various life events correspond to an 1848 birth year. Because of the possibility that a census-taker recorded a year incorrectly, or of Albert's father inadvertently saying the wrong year when interviewed, until further evidence emerges, I am sticking with the 1848 date that Albert and his family claimed. Regardless of his birth year, 1845 or 1848, he was underage at the time he joined the Confederate military, and it changes nothing about the substance of anything I argue in this section. For Jones's claim, see Jones, *Goddess of Anarchy*, 6, 362n4.

7. David Silkenat, *Raising the White Flag: How Surrender Defined the American Civil War* (Chapel Hill: University of North Carolina Press, 2019); John H. Eicher and David J. Eicher, *Civil War High Commands* (Stanford, CA: Stanford University Press, 2001); Parsons, *Life of Albert R. Parsons*.

8. Parsons, *Life of Albert R. Parsons*, 9.

9. Parsons to Schilling, 218.

10. Ibid., 216.

11. Ibid.

12. Ibid., 217.

13. Ahrens, *Lucy Parsons*; Ashbaugh, *Lucy Parsons*; Jones, *Goddess of Anarchy*.

14. Jones, *Goddess of Anarchy*, 11–12.

15. "Lucy Parsons Is Mild," *Sunday Inter-Ocean*, August 12, 1900, 33.

16. Jones, *Goddess of Anarchy*, 5.

17. *Waco Daily Examiner*, May 9, 1886.

18. Ibid.

19. Ibid.

Notes to Chapter 5    227

20. Ibid.

21. Parsons to Schilling, 218.

22. Ibid.

23. Parsons, *Life of Albert R. Parsons*, 9.

24. *Biographical Encyclopedia of Texas* (New York: Southern, 1880), 185; James Lafayette Walker and C. P. Lumpkin, *History of the Waco Baptist Association of Texas* (Waco, TX: Byrne-Hill, 1897), 43, 64; Betty McCartney McSwain, ed., *The Bench and Bar of Waco and McLennan County* (Waco, TX: Texian Press, 1976).

25. Parsons to Schilling, 217.

26. Ibid.

27. Ibid., 218.

28. Merline Pitre, *Through Many Dangers, Toils, and Snares: Black Leadership in Texas, 1868–1898*, 3rd ed. (Austin: Texas A&M University Press, 2016); Alwyn Barr and Robert A. Calvert, eds., *Black Leaders: Texans for Their Times* (Austin: Texas State Historical Association, 1985); Ashbaugh, *Lucy Parsons*; Parsons, *Life of Albert R. Parsons*.

29. Lucy Parsons, "Southern Lynchings," in Ahrens, *Lucy Parsons*, 70, originally published in *Freedom*, April 1892.

30. Parsons, "Southern Lynchings," 70.

31. Lucy Parsons, "The Negro: Let Him Leave Politics to the Politician and Prayers to the Preacher," *The Alarm*, April 3, 1886, in Ahrens, *Lucy Parsons*, 54.

32. Parsons, "Southern Lynchings."

33. Akinyele Omowale Umoja, *We Will Shoot Back: Armed Resistance in the Mississippi Freedom Movement* (New York: New York University Press, 2013); Charles E. Cobb Jr., *This Nonviolent Stuff'll Get You Killed: How Guns Made the Civil Rights Movement Possible* (New York: Basic Books, 2014); Robert F. Williams, *Negroes with Guns* (New York: Marzani and Munsell, 1962); Nicholas Johnson, *Negroes and the Gun: The Black Tradition of Arms* (Amherst, NY: Prometheus, 2014); Lance Hill, *The Deacons for Defense: Armed Resistance and the Civil Rights Movement* (Chapel Hill: University of North Carolina Press, 2004); Joshua Bloom and Waldo E. Martin Jr., *Black against Empire: The History and Politics of the Black Panther Party* (Oakland: University of California Press, 2016); Sundiata Keita Cha-Jua, "'A Warlike Demonstration': Legalism, Armed Resistance, and Black Political Mobilization in Decatur, Illinois, 1894–1898," *Journal of Negro History* 83, no. 1 (Winter 1998): 52–72.

34. Warsan Shire, "Conversations about Home," in *Teaching My Mother How to Give Birth* (London: Flipped Eye, 2011), 24.

35. Ashbaugh, *Lucy Parsons*, 15.

36. Ashbaugh, *Lucy Parsons*, 16.

37. Jones, *Goddess of Anarchy*, 46–47.

38. *Report of the Chicago Relief and Aid Society to the Common Council of the City of Chicago* (Chicago: Horton and Leonard, 1872), 87.

39. Adams discussed his views on "the importation of ready-made foreign labor" in "City Slave Girls," *Chicago Times*, August 21, 1888.

40. Kathleen D. McCarthy, *Noblesse Oblige: Charity and Cultural Philanthropy in Chicago, 1849–1929* (Chicago: University of Chicago Press, 1982); Karen Sawislak, *Smol-*

dering City: Chicagoans and the Great Fire, 1871–1874 (Chicago: University of Chicago Press, 1995); Michael B. Katz, In the Shadow of the Poorhouse: A Social History of Welfare in America, 10th anniv. ed. (New York: Basic Books, 1996); Ashbaugh, Lucy Parsons.

41. Lucy Parsons, "The Negro." 54.

42. See, for example, DuVernay, 13th; Michelle Alexander, The New Jim Crow: Mass Incarceration in the Age of Color Blindness (New York: New Press, 2012).

43. Ahrens, Lucy Parsons; Ashbaugh, Lucy Parsons; Jones, Goddess of Anarchy.

44. Parsons, Life of Albert R. Parsons, 10.

45. Quoted in Jones, Goddess of Anarchy, 65–66.

46. Ashbaugh, Lucy Parsons, 16.

47. Parsons, Life of Albert R. Parsons, 6–12.

48. Ibid., 12.

49. Ibid., 11–12.

50. Ibid., 11.

51. Ibid., 12–13.

52. Ibid.

53. Ibid., 13–14.

54. Ibid., 15.

55. Ibid.

56. Ibid.

57. Avrich, Haymarket Tragedy; Jones, Goddess of Anarchy; Ashbaugh, Lucy Parsons; Ahrens, Lucy Parsons; Parsons, Life of Albert R. Parsons.

58. Mary Harris Jones, The Autobiography of Mother Jones, ed. Mary Field Parton (Chicago: Charles H. Kerr, 1996), 16.

59. Sam Mitrani, The Rise of the Chicago Police Department: Class and Conflict, 1850–1894 (Urbana: University of Illinois Press, 2013), 112.

60. For a more focused study of German anarchists in the United States, see Tom Goyens, Beer and Revolution: The German Anarchist Movement in New York City, 1880–1914 (Urbana, IL: University of Illinois Press, 2007).

61. The number of participants in the Lehr und Wehr Verein is unclear. The Haymarket martyr August Spies, who was a leader in the Verein, numbered it at fifteen hundred, but some historians number it between five and seven hundred. See August Spies, August Spies' Autobiography; His Speech in Court and General Notes (Chicago: Nina Van Zandt, 1887), 11; John Jentz and Richard Schneirov, Chicago in the Age of Capital: Class, Politics, and Democracy during the Civil War and Reconstruction (Urbana: University of Illinois Press, 2012); Flinn and Wilkie, History of the Chicago Police; Avrich, Haymarket Tragedy; Mitrani, Rise of the Chicago Police.

62. Arbeiter-Zeitung, August 3, 1880, quoted in Mitrani, Rise of the Chicago Police Department, 119.

63. Spies, August Spies' Autobiography, 11.

64. Parsons, Life of Albert R. Parsons, 16–17.

65. Mitrani, Rise of the Chicago Police, 119.

66. Presser v. Illinois, 116 U.S. 252 (1886); Mitrani, Rise of the Chicago Police, 119.

67. Cynthia Deitle Leonardatos, "California's Attempt to Disarm the Black Panthers,"

*San Diego Law Review* 36, no. 4 (Fall 1999): 947–96; Dunbar-Ortiz, *Loaded*; Adam Winkler, *Gunfight: The Battle over the Right to Bear Arms in America* (New York: W. W. Norton, 2011); Ward Churchill and Jim Vander Wall, *Agents of Repression: The FBI's Secret Wars against the Black Panther Party and the American Indian Movement*, 2nd ed. (Cambridge, MA: South End, 2002).

68. Falk et al., *Emma Goldman*, 571–72.

69. Trautmann, *Voice of Terror*, 78–79; Goyens, *Beer and Revolution*.

70. Zimmer, *Immigrants against the State*, 3.

71. Alan Dawley, "The International Working People's Association," in *Haymarket Scrapbook*, ed. Franklin Rosemont and David Roediger (Chicago: Charles H. Kerr, 1986), 85.

72. *The Alarm*, November 1, 1884.

73. Zimmer, *Immigrants against the State*, 4.

74. Anderson, *Under Three Flags*, 2.

75. Robert C. Tucker, ed., *The Marx-Engels Reader*, 2nd ed. (New York: W. W. Norton, 1978), 475.

76. "Price, Hiram (1814–1901)," in *Biographical Directory of the United States Congress, 1774-Present*, http://bioguide.congress.gov/scripts/biodisplay.pl?index=P000525.

77. US Department of the Interior, *Report of the Secretary of the Interior for the Fiscal Year Ending June 30, 1887*, vol. 2 (Washington, DC: Government Printing Office, 1887), 1001.

78. Ibid.

79. Ibid., 2: 1003.

80. Ibid., 2: 957.

81. *Second Annual Address to the Public of the Lake Mohonk Conference, Held at Lake Mohonk, N.Y., September, 1884, in Behalf of the Civilization and Legal Protection of the Indians of the United States* (Philadelphia: Executive Committee of the Indian Rights Association, 1884), 7–11, quoted in John M. Rhea, *A Field of Their Own: Women and American Indian History, 1830–1941* (Norman: University of Oklahoma Press, 2016), 100.

82. *Second Annual Address to the Public of the Lake Mohonk Conference, Held at Lake Mohonk, N.Y., September, 1884, in Behalf of the Civilization and Legal Protection of the Indians of the United States*, 3–22; Joan Mark, *A Stranger in Her Native Land: Alice Fletcher and the American Indians* (Lincoln: University of Nebraska Press, 1988); Rhea, *Field of Their Own*.

83. US Department of the Interior, *Report of the Secretary of the Interior for the Fiscal Year Ending on June 30, 1887*, 2: 1001.

84. Ibid., 2: 1003.

85. *Annual Report of the Commissioner of Indian Affairs to the Secretary of the Interior for the Year 1884* (Washington, DC: Government Printing Office, 1884), III.

86. *The Alarm*, November 8, 1884.

87. Ibid.

88. Ibid., April 18, 1885, quoted in Steven Sapolsky, "The Making of Honore Jaxon," in Rosemont and Roediger, eds., *Haymarket Scrapbook*, 103.

89. Smith, "Great Guns!"; Stigger, "Reconsideration"; Keller, *Mr. Gatling's Terrible Marvel.*

90. *The Alarm*, November 28, 1885, quoted in Sapolsky, "The Making of Honore Jaxon," 103.

91. Lombroso, *L'Homme criminel: atlas*, 2: plates 49–50.

92. Donald B. Smith, *Honoré Jaxon: Prairie Visionary* (Regina, SK: Coteau, 2007), 74.

93. Sapolsky, "Making of Honore Jaxon," 105.

94. Smith, *Honoré Jaxon*, 75; Ashbaugh, *Lucy Parsons*, 168.

95. For more on Jaxon, see Smith, *Honoré Jaxon*; Ashbaugh, *Lucy Parsons*, 167–69; Sapolsky, "Making of Honore Jaxon"; Rudolf Rocker, *The London Years*, trans. Joseph Leftwich (Oakland, CA: AK Press, 2005), 140.

96. *The Alarm*, December 26, 1885.

97. Ibid.

98. Ibid.

99. For an example, see Lucy Parsons's letter to the editor of *The Socialist*, Chicago, February 1, 1879, in response to a *Scribner's Magazine* article instructing wealthy white women how to choose house servants, included in Ahrens, *Lucy Parsons*, 42–43.

100. *The Alarm*, December 26, 1885.

101. Ibid.

102. Ibid.

103. Goldman, *Anarchism and Other Essays*, 184–85. See also Margaret S. Marsh, *Anarchist Women, 1870–1920* (Philadelphia: Temple University Press, 1981).

104. The quote is from de Cleyre's 1896 essay "Sex Slavery," reproduced in Brigati, *Voltairine de Cleyre Reader*, 101.

105. *The Alarm*, December 26, 1885.

106. Ibid.

107. Ibid.

108. Migrant Italian anarchists in the United States often made similar inversions. See Zimmer, *Immigrants against the State*; Guglielmo and Salerno, *Are Italians White?*.

109. *The Alarm*, August 8, 1885, reproduced in Ahrens, *Lucy Parsons*, 45.

110. For discussion of the relationship between whiteness and property, see Cheryl I. Harris, "Whiteness as Property," *Harvard Law Review* 106, no. 8 (June 1993): 1707–91.

111. Lucy Parsons, May 1885, quoted in Ashbaugh, *Lucy Parsons*, 59.

112. "To Whom Does the World Owe a Living?," *Chicago Tribune*, July 29, 1877; Lucy Parsons, quoted in Ashbaugh, *Lucy Parsons*, 60.

113. Ashbaugh, *Lucy Parsons*, 60; "Lucy Parsons Is Mild," *Sunday Inter-Ocean*, August 12, 1900.

114. *The Alarm*, December 8, 1888. See also the discussion of Lucy Parsons, Indigeneity, and race in Lauren L. Basson, *White Enough to Be American? Race Mixing, Indigenous People, and the Boundaries of State and Nation* (Chapel Hill: University of North Carolina Press, 2008).

115. Spies, *August Spies' Autobiography*, 1.

Notes to Chapter 5      231

116. Basson, *White Enough to Be American?*, 168.

117. Ashbaugh, *Lucy Parsons*, 1976, 60.

118. Jones, *Autobiography*, 18.

119. Ibid., 18–19.

120. Ibid.

121. "Lucy Parsons Is Mild."

122. *The Liberator*, October 29, 1905; Ahrens, *Lucy Parsons*, 107–10.

123. Hay to Amasa Stone, March 11, 1883, in Hay, *Letters of John Hay*, 2: 83.

124. Thayer, *Life and Letters of John Hay*, 1: 2.

125. Parsons, *Life of Albert R. Parsons*, 7.

126. Thayer, *Life and Letters of John Hay*, 1: 3.

127. Parsons, *Life of Albert R. Parsons*, 7.

128. Albert Parsons to Justus Schwab, September 21, 1887, in Parsons, *Life of Albert R. Parsons*, 219.

129. Lucy Parsons, *Life of Albert R. Parsons; with a Brief History of the Labor Movement in America* (Chicago: Lucy Parsons, 1903), 248. Note that this is a different edition of this book than is cited elsewhere in this study, being the 1903 rather than the 1889 edition. The 1889 edition page numbers do not match up with the 1903 edition and the 1889 edition does not include the letter quoted here.

## Chapter 6. The Respectable Mob

1. Avrich, *Haymarket Tragedy*, 422–27.

2. "Liberty Is Dead in San Diego," *Industrial Worker*, April 4, 1912, 1.

3. Joan W. Scott, "Gender: A Useful Category of Historical Analysis," *American Historical Review* 91, no. 5 (December 1986): 1053–75.

4. Kristin L. Hoganson, *Consumers' Imperium: The Global Production of American Domesticity, 1865–1920* (Chapel Hill: University of North Carolina Press, 2007); McDuffie, *Sojourning for Freedom*; Bederman, *Manliness and Civilization*; Moreton-Robinson, *White Possessive*; Barker, *Critically Sovereign*; Simpson, *As We Have Always Done*; Gilmore, *Gender and Jim Crow*; Guglielmo, *Living the Revolution*; Moreton-Robinson, *Talkin' Up*; Newman, *White Women's Rights*; Rhea, *A Field of Their Own*; Hane, *Reflections on the Way to the Gallows*.

5. Audra Simpson, "The State Is a Man: Theresa Spence, Loretta Saunders and the Gender of Settler Sovereignty," *Theory and Event* 19, no. 4 (2016), muse.jhu.edu/article/633280; Dian Million, *Therapeutic Nations: Healing in an Age of Indigenous Human Rights* (Tucson: University of Arizona Press, 2013); Kim Anderson, *A Recognition of Being: Reconstructing Native Womanhood*, 2nd ed. (Toronto: Women's Press, 2016); Jennifer Nez Denetdale, "Securing Navajo National Boundaries: War, Patriotism, Tradition, and the Dine Marriage Act of 2005," *Wicazo Sa Review* 24, no. 2 (Fall 2009): 131–48; Moreton-Robinson, *White Possessive*.

6. "City Council Protests against State Interference: Prepares Memorial to Governor Outlining I.W.W. Situation in This City," *San Diego Weekly Union*, April 25, 1912.

7. "City Council Protests."

8. "City Council Protests."

9. Dubofsky, *We Shall Be All*.

10. "The San Diego Outrages," *Freedom*, July 1912, 54.

11. "San Diego Must Continue Law-Abiding," *San Diego Union*, March 3, 1912; "Civil War Veterans Appear against I.W.W.," *San Diego Union*, April 20, 1912.

12. For general facts on this historical episode, see Dubofsky, *We Shall Be All*; Elizabeth Gurley Flynn, *The Rebel Girl: An Autobiography, My First Life, 1906–1926*, rev. ed. (New York: International, 1973); Drinnon, *Rebel in Paradise*; Falk, *Love, Anarchy, and Emma Goldman*; Bruns, *Damndest Radical*; Falk et al., eds., *Emma Goldman: A Documentary History of the American Years*, vol. 3, *Light and Shadows, 1910–1916* (Stanford, CA: Stanford University Press, 2012).

13. Pliny Castanien, *To Protect and Serve: A History of the San Diego Police Department and Its Chiefs, 1889–1989* (San Diego, CA: San Diego Historical Society, 1993); A. E. Jansen, "Keno Wilson: A Lawman's Lawman," *San Diego Historical Quarterly* 8, no. 4 (October 1962): 50–53.

14. "Why This Encouragement of San Diego's Peace Disturbers?," *Evening Tribune* (San Diego), April 22, 1912.

15. "San Diegans to Drive Lawless Element Forth," *The Call*, May 17, 1912.

16. "Anarchists Must Leave San Diego," *The Call*, May 17, 1912.

17. Oliver C. Cox, "Lynching and the Status Quo," *Journal of Negro Education* 14, no. 4 (Autumn 1945): 576–88.

18. Cox, "Lynching and the Status Quo," 581. ·

19. "Horsewhip Vigilantes Urged to Drive Back Industrial 'Workers,'" *San Diego Union*, February 10, 1912.

20. Cox, "Lynching and the Status Quo," 576.

21. "The Passing Show," *Evening Tribune* (San Diego), January 8, 1912.

22. Letter from Emma Goldman (Los Angeles) to Ellen A. Kennan (Denver), May 22, 1913, *The Emma Goldman Papers: A Microfilm Edition*, reel 7 (Alexandria, VA: Chadwyck-Healey, 1991).

23. "Criticizing in Ignorance," *San Diego Union*, April 23, 1912.

24. Cox, "Lynching and the Status Quo," 580.

25. "Criticizing in Ignorance."

26. "San Diegans to Drive Lawless Element Forth."

27. "Anarchists Must Leave San Diego."

28. Ben Reitman, "Respectable Mob," *Mother Earth*, June 1912, 110.

29. Ibid., 109.

30. Ibid.

31. Emma Goldman, "The Outrage of San Diego," *Mother Earth*, June 1912, 117.

32. Ibid.

33. Ibid.

34. "Leaders of the Murderous Vigilantes Pilloried: Some of the Participants in the Outrages against Life and Liberty Perpetrated in San Diego," *Mother Earth*, June 1912, 108; Falk et al., *Emma Goldman*, 3: 370n9; Clarence Alan McGrew, *City of San Diego and San Diego County: The Birthplace of California*, vol. 2 (Chicago: American Historical

Society, 1922), 70–72; Earnest E. Kirk, "People of the State of California v. Earnest E. Kirk: Affidavit," May 18, 1912, 6, Emma Goldman Papers.

35. "Leaders of the Murderous Vigilantes Pilloried: Some of the Participants in the Outrages Against Life and Liberty Perpetrated in San Diego," 108.

36. James M. Inverarity, "Populism and Lynching in Louisiana, 1889–1896: A Test of Erikson's Theory of the Relationship between Boundary Crises and Repressive Justice," *American Sociological Review* 41, no. 2 (April 1976): 262–80.

37. Ibid.

38. "Preamble and Constitution of the Industrial Workers of the World" (n.p.: Industrial Workers of the World, 1912), 3, http://www.workerseducation.org/crutch/constitution/1912.pdf.

39. Flynn, *Rebel Girl*, 177.

40. "Hermetet Injured by J. Keno Wilson," *Industrial Worker*, May 23, 1912, 3.

41. "Liberty Is Dead," 1, 4; "San Diego Workers Armed for Defense," *Industrial Worker*, April 16, 1912, 1, 4; "Free Speech Is the Issue," *Industrial Worker*, May 16, 1912, 1, 4; "San Diegans to Drive Lawless Element Forth"; "'Free Press' in San Diego," *Industrial Worker*, May 23, 1912, 3; Falk et al., *Emma Goldman*, 3: 634–35.

42. "San Diegans to Drive Lawless Element Forth."

43. Kirk, "People of the State of California v. Earnest E. Kirk: Affidavit," 5.

44. Ibid., 6.

45. Bruns, *Damndest Radical*, 129.

46. Wildwood, *Thrilling Adventures*, 5–6.

47. Richard Drinnon, *Facing West: The Metaphysics of Indian-Hating and Empire-Building* (Norman, OK: University of Oklahoma Press, 1997); Dunbar-Ortiz, *Indigenous Peoples' History*; Daniel Bender, *American Abyss*; Slotkin, *Fatal Environment*; Slotkin, *Gunfighter Nation* ; Bederman, *Manliness and Civilization: A Cultural History of Gender and Race in the United States, 1880–1917* (Chicago: University of Chicago Press, 1995); Joel Kovel, *Red Hunting in the Promised Land: Anticommunism and the Making of America* (London: Cassell, 1997); Michael Rogin, *Fathers and Children: Andrew Jackson and the Subjugation of the American Indian* (New York: Alfred A. Knopf, 1975); Michael Rogin, *Ronald Reagan the Movie and Other Episodes in Political Demonology* (Berkeley: University of California Press, 1987); Matthew Frye Jacobson, *Barbarian Virtues: The United States Encounters Foreign Peoples at Home and Abroad, 1876—1917* (New York: Hill and Wang, 2000); Lauren Basson, *White Enough to Be American?: Race Mixing, Indigenous People, and the Boundaries of State and Nation* (University of North Carolina Press: Chapel Hill, 2008).

48. "San Diegans to Drive Lawless Element Forth." Woodbey was not actually a member of the IWW. He was a Baptist minister and a member of the Socialist Party of America, but he worked with the IWW during the 1912 free-speech fights. To outsiders, he likely appeared to be an IWW leader because he took a leading role in the mobilizations against the speech ordinance.

49. "I.W.W. Band Retreats to Camp near Capistrano," *San Diego Weekly Union*, April 25, 1912.

50. Reitman, "Respectable Mob," 110.

51. "A Dangerous Proposal," *San Diego Union*, February 5, 1912.

52. "San Diego Solving the Anarchist Problem," *San Diego Union*, May 9, 1912.

53. "Criticizing in Ignorance."

54. Quoted in Bruns, *Damndest Radical*, 131.

55. "San Diego Commended for Its Method of Handling Anarchists," *Evening Tribune* (San Diego), April 20, 1912.

56. "Orator Surprised When Policeman Arrests Him," *San Diego Union*, March 3, 1912.

57. "Dangerous Proposal."

58. Ibid.

59. Goldman, "Outrage of San Diego," 122; Flynn, *Rebel Girl*, 177.

60. "San Diego Must Continue Law-Abiding."

61. "No Room in the Land for Red Flag," *San Diego Union*, May 6, 1912.

62. "Room for Only One Flag, Says Pastor," *San Diego Union*, May 6, 1912.

63. Ibid.

64. "Suggests Patriotic Display in Parade," *San Diego Union*, May 9, 2014.

65. "Protect the Flag from Insult," *San Diego Union*, May 7, 1912.

66. "Civil War Veterans Appear against I.W.W."

67. "Police Murder in San Diego," *Industrial Worker*, April 11, 1912, 1.

68. Bruns, *Damndest Radical*, 121. See also "Forced to Kiss the Flag: 100 Anarchists Are Then Driven from San Diego," *New York Times*, April 5, 1912, 1.

69. "Liberty Is Dead," 1.

70. Ibid., 4.

71. "San Diego Commended."

72. The best scholarly treatment of the relationship between Goldman and Reitman is Falk, *Love, Anarchy, and Emma Goldman*.

73. Emma Goldman to Fred G. Bonfils, May 16, 1912, in Falk et al., *Emma Goldman*, 3: 359.

74. Ibid., 360.

75. Flynn, *Rebel Girl*, 177.

76. "Blood Shed in San Diego," *Industrial Worker*, May 16, 1912, 4.

77. Aileen Moreton-Robinson, *White Possessive*; Joanne Barker, ed., *Critically Sovereign: Indigenous Gender, Sexuality, and Feminist Studies* (Durham, NC: Duke University Press, 2017); Simpson, *As We Have Always Done*; Audra Simpson, "The State Is a Man"; Dian Million, *Therapeutic Nations: Healing in an Age of Indigenous Human Rights* (Tucson: University of Arizona Press, 2013).

78. Marsh, *Anarchist Women*.

79. For more on masculinity and manliness as they relate to empire and race in the era, see Bederman, *Manliness and Civilization*; Kristin Hoganson, *Fighting for American Manhood: How Gender Politics Provoked the Spanish-American and Philippine-American Wars* (New Haven, CT: Yale University Press, 1998); Jacobson, *Barbarian Virtues*; John Kasson, *Houdini, Tarzan, and the Perfect Man: The White Male Body and the Challenge*

*of Modernity in America* (New York: Hill and Wang, 2001); Glenda Gilmore, *Gender and Jim Crow: Women and the Politics of White Supremacy in North Carolina, 1896–1920* (Chapel Hill: University of North Carolina Press, 1996).

80. "Boy Scouts Not Military?," *Industrial Worker*, April 11, 1912, 3.

81. *Industrial Worker*, March 28, 1912, 1.

82. Emma Goldman to Ben Reitman, July 10?, 1912, *The Emma Goldman Papers: A Microfilm Edition*, reel 6.

83. Robert Baden-Powell, *Scouting for Boys* (London: Arthur Pearson, 1908), 77–78.

84. Ibid., 286.

85. To show that these notions endure into the present, note that "helping police" is exactly what the armed vigilantes in Kenosha, Wisconsin, in late August 2020 conceived of themselves as doing against the threat of multiracial protests against racist police violence. One of the vigilantes, a seventeen-year-old boy wielding a semiautomatic rifle fatally shot two people and injured a third. He has since become a celebrated hero to the US conservative movement.

86. Bederman, *Manliness and Civilization*.

87. Amy Louise Wood, *Lynching and Spectacle: Witnessing Racial Violence in America, 1890–1940* (Chapel Hill: University of North Carolina Press, 2009).

88. Reitman, "Respectable Mob," 109.

89. "Emma Goldman and Ben Reitman Tell of San Diego Experience," *Industrial Worker*, June 6, 1912, 4.

90. Ibid.

91. Reitman, "Respectable Mob," 110.

92. Ibid.

93. Ibid., 110–11.

94. Ibid., 111.

95. "Emma Goldman and Ben Reitman Tell of San Diego Experience"; Reitman, " Respectable Mob"; Falk et al., *Emma Goldman* 3: 366.

96. John D. Barry, "Ways of the World," *Bulletin* (San Francisco), May 23, 1912, 6.

97. Falk, *Love, Anarchy, and Emma Goldman*; Bruns, *Damndest Radical*.

98. Emma Goldman (Los Angeles) to Ellen A. Kennan (Denver), May 22, 1913, *The Emma Goldman Papers: A Microfilm Edition*, reel 7.

99. "Emma Goldman In; Hooted by Crowd; Can't Get a Hall," *San Diego Sun*, May 14, 1912.

100. "San Diegans Assail Emma Goldman: Her Manager Is Tarred, Feathered and Burned by Vigilantes," *Bulletin* (San Francisco), May 15, 1912.

101. "Emma Goldman In."

102. "Emma Goldman and Ben Reitman Tell of San Diego Experience," 4.

103. Ibid.

104. Goldman, "Outrage of San Diego," 120.

105. "Anarchists Must Leave San Diego."

106. Quoted in Bruns, *Damndest Radical*, 131.

107. It should be acknowledged that Sanger began her career among anarchists,

socialists, and Wobblies but later distanced herself from the radical left to become a respectable progressive and a proponent of some odious positions on race and eugenics.

108. Falk et al., *Emma Goldman*, 3: 666–67; Drinnon, *Rebel in Paradise*, 134–37.

109. Reitman, "Respectable Mob," 112.

110. Alexander Berkman, Hippolyte Havel, and Harry Kelly, "A Protest and a Warning," *Mother Earth*, June 1912, 123.

111. bell hooks, *The Will to Change: Men, Masculinity, and Love* (New York: Simon and Schuster, 2004), 17.

## Chapter 7. Aliens and Mobs

1. *Proceedings and Debates of the Second Session of the Sixty-Sixth Congress of the United States of America, Congressional Record*, vol. 59, pt. 1 (Washington, DC: Government Printing Office, 1920), 977.

2. Ibid.

3. Roosevelt, *Thomas Hart Benton* (Boston: Houghton, Mifflin, 1889), 216.

4. They were not all ethnic Russians, but they were all born within the borders of the Russian Empire of the time. For a more focused study on the Buford deportees, see Kenyon Zimmer, "The Voyage of the Buford: Political Deportations and the Making and Unmaking of America's First Red Scare," in *Deportation in the Americas: Histories of Exclusion and Resistance*, edited by Kenyon Zimmer and Cristina Salinas (College Station: Texas A&M Press, 2018).

5. *New York Tribune*, December 22, 1919.

6. *Proceedings and Debates of the Second Session of the Sixty-Sixth Congress of the United States of America, Congressional Record*, vol. 59, part 1, 990.

7. William Z. Foster was an Irish American socialist and a syndicalist who at the time was a key organizer of an ongoing major steel strike. He later went on to serve as the general secretary of the Communist Party USA from 1945 to 1957. He is buried at Forest Home Cemetery, Chicago, near the graves of the Haymarket martyrs, Emma Goldman, Lucy Parsons, Voltairine de Cleyre, and dozens of other "reds" from the era, in a section of the cemetery called Radical Row.

8. *Proceedings and Debates of the Second Session of the Sixty-Sixth Congress of the United States of America, Congressional Record*, vol. 59, part 1, 990–91.

9. Katherine Benton-Cohen, *Borderline Americans: Racial Division and Labor War in the Arizona Borderlands* (Cambridge, MA: Harvard University Press, 2009); Philip J. Mellinger, *Race and Labor in Western Copper: The Fight for Equality, 1896–1918* (Tucson: University of Arizona Press, 1995).

10. J. Edgar Hoover, "Memorandum for Mr. Creighton, Re Berkman and Goldman," August 23, 1919, Department of Justice, Record Group 60, file 186233–13, US National Archives and Records Administration, Washington, DC.

11. Richard Gid Powers, *Secrecy and Power: The Life of J. Edgar Hoover* (New York: Free Press, 1987); Curt Gentry, *J. Edgar Hoover: The Man and the Secrets* (New York: W. W. Norton, 1991); Weiner, *Enemies*; Kristian Williams, *Our Enemies in Blue: Police*

*and Power in America*, 3rd ed. (Oakland, CA: AK Press, 2015); Ward Churchill and Jim Vander Wall, *Agents of Repression: The FBI's Secret Wars against the Black Panther Party and the American Indian Movement* (Boston: South End, 1988); Barton, "Global War on Anarchism"; Jensen, *Battle against Anarchist Terrorism*.

12. Powers, *Secrecy and Power: The Life of J. Edgar Hoover*; Gentry, *J. Edgar Hoover: The Man and the Secrets*; Weiner, *Enemies: A History of the FBI*, 2012.

13. Paul Avrich, *Anarchist Portraits* (Princeton, NJ: Princeton University Press, 1988); Kenyon Zimmer, *Immigrants against the State: Yiddish and Italian Anarchism in America* (Urbana: University of Illinois Press, 2015); Kenyon Zimmer, "Voyage of the Buford"; *The Blast*, February 19, 1916, 4.

14. Avrich, *Anarchist Portraits*; Paul Avrich, *Anarchist Voices: An Oral History of Anarchism in America* (Edinburgh, Scotland: AK Press, 2005).

15. Wolfe, "Settler Colonialism," 388.

16. Charles L. Lumpkins, *American Pogrom: The East St. Louis Race Riot and Black Politics* (Athens: Ohio University Press, 2008); Malcolm McLaughlin, *Power, Community, and Racial Killing in East St. Louis* (New York: Palgrave Macmillan, 2005); Johnson, *Broken Heart of America*; Harper Barnes, *Never Been a Time: The 1917 Race Riot That Sparked the Civil Rights Movement* (New York: Walker, 2008).

17. Martha Gruening, "Speaking of Democracy," *Mother Earth*, August 1917, 213–18.

18. W. E. Burghardt Du Bois and Martha Gruening, "The Massacre of East St. Louis," *The Crisis*, September 1917, 219–38.

19. Gruening, "Speaking of Democracy,".

20. Ibid.

21. Du Bois and Gruening, "Massacre of East St. Louis," 222.

22. Gruening, "Speaking of Democracy"; Du Bois and Gruening, "Massacre of East St. Louis"; Jackson, *A Century of Dishonor*.

23. Weber, "'Different Plans': Indigenous Pasts, the Partido Liberal Mexicano, and Questions about Reframing Binational Social Movements of the Twentieth Century"; Weber, "Keeping Community, Challenging Boundaries: Indigenous Migrants, Internationalist Workers and Mexican Revolutionaries, 1900–1920"; Weber, "Wobblies of the Partido Liberal Mexicano: Reenvisioning Internationalist and Transnational Movements through Mexican Lenses."

24. Weber, "Different Plans"; Weber, "Keeping Community"; Weber, "Wobblies of the Partido Liberal Mexicano."

25. Cappelletti, *Anarchism in Latin America*, 9–10.

26. Benton-Cohen, *Borderline Americans*; Mellinger, *Race and Labor*; Weber, "Keeping Community."

27. Benton-Cohen, *Borderline Americans*; Mellinger, *Race and Labor*.

28. Frederick Allen, "Montana Vigilantes and the Origins of 3-7-77," *Montana* 51, no. 1 (Spring 2001): 2–19; Frederick Allen, *A Decent, Orderly Lynching: The Montana Vigilantes* (Norman: University of Oklahoma Press, 2013).

29. Streeby, *American Sensations*; Denning, *Mechanic Accents*.

30. Wildwood, *Thrilling Adventures*, 5–6.

31. Jane Little Botkin, *Frank Little and the IWW: The Blood That Stained an American Family* (Norman: University of Oklahoma Press, 2017).

32. Botkin, *Frank Little*; Arnon Gutfeld, "The Murder of Frank Little: Radical Labor Agitation in Butte, Montana, 1917," *Labor History* 10, no. 2 (Spring 1969): 177–92; Patrick Renshaw, *The Wobblies: The Story of the IWW and Syndicalism in the United States* (Chicago: Ivan R. Dee, 1999).

33. Allen, "Montana Vigilantes," 17.

34. The Southwest Montana Official Website, https://southwestmt.com/itineraries/vigilantetrail/.

35. 120th Airlift Wing Official Website, https://www.120thairliftwing.ang.af.mil/.

36. "Montana National Guard to Recognize Aviation Support Battalion," *NBC Montana*, April 3, 2014, https://nbcmontana.com/news/local/gallery/montana-national-guard-to-recognize-aviation-support-battalion#photo-1.

37. Montana Highway Patrol Official Website, https://dojmt.gov/highwaypatrol/.

38. *Proceedings and Debates of the Second Session of the Sixty-Sixth Congress of the United States of America, Congressional Record*, vol. 59, pt. 1: 1014.

39. Benevolent Protective Order of Elks, "Flag Day Resolution," July 9, 1919, Internet Archive, https://web.archive.org/web/20060109092240/http://www.salisburyelks.org/Elks%20history/FlagDayResolution1919.jpg.

40. *Proceedings and Debates of the Second Session of the Sixty-Sixth Congress of the United States of America, Congressional Record*, vol. 59, pt. 1, 1014.

41. William E. Unrau, *Mixed-Bloods and Tribal Dissolution: Charles Curtis and the Quest for Indian Identity* (Lawrence: University Press of Kansas, 1989); Don C. Seitz, *From Kaw Teepee to Capitol: The Life Story of Charles Curtis, Indian, Who Has Risen to High Estate* (New York: Frederick A. Stokes, 1928).

42. Seitz, *From Kaw Teepee to Capitol*; Unrau, *Mixed-Bloods and Tribal Dissolution*.

43. *Proceedings and Debates of the Second Session of the Sixty-Sixth Congress of the United States of America, Congressional Record* vol. 59, pt. 1: 1014–17.

44. Ibid.

45. Robert W. Walker, *The Namesake, the Biography of Theodore Roosevelt Jr.* (New York: Brick Tower, 2014); Eleanor Butler Roosevelt, *Day before Yesterday: The Reminiscences of Mrs. Theodore Roosevelt, Jr.* (New York: Doubleday, 1959); Tim Brady, *His Father's Son: The Life of General Ted Roosevelt Jr.* (New York: New American Library, 2017); William Pencak, *For God and Country: The American Legion, 1919–1941* (Boston: Northeastern University Press, 1989); Thomas B. Littlewood, *Soldiers Back Home: The American Legion in Illinois, 1919–1939* (Carbondale: Southern Illinois University Press, 2004).

46. Ralph Chaplin, *The Centralia Conspiracy: The Truth about the Armistice Day Tragedy*, 3rd ed. (Chicago: General Defense Committee, 1924), 8. Ralph Chaplin (1887–1961) was a highly influential figure in the labor movement whose work continues to be part of labor and people's movement struggles into the present. For example, Chaplin wrote the lyrics of the song "Solidarity Forever," which is sung on picket lines and in social struggles globally. He also designed the iconic anarcho-syndicalist black cat image-also

Notes to Chapter 7     239

known as "sabo cat," "sab cat," and "sabo-tabby"—which labor groups continue to use as a symbol for syndicalism, working-class militancy, and wildcat strikes in the present.

47. Chaplin, *The Centralia Conspiracy*; Tom Copeland, *The Centralia Tragedy of 1919: Elmer Smith and the Wobblies* (Seattle: University of Washington Press, 1993); John McClelland, *Wobbly War: The Centralia Story* (Tacoma: Washington State Historical Society, 1987); James W. Loewen, *Lies across America: What Our Historic Sites Get Wrong* (New York: Simon and Schuster, 1999), 64; American Legion website, "Preamble to the Constitution," https://www.legion.org/preamble.

48. Parsons, *Life of Albert R. Parsons*.

49. Louis Lingg committed suicide in his jail cell on November 10, the night before the execution of the other Haymarket martyrs.

50. *Daily Illini*, November 3, 1936, 4. For more discussion of the incident, see Nick Goodell, "Attacks on the Campus Left Then and Now: Fighting Student Activists on Illinois' Campus in the 1930s," *Public i*, May 2019, http://publici.ucimc.org/2019/05/attacks-on-the-campus-left-then-and-now-fighting-student-activists-on-illinois-campus-in-the-1930s/.

51. Roosevelt, *Thomas Hart Benton*, 216.

52. Patricia Bernstein, "Lynching in America: A History in Documents (Review)," *Southwestern Historical Quarterly* 110, no. 3 (January 2007): 425.

53. Michael Scherer and Alex Altman, "Bigots Get a Boost from the Bully Pulpit after Charlottesville," *Time*, August 17, 2017, https://time.com/4904281/bigots-boosted-by-the-bully-pulpit-charlottesville/.

54. Woodrow Wilson, *A History of the American People*, vol. 5 (New York: Harper and Brothers, 1908), 58–60. The words on the intertitle were mostly Wilson's words, but they do not appear in the book exactly as they did on the intertitle. The words on the intertitle were cobbled together from a few places on pages 58–60 of the book. The only place they strayed from Wilson's exact phrasing was the phrase "veritable empire of the South." In the book, Wilson wrote it as "Invisible Empire of the South [*sic*]."

55. Ibid., 5: 58–64.

56. Ibid., 5: 63.

57. Valerie Strauss, "Trump's Newest Assault on America's Public Schools: They Teach Kids to 'Hate Their Own Country,'" *Washington Post*, July 5, 2020, https://www.washingtonpost.com/education/2020/07/05/trumps-newest-assault-americas-public-schools-they-teach-kids-hate-their-country/.

58. Wilson, *History of the American People*, 5: 58–64.

59. Lena V. Groeger et al., "What Parler Saw during the Attack on the Capitol," *ProPublica*, January 17, 2021, https://projects.propublica.org/parler-capitol-videos/.

60. Wilson, *History of the American People*, 5: 58–64.

61. "Radicals: IWW vs. KKK," *Time Magazine*, July 30, 1923.

62. Lauren Coodley, "Upton Sinclair, the 1923 San Pedro IWW Maritime Strike, and the Battle of Liberty Hill," University of Washington IWW History Project, 2015, https://depts.washington.edu/iww/liberty_hill.shtml; Mike Davis, "Sunshine and the Open Shop," in *Metropolis in the Making: Los Angeles in the 1920s*, ed. Tom Sitton and William Deverell, 96–122 (Berkeley: University of California Press, 2001).

63. "K.K.K. and I.W.W. Wage Drawn Battle in Greenville," *Portland Press Herald*, February 5, 1924.

64. Groeger et al., "What Parler Saw."

65. Moreton-Robinson, *White Possessive*.

## Conclusion

1. A. Naomi Paik, *Bans, Walls, Raids, Sanctuary: Understanding U.S. Immigration for the Twenty-First Century* (Oakland: University of California Press, 2020), 3.

2. Césaire, *Discourse on Colonialism*, 31.

3. There has been some good work along these lines in recent years, such as Stuart Schrader's *Badges without Borders: How Global Counterinsurgency Transformed American Policing* (Oakland: University of California Press, 2019), which looks at how US imperialism during the Cold War contributed to police in the United States and globally, increasingly applying anticommunist counterinsurgency approaches to internal policing. This study, however, suggests that the story of police as counterinsurgents begins much earlier than the post–World War II period, and that police conceived of themselves as anticommunist counterinsurgents as early as the nineteenth century, when modern police departments were new institutions. As earlier chapters discuss, the imperialist ventures the police drew from to inform their urban policing were the Indian Wars, which suggests that settler colonialism is a central framework from which policing developed.

4. Julian Go, "The Imperial Origins of American Policing: Militarization and Imperial Feedback in the Early 20th Century," *American Journal of Sociology* 125, no. 5 (2020): 1193–1254.

5. Richard Trumka, "Dakota Access Pipeline Provides High-Quality Jobs," press release, September 15, 2016, AFL-CIO, https://aflcio.org/press/releases/dakota-access -pipeline-provides-high-quality-jobs.

6. "GEO Calls for AFT/IFT Solidarity with Palestine," press release, June 19, 2018, Graduate Employees Organization at University of Illinois at Urbana-Champaign, https://www.uiucgeo.org/solidarity-statements-and-press-releases/2018/06/19/geo-calls -for-aftift-solidarity-with-palestine?fbclid=IwAR16PDIIYLUaBOe5IJP8_OIvqcQ WO0lbO88WHd1Uq3FxYqDevMu8QR_luvM; Jeff Schuhrke, "U.S. Unions Are Voicing Unprecedented Support for Palestine," *In These Times*, May 26, 2021, https://inthesetimes .com/article/palestine-israel-labor-unions-afl-cio-aft-bds-gaza.

7. Walia, *Border and Rule*.

8. Jake Lahut, "Biden Still Wants to Increase Funding for Police Departments by $300 Million to 'Reinvigorate Community Policing,'" *Business Insider*, June 10, 2020, https://www .businessinsider.com/biden-300-million-for-reshaped-police-departments-in-op-ed -2020–6; Alice Speri, "As Calls to Defund the Police Grow Louder, Joe Biden Wants to Give Them More Money," *Intercept*, June 11, 2020, https://theintercept.com/2020/06/11/defund- the-police-joe-biden-cops/; Lee Fang, "In Her First Race, Kamala Harris Campaigned as Tough on Crime and Unseated the Country's Most Progressive Prosecutor," *Intercept*, February 7, 2019, https://theintercept.com/2019/02/07/kamala-harris-san-francisco

-district-attorney-crime/; Nicholas Reimann, "Biden Picked a 'Cop': Some on Left Slam Choice of Kamala Harris for VP," *Forbes*, August 11, 2020, https://www.forbes.com/sites/nicholasreimann/2020/08/11/biden-picked-a-cop-some-on-left-slam-choice-of-kamala-harris-for-vp/?sh=1b71f9972b23.

9. Igor Derysh, "Joe Biden to Rich Donors: 'Nothing Would Fundamentally Change' If He's Elected," *Salon*, June 19, 2019, https://www.salon.com/2019/06/19/joe-biden-to-rich-donors-nothing-would-fundamentally-change-if-hes-elected/.

10. "Biden: 'I Will Not Ban Fracking. Period,'" *Washington Post*, October 24, 2020, https://www.washingtonpost.com/video/politics/biden-i-will-not-ban-fracking-period/2020/10/24/a0533c7b-a30c-4948-b81f-67b84cff57c8_video.html.

11. Ibid.

12. "Biden Will Recognize Guaido as Venezuela's Leader, Top Diplomat Says," *Reuters*, January 19, 2021, https://www.reuters.com/article/us-usa-biden-state-venezuela/biden-will-recognize-guaido-as-venezuelas-leader-top-diplomat-says-idUSKBN29O2PE; Alex Ward, "The 'Ridiculous' Failed Coup Attempt in Venezuela, Explained," *Vox*, May 11, 2020, https://www.vox.com/2020/5/11/21249203/venezuela-coup-jordan-goudreau-maduro-guaido-explain; "Venezuela's Maduro: Americans Captured in Failed Coup Plot," *Al Jazeera*, May 5, 2020, https://www.aljazeera.com/news/2020/5/5/venezuelas-maduro-americans-captured-in-failed-coup-plot.

13. 8 U.S.C. 1424.

14. This is not to suggest that it does not matter who is in office or that people should not engage with the political system. Clearly there are key policies—on criminal sentencing and reproductive rights, for example—that can change significantly as a matter of who is in office and who gets appointed to influential positions, which have deep, lasting material consequences in ordinary people's lives. The question is not *whether* people should engage the political system, but *how* to do so effectively and in ways that do not inadvertently strengthen the very systems and hierarchies at the root of the problem. Even the most conservative politicians' reactionary policies can be rendered obsolete by social movements made up of ordinary people collectively building power "from below." On this, see Maya Schenwar and Victoria Law, *Prison by Any Other Name: The Harmful Consequences of Popular Reforms* (New York: New Press, 2020); Mariame Kaba, *We Do This 'til We Free Us: Abolitionist Organizing and Transforming Justice* (Chicago: Haymarket, 2021); James Kilgore, *Understanding E-Carceration: Electronic Monitoring, the Surveillance State, and the Future of Mass Incarceration* (New York: New Press, 2022).

# Libraries and Archives Utilized

Anarchy Archives: An Online Research Center on the History and Theory of
    Anarchism, http://pzacad.pitzer.edu/Anarchist_Archives/
Chicago Historical Society
    Haymarket Affair Digital Collection
Forest Home Cemetery, Forest Park, Illinois, sections N and M (Radical Row)
George Mason University Libraries
    Arlington Campus Library, Arlington, Virginia
    Fenwick Library, Main Campus, Fairfax, Virginia
    Law Library, Arlington, Virginia
Institute of International Studies, University of California, Berkeley
    Emma Goldman Papers Project
International Institute of Social History, Amsterdam, Netherlands, https://iisg
    .amsterdam/en" https://iisg.amsterdam/en
    Alexander Berkman Papers
    Emma Goldman Papers
    FBI File on Emma Goldman and Alexander Berkman Archives
Internet Archive: archive.org
Kate Sharpley Library, https://www.katesharpleylibrary.net/
KU Natural History Museum, University of Kansas, Lawrence, Kansas
Library of Congress, Washington, DC
    Chronicling America, Historic American Newspapers
    Directory of US Newspapers in American Libraries
    Rare Book and Special Collections Division
        Anarchism Collection
        M and S Collection
        Paul Avrich Collection
        Radical Pamphlets Collection
Marxists Internet Archive, https://www.marxists.org/

Project Gutenberg, https://www.gutenberg.org/
South Asian American Digital Archive, https://www.saada.org/
Gadar Party Collection
The Anarchist Library, https://theanarchistlibrary.org/special/index
United States National Archives, Washington, DC
Record Group 60, General Records of the Department of Justice
University of Illinois at Urbana-Champaign University Library
History, Philosophy, and Newspaper Library
International and Area Studies Library
Main Stacks
Rare Book and Manuscript Library
University of Michigan Library, Special Collections and Archives, Ann Arbor,
Michigan
Joseph A. Labadie Collection
Walter P. Reuther Library, Archives of Labor and Urban Affairs, Wayne State
University, Detroit, Michigan
Industrial Workers of the World Records

# Index

Abel, Elijah, 107
Abrams, Jacob, 174
Adams, J. McGregor, 128
Agassiz, Louis, 57
*Alarm, The,* 137, 139–40, 146, 148; "Christmas Story" in, 141–46
Alexander II, Czar, 135
Alien Immigration Act of 1903, 56–57, 83
Altgeld, John, 30, 82, 151
American Civil Liberties Union, 57
American Federation of Labor (AFL), 13, 14, 23, 175
American Federation of Teachers, 193
*American Holocaust,* 64–65
American Indian Movement, 174
American Legion, 183–86
anarchism, 4; assassinations and, 77–82; challenges to racial, economic, and colonial order in, 18–23; "Christmas Story" and, 141–46; and deportations of anarchists, 172–78; Indigenous people and, 24, 36–37; institutes of, 21–22; Italian, 18; Jewish, 16, 21; language of dirt and disease used against, 63–66, 75–77; laws excluding, 172–75; legislation against, 171–72, 181–83; martyrs of, 140–41; Mother Jones and, 133, 146–48; newspaper coverage of, 38, 45–46, 50, 52–53, *53,* 63; origins of, 22; outside the United States, 77, 100–103; race science and, 52–58, *53;* racial diversity of, 20–22; racialization and, 18–19; red sisterhood and, 43–51; in San Diego (*see* San Diego [1912]); sexual violence and, 28;

state responses to, 36–43; subverting the ruling class narratives, 146–48; women and, 25–29, 43–51; worldwide influence of, 22–23
*Anarchism and the Black Revolution,* 11
Anarchist Exclusion Act, 21, 56, 83
*Anarchy and Anarchists,* 37–38
Anderson, Benedict, 22–23, 137
Angiolillo, Michele, 77
anti-Blackness, 12–15, 79
anticolonialism, 4; of anarchists, 19–20
anticommunism-antianarchism, 1–2, 171–72; anti-Blackness and, 12–15; Cold War roots of, 31; development in the United States, 31–33; directed at Indigenous people, 34–36, 90; language of, 63–66; rhetoric of, 3–4; Theodore Roosevelt and, 80–85; working class history and, 5–6
anti-Mormonism, 74
anti-Semitism, 64
Appel, David, 91
*Arbeiter-Zeitung,* 50, 131, 146
Argentina, 102
Ashbaugh, Carolyn, 120
assassinations, 77–82
attentat, 77–79
Avrich, Paul, 76, 86, 151

Baden-Powell, Robert Stephenson Smyth, 164, 165
Baker, Simon, 24
Bakunin, Mikhail, 21, 54
Bakunin Institute, 21–22

Barnett, James, 112
Battle of Little Bighorn, 93
Becker, August, 32
Beckert, Sven, 93
Bende, Daniel, 41
Benton, Thomas Hart, 84
Berger, Victor, 173
Berkman, Alexander, 19, 22, 28, 168, 171; deportation of, 172, 173–74; language of dirt and disease used against, 65
Bernstein, Ethel, 65, 173
Betances, Ramón Emeterio, 77
Biden, Joe, 194–95
Bierman, Francis, 156
Biggy, William, 60
*Birth of a Nation, The,* 13, 68–69, 186–87
Bisbee Deportation (1917), 173, 176–78
Black Americans: East St. Louis Pogrom and, 175–76; elected to political office during Reconstruction, 126; during the Reconstruction era, 123–24; violence against (*see* lynchings and massacres); voting rights of, 125–26
Blackhawk, Ned, 92
Black Horse Troop, 112–13
Black International, 135–41
Black left feminism, 25–26
*Black Marxism,* 11–12
Black Panther Party, 134–35, 174
Black workers: communist, 19; feminism and, 25–26; Industrial Workers of the World (IWW) and, 12–14, 23; Railroad Uprisings (1877) and, 8–9; Reconstruction and, 14–15
Blauner, Robert, 20
Boggs, Lilburn W., 104
Bolton, Charles, 112
Boone, Daniel, 38
border security and immigration laws, 194–96
boundary crisis, 157–59
bourgeoisie, the, 97–98; attention on events outside the United States, 100–103; of Chicago, 128; the proletariat and, 15–16; responses to labor strikes, 114–17; rise of, 11–12
Boycott, Divestment, and Sanctions movement (BDS), 193
Boy Scouts, 164, 165
Braly, Clark, 156
Brave Bird, Mary, 75
*Breadwinners, The,* 90, 103–4, 114
Bresci, Gaetano, 77

Breshkovskaya, Katerina, 46
*Broken Heart of America, The,* 3
Buford, John, 67
Burden-Stelly, Charisse, 12
Buwalda, William, 60–62

*Call, The,* 154, 156, 160
Capilano, Joe, 24
capitalism, 2, 3, 4, 7, 8; the bourgeoisie and the proletariat in, 15–16; in Central American and Southern Cone countries, 101–2; development of, 11–12; gender and, 25–29; John Hay and, 90; massacres and, 79; mode of production and, 24–25; private property system and, 89, 92–93; racial, 12; racism endemic in, 11
capitalist class, 15; Civil War and, 121–25; suppression of railroad uprisings by, 117–18
Caraway, Thaddeus Horatius, 172
Carlisle Indian Boarding School, 138
Carnot, Marie François Sadi, 77
Cartwright, Samuel, 89
Caserio, Sante Geronimo, 77
Castillo, Antonio Cánovas del, 77
Césaire, Aimé, 65–66, 191
*Chambre Syndicale,* 44
Cheyenne people, 92
Chicago Citizens' Association, 120
*Chicago Times,* 130, 131
*Chicago Tribune,* 96, 143, 146; Albert Parsons and, 131–32; on the Indian Wars, 118–20; on labor strikes, 114–18
Chinese Exclusion Act, 82
Chivington, John, 72–73
Christian civilization and missionaries, 142–46
Christianity, liberal, 138–39
"Christmas Story, A," 141–46
Civil War, the, 93–94, 121–25; Reconstruction era after, 14–15, 98, 121–27, 149
Cleveland, Grover, 36
*Cleveland Leader,* 115
Cody, William "Buffalo Bill," 154
Cold War, 31, 114
Cole, Peter, 21
colonialism-imperialism, US, 1, 191–96; capitalism and, 11–12; Enlightenment justifications for, 88–89; gender and, 25–29; Indigenous peoples and, 1–3, 5, 24, 34–36; language of dirt and disease used in, 64; language of extermination in, 70–71; notion of "infestation" in, 71–75; portrayed

in *The Navigator,* 67–70; private property system and, 89, 92–93; racism in, 11–12; sexual violence and, 28; turned inward, 3; USAT *Buford* as instrument and symbol of, 66–70; War for Independence and, 2; Wild West cultural narrative in, 159–63

Columbus, Christopher, 17, 18, 41

*Comanche: The Story of America's Most Heroic Horse,* 91

Comstock laws, 28, 163, 169

concentration camps, 35, 58, 64, 82, 195

*Congressional Record,* 6, 7, 33

Coote, Charles, 71

Couden, Henry Noble, 171

counterinsurgency policy, 4–7, 21, 23, 30, 75, 89, 113–14, 118, 120, 125, 191–92

cowboys, 84–85, 87

Cowles, Anna Roosevelt, 85

Cox, Oliver Cromwell, 30, 108–9, 154–56

Crabtree, W. E., 161

Cravello, Ernestina, 50

Criminal Anarchy Act, 1902, 83

criminality, 47, 54–56, 80

*Crisis, The,* 176

Critical Race Theory, 187

Crockett, Davy, 38

Cromwell, Oliver, 6, 71–72

Crosby, 82

Cuba, 6, 67, 72

Curtis, Charles, 182–83

Custer, George, 94, 99

Czołgosz, Leon, 77–81

*Daily Illini,* 186

*Daily News* (Galveston), 122

Dakota people, 34–36

Dana, Charles, 115

Darrow, Clarence, 57

David, Marie Louise, 52

Davis, Angela, 174

Davis, Edmund Jackson, 125

Davis, Ewin Lamar, 173

Dawes, Henry, 35, 137–38

Dawes Act, 1887, 35, 36, 92, 137–38

Dawley, Alan, 136

Dayal, Har, 19, 21–22

Debs, Eugene, 41

de Cleyre, Voltairine, 27, 46–47, 50, 78–79, 163

Deer, Sarah, 28

*Degeneration,* 53

Democratic Party, the, 1, 196

Denning, Michael, 39, 179

*Denver Post,* 163

deportations of anarchists, 172–75; Bisbee Deportation (1917), 173, 176–78

Detroit Rebellion, 1967, 23

Dexter, Wirt, 128

Dickinson, Joseph, 62

Dixon, Thomas, 13

*Documents d'études sociales sur l'anarchie,* 100–101

Dodge, John Mason, 156

Dorame, Rosendo, 177

Douglas, Mary, 70–71

Down, J. Langdon, 55

Down syndrome, 55

*drapetomania,* 89

Drinnon, Richard, 85–86

Du Bois, W. E. B., 176

Dunbar-Ortiz, Roxanne, 2–3, 40, 93, 109, 135

Dyche, Lewis Lindsay, 91

East St. Louis Pogrom, 175–76

Echidna, 53

Edison, Thomas, 81

*El soldado argentino,* 102

empire, US: gender and capitalism in, 25–29; state violence and, 29–30; under William McKinley, 78–79. *See also* colonialism-imperialism, US

*End to the Neglect of the Problems of the Negro Woman!, An,* 26

*Enemy of the People, An,* 169

Engels, Friedrich, 137

Enlightenment philosophy, 88–89

Erikson, Kai, 157

Ervin, Lorenzo Kom'boa, 11

Evans, George Henry, 32

*Evening Tribune,* 155, 160–63

Everest, Wesley, 183–86, 190

execution of Leon Czołgosz, 81

extermination: John Hay, "Indian Wars," and "Railroad War," 90–99; language of, 70–72; of Mormons, 104–8

Fairbank, Nathaniel Kellogg, 128

Fanon, Frantz, 12

Farnham, Arthur, 111, 114

fascism, 65–66

*Fatal Environment, The,* 99

Faure, Sébastien, 101

feminism: Black left, 25–26; Indigenous, 27, 28

Fennell, Frederick, 113

Ferguson, Kathy, 18, 63, 65

Index     247

Ferrer, Francisco, 21
Ferrero, William, 47
Ferris, Carl, 156
Fielden, Samuel, 140
Fishburn, George, 156
Fitzhugh, George, 89
Fletcher, Alice, 138
Flint, John Thompson, 126
Floyd, George, 196
Fort Dearborn massacre, 39–42
Fort Laramie Treaty, 1868, 5
Fort Sheridan, 42
Free Speech League, 57
French, William, 99
*Fresno Morning Republican,* 52
frontier settlers and stories, 38–39, 84–85
Funston, Frederick, 62

Garfield, James A., 137
Gatling guns, 110–11, 120, 125, 133
Geneva Conventions, 123
George, Dan, 24
Ghadr Party, 21
Gilded Age, 36, 45, 109, 134
Gilmore, Ruth Wilson, 11
Goldman, Emma, 16, 22, 27, 28, 29, 38, 176;
    Ben Reitman and, 163–68; on capitalist
    massacres, 79; deportation of, 171, 172,
    173–74; John Turner and, 57; language
    of dirt and disease used against, 65; on
    patriotism, 61–62; portrayed as terrorist,
    46; race science and, 52–53; in San Diego,
    158–59, 161, 163–69; San Diego lynch mob
    and, 50; on San Diego's citizen's commit-
    tee, 155; on sex work, 144; on suffragists,
    47–48; visit to San Francisco, 60–61
Goodspeed, William, 112
Gookin, Daniel, 48
Gould, Stephen Jay, 55
Grandin, Greg, 85
Grant, Ulysses S., 93–94
Great Fire of 1871, 128
Green, James, 64
Greene, John Priest, 82
Grenier, John, 40
*grido degli oppressi, Il,* 18
Griffith, D. W., 13, 68–69
Gruening, Martha, 176
Guaido, Juan, 194
Guglielmo, Jennifer, 17, 18, 19, 25
Guha, Ranajit, 4
*Gunfighter Nation,* 86, 114
gun-rights advocates, 109–10, 134–35

Gurley Flynn, Elizabeth, 46, 157–58, 161, 163
Guyana, 24–25

Hammersmark, Samuel, 185–86
Harding, Warren G., 185, 186
Harman, Moses, 163
*Harper's Weekly,* 99
Harris, William, 112
Harrison, Benjamin, 41, 42
Harrison, William Henry, 40, 41
Hawn's Mill Massacre, 74
Hay, John, 7, 44, 50, 90–99, 109, 110, 114,
    148–49, 194; *The Breadwinners* by, 90,
    103–4; Mormons and, 104–8; on organized
    labor, 98–99, 116–18
Haymarket Riots, 37–38, 46, 54–55, 56, 64,
    85–86, 115; pardoning of defendants after,
    30, 151
Haywood, "Big" Bill, 158
Heatherton, Christina, 21
Henry, Émile, 77
Hernández, Kelly Lytle, 85
Hickey, Michael, 131
*History of the American People,* 187
*History of the Chicago Police,* 39, 42
Hitler, Adolf, 64, 65
Hoar, George Frisbie, 82–83
Hobsbawm, Eric, 22
Hoey, Michael, 152, 162
Holmes, Lizzie, 27, 50
hooks, bell, 169–70
Hoover, Herbert, 182
Hoover, J. Edgar, 19, 65, 173–74, 190
Horne, Gerald, 71–72
Horton, Johnny, 91
*Houston Daily Telegraph,* 121
Howard, Oliver, 99
Howells, 82
*How the Irish Became White,* 16–17
*How the Other Half Lives,* 82
Hunter, Robert, 33–34
*hysteria,* 56

Ibsen, Henrik, 169
Ignatiev, Noel, 16–17
*Immigrants against the State,* 18
imperial feedback, 7
Indian Wars, 1, 8, 29, 36–37, 90–99; news-
    paper coverage of, 118–20; Wild West cul-
    tural narrative and, 160
Indigenous peoples, 1–3; Albert Parsons
    on, 137–40; American Civil War and,
    93–94; anarchism and syndicalism and,

248    Index

24, 36–37; anticommunism and, 34–36, 90; boarding schools for, 138–39; Dawes Act and, 35, 36, 92, 137–38; "enlightened" reformers and, 138–39; femininity/masculinity and, 48; feminism and, 27, 28; Gatling guns used against, 110–11; hatred toward, 90–99; language of dirt and disease used against, 64–65; newspaper portrayals of, 114–20; race science and, 57–58; resistance by, 5; state violence against, 35–36, 39–43, 58–59, 72–73; Theodore Roosevelt and, 83–85; white construction of "wild Indian" image of, 89, 113–14

*Industrial Worker,* 162, 163

Industrial Workers of the World (IWW), 12–14, 19, 21, 23, 102, 136, 169; American Legion and, 184; attorneys defending, 158–59; Bisbee Deportation and, 176–78; Frank Little and, 178–80; Ku Klux Klan and, 188–89; San Diego and, 153–59, 161–62

International Workingmen's Association, 45

International Working People's Association (IWPA), 135–41, 146–48

*Inter-Ocean,* 53, 53, 130, 146, 148

interracial marriage, 124–25

Inverarity, James, 156–57

Irish immigrants, 16–17

Isaac, Abraham, 78, 109–10

Italian immigrants: anarchist, 18, 25; whiteness of, 17

Jackson, Andrew, 32, 186

Jackson, Helen Hunt, 72–73, 91, 176

Jackson, William Henry, 141

Jacobson, Matthew Frye, 16

James, William, 70

Jaxon, Joseph, 141

Jay, John, 15

Jefferson, Thomas, 2, 88, 92

Jewish anarchists, 16, 21; deportations of, 174

Jews, Nazi vilification of, 64, 65

Jiménez, Camilo, 177

Johnson, Amy, 156, 159

Johnson, Walter, 3

Jones, Claudia, 26

Jones, Jacqueline, 124, 128

Jones, Mary Harris, 133, 147–48

Kakel, Carroll, 64

Kane, Kathleen, 74–75

Kearney, Denis, 95

Keating, Ann Durkin, 40, 41

Keaton, Buster, 67, 69

Keller, Julia, 111

Keogh, Miles, 91, 94, 118

Kicking Bear, 41–42

King, Henry W., 128

King, Martin Luther, Jr., 28

Kirk, Earnest E., 158–59

Knights of Labor, 130, 175

Kraut, Julia Rose, 57

Kropotkin, Peter, 45

Ku Klux Klan, 69, 121, 125–27, 150, 176; Woodrow Wilson and, 186–90

Kurds, 100

*Labor Leader,* 158

*Labor Standard, The,* 96

Lachowsky, Hyman, 174

Lake Mohonk Conference, 138–40

Lakota people, 5, 41–42, 75, 92

Lamia, 53

*Land and Liberty,* 21

language: of anticommunism and antianarchism, 75–77; of dirt and disease, 63–66; of extermination, 70–71, 75; of infestation, 71–75; of "war with relentless efficiency," 83–85

Lause, Mark, 85

law enforcement, 37–40, 43–44, 50, 192, 193–94

League of Revolutionary Black Workers, 23

Lehr und Wehr Verein, 133–35

*L'era nuova,* 18

Lewis, Q. Walker, 107

liberalism, Enlightenment, 88–89

*Liberator, The,* 129

*Life,* 102

Lincoln, Abraham, 35, 90, 122, 150

Lingg, Louis, 56

Lipkin, Dora, 173

Lipman, Samuel, 174

Lippard, George, 33

Little, Frank, 169, 178–80, 190

Little Crow, 36

Litzenberg, W., 156

*Loaded: A Disarming History of the Second Amendment,* 109

Locke, John, 88–89, 92

Locofocos, 32

Lodge, Henry Cabot, 81–82

Lombroso, Cesare, 47, 54–56, 58, 80, 100–101, 140–41

Long Depression, 94, 127

*Los Angeles Times,* 46

Louisiana, boundary crisis in, 157

Lucheni, Luigi, 77
Ludlow Massacre, 87
lynchings and massacres, 29–30, 39–43, 126–27, 169; boundary crisis and, 157–59; of Frank Little, 169, 178–80; justifications of, 86; of Mormons, 105–8; in San Diego (1912), 154–59; settler death squads and, 178–80; vigilantism and, 108–14; of Wesley Everest, 183–86; Wild West cultural narrative and, 159–63. *See also* state violence; vigilantism

Madison, James, 88
Magón, Ricardo Flores, 29, 113, 145–46
Malatesta, Errico, 78
Malcolm X, 127
Manifest Destiny, 92, 139
*Manifesto of the Communist Party,* 32, 137
Maratija, Domingo, 60
Marx, Karl, 32, 33, 137, 161
Marxism, 4, 22–23, 137; concept of the working class in, 16; rise of the bourgeoisie and, 11–12
Mason, Edward, 42
Massacre of Drogheda, 71
Mbah, Sam, 11
McAliskey, Bernadette Devlin, 17
McCarran Act, 1950, 57
McCarran-Walter Act, 1952, 57
McKinley, William, 77–82, 90
McLean, Nathaniel, 35
Medusa, 48–49, 53
*Mein Kampf,* 65
*Merchants' Magazine,* 89
*Messenger, The,* 13–14
Métis Rebellion, 140–41
Mexico, 31–32, 33, 112–13; deportations to, 176–78
Meyer, Edward, 112
Michel, Louise, 44–45, 50–51, 54, 148
Mikolasek, Joseph, 152
Miles, Nelson, 110
"Miles Keogh's Horse," 91
militia movement, 134–35
Million, Dian, 28, 49
Minkin, Helene, 76
*Mismeasure of Man, The,* 55
*Missouri Republican,* 97, 99
Missouri State Militia, 74
Mitchell, Darryl, 23
mode of production, 24–25
Montana: lynching of Frank Little in, 169, 178–80; vigilante code in, 180–81

Moon-Ho Jung, 79
Moore, Fred, 158
Moore, Walter P., 156, 159
Moreton-Robinson, Aileen, 27, 93, 190
Mormons and anti-Mormonism, 74, 104–8
Most, Johann, 54, 76–77, 135–36
Most, John Jr., 76
*Mother Earth,* 156, 176
Mount Rushmore, 5
Mulberry Creek Massacre, 58
Mullens, Sheppard, 126
Muñoz Martinez, Monica, 106, 112–13
Mussolini, Benito, 19

Nash, Gary, 113–14
National Association for the Advancement of Colored People (NAACP), 176
National Rifle Association, 134
*Nauvoo Expositor,* 105
*Navigator, The,* 67–70
Nazi Germany, 64, 65
Neebe, Oscar, 50
*New York Times,* 66, 97, 100
*New York Tribune,* 44, 146; on communism, 98; on deportations of "alien anarchists," 172; on Indigenous people, 71, 91; on labor strikes, 8, 97, 116; on railroad uprisings, 47, 99
*New York World,* 38, 52
"nits make lice," 71–75
Nordau, Max, 53
Northwest Ordinance, 2

Obama, Barack, 28
Order of the Red Flag, 21
organized labor, 89, 193; in 1876–1877, 94–95; bourgeoisie fear of, 97–98; Industrial Workers of the World (IWW) and, 12–14, 19, 21, 23, 102, 136; International Working People's Association (IWPA) and, 135–41; labor unrest and, 86–87, 136–37; newspaper coverage of, 96; railroad workers and, 8–9, 15, 29, 47, 95, 114–15; strikes by, 96, 98–99, 114–16, 125, 132–35; viewed as tied to communism, 98
Owen, Chandler, 13

Pagden, Anthony, 88
Pakistan, 28–29
Palestine, 193
Palmer, A. Mitchell, 31, 178, 190
Palmer Raids, 1919, 31, 57, 66
Palomares, Fernando, 177

Panic of 1873, 94, 127
Paris Commune, 14–15, 44, 97, 148
Parker, James Benjamin, 79
Parsons, Albert, 7, 14, 27, 114–15, 146, 148–49; in Chicago's labor movement, 128–35; Civil War and Reconstruction and, 121–27; execution of, 150; on the "Indian problem," 137–40; International Working People's Association (IWPA) and, 135–41
Parsons, Lucy, 7, 14, 27, 29, 36, 50, 148; in Chicago's labor movement, 128–35; "Christmas Story" by, 141–46; Civil War and Reconstruction and, 121–27; International Working People's Association (IWPA) and, 135–41; race science and, 53, 53; on white racial identity, 146–47
Parsons, Richard, 122–23
Parsons, William Henry, 122–23
Patagonia Rebelde (1920–22), 101–2
Patriot Act, 2001, 57
patriotism, 60–63, 161–63
Paull, Andy, 24
Pease, Bob, 189
Perovskaya, Sophia, 54
Philippines, the, 60–62, 72, 78, 81
*Phrenological Journal of Science and Health,* 52
phrenology and physiognomy, 52–58
Pickford, Ed, 16
*Plebian,* 32
Porter, John M., 156, 159
Potawatomi people, 40–41
Powderly, Terrence, 147
Presser, Herman, 134
*Presser v. Illinois,* 134
Price, Hiram, 137, 139
Price, William S., 89
private property system, 89, 92–93
Progressive Era, 36, 45
proletariat, 15–16, 97
Proudhon, Pierre-Joseph, 14, 27
psychopathology, 12, 52–58, 80–85, 100–101
*Puck,* 102
Pullman, George, 41, 128
Pullman Strike, 41
*Punch,* 48, 49
*Purity and Danger,* 70
Putlizer, Joseph, 38

*questione sociale, La,* 19

race, 11–12; anarchism and, 18–24; anticommunism and, 12–15; bourgeoisie and proletariat and, 15–16; interracial marriage and, 124–25; mode of production and, 24–25; notions of manliness and, 164–65; subverting the ruling class narratives and, 146–48; white identity and, 16–17, 19–20
race science, 52–58, 53
racial capitalism, 12; anti-Blackness and anticommunism in, 12–15
racialization: anarchism and, 18–19; language of, 63
Radical Republicans, 121, 123–26, 129
Railroad Uprisings, 1877, 8–9, 15, 29, 47, 95, 114–15; Albert Parsons and, 132–33; suppress by the capitalist class, 117–18
Railroad War, 90–99
Ramnath, Maia, 21
Ramsey, Alexander, 34–35
Rand, Ayn, 90
Randolph, Philip, 13
rape, 28
Reagan, Ronald, 134
"reconcentration camps," 82
Reconstruction era, 14–15, 98, 121–27, 149
*Red, White, and Black,* 113–14
Red Scare, 3, 5, 7, 14, 31, 186
Reeve, Paul, 74
*Regeneración,* 21, 113
Reitman, Ben, 28, 50, 62, 156, 159, 169; sexual assault on, 163–67
Relief and Aid Society, 128–29
Republican Party, the, 1, 90, 149, 195; Black southerners and, 14–15
Rhett, Robert Barnwell, 33
Rhodes, James Ford, 98
Richards, A. C., 8–9
Richardson, Heather Cox, 14–15
Richardson, Willard, 122–23
Riel, Louis, 54, 140–41
Riis, Jacob, 82
Robbins, Marcus, 158
Roberts, Donald Abdul, 23
Robinson, Cedric, 11–12
Rodney, Walter, 24–25
Roediger, David, 25
Rohl-Smith, Carl, 41
Rome Statute of the International Criminal Court, 123
Roosevelt, Theodore, 4, 6, 21, 90, 165, 184, 194; Alien Immigration Act (1903) and, 56; on anarchists, 76–77; influence of Cromwell on, 72; pardon of William Buwalda by, 62; "war with relentless efficiency," 80–85; white settlers supported by, 171–72

Index    251

Roosevelt, Theodore, Jr., 184
Rosemont, Franklin, 36
Rousseau, Jean Jacques, 161
ruling class, 15; boundary crisis and, 157–59; subversion of narratives of, 146–48
Rusk, Jeremiah, 86
Russian Bolshevism, 12, 22, 70
Russo-Turkish War, 1877, 100

Salinas, Cristina, 21
Sanchini, Irma, 50–51
Sandburg, Carl, 76
Sand Creek Massacre, 58, 72–73, 84, 176
San Diego (1912), 151–52, 169–70; lynching and the status quo in, 154–59; Ordinance 4623 passed in, 152–54; sexual violence in, 163–68; Wild West cultural narrative in, 159–63
*San Diego Herald,* 158
*San Diego Sun,* 50, 167
*San Diego Union,* 153, 155–56, 160–62
*San Diego Weekly Union,* 160
*San Francisco Bulletin,* 50
*San Francisco Chronicle,* 63
Sanger, Margaret, 169
Sapolsky, Steven, 141
Sauer, Abram, 158
Schaack, Michael, 37–38, 43, 48, 54, 58, 75
Schenck, Joseph, 67
Schnaubelt, Rudolph, 86
science, race, 52–58, *53*
Scott, Janny, 114
Scott, Joan, 152
Scott, Thomas, 114, 115
*Scouting for Boys,* 164, 165
Second Amendment, 109, 134–35, 139
*Second Treatise of Government,* 88
Sehon, John, 154
sexual freedom, 27–28
sexual violence, 28, 50, 126, 163–68
sex workers, 144
Shaffer, Kirwin, 21
Shantz, Jeff, 24
Sheridan, Philip, 42, 74–75, 84
Sherman, William Tecumseh, 93–94, 119
Shire, Warsan, 127
Short Bull, 41–42
Sinclair, Upton, 76
Sioux War, 99
Skidmore, Thomas, 32
slavery, 3, 5, 89; anticommunism and, 33–34; Joseph Smith on, 107. *See also* Civil War, the

Slotkin, Richard, 86, 99, 114
Smith, Barbara, 26
Smith, Hoke, 13
Smith, Hyrum, 105, 108
Smith, Joseph, 105–8
socialism, 32–33, 94, 97, 130, 134–35; International Working People's Association (IWPA) and, 136
Sousa, John Philip, 113
*South West,* 122
"Soviet Ark," 174–75
Spanish-American War, 67
*Spectator,* 121
Spies, August, 135, 140–41, 147
Squamish workers, labor organizing by, 24
SS *Estonia,* 174
Stannard, David, 65
Stanton, Edwin, 57
*Statesboro News,* 81
state violence, 29–30, 35–36, 193–94; against Indigenous people, 39–43, 58–59, 72–73; against the Irish, 71–72; against Mormons, 74, 104–8; vigilantism and, 108–14, 117, 125, 150, 151–59; against women, 50–51. *See also* lynchings and massacres; vigilantism
Steimer, Molly, 174
Stokes, Rose Pastor, 46
Stone, Amasa, 97, 109, 111
Streeby, Shelley, 32, 39, 179
strikes, labor, 96, 98–99, 114–16, 125, 132–35
Struthers, David, 21
Subaltern Studies, 4
*Subterranean,* 32
suffragists, 47–48
Sugako, Kanno, 19
*Sun,* 86, 115, 117
Swain, Joseph, 48, 100
syndicalism, 21, 24

Taliaferro, Thomas J., 124
Tarde, Gabriel, 58
Taylor, Zachary, 34, 104, 122
Texas Rangers, 38, 112–13
Thuŋkášila Šákpe (Six Grandfathers), 5
Thayer, William Roscoe, 90, 92, 98, 104
Thirteenth Amendment, 129
Thomas, David Hurst, 58
Thomson, Rodney, 102–3
Thorp, Willard Brown, 161
*Thrilling Adventures among the Early Settlers,* 38, 159, 179
Toland, John, 64

Tolstoy, Leo, 61, 82
Tom Quick folklore, 74
*Tonka,* 91
Treaty of Guadalupe Hidalgo, 32
Treaty of Walla Walla, 99
Trumka, Richard, 192
Trump, Donald, 1–2, 5, 8, 186, 194–96
Tsleil-Waututh workers, labor organizing by, 24
Ture, Kwame, 127
Turner, John, 57
Twiggs, David E., 122–23

Umberto I, King, 77
*Under Three Flags,* 137
Union of Russian Workers (UORW), 66
United Nations Convention on the Rights of the Child, 123
USAT *Buford,* 66–70, 174–75
Ute people, 91–92

Vaile, William, 65, 66, 71
Vaillant, Auguste, 77, 101
Vancouver waterfront, 24
van der Walt, Lucien, 23
*Vanity Fair,* 102
Vardaman, 13
vigilantism, 108–14, 117, 125, 150; boundary crisis and, 157–58; East St. Louis Pogrom and, 175–76; in San Diego (1912), 151–59; sexual violence and, 163–68; vigilante code and, 180–81. *See also* lynchings and massacres; state violence
von Luschan, Felix, 52, 58

*Waco Daily Examiner,* 124
Walsh, R. J., 156
War for Independence, 2
*Warsaw Signal,* 105, 108
Washington, George, 149
Washington, Mary Helen, 25
*Washington Post,* 63, 70, 75
*Was wollen die Kommunisten?,* 32
Weingarten, Randi, 193

Wheeler, Harry, 177–78, 190
White, Richard, 93
white identity, 16–17, 19–20; policing of sexual relationships and, 27–28
*White Possessive, The,* 190
Whitman, James, 64
Wild West cultural narrative, 159–63
Wildwood, Warren, 38–39
Williams, John Sharp, 13
Wilson, Keno, 154
Wilson, Woodrow, 68, 176, 190; Ku Klux Klan and, 186–90
Wobblies. *See* Industrial Workers of the World (IWW)
Wolfe, Patrick, 53
women: capitalism, empire and, 25–29; criminality of, 47; Indigenous, 48; masculinity and, 48; massacres of, 73; portrayed as hideous creatures, 48, *49*; portrayed as terrorists, 46–47; race science and, 52–53; red sisterhood and, 43–51; republican motherhood and wifehood ideals of, 47; sexual violence against, 28, 50, 126, 163–64; sex work by, 144; as suffragists, 47–48
Wood, Amy, 81
Woodbey, George Washington, 160
working class, the, 5–6, 7, 16; Black left feminism and, 25–26; boundary crisis and, 157–59; in Chicago, 128–35; Italian anarchists and, 18; outside the United States, 101; rise of socialism among, 32–33; white identity and, 16–17, 19–20
*Working Man's Advocate,* 32
Workingmen's Party, 32, 130, 131
Wounded Knee, 75

Young, Brigham, 107
Yousafzai, Malala, 28

Zagarri, Rosemary, 47
Zalacosta, Francisco, 177
Zimmer, Kenyon, 18, 21, 54, 136
Zola, Émile, 77
Zouaves, 101

TARIQ D. KHAN is a lecturer in the
history of psychology at Yale University.

The University of Illinois Press
is a founding member of the
Association of University Presses.

---

University of Illinois Press
1325 South Oak Street
Champaign, IL 61820-6903
www.press.uillinois.edu